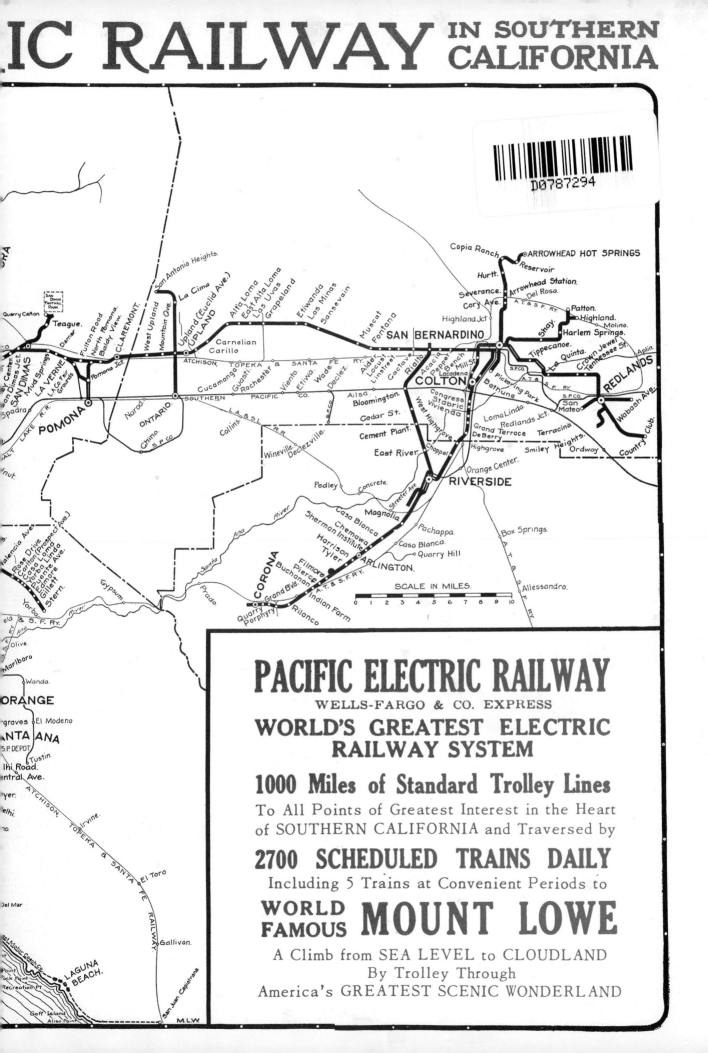

IC RAILWAY IN SOUTHERN CALIFORNIA

D0787294

I am a foresighted man, and I believe Los Angeles is destined to become the most important city in this country if not in the world. It can extend in any direction as far as you like . . . We will join this whole region into one big family.

HENRY E. HUNTINGTON
President of the Pacific Electric, 1901-1910

The Pacific Electric will bring you, I hope, all that your honest hopes have anticipated; it will do all it can do to continue to bring the thousands of strangers that come to California down the main street of your city . . . .

PAUL SHOUP
President of the Pacific Electric, 1912-1929

In our own section, this railway has been the greatest reliance of and greatest single element in promoting the growth and progress of over forty-five cities and their adjacent territory. It was not only the pioneer, but the permanent resident.

DAVID W. PONTIUS
President of the Pacific Electric, 1929-1937

RIDE THE BIG RED CARS

How Trolleys Helped Build Southern California

Also by Spencer Crump:

Henry Huntington and the Pacific Electric
A Pictorial Album

California's Spanish Missions Yesterday and Today

252 Historic Places You Can See in California

Redwoods, Iron Horses, and the Pacific
The Story of the California Western "Skunk" Railroad

Black Riot in Los Angeles
The Story of the Watts Tragedy

Western Pacific

The Fundamentals of Journalism

Suggestions for Teaching the Fundamentals
of Journalism in College

Rail Car, Locomotive, and Trolley Builders:
An All-Time Directory

In Preparation:
In the Wake of the Big Red Cars

A Red Car Rides the Coast near Huntington Beach

PHOTOGRAPH BY JOHN LAWSON

RIDE THE BIG RED CARS

How Trolleys Helped Build Southern California

by SPENCER CRUMP

 TRANS-ANGLO BOOKS

Library of Congress Cataloging in Publication Data

Crump, Spencer.
  Ride the Big Red Cars.

  Bibliography: p. 9
  Includes index.
  1. Street-railroads--California, southern. 2. Los
Angeles--Transit Systems. 3. Pacific Electric Railway
Company. I. Title.
HE5425.C2C7   388.4609749   77-72017
ISBN 0-87046-047-1

RIDE THE BIG RED CARS
How Trolleys Helped Build Southern California

Copyright © MCMLXII, MCMLXV,
MCMLXX by Spencer Crump

FIFTH EDITION (Revised)

Library of Congress Catalog
Card Number: 77-72017

ISBN 0-87046-047-1

A Vic-Jac Production: Published by Trans-Anglo Books,
Post Office Box 38, Corona del Mar, California 92625

Printed and Bound in the United States of America

A two-car Pacific Electric train stops for passengers at Venice, just an hour (including stops) via trolley from downtown Los Angeles. Note the private right-of-way. (Stephen D. Maguire Collection)

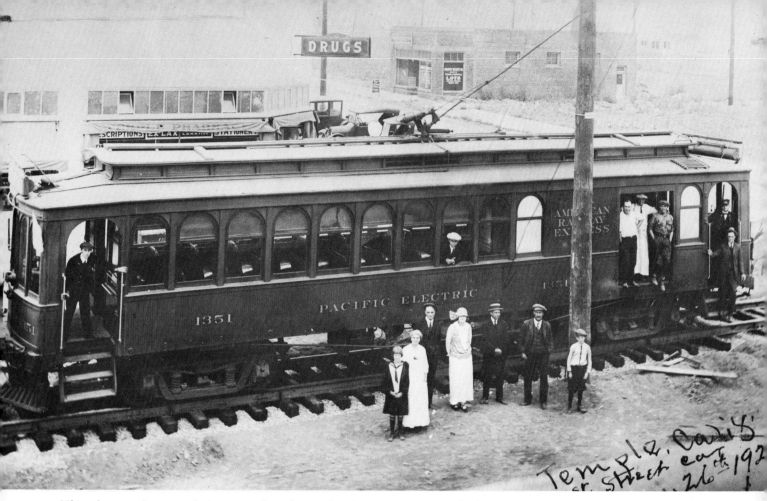

This photograph was made in 1924 when the Pacific Electric's last extension — from San Gabriel to Temple City — was opened. Construction of trolley lines always brought new residents to areas because of the ease in travelling.

INTRODUCTION

This book is a history of the Pacific Electric, which for more than half a century served Southern California commuters. It could honestly boast that it was the largest and most efficient electric interurban system in the world.

The volume was written so that the text could stand alone. Illustrations were added with the knowledge that photographs, maps, and charts graphically help tell a story.

Southern California once was an arid area known chiefly for its big ranches and fine cattle.

Then came the technology of electric interurbans, and far-sighted entrepreneurs began laying trolley tracks over the countryside. Wherever the tracks stretched, villages developed and grew; the fast, efficient electric cars made travel easy between the business center of downtown Los Angeles and the surrounding communities.

This book is a study of the impact of electric interurban transportation on the life and growth of Southern California from the trolleys' arrival in 1895 until their departure in 1961. Although over the years the trolleys were garbed in many colors — green, olive, yellow, and perhaps other hues lost in history — the most famous, most important, and most symbolic of the era were the Big Red Cars of the Pacific Electric.

No other electric interurban system in America achieved the place in history accorded the Big Red Cars. This situation resulted from the immense and varied impact which these trolleys made on Southern California. The Big Red Cars were a variety of things to a variety of people. To the commuters, they meant jobs in Los Angeles coupled with the pleasure of homes in the suburbs; to the business community, they brought customers and prosperity, and to the country dweller, they placed the culture of a metropolis within easy reach. To this author, whose family was among those which could not afford the luxury of an automobile during the Depression of the 1930's, they brought many memorable days of sightseeing through the orange groves, in Southern

California cities, and at the Spanish missions. Accompanying the author were his grandparents, John and Margaret Person, and his mother, Mrs. Jessie Person Crump. The Big Red Cars also provided the author, aspiring as a child to be a writer, with his first glimpse into the editorial department of a newspaper as the Pacific Electric cars climbed the elevated tracks to the Los Angeles station and rolled past the open windows of the Los Angeles Daily Record's building adjacent to the right-of-way.

The Big Red Cars became a symbol of an era when there was no smog and the snow-capped mountains backdropping Southern California sparkled almost every day in the sunlight, when automobile traffic jams were rare, and when the area's growth was a popular topic of conversation at a time that the general public was not aware of pending crises in urban development.

The approach in this book has been as a general history of Southern California and the impact of interurbans on the area and its people. Particular pains have been taken to avoid technical terms peculiar to the electric railroad systems, since there are numerous volumes intended for transportation experts. Similarly, it was not the intention of this book to record detailed histories of individual lines. The purpose of this study, rather, has been to capture the more human aspects of the trolley era.

While this book analyzes important factors in the area's growth, the author has avoided temptations to assess the methods used by the boosters in selling real estate; neither was an effort made to evaluate the economic or sociological end product resulting in the City of Southern California. These are studies which have been, and are being, undertaken by other writers.

Most people, however, who begin their Southern California residency as late as the early 1950's — when the Big Red Cars were still rolling agree that the immense growth transformed the area into an increasingly unpleasant place to live.

When "pioneer" residents, meaning those who went to Southern California during the 1940's or before, talk nostalgically about the Big Red Cars, they frequently forget to mention the miles of solid orange groves, the farms, fields of wildflowers and mustard, and the towns, each with individuality, which made it pleasant to ride over the Pacific Electric system. "Progress" doomed these beautiful attractions.

While this growth brought monetary wealth to the larger merchants, land developers, and industrialists, its only fruit for Mr. and Mrs. Average has been bigger tax bills and perplexing travel problems.

Growth is destroying a beautiful area. Row after row of unimaginative new tract homes, sprawling apartments, monotonous shopping centers, and crowded freeways eat up the countryside. Few provisions are made for parks or for the preservation of wlid life.

If this disregard continues, Southern Californians of the next century may desperately put decks over the freeways to provide room for farming and recreation; at the same time, citizens will be forced to re-plan cities and erect skyscrapers surrounded by parks where housing tracts and stores previously were built in a wasteful use of land.

Southern California presented many perplexing paradoxes in the 1970's. Here are digests of a few of them:

1. Long Beach, which grew from a village after being connected to Los Angeles by the Pacific Electric, in the 1970's was spending millions of dollars in tidelands oil revenue to make the rusty ocean liner Queen Mary into a garish tourist "attraction." The city attempted to justify these immense expenditures on the ground that the ship would help rehabilitate its downtown area, decaying since suburban centers began luring business in 1952. Instead of spending these tens of millions of dollars on the old ship, it would be more realistic to spend the money on the rapid transit or slum clearance programs that would benefit more people. Changes in state laws could be made easily to allow these more beneficial expenditures.

2. Boosterism may have been an attribute in early day Southern California, but its continuance these days only despoils the area. Yet, the Southern California Visitors Council (formerly the All-Year Club) and Chamber of Commerces even in the 1970's were still attempting to lure more people to the area. Citizens should demand that these groups stop this activity and use their energies to solve the problems created by so many residents already being here.

3. While many Southern Californians are concerned, rightfully, about crime in the streets, they oppose spending money for the parks and recreational facilities that in the long run would reduce the causes of delinquency.

4. The demise of the Big Red Cars brought a frantic increase in the construction of freeways, most of which became jammed almost as soon as completed. Freeways are expensive to build. Moreover, they are also costly because of the high prices of the business and residential property condemned for the right-of-ways. Yet, local and state officials failed to provide the leadership of making space for rail facilities on freeways. The Chicago area has done just that, building an efficient rail artery in the center of key turnpikes.

WATER COLOR BY JESSIE PERSON CRUMP

The Red Cars Arrive

There were paradoxes nationally, too. Vast expenditures were earmarked for the military in the name of "defense" even though nuclear power has antiquated war and made it a virtual guarantee of the end of civilization. Moreover, despite the earth's problems of poverty, war and peace, transportation, and ecology, vast funds were being spent for space exploration.

Southern Californians, noted during the early twentieth century for extravagant praise of their beautiful countryside, had changed by the 1970's into a people distinguished by their complaints of property taxes, traffic jams, and smog-laden air.

Little optimsim could develop over a successful solution to Southern California's traffic situation.

The author has given numerous talks on the Big Red Cars since the first edition of this book appeared, and those in the audience frequently suggest that preservation of the Pacific Electric system would have served modern-day commuter needs. Let's make no mistakes. The P. E. was constructed for slower electric cars. Too much of its track was laid in the streets where it would impede traffic, and its curves were too sharp for the mile-a-minute speed necessary for today's rapid transit systems.

The Pacific Electric system could have been modernized, however, by using its precious rights-of-way as the nucleus for an efficient system serving commuters. Public officials made a sad and expensive mistake in permitting these rights-of-ways to be converted into places for building more apartments or to be consolidated into street systems.

Modernizing the P. E. system and at the same time providing space for rail facilities on every new freeway would

7

have saved the taxpayers millions — perhaps billions — of dollars.

This area's answer to public transportation has been the Southern California Rapid Transit District, a public agency formed in 1964 to replace the Metropolitan Travel Authority after that unit failed to provide answers. The District proved, at least by the early 1970's, to be "rapid" in name only and operated an undistinguished bus system which made the streets and freeways more crowded.

Rapid transit is expensive: construction is costly, there is a high price tag on today's sophisticated equipment, and the manpower to operate it requires money. Even publicly-owned rapid transit systems lose money. Southern Californians must realize that the deficit must be paid by some kind of tax.

The tax logically should be levelled against those who have, and are, profiting from Southern California's growth.

The little people have not profited.

They have lost.

Some day, rapid transit undoubtedly will be regarded as a public utility and necessity — with free rides to everyone who must travel.

While Southern Californians did nothing about rapid transit problems, other areas moved ahead. Washington, D. C., and San Francisco started on rapid transit programs and other cities in North America already were operating such systems. Despite the criticism levelled at it, the New York City subway system performs an excellent job of carry-in commuters. Rapid transit systems in Boston, Cleveland, Chicago, Toronto, Montreal, and Mexico City also solve travel problems by taking passengers under — or over — street traffic.

After having seen and ridden most of these systems, the author is unable to understand why Southern Californians — who boast of the area's progressiveness — have done nothing to solve the problem of commuting.

But as history shows, the City of Southern California once had a great transportation system. It was one that helped build ranch lands into a city over a relatively short span of time.

This book is the story of that past success in rapid transit: the famous Big Red Car system that made travel a pleasure.

The research yielded numerous basic sources of information. The temptation to cite all individual sources has been resisted. Footnotes have been used sparingly and only when necessary to make the book more readable.

Appreciation is hereby expressed for the use of research facilities at the University of Southern California and the University of California at Los Angeles. The use of early twentieth century U.S.C. graduate studies pertaining to community growth, economic impact of streetcars, and sociological aspects of railway employment proved most valuable for this study. Gratitude also goes to the efficient library staffs of communities too numerous to mention throughout Southern California. Particular thanks go to the Los Angeles Public Library, the Los Angeles County Museum of Natural History, and the New York Public Library.

The author also is grateful to the Henry E. Huntington Memorial Library and Art Gallery for granting permission to use its research facilities.

Acknowledgement for the greatly appreciate use of historical pictures is given to Victor Plukas of Security Pacific National Bank, and to Clyde Simpson, associated with the bank until his retirement; Mrs. Jessie Kitching of the Title Insurance and Trust Company; Mrs. Barbara J. Blankman of First American Title Insurance and Trust Company, and Donald Duke of Pacific Railroad Publications.

The author also thanks Carl Blaubach, John Lawson, Steve Maguire, Robert McVay, John Lawson, Craig Rasmussen, Maxine Reams, Vernon J. Sappers, and Charles Seims for making illustrations available from their private collections. Appreciation also is expressed to the other individuals and organizations whose photographs have been credited where used in this book.

The assistance of Mrs. Don (Clara) Nixon, sister-in-law of President Nixon, in making photographs and information available was appreciated. The President's father once served as a P. E. motorman.

I also thank Harold Lloyd, whose motion picture comedies have pleased so many people, for making photographs available.

The use of files of newspapers, those detailed records of history, throughout California was of great assistance for the research, as were the court and other public records in the Counties of Los Angeles, Orange, Riverside, and San Bernardino.

The author made many personal contacts in preparing this book in the 1950's and early 1960's. Thinking in retrospect while making revisions for this third edition in 1970, it was fortunate that these contacts occurred when they did. Many of those associated with Henry Huntington or the early days of the Pacific Electric would have been reluctant to have told their stories a decade before, but were pleased to do so when the author explained his project. Now, unfortunately, many of these people who were so helpful no longer are with us.

Thanks are offered to many former Pacific Electric motormen, conductors, and other employees too numerous to identify individually for the assistance they gave so enthusiastically at many points during the research.

Acknowledgement and appreciation also is expressed to many individuals who helped this research in varying ways. Among those assisting were O. A. Smith, who began his career as a stenographer for Henry Huntington and eventually became president of the Pacific Electric; I. W. Hellman, whose famed grandfather, Isaias W. Hellman, helped Huntington finance his initial interurban construction; Howard Huntington, grandson of Huntington, and Harry O. Marler, one-time office boy for pioneer trolley builders Eli Clark and Moses Sherman who became general passenger agent for the Pacific Electric.

Others who provided information include Dr. Carl Shoup, professor of economics at Columbia University and son of Paul Shoup, president of the Pacific Electric during its peak years; Mrs. Anna Huntington, daughter-in-law of Mrs. Arabella Huntington and herself internationally famed as a sculptress; William Hertrich, first associated with Huntington in 1904 as horticulturist for his San Marino estate; Don Belding, who directed the "Big Red Car" advertising campaign of the 1920's; Mrs. Isaac Marcosson, widow of Huntington's biographer; Terry Stephenson, son of Orange County historian Terry Stephenson, and Mellicent M. Epps, librarian at the Huntington Memorial Library in Oneonta, New York. Cooperation also was given by Miss Anne Patton, daughter of George Patton, neighbor and business associate of Huntington; R. J. Pajalich, secretary to the California Public Utilities Commission (successor to the State Railroad Commission); Edward Margolin, director of the bureau of transport economics and statistics of the Interstate Commerce Commission; Jane F. Smith, chief of the social and economic branch of the United States National Archives, and Robert King, member of the public relations department of the Southern Pacific.

Particular thanks also go to a trio who as nonagenarians in 1962 used the memories of their rich lives to aid in the research: Horace Dobkins, whose bicycle freeway was an 1899 experiment; C. M. Pierce, whose trolley sightseeing trips became famous, and Dr. Rockwell D. Hunt, for many years the dean of the U.S.C. Graduate School and a friend of many early Californians.

Miss Hortense White, daughter of Senator Stephen White, graciously provided much background material on early Los Angeles and in regard to her famous father who did so much to help build the City of Southern California.

Gratitude for invaluable advice and suggestions also is expressed to Hank Johnston, E. Delwin Jones, Will Kern, Clyde Snyder, and William Tetzlaff.

The author's family also was helpful with encouragement and advice. I thank my mother, Mrs. Jessie Person Crump; my wife, Mrs. Mary Dalgarno Crump, and my children, John Spencer and Victoria Elizabeth Margaret.

Mrs. Sandra Tetzlaff was very helpful for her many hours of service as both a research assistant and editorial aide.

For additional reading about the Big Red Cars, see the author's "Henry Huntington and the Pacific Electric," a book which emphasizes the pictorial aspects of the P. E. Most of the illustrations in this book are unduplicated in "Ride the Big Red Cars."

Spencer Crump

Bibliography

This bibliography lists the books and other publications used in the research for this volume. The list also includes additional reading in the field of electric railroads as well as in the area of California history.

Alexander, J. A., *The Life of George Chaffey;* Melbourne: 1928.

Bancroft, Hubert, *History of California,* (Vols. XVIII through XXIV of *Bancroft's Works*); San Francisco: 1884 to 1890.

Bigger, Richard, and James D. Kitchen, *Metropolitan Los Angeles: II How the Cities Grew;* Los Angeles: 1952.

Burton, G. W., *California and Its Sunlit Skies of Glory;* Los Angeles: 1909.

California State Public Utilities Commission, *Case No. 4863: Report on Engineering Survey of Operations and Facilities of Pacific Electric Railway Company;* Sacramento: 1947.

California State Railroad and Public Utilities Commission, *Annual Reports;* Sacramento: Various annual editions 1905 to 1954.

Carr, Harry, *Los Angeles: City of Dreams;* New York: 1935.

Clover, S. T., (Editor) *Constructive Californians,* Los Angeles: 1926.

Crump, Spencer, *Black Riot in Los Angeles: The Story of Watts Tragedy;* Los Angeles 90053: 1966.

Crump, Spencer, *Henry Huntington and the Pacific Electric: A Pictorial Album;* Costa Mesa, California 92626: 1970.

Duke, Donald, *Pacific Electric Railway;* San Marino: 1958.

Dumke, Glenn S., *The Boom of the Eighties;* San Marino: 1944.

Friis, Leo J., *Orange County through Four Centuries;* Santa Ana, California: 1965.

Gibson, George H., *High Speed Electric Interurban Railways,* Smithsonian Institution Annual Report for 1903; Washington, D. C.: 1904.

Goff, Frances A., *The Trolley Man and The Angel Hosts;* Sunset Magazine: April, 1913.

Graves, J. A. *My Seventy Years in California;* Los Angeles: 1928.

Hertrich, William, *The Huntington Botanical Gardens: 1905-1949;* San Marino: 1949.

Hilton, George W. and John F. Due, *The Electric Inter-urban Railways in America;* Stanford: 1960.

Hunt, Rockwell D., *California and Californians;* Los Angeles: 1926.

Johnson, Arthur T., *California: An Englishman's Impressions of the Golden State;* London: 1913.

Johnston, Hank, *The Railroad That Lighted Southern California;* Los Angeles 90053: 1966.

Kennan, George, *E. H. Harriman: A Biography;* Boston: 1922.

Lanigan, Mary, *Second Generation Mexicans in Belvedere;* Master's Thesis for the University of Southern California Department of Sociology: 1932.

Marcosson, Isaac F., *A Little Known Master of Millions;* Boston: 1914.

Martin, James R., *The University of California in Los Angeles: A Resume of the Selection and Acquisition of the Westwood Site;* Los Angeles: 1925.

McEuen, William Wilson, *A Survey of the Mexicans in Los Angeles;* Master's Thesis for the University of Southern California Department of Economics and Sociology: 1914.

Meyer, Samuel A., *Fifty Golden Years: A History of the City of Newport Beach—1906 to 1956;* Newport Beach: 1957.

Moody's Manual of Public Utilities; New York: Various annual editions from 1910 to 1954.

Mosher, Leroy E., *Stephen M. White: His Life and His Work;* Los Angeles: 1903.

Nadeau, Remi, *City-Makers: The Story of Southern California's First Boom;* Costa Mesa, California: 1965.

Newmark, Harris, *Sixty Years in California: 1853-1913;* Boston: 1930.

Nordhoff, Charles, *California: For Health, Pleasure and Residence;* New York: 1874.

Pacific Electric, *Pacific Electric Magazine;* Los Angeles: 1916 to 1953.

Redinger, David H., *The Story of Big Creek;* Los Angeles: 1949.

Rowsome, Frank Jr., and Stephen D. Maguire, *Trolley Car Treasury,* New York: 1956.

Schad, Robert O., *Henry Edwards Huntington: The Founder and The Library;* San Marino: 1948.

Shonerd, Roscoe E., *Investigation of Los Angeles Electric Railway Traffic Conditions;* Bachelor of Arts in Electrical Engineering Thesis for the University of Southern California: 1914.

Sprague, Frank J., *Some Facts and Problems Bearing on Electric Trunk-line Operation;* Smithsonian Institution Annual Report: 1907; Washington, D. C.: 1908.

Stephenson, Terry, *Orange County History Series;* Santa Ana: 1939.

Swanner, Charles D., *Santa Ana: A Narrative of Yesterday—1870-1910;* Claremont: 1953.

Swett, Ira, *Interurbans;* Los Angeles: 1943 to 1965.

Tuthill, John Kline, *Transit Engineering: Principles and Practice;* St. Louis: 1935.

Vining, Edward Payson, *An Inglorious Columbus; or Evidence That Hwui Shan and a Party of Buddhist Monks from Afganiston Discovered America in The Fifth Century A. D.;* New York: 1885.

Walker, H. D. (Editor), *Walker's Manual of California Securities and Directory of Directors;* San Francisco: Various issues from 1908 through 1930.

Wiley, John L., *History of Monrovia;* Pasadena: 1927.

Wolfe, Wellington C. (Editor), *Men of California;* San Francisco: 1901.

Workman, Boyle, *The City That Grew;* Los Angeles: 1926.

Works Project Administration (Sponsor) *California: A Guide for the Golden State;* New York: 1939.

NEWSPAPERS: Files of weekly and daily newspapers throughout California from 1890 to 1962 were used extensively. Specific issues of various newspapers have been cited in footnotes.

A photograph taken in June, 1941, shows a PCC, most modern trolley ever used by the Pacific Electric, operating on the Glendale line. The car was on Glendale Boulevard near Bonnie Brae. (Photo by Vernon J. Sappers)

TABLE OF CONTENTS

1. Queen of the Cow Counties 13
2. Prelude to Progress: The Iron Horse Arrives 19
3. "Speed" by Sprague 27
4. The Man Behind the Millions: What Behind the Man? 39
5. Trolleys to Long Beach: The P. E. Makes a Story 47
6. Triumph for Trolleys 55
7. The Electrics Expand 63
8. Huntington vs. Harriman 71
9. Huntington's Surprise Firecracker 79
10. The Million Dollar Divorce 85
11. The Great Merger 91
12. A Catalyst for the Cow Counties 97
13. Lines to Last 105
14. The Rails and Real Estate, and Hollywood, Too 109
15. A Day for a Dollar 127
16. The Trolleymen: My Red Coat, My Red Flag 135
17. A Bride for the Builder 145
18. When Death Rode the Rails 149
19. Invasion of the Tracks 157
20. The P. E. Hits the Peak 173
21. "Ride the Big Red Cars" 179
22. The Huntington Heritage 183
23. The Rolling Stock, Fares, and Finances 187
24. The Thrifty Thirties: Toward the End of the Line 203
25. The Legacy of the Big Red Cars 211
26. Goodbye, Red Cars 221

THE APPENDIX
    A. Where the Trolleys Ran — When and How Often 225
    B. 1909 P. P. Articles of Incorporation 235
    C. 1911 P. E. Articles of Incorporation 236
    D. Population of Area Served by the Red Cars 248
    E. Digest of P. E. Financial Reports 250
    F. Los Angeles "Local" Trolley Service 252

INDEX 253

This P. E. emblem was used in the 1920's and 1930's.

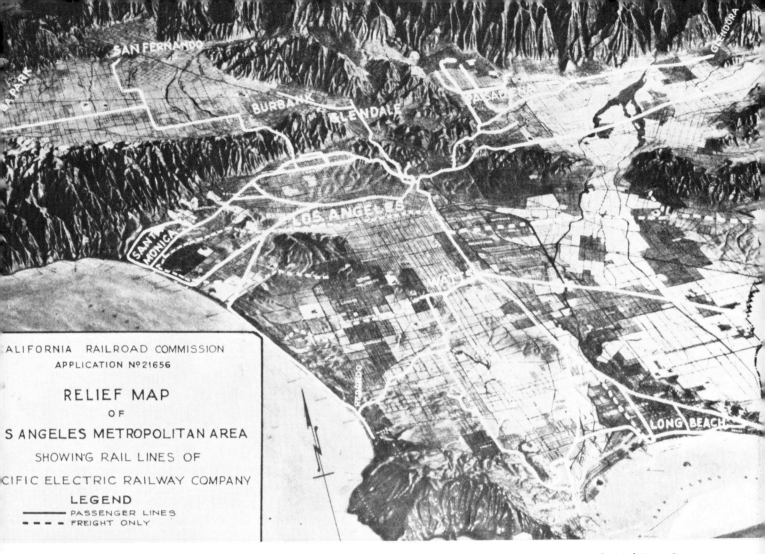

CALIFORNIA RAILROAD COMMISSION
APPLICATION Nº 21656

RELIEF MAP
OF
S ANGELES METROPOLITAN AREA

SHOWING RAIL LINES OF

CIFIC ELECTRIC RAILWAY COMPANY

LEGEND
———— PASSENGER LINES
- - - - FREIGHT ONLY

This 1939 relief map shows the Pacific Electric routes radiating from Los Angeles. Dotted lines were freight routes form- *erly carrying passengers. Routes continued (right) to San Bernardino, Riverside, and Santa Ana.*

1. Queen of the Cow Counties

One day shortly after the birth of the twentieth century, Henry Edwards Huntington, in the process of building his Big Red Car electric interurban system in Southern California, was chatting with William M. Garland, rated as one of the most enthusiastic real estate brokers in a place and era when enthusiasm ran high.

Garland had come to Los Angeles from Chicago in 1890 when 24 years old and, envisioning great strides for the area, entered the real estate business. His firm was becoming locally famous, although at times ridiculed, by its red and white signs which flatly stated that the population of Los Angeles would be 250,000 in 1910.

Angelenos even then were noted nationally as ardent boosters of their mild climate and rate of growth.

However, they were quite pleased when the 1900 census gave Los Angeles 102,479 residents and laughed at Garland because they thought his signs were too optimistic.

Henry Huntington disagreed with them.

"You're too conservative, Bill," Huntington told Garland as they discussed the signs.[1]

Huntington, already nationally recognized as a financial giant, recently had entered the Southern California scene by purchasing trolley lines and considerable

1. Seated with the pair was Oscar A. Smith, who went to work as Huntington's stenographer after attending Southern California Business College in 1904. He reported the conversation to the author during an interview in 1962.

amounts of real estate. His blue eyes twinkled as he talked with Garland.

"Make your signs read that the population of Los Angeles some day will be ten times 250,000," Huntington said, "and you'll still be too conservative!"

The vision of a City of Southern California was within the realm of achievement in the twentieth century to Huntington and Garland, as it was to other men who would lead the way: George Chaffey and William Mulholland, who were to bring water to the arid area; Eli Clark and Moses Sherman, who built the first electric interurban lines; Harrison Gray Otis and Harry Chandler, who invested in Southern California real estate as they published the Los Angeles Times, and Frank Wiggins, the Chamber of Commerce manager who reigned as king of the boosters.

Huntington's proposal of such growth would have been most unbelievable less than a half century before to the residents of the sleepy little village which the Spanish pioneers had majestically named La Ciudad de Nuestra Señora, la Reina de los Angeles de Porciuncula. The population of Los Angeles was less than 2,000 when California was admitted to the United States in 1850, and its residents held little hope that the village could become more than a cattle town.

As the twentieth century passed its midpoint, however, the City of Southern California stretched from the San Gabriel Mountains down the Los Angeles alluvial plain to the shores of the Pacific Ocean. Endless acres of homes, shops, and factories which decades before had engulfed coastal valley were expanding over the San Gabriels into the Mojave Desert as the wave of the City's growth seemed endless. It was an ever-growing collection of many individual municipalities separated only by the technicality of legal boundary lines.

Logic maintained there should be no metropolis where the City of Southern California developed: at the start the countryside was arid, the area had mud-flats instead of a harbor, and only the most primitive of transportation facilities served the territory.

Seven major factors made Henry Huntington's prediction come true and combined as the vital forces which moved Southern California toward a place among the great cities of the world.

Having long since forgotten the reasons why it could not become a metropolis, the City of Southern California at the mid-century mark bulged with 6,000,000 residents who, with varying amounts of enthusiasm, resignation, and despair had accepted the destiny that the area was to become the largest population center in the world.

The forces which nurtured the spectacular growth in less than a century were these:

1. The mild and desirable climate, coupled with a scenic countryside holding the contrasts of mountains, beaches, and deserts.

2. The transcontinental railway links which ended the area's isolation from other American population centers.

3. Construction of deep-water Los Angeles - Long Beach Harbor from what had been mud-flats.

William May Garland's colorful ads predicted that Los Angeles' population would reach 250,000, in 1910 — although the 1900 census gave the city barely 100,000 people. Huntington thought Garland was too conservative.

14

William M. Garland (above) believed Los Angeles' growth had just started — and said so in real estate ads. (Security Pacific National Bank) Harrison Gray Otis published the Los Angeles Times and invested in Southern California property. (Los Angeles Public Library)

4. Completion of the Panama Canal concurrently with the awakening of world trade which followed the industrial revolution.

5. The development of aqueducts to bring water supplies from interior regions.

6. The Los Angeles boosters, who dauntlessly envisioned the area's potential and then with enthusiasm coupled with practical action made the dream of a city a reality.

7. The electric interurban trolleys, which made it possible for migrants to spread into comparatively remote suburban residential areas that otherwise would have been undeveloped for decades.

While the electric interurban was to become familiar in most sections of the world, its influence was the greatest in creating the City of Southern California. In other regions of America the interurbans came after the areas had been settled generally and they did little more than supplement development.

The advent of the technology of the electric interurban came as Southern California was on the verge of its most important growth period. The trolley not only set a pattern for the area's geographical development but it also helped to establish traditions of suburban living that remained long after the final departure of the interurban.

In Southern California, the interurban was the pioneer. After its arrival, the population followed.

Had the trolley been perfected fifteen years later, its era probably would never have developed. The automobile would have supplanted it just as it later replaced it.

When the network of Southern California's interurban trolley lines eventually was consolidated into the Pacific Electric Railroad, the system's peak 1,164 miles of track made it the largest electric railway in the world. Linking more than fifty communities, the trolleys spanned miles of coastline, climbed into two separate mountain ranges, and the Big Red Cars became as familiar in the farmlands as they were on the streets of Los Angeles.

Southern California's four major counties —Los Angeles, Orange, Riverside, and San Bernardino—were forged into what became virtually a single city of homes, stores, industries, and recreational areas.

The Big Red Cars sped through semi-desert terrain where the thermometer hit 110 degrees and plowed through banks of snow in the mountains. They carried actors to the Hollywood motion picture studios and pickers to the always-green orange groves.

The long, deep blasts of the interurban air horns became familiar to three generations of Southern Californians as they transported commuters, shoppers, and sightseers over the countryside of vineyards, orange groves,

This horse-power line to the Raymond Hotel in Pasadena, pictured in the late 1880's, eventually was electrified and became part of the Pacific Electric. Note the unpaved streets and unpaved land. (Security Pacific National Bank)

and palm-lined lanes backdropped by the snow-capped mountain ranges.

The trolley tracks become more than mere means of transportation: the bright steel rails tying cities together symbolized the growth, culture, and economic progress which nourished this period of life in Southern California.

Let's take a brief look at how the area was settled.

Although the existence of the land to be called California was known shortly after the beginning of the Christian Era, its development did not start until the time of the American revolution against the English Crown on the relatively thickly settled Atlantic Seaboard. California's settlement eventually was launched through the efforts of a handful of Spaniards whose material resources were considerably less than those which had been available for the conquests of Mexico and South America.

It was this lag in settlement that held Southern California in virtually undeveloped status almost until the advent of the Big Red Cars destined to be important tools for a most spectacular growth period.

Southern California's comparative isolation from Europe and South America can be blamed for the small attention it was accorded initially. Travel difficulties from the United States' eastern population centers later made it unattractive.

California might have been settled centuries before

the Atlantic Seaboard if the Orient's sociological and philosophical development had varied. The archives of China held evidence that a group of Buddhist monks from Afghanistan sailed along the Pacific Coast in the Fifth Century, A.D., making their way along the logical and easy route across the Bering Straits and down the coast of Alaska. They probably never were beyond sight of land. Even though these explorers wrote details of their journey on arriving in China after the trip, the Orient fostered no breed of conquistadores who would seek the mysteries of a new world. The philosophy of the Orient had turned inward and to the past through the teachings of Confucius. Scholars were content to note academically that a far distant land existed.[2]

It was in 1542, just fifty years after Columbus' first voyage to America, that the Spanish discovered California. However, its arid terrain and apparent lack of gold discouraged Spanish ambitions for two centuries.

Meanwhile, the Atlantic Seaboard had been settled and was noted for its great cities as well as its growing culture.

Finally turning their interests to California, the Spanish began a plan of settlement in 1769. The undertaking was directed primarily by priests of the Franciscan order, backed by the military force of small detachments of soldiers. The frontier was secured by the founding of missions, of which twenty-one ultimately were constructed along the coastal region from San Diego to San Francisco Bay.

Among the remarkable personages of the Spanish era was Captain Juan Bautista de Anza, a frontiersman who was given the difficult task of blazing the first overland trail to California over a desert that was to claim thousands of American lives during the gold rush nearly a century later. He proved his mastery of the desert and the men and women persuaded to join the trek proved their gallantry: the journey started with 240 people and arrived on the coast with a contigent of 242—one mother had died in childbirth but three babies were born enroute.

Members of the party became the settlers of the villages of Los Angeles and San Francisco.

Colonization generally was minimized, however. Contrary to popular opinion the so-called "rancho" period, which has been greatly romanticized, did not reach a peak until California along with Mexico won freedom

from Spain. Most of the important land grants were made by the Mexican Government.

The Spanish period became regarded of interest culturally to Southern California because it fostered the popularized "mission" architecture, differing radically from its prototypes in Arizona, New Mexico, Texas, and Mexico. Members of the Jesuit Order, who planned the settlements in the Southwest and Mexico, had been trained not only as missionaries but also as architects and builders. The Franciscans, who succeeded them, were trained basically as scholars. The circumstances forced them to assume duties as architects and builders of the California Mission Chain.

The crudeness which gave beauty to these missions stemmed from the improvised methods forced on the builders. Timbers across the tops of doorways were substituted for the architecturally advanced keystone of missions in other areas. Likewise, the width of chapels was limited to the longest timber available in nearby forests. The engineering skills were not available for the stresses required to create larger buildings.

Skills to be utilized for intricate work aparently could not be developed in the California Indians. It was perhaps this lack of culture which led to their early subjugation by the Spanish, their reduction to virtual serfdom under the mission system, and their eventual decimation under the Americans.

Yet the romanticized lore of the Indians and their missions became practical tools not only for the land developers who used "Spanish" architecture to interest home buyers but also for the operators of the trolleys that were to help build Southern California.

The downfall for the Indians and the start of a change for all California came with the discovery of gold in 1848 on the American River near Sacramento. Various forces already were at work to seize California from Mexico, and the mass arrivals of Americans secured the area for the United States.

The famous gold rush, bringing most of the pioneers to the northern section of the state, quickly made San Francisco a major city and its harbor a thriving port.

The impetus of the gold rush boomed San Francisco, a village of 812 people in 1848, into a metropolis of more than 50,000 within the next ten years.

San Francisco took an undisputed place as the principal shipping port and financial center for a major portion of the West as Nevada and adjacent territory began to develop.

Southern California was not forgotten. The southern section of the state, with cattle thriving on the ranches stretching along the coastal planes and valleys, provided the gold country with its supplies of beef.

2. Documents relating to Oriental explorations along the Pacific Coast during pre-Columbian times are discussed by Edward Payson Vining in "An Inglorious Columbus; or Evidence That Hwui Shan and a Party of Buddhist Monks from Afghanistan Discovered America in the Fifth Century, A.D.," (New York: 1885).

The south became amusingly known as the "cow counties," for sophisticated San Franciscans regarded the arid area as of little value for anything but raising cattle.

Los Angeles, with a population of 1,500 in the 1850 census, was the largest city in the southern section and therefore was accorded the title of "Queen of the Cow Counties" by flippant San Franciscans.

While the northern section of the state grew and prospered during the years immediately following the gold rush, Southern California remained largely pastoral in character. The reason for the inactivity was not only the remoteness from the main stream of the state's development but also the fact that much of the area's land was in large ranches.

Three factors in the 1860's reversed this situation. The first division of large land holdings came with foreclosures against many ranches whose owners were unable to make payments on mortgages made with ridiculously high interest rates by wily American money lenders.

A severe drought hit Southern California in 1861-62, resulting in financial disaster for many ranchers. Livestock died for want of pasture. Thousands of cattle were slaughtered for the small amounts of money which their hides could bring. The crisis forced more land on the market.

The third factor was the encouragement of agriculture through state subsidies, which further reduced large land holdings.

The availability of small farms, together with a growing appreciation of Southern California's mild climate, began to attract residents to the area. Los Angeles' rate of growth remained small, however, and the 1870 census gave it only 5,614 residents.

Farming on the surrounding plains grew so that by 1872 Charles Nordhoff, the famous California booster, was able to note that as he arrived in Los Angeles he met a farm wagon "carrying to market oranges, pumpkins, a lamb, corn, green peas in their pods, sugar-cane, lemons and strawberries. . . . Below us, as we looked off a hill-top, lay the suburbs of Los Angeles, green with the deep green or orange groves, and golden to the nearer view with their abundant fruit." [3]

However, he was forced to add:

The Pueblo de Los Angeles—the town of the angels—is not, in its present state, a very angelic place. It is irregularly built, the older part having but one principal street . . . if you walk down this street, you will be surprised at the excellence of the shops . . . which will surprise you if you have listened to the opinion of San Franciscans about this metropolis of Southern California.

The old Spanish town, nicknamed Sonora, lies at one end near the mission church, the somewhat discordant clangor of whose bells startles you out of your sleep early in the morning as they summon the faithful to prayers. Next to this comes the business streets, and beyond these the American part of the town. Orange groves surround the town almost, and vineyards are numerous.

Nordhoff noted that real estate prices already were climbing in anticipation of a boom: [4]

The price of land at first strikes the stranger as high. Near Los Angeles they ask from thirty to a hundred dollars per acre for unimproved farming land. I thought they were already discounting the railroad which is coming to them . . . As I had seen in the East the rise in prices following the mere announcement of a new railroad, it was natural for me to think that prices here had been affected by the same cause. But I am satisfied that they are, on the whole, not too high.

Of course, when men ask fifty or a hundred dollars per acre for land, it is "with water." Land which has little water is sold for from one to three dollars per acre, in large quantities, for herding sheep or cattle.

As the ranches were divided into small farms, the subdividers made their way to San Francisco, where they button-holed new arrivals as they left ships. The promoters told of land being sold at bargain prices in an area which was on the verge of a boom.

The City of Southern California had given birth to its first boosters, a breed that was to multiply and send the message of seemingly endless growth down through the decades.

---

3. Charles Nordhoff, "California: For Health, Pleasure, and Residence," (New York: 1874), p. 137.

4. Nordhoff, p. 139.

Streetcars drawn by horses or mules became commonplace in Southern California communities after the success of Judge Widney's line in Los Angeles. This one, at Ontario, was equipped with a rear platform so the animal could ride "free" during the downhill return trip from San Antonio Heights. (Title Insurance and Trust Co.)

2. Prelude to Progress: The Iron Horse Arrives

The awakening of Southern California following the division of ranches into farms which in turn were to become cities produced the man who is credited with opening the first real estate office in Los Angeles.

Appropriately, it was this same individual who was to organize the area's initial streetcar company—the first of nearly a hundred individual transportation firms which eventually were consolidated into the vast Pacific Electric interurban system.

This entrepreneur was Judge Robert Maclay Widney, a man of many talents who was to leave deep imprints on the cultural and commercial life of Southern California.

A native of Ohio, Widney had been a hunter on the plains prior to coming to California in a covered wagon in 1857 when nineteen years of age. Widney demonstrated the drive which was to mark his life when on arriving he applied for a job paying $1.50 for each cord of wood that he could cut. He was asked how soon he could go to work.

"Just as soon as I can get to the first tree," he replied.

Widney saw greater opportunities in California, however. The year after his arrival he enrolled at the University of the Pacific at Santa Clara. He was graduated in 1863 as valedictorian of his class and immediately joined the University's faculty, teaching subjects ranging from mathematics and astronomy to botany and civil engineering. At the same time he studied law and was admitted to the state bar.

Seeking opportunities to apply his varied talents, Widney was among the first to sense the boom developing in Southern California as the ranch era ended. He settled at Los Angeles in 1868 and immediately became active in its affairs. Three years after his arrival he won an appointment as district judge for a territory covering most of Southern California. The position allowed time for other activities, and Widney put his talents to good use.

Widney had opened a real estate office and he

19

Judge Robert M. Widney built Los Angeles' first streetcar line so he and neighbors could ride to their homes.

extended its activities throughout Southern California. Putting his literary talents to use, he launched a publication, "The Southern California Real Estate Advertiser," to boast the area's natural attractions in general and his land offerings in particular to prospective buyers throughout the nation.

Judge Widney also directed the incorporation of the first Los Angeles Chamber of Commerce in 1873. The same year he used his engineering skills to make specifications for the breakwater needed to develop a deep water harbor at San Pedro.

It was Widney who led the party that staked out the route for a railroad through Cajon Pass, above San Bernardino, only two hours before engineers from the Southern Pacific arrived for the same purpose. His action prevented the possibility of a railroad monopoly in Southern California.

One evening in 1879 he invited the Rev. A. M. Hough, a Methodist minister, to his home near Bunker Hill to discuss needs of a college for the community. The meeting produced the University of Southern Cali-

fornia, for which Judge Widney drew the articles of incorporation in 1880 and became one of its first trustees.

The City of Southern California was growing.

But the problem of transportation was beginning to perplex Judge Widney, just as it was to puzzle generations of Southern Californians to follow him.

The judge's neighbors in the vicinity of Third and Hill Streets, regarded as "out in the country," agreed the distance from the business section called for some form of convenient public transportation. They agreed to contribute 50 cents for each front foot of their property to build a horsecar line, at the time considered the ultimate in city travel.

Widney's single-track Spring Street and Sixth Street Railroad, stretching for 2½ miles from the Mission Plaza down Main and Spring Streets to Sixth Street, was opened in 1874.

The first link had been formed in the network of tracks that was to connect communities and help build Southern California.

Rides were ten cents each; "commuters" could purchase twenty tickets for a dollar. The streetcars stopped at the passengers' convenience on the route without regard to intersections; there was no traffic congestion problem.

"While the single horse or mule jogged along slowly," recalled Harris Newmark, the Los Angeles pioneer, "the driver, having wound his reins around the handle of the brake, would pass through the never-crowded vehicle and take up fares." [1]

Rains frequently brought troubles, however, for the railroad's ties had been laid on the surface of the unpaved streets. Wet weather either suspended service entirely or caused cars to become stuck in the mud. As primitive as Judge Widney's streetcar system was, it became enthusiastically accepted by the public. Its financial success brought construction of similar enterprises to other communities in Southern California.

Unlike most men, the remarkable Judge Widney was able to see the seeds that he had sown grow and blossom into creations exceeding his greatest dreams.

Before he died in the early 1930's, the tracts he had planned grew into major cities, the university he helped to found had become one of the nation's leading institutions for learning, and the basic drawings he made for a harbor became the foundation for an important seaport.

And the single-track, horse-drawn streetcar system he started had grown into the biggest interurban operation in the world, knitting a great area together.

1. Harris Newmark, "Sixty Years in Southern California: 1853-1913," (Boston: 1930), p. 460.

Puffing and steaming, locomotives brought Southern California its first boom. This train was part of the Los Angeles *and San Gabriel Valley Railroad, a short line built during the 1880's. (Security Pacific National Bank)*

The results of the 1870 census brought good news to San Francisco, which was given a population of 149,473. Only 5,728 residents were reported in Los Angeles, where boosters were clamoring for a bigger share of the increasing numbers of easterners who headed west after completion of the transcontinental railroad.

Networks of steam railroads had stretched over the midwestern and eastern United States during the three decades preceding the American Civil War. A tremendous impetus was given to the development of farming communities and industrial centers wherever railroads were built.

The famous ceremony for the driving of the gold spike at Promontory Point, Utah, celebrated completion of the nation's first transcontinental route, the Central Pacific, in 1869—just a century after the founding of the first California mission by the Spanish. The rail link started a transcontinental migration which would have made the Spanish pioneers blink in amazement. The population boom warmed the hearts of boosters throughout California.

The driving force behind the Central Pacific was

Collis P. Huntington, who went to California during the gold rush armed with sound business advice from his older brother, Solon Huntington, owner of a hardware store in Oneonta, New York.

Huntington, however, did not dig in the Mother Lode to find his gold. Instead, he became a hardware merchant in Sacramento, second only to San Francisco in commercial importance for California. He sold to the miners who willingly paid inflated prices during the gold rush. Huntington became associated with three other men who realized that ownership of a transcontinental rail system would be a bonanza more valuable than a gold mine. Huntington, Charles Crocker, Leland Stanford, and Mark Hopkins—The Big Four—formed the Central Pacific. The railway, heavily financed by federal subsidies, was completed after six years of construction and linked booming San Francisco with the Atlantic Coast.

It had taken the pioneers up to six months to reach California in covered wagons after leaving the "jumping-off place," St. Joseph, Missouri.

"The traveling time from New York to San Fran-

Crowds enjoy one of the barbecues staged during the 1880's by real estate promoters to attract potential buyers arriving on the new transcontinental rail lines. Southern California land prices soared. (Security Pacific National Bank)

cisco, if you go through without stopping, is seven days," reported that enthusiastic booster of California migration, Charles Nordhoff.

Describing the transcontinental trip, he continued: [2]

In the East a railroad journey is an interruption to our lives. We submit to it because no one has yet been ingenious enough to contrive a flying machine. . . . No Eastern man knows the comfort or pleasure of traveling by rail until he crosses the Plains . . . you leave care behind in the depot, and make yourself comfortable, as one does on a sea voyage . . .

. . . You may lie down at full length or sit up, sleep or awake . . . your dinner is sure to be abundant, very tolerably cooked, and not hurried . . . you are pretty certain to make acquaintances on the car . . . you write very comfortably at a table in a little room called a drawing room . . .

. . . About eight o'clock . . . the porter, in a clean gray uniform, like that of a Central Park Policeman, comes in to make up the beds. The two easy chairs are turned into a berth; the sofa undergoes a similar transformation. . . . The freshest and whitest of linen and brightly colored blankets complete the outfit; and you undress and go to bed as you would at home, and, unless you have eaten too heartily of antelope or elk, will sleep as soundly.

. . . From Chicago three railroads . . . lead to Omaha. . . . You are to understand that all these lines make connection with the Pacific Railroads, and that all roads lead to San Francisco.

The railroad was regarded as the harbinger of prosperity and growth. The boosters of Los Angeles

were unhappy because their metropolis had none.

Fears that the city would be relegated to indefinite anonymonity grew after the report that the Southern Pacific, by this time the successor to the Central Pacific, planned to pass Los Angeles in constructing a route from San Francisco through the San Joaquin Valley toward Arizona and thence eastward.

Delegations of Los Angeles businessmen contacted the railroad with pleas for a change in the route. The company remained adamant in plans to bypass the village —unless townspeople agreed to pay $600,000, an amount equal to five percent of the city's assessed valuation, to reimburse the costs of building to the pueblo. Conservative citizens vigorously opposed the subsidy, maintaining that the railroad really intended to include Los Angeles on its southern route and made the monetary demand only to coerce the community.

The boosters were concerned, however, and contended that the city would be benefited by prosperity valued at many times the subsidy when it obtained rail connections. If the Southern Pacific bypassed Los Angeles, they argued, some community fortunate enough to be on the line would become the metropolis of Southern California.

The controversy was placed on a ballot in 1872 and by a vote of 1,896 to 650 the people of Los Angeles

2. Nordhoff, pp. 20, 23, 25.

This brass band added to the festivities greeting the arrival of the first Southern Pacific train to Los Angeles in 1876.

Completion of the rail link brought new residents. (Los Angeles Public Library)

approved the subsidy. The last spike connecting Los Angeles with San Francisco was driven on September 6, 1876—just two years after Judge Widney had opened his streetcar line—and connections to the Texas Pacific Railroad were completed eight months later.

The effect of the rail system linking Southern California with San Francisco and subsequently the eastern United States was to launch a steadily increasing flow of migrants of two classes: one came to settle and the other to speculate on the spiralling prices of land.

The result was what has popularly been called the "Boom of the Eighties," but which really was a series of booms starting with the completion of the Southern Pacific link. Every pasture became a potential metropolis, at least in the minds of the buyers if not in the practical beliefs of the developers.

The land boom heightened in 1885 with the completion of a second transcontinental rail link, the Atchison, Topeka, and Santa Fe Railroad, which entered the Los Angeles basin through the Cajon Pass route staked out by Judge Widney.

A passenger fare rate war developed between the Southern Pacific and the Santa Fe, adding to the frenzied real estate activity for which there seemed to be no peak. A ticket from the Mississippi River to Los Angeles had been $125 when the Southern Pacific held its monopoly; the fare dropped to $100 shortly after arrival of the Santa Fe.

It was on March 6, 1887, that the battle between the railroads reached its peak. That morning the fare from Kansas City had been $12; shortly before noon the Santa Fe reduced the fare to $10 and when the Southern Pacific met the competition, the Santa Fe cut the tariff to $8. During the remainder of the day the Southern Pacific cut its rates three times—finally selling tickets for the all-time low of $1 for the trip west. Although both railroads almost immediately began increasing fares slightly, it was possible for nearly a year to purchase a ticket to Los Angeles for $25 or less.

The depressed fares proved the incentive needed to bring thousands of people who ordinarily would have not made the journey to California. Real estate developers regarded these new arrivals as fair game. Lots were sold at higher prices and speculators counted increasingly high paper profits on the expectation that each train would bring more enthusiastic buyers from the East.

Real estate developers built railroad short lines to points in Southern California wherever they might be selling land. They counted on the availability of such transportation to boost the sales potentials of property in the new "cities." Barley and wheat fields were laid out as pretentious municipalities, at least on paper. If all lots plotted had been sold and built upon, it is probable that Southern California's population would have soared toward the five million mark — substantially de-populating many eastern cities.

But the influx of migrants expected in late 1888 failed to develop. Ambitious building projects which had been announced for the new communities were dropped. Real estate sales slowed and many speculators unhappily discovered that their property was useful only for farming. The few settlers who did arrive in Southern California shunned the recently formed villages and displayed a marked preference for Los Angeles itself, which boasted the business center and cultural offerings not available in the smaller communities.

The wake of Southern California's growth brought increased emphasis in the transportation field. The Southern Pacific and Santa Fe railroads, not content with merely reaching Los Angeles, started to extend tracks to the outlying communities founded during the growth periods. The automobile was as yet a dream and lucrative profits from passenger and freight service were expected from the rail investments with the continuing westward trek.

As part of their expansion, the two transcontinental railroads acquired many of the short lines started by real estate developers to promote their tracts. The two companies expected the lines to feed passengers and freight into their systems as Southern California grew.

Railroads nationally and local were highly profitable investments because of the fact that they enjoyed a virtual monopoly in transporting passengers and freight. Railroads could, and frequently did, charge whatever the traffic would bear because of the absence of competition. The term "robber barons" was applied to the tycoons that consolidated rail systems and formed such monopolies in order to boost rates. As the nineteenth century closed, there was general public feeling against railroads in general. The trust-busters, typified and led by President Theodore Roosevelt, began action to break monopolies. At the same time, heavy taxes were imposed on the railway companies, all making handsome profits.

Among those who moved to board the band wagon of profits was United States Senator William A. Clark of Montana, distinguished in appearance by his beard

Senator Stephen M. White successfully opposed Huntington and obtained funds for a harbor at San Pedro.

and ample head of hair. Early in 1900 he formed the Salt Lake Railroad (a predecessor of the Union Pacific) with the intent of forging a new rail link across the desert to Southern California to compete with the existing railroads in the profitable traffic. As part of his successful plan he purchased the Los Angeles Terminal Railroad, a line running between Los Angeles, Long Beach, San Pedro, Pasadena, and Glendale.

The Southern Pacific had not been idle following completion of its tracks to Los Angeles, but its efforts had turned to a new goal: development of a deep-water harbor which inevitably would be needed to serve the increasing commerce of the City of Southern California. Los Angeles business interests agreed that a port was needed for the metropolis and the only debate was as to where the harbor would be located. Unlike San Francisco, Southern California had no natural deep-water harbor. It would be necessary for Los Angeles to carve

Electric streetcars were a familiar sight in Los Angeles when this picture was made at the corner of First and *Spring Streets shortly after the birth of the twentieth century. (Pacific Railroad Publications)*

a port from mudflats or shape it with breakwaters and piers at one of the beach communities.

Every seaside village envisioned itself as the site for the port of the Metropolis, for such selection would give it immense growth. There were shallow harbors at Newport, Anaheim Bay (adjacent to what was to become Seal Beach), Alamitos Bay (at Long Beach), at San Pedro, and at Ballonna Bay (adjoining Venice), all of which local groups advocated dredging. In addition the construction of piers for large vessels were advocated at Long Beach, Redondo Beach, Santa Monica, and the

area which was to become Huntington Beach.

A report by the Army Corps of Engineers favored building the port at San Pedro, a proposal endorsed by the majority of Los Angeles interests. In addition to allowing ample area for expansion, diversified ownership of the area assured free access for all railroads in order to promote competition.

However, the Southern Pacific controlled most of the seaside land at Santa Monica, which it designated "Port Los Angeles" in anticipation of its development. During the 1890's Collis P. Huntington as president of the railroad exercised his extensive and personal influence in an effort to pressure Congress to allocate federal funds for a port at Santa Monica. Los Angeles interests were stymied as they sought funds to build a harbor at San Pedro.

Collis Huntington found a formidable and unyielding opponent in the person of United States Senator Stephen Mallory White, a young San Franciscan who had settled in Los Angeles and embarked on a political career to fulfill a boyhood ambition to be a Senator from California.

Stephen White surmounted obstacles as he sought the office he craved. He was a Catholic in a state dominated by Protestants at a time of religious bigotry and a Democrat when the party was weak. Yet he had ability that won the admiration even of the Los Angeles Times, an ultra-Republican newspaper.

White took his seat in the Senate in 1893 and began the fight for federal funds for a harbor at San Pedro. Collis P. Huntington was a powerful lobbyist and the fight was to continue for five years. White later recalled a conversation with the magnate: [3]

He (C. P. Huntington) asked if there was no way for us to get together on the harbor business. I said that I did not see any way to do so—that I did not think he would give up, and I knew I would not.

Said he (Huntington) I do not see why. It might be to your advantage not to be so set in your opinion. I then said to him: Mr. Huntington, if that harbor were my personal possession and you wanted it then it would be an easy way for us to get together and one or both of us make some money. But as that harbor belongs to the people, and I am merely holding it in trust for them, and have no right to give it away, I do not see how we can come to any understanding.

By powerful oration and strong logic, Senator White won Congressional endorsement for the harbor at San Pedro in 1898 and the following year President William McKinley pressed a button in Washington, D.C., which sent an electrical impulse dumping the first rock for the great port.

After the battle was won, Collis Huntington approached the Senator and said: [4]

White, I like and respect you. You are almost always against us, but it is not for what you can make out of us to come over. You have a steadfast principle and you fight like a man, in the open and with weapons. I cannot say that of all the public men I have had to deal with.

Subsequent chiefs of the Southern Pacific were as dedicated as Collis P. Huntington in seeking a monopoly for traf-

3. Leroy E. Mosher, "Stephen M. White: His Life and His Work," (Los Angeles: 903), p. 12.

4. Mosher, p. 12.

Collis P. Huntington of the Southern Pacific fought Los Angeles groups seeking to build a harbor at San Pedro.

fic to Los Angeles' harbor as it developed in the early 1900's. The particular nemesis of the S. P. was to be none other than C. P.'s nephew, Henry E. Huntington.

When Henry Huntington began to battle the Southern Pacific in the Los Angeles area, he associated himself with many of the civic leaders who had been allied with Stephen Mallory White in his opposition to the railway monopoly prior to his death in 1901.

Senator White's daughter, Miss Hortense White, told me in a 1967 conversation that her father and Henry Huntington had many interests in common. If the Senator had lived, she said, he and Henry Huntington certainly would have formed an alliance in a battle to provide ample competition for the Southern Pacific.

Henry Huntington's plans — and the development of the City of Southern California — might have been radically different if it had not been for the invention unveiled by a young man named Frank J. Sprague.

That invention — the electric interurban — was to help shape Southern California into an immense horizontal community rather than a vertical, compact city of skyscrapers.

The Angel's Flight Railway, pictured here shortly after its opening, provided easy access to Bunker Hill, at the time *an exclusive Los Angeles residential area. Atop the hill was an observation tower. (Security Pacific National Bank)*

3. "Speed" by Sprague

The growth of major cities throughout the world brought many problems, and chief among them was transportation for the people who could not afford to buy and maintain horses and carriages. One of the early solutions for this need had been the birth in 18th century London of the Omnibus, which was in fact an over-sized stagecoach offering transportation to the public over basically formalized routes. Riders crowded into the vehicles in much the same manner as commuters of other eras were to use streetcar and subway systems.

The coming of the railroads in the 1830's not only provided inter-city travel, but it also provided the idea of tracks which formed the basis for the horse and mule

streetcars that served the public for local transportation.

The conveyance which provided transportation during the transition between horse-drawn streetcars and the electric interurban was the cable car, that unique vehicle which had its birth and greatest fame in San Francisco. Andrew Hallidie, a Scot, arrived in San Francisco in 1852 when 16 years old. Eventually he became the proprietor of a wire rope manufacturing company. Hallidie had an inventive mind and was issued several patents, including one for a wire rope suspension bridge.

His most famous invention, however, was the cable car street transportation system.

Hallidie had seen countless accidents involving horse-

27

drawn streetcars on the steep hills of San Francisco. His solution involved a cable concealed in a slot in the middle of the streetcar tracks; power from a steam plant kept the cable moving continuously and the car moved as the operator engaged a lever to connect the vehicle to the cable.

The first installation, on San Francisco's Clay Street, opened in 1873 and was declared a success.

Similar systems were installed in other American cities including Los Angeles. There were shortcomings to cable systems, however; these included high initial costs and rapid deterioation because of water filling the slot and rusting the heavy cable.

It should be noted at this point that the pattern of Southern California's transportation development at the turn of the century was by no means limited to conventional rails. Travelers took to incline cable railways and, briefly, even a freeway for bicycles.

Among the arrivals during the boom following completion of the Southern Pacific was Professor Thaddeus

S. C. Lowe, who had distinguished himself during the Civil War in the unusual role of a balloonist for the Union forces. On settling in Southern California, he was inspired by the majesty of the San Gabriel Mountain range whose lofty peaks were inaccessible to most travelers. He decided to build a railway into the mountains from a point near Pasadena.

Conventional railroad construction obviously couldn't conquer the steep mountain grades. Lowe therefore called on the technical abilities of Andrew Hallidie, the Scot who invented the cable railway system to conquer the hills of San Francisco.

After more than a year of construction, the facility was opened officially on July 4, 1893 and immediately proclaimed as one of Southern California's greatest tourist attractions. Its most spectacular feature was The Great Incline, a cable system which transported passengers approximately 1,500 feet from a pavilion in Rubio Canyon at 2,000 feet above sea level up a sixty percent grade to the summit of Echo Mountain. Two cable cars, designed so that passengers always would be at a level

Trolleys dominated downtown Los Angeles streets when this photo was made in the early twentieth century. Street- *cars helped workers travel from suburbs in this era when there were few autos. (Security Pacific National Bank)*

Passengers posed for this historic photograph when the first trolley line linking Santa Monica with Los Angeles and   *Pasadena was opened in 1896. The speedy trolley service made Santa Monica grow. (Title Insurance and Trust Co.)*

despite the steep grade, balanced each other so that a minimum of power would be required for operation.

From Echo Mountain, at 3,500 feet above sea level, travelers rode trolley cars around 127 curves and eighteen trestles to the base of Mount Lowe, at 5,000 feet above sea level. Here were restaurant facilities as well as a hotel and cabins for those who wished to spend extended vacations.

The system became immensely popular not only for the scenic rides but also for the spectacular view: in those pre-smog days it was possible to look down on the mountain onto the growing City of Southern California as well as to Catalina Island twenty miles offshore. Most winters brought snow to Mount Lowe and Southern Californians, accustomed to the year-long mild climate, found a pleasant contrast in the apline area.

Subsequent advertising of the resort proclaimed it to be the "Sierra Madre Mountains," a misnomer for the range destined to continue for years. There was, in fact, no Sierra Madre range in California; the peaks by Pasadena were named the San Gabriel Mountains. The Angel's Flight Railway in Los Angeles was another funicular cable system. It opened on December 31, 1901, to carry passengers from Third and Hill Streets up the steep grade to Bunker Hill, which at the time was one of the city's exclusive residential districts. The builder was Colonel J. W.

Eddy, 69 years of age when the little railway was opened. His career included experience as a lawyer as well as an engineer. He proudly told friends he had been a friend of President Abraham Lincoln.

Colonel Eddy's railway climbed a thirty-three percent grade in 335 feet, a system not nearly as spectacular at the Mount Lowe incline but one highly popular with its one cent fare for those who otherwise had to climb the tedious 207 steps adjoining the rails.

Bicycles were becoming popular means of transportation at the turn of the century and in 1899 a 33-year-old businessman named Horace Dobkins decided to capitalize on the fad. He decided to build an elevated road of lumber which would stretch from Pasadena to Los Angeles, a distance of ten miles. The facility, which he named "The Cycleway," would have a maxium grade of three percent and, spanning the countryside, would allow bicyclists to travel uninterrupted by turns, pedestrians, or other vehicles. The cost of using the bicycle freeway was set at five cents per trip.

The Cycleway's first 1,000 feet opened on New Year's Day of 1900 and more than 500 bicyclists paid to use the facility. Dobkins was overjoyed and beginning planning extensions of the Cycleway throughout Southern California. But by the end of the week traffic had dwindled to four to five rides daily and Dobkins realized

29

the initial enthusiasm had been caused only by the novelty of his brain child. He began to dismantle the great wooden overhead freeway.

It was evident that Southern Californians preferred to travel by rail car.

Meanwhile, experimenters in other parts of the nation were seeking more efficient ways to carry commuters.

Experiments with the use of electric motors to operate streetcars had been conducted as early as 1835 without production of a commercially useable vehicle. Among the experimenters had been Leo Daft of Greenville, New Jersey, whose 1883 electric locomotive drew its 120 volt current from an exposed third rail in a street at Baltimore. To overcome objections of dangers presented by the exposed rail, Daft then used a system carrying the current by two overhead wires.

Riding over the wires to pick up the current for the streetcars were small trucks called trollers—which promptly were corrupted into "trolleys" and gave a popular name to the system. "Trolleys" became the shortened term for both interurban and local electric streetcars.

The electric interurban system that was becoming popularly used, however, was that of Frank J. Sprague, whose techniques solved the problems of safety, efficiency, and economy not available in competing inventions. The electric streetcar was quickly accepted but was antiquated almost as promptly by the invention of the automobile.

After graduating from the United States Naval Academy in 1878 Sprague spent five years in electrical experimentation on active naval duty, during the course of which he went to London. When he saw the London underground filled with the smoke of locomotives, the idea came to him that electric power could be used for transportation. Leaving the navy, he worked as an assistant to Thomas Edison in experiments perfecting the electric light.

The young man terminated the Edison association after a year in order to form the Sprague Electric Railway and Motor Company. The firm was to manufacture and market Sprague's invention, the electric streetcar. Although unable to interest the New York elevated railroads in his system, he obtained a contract in 1887 to install his invention on the Union Passenger Railway at Richmond, Virginia.

The installation, completed in 1888, included twelve miles of track, an electric powerhouse, and forty electric cars. The system was pronounced a success and a second installation was made in Boston.

Sprague was then deluged by orders.

Transportation men hailed the superiority of the electric railroad over horse and mule drawn cars, which required expensive facilities for feeding and care of the

Frank J. Sprague's invention of the electric streetcar opened the way for vast improvements in community transportation.

animals and could never hope to provide the speed possible with Sprague's invention.

Trolleys could travel easily up steep grades impossible for horse-drawn streetcars and difficult for steam locomotives. Soon after the invention was unveiled, numerous improvements in technology—notably a multiple-unit control system allowing one motorman to operate a train of several electric cars—made the trolleys increasingly practical for interurban service.

During the next ten years horse and cable streetcar systems, including those in Los Angeles, were replaced by the trolley. New systems were built using Sprague's invention.

On the eve of the advent of the electric interurban, Los Angeles had finally achieved the status of a true city and could no longer be called a village.

The booms following the arrival of the Southern Pacific gave the city an 1880 population of 25,000, a four-fold increase since 1870. By 1890 Los Angeles had a population of 50,395—double the number of residents a decade before but substantially less than the boosters anticipated as the boom was hitting its peak. More

Even suburban areas were within easy — and pleasant — travel time from Los Angeles when the Pacific Electric's Big Red Cars rolled and reigned. This scene was near Etiwanda. (Photograph by the Author)

important, towns had developed in the surrounding areas previously devoted to farmlands. The 1890 census gave the Los Angeles County area outside of Los Angeles a population of 51,059 as compared to only 8,000 in 1880. San Bernardino and Riverside Counties had a total population of 25,497, a spectacular increase from the 7,786 residents of 1880.

Despite the general depression which hit America in the 1890's, successful subdivisions began to replace orange groves and corn fields surrounding Los Angeles. Horse-drawn streetcar lines as well as cable systems frequently were built by the land developers to attract buyers. Among the groups developing land during the boom of the eighties was one headed by Charles H. Howland, a man who was to become noteworthy for an innovation rather than his singular success. Howland's investment group had purchased land for a subdivision in a farming area west of Vermont Street and north of Pico Street, a district regarded as rural. In an effort to make the tract more saleable Howland produced an idea which was indeed original: an electric streetcar line would be built to the area. The subdivision appropriately was named "The Electric Railway Homestead Association Tract" in order to capitalize on the innovation.

Frank Sprague's efficient electric streetcar system was as yet unveiled, so Howland used the principle developed by Leo Daft in which two overhead wires were used for the cars to receive and return the electricity. The electric streetcars ran for the first time on January 4, 1887, causing a sensation among Los Angeles residents, a large number of whom were prompted to enjoy the thrill of riding the electric cars.

The city's initial electric railway was doomed to failure, however, because of technical difficulties in its operation. Prospective purchasers eventually were taken to inspect the tract in horse-drawn streetcars. Howland's system became important in the ultimate development of interurban transportation in Southern California not only because of the innovation itself but also because of the men it eventually attracted.

The streetcar line was purchased early in 1890 by a group of Kansas investors, who decided to modernize it with the Sprague electric cars being acclaimed nationally. The work of rebuilding the line along Pico Street attracted more than passing attention from General Moses H. Sherman, a 37-year-old native of Vermont. He had left his home in Arizona for a vacation in Los Angeles.

It was the Pico Street line which was to induce Sherman to make his trip to Los Angeles more than a mere vacation. Sherman's interest resulted in the first link of an electric interurban system eventually making Southern California a single community.

The Cycleway spanned this Pasadena street in a turn-of-the-century venture designed to carry bicyclists over the country-side to Los Angeles. The convenience of trolleys helped doom the project. (Security Pacific National Bank)

A Los Angeles Railway Company trolley awaits passengers at the ornate La Grande Station in Los Angeles. The firm *was Henry Huntington's initial investment in the area's electric rail field. (Security Pacific National Bank)*

General Moses H. Sherman's summer visit to Southern California was extended to cover the remainder of his life and to mark him, along with his brother-in-law, Eli P. Clark, among the great builders of the City of Southern California.

Sherman, who had visited Los Angeles briefly in 1876 while enroute to settle in Arizona, was greatly impressed by the opportunities the city promised in 1890 as it emerged from its recent booms. The construction of the electric railway particularly interested him for he envisioned profitable extensions throughout the area. Eli Clark agreed on the potentials and the pair purchased the Howland line — launching in Southern California association extending for nearly forty years.

Sherman and Clark were among those young men who had turned to the growing west for their futures:

both shared a common background as school teachers who adapted themselves to a variety of interests.

Moses Sherman had been a teacher in a rural school in New York before moving to Arizona. It was in Prescott, where he taught school, that his sister, Lucy, married Eli Clark, a former teacher from Iowa who had become a merchant and acting postmaster for the city. Sherman was appointed state superintendent of public instruction by Arizona's territorial Governor John C. Fremont, the controversial figure identified with the struggle for California with the Mexican Government and subsequently an unsuccessful candidate for the U.S. Presidency.

General Sherman received his military title through service as adjutant in the Arizona state militia. In 1884 he established the Valley Bank of Phoenix and built

33

Eli P. Clark (above) and his brother-in-law, Moses H. Sherman, acquired Los Angeles area trolley systems in the 1890's and forged them to link Pasadena and Santa Monica via Los Angeles. (Los Angeles Public Library)

the Phoenix Railway, linking the city to the adjacent community of Glendale. Eli Clark also had fared well in Arizona. He won an appointment as territorial auditor, established a lumber firm, and was an officer in the Prescott and Arizona Railroad, built in 1886.

The brothers-in-law proceeded to expand their Los Angeles transit interests after purchasing the city's initial electric streetcar system. Acquiring horse-car and cable-car systems, they unified them into the Los Angeles Consolidated Electric Railway, called LACE by its patrons. The company's initial streetcar building project was the University Line, securing strategic areas in the southwestern section of Los Angeles—including the University of Southern California founded a decade before by Judge Widney and his associates.

LACE's main competition became William Spencer Hook, a Chicago banker who in 1894 came to Los Angeles for a summer vacation as had Sherman four years previously.

Hook, a lanky, lean-faced midwesterner, also envisioned a vast electric streetcar transportation system pacing the area's growth. He formed the Los Angeles Traction Company, bringing such vigorous competition that Sherman and Clark soon found it difficult to obtain credit for expansion.

The Hook and Sherman-Clark interests competed in Los Angeles not only in electrifying cable and horse railways but also in building new trolley lines.

Until this time Southern California's streetcar construction projects had been concerned with providing transportation within the cities. Horsecar lines had opened in Pasadena, Pomona, Ontario, Santa Monica, and San Bernardino as well as in Los Angeles to encourage the purchase of housing tracts.

Elsewhere in the United States, however, Frank Sprague's electric cars had been put to use in linking cities through interurban lines. As early as 1893 Oregon's East Side Railway Company had completed its line between Portland and Oregon City and Ohio's Sandusky, Milan and Norwalk Electric Railway had linked Sandusky and Norwalk. Other inter-city electric lines were being built in Maine, Massachusetts, Illinois, Iowa, and Missouri.

The term applied to these lines, "interurban" (Latin for "between cities"), had been used as early as 1890 in regard to the electric streetcar line which connected Minneapolis and St. Paul. It was popularized in 1893 by Charles L. Henry, an Indiana transit developer. As the years passed "interurban" generally was to refer to systems built on private rights-of-way and connecting cities as contrasted to those using public streets and usually serving a single city.

Observing the success of interurbans elsewhere in the nation, Sherman and Clark decided to initiate a system for Southern California. The first step, they decided, would be a link to Pasadena.

Pasadena, only ten miles northeast of Los Angeles, was a quiet little residential community on the piedmont of the San Gabriel mountains. The town was founded by a group of migrants from Indiana in 1874, two years before the arrival of the Southern Pacific. Pasadena had prospered during the booms of the seventies and eighties and by 1890 had nearly 5,000 residents. Its progress had slowed somewhat with the collapse of the boom.

Borrowing money from San Francisco banks, the brothers-in-law purchased all of the streetcar lines in Pasadena in 1894. They not only obtained a local transportation monopoly in the growing city but, most important, they could use portions of the local lines to forge an interurban connection to Los Angeles. Meanwhile, Sherman and Clark met financial difficulties in operation of their Los Angeles streetcar lines. Early in 1895 bondholders ousted them from control of LACE and formed the Los Angeles Railway Company which took over the system.

Despite the financial reverses Sherman and Clark retained control of their Pasadena investment. Forming the Los Angeles and Pasadena Railway Company, they began linking the local lines into what was to become Southern California's first interurban system. The line was dramatically opened on May 4, 1895 as ten electric cars sped along the route from Pasadena through South Pasadena and thence into Los Angeles.

The route that this pioneer trolley system followed could hardly be recognized today because of the area's growth, track removal, and street paving programs. The car barns were at North Fair Oaks and Mary Street in Pasadena, and the trolleys went down Fair Oaks. They entered Los Angeles from the north via Broadway and Main and Spring Streets. (Under the Pacific Electric banner, the route became known as the "Pasadena Short Line," appropriately named because it was the system's shortest route between Los Angeles and Pasadena. While the line used Fair Oaks until service was discontinued in 1951, other portions of the route varied during the years.)

The interurban line was an immediate success. One reason that it was able to gather a loyal force of riders who subsequently could carry word of the electric interurban's efficiency was the fact that Sherman and Clark had been able to forge the link several weeks before the Southern Pacific line was completed to Pasadena from Los Angeles. This fact also gave great prestige to the potential of the interurban.

There was no problem of crowds when this picture was taken during the early twentieth century at Santa Monica, but the convenience of electric interurbans was beginning to draw inlanders. (Security Pacific National Bank Collection)

Electric streetcars replaced cable and horse lines during the early 1890's. This Los Angeles Consolidated Electric Rail- *way car went to University of Southern California and Agricultural (Exposition) Park. (Title Insurance & Trust)*

The trolley line proved so successful that by the end of the year a second track was laid on the route so that additional cars could operate without a passing problem.

The electric interurban had proved its place in Southern California.

If there had been any questions as to the extent of the ambitions of Sherman and Clark for future interurban construction, they were answered when the first cars arrived for the Los Angeles and Pasadena Railway.

Emblazoned on the interurbans which were to run between Los Angeles and Pasadena was the name "Pasadena and Pacific."

The fact that the brothers-in-law had been contemplating an extension to the Pacific Ocean also is apparent in public records which show that early in 1894—a year before opening of the Pasadena line— they quietly incorporated the Pasadena and Pacific Railway Co. in Arizona. In the summer of 1895, immediately after opening of their Pasadena line, Sherman and Clark

went to work on an interurban line connecting Santa Monica with Los Angeles. Following the pattern so successful in the Pasadena venture, Sherman and Clark acquired four small railroad companies whose tracks were to be rebuilt and linked for the interurban system.

The project immediately caught the public's attention, and newspapers, recalling the Civil War general's movement to Atlanta, paraphrased the construction as "General Sherman's March to the Sea." Selection of Santa Monica as a goal for the interurban amused the cynics, for the town, fifteen miles southwest of Los Angeles and boasting approximately 2,000 residents, was substantially more distant and smaller than Pasadena. Moreover, said the cynics, the passenger service provided by the Southern Pacific and Santa Fe railroads was quite adequate.

Santa Monica had been a sleepy seaside village since it came into existence in 1871 as a tent city summer resort. The townsite had been laid out in 1875 by Senator John P. Jones of Nevada, who had started con-

This trolley, photographed in the early twentieth century in downtown Los Angeles, took passengers to the Southern Pa- *cific's Arcade Depot at Fifth and Central. Note the absence of autos. (Security Pacific National Bank Collection)*

struction of the Los Angeles and Independence Railway as a proposed transcontinental system with its terminus at a great port to be built at Santa Monica. The Southern Pacific later consolidated the Los Angeles and Independence into its system. The prospect of an interurban railroad link gladdened the hearts of Santa Monicans, however, who foresaw new progress for their community with increased transportation.

Property owners along the interurban route encouraged Sherman and Clark by presenting them with 225 acres of land, knowing that the rail line would bring more settlers and increase the value of their ranch holdings. The interurban developers promptly sold the land—which became the town of Sawtelle—and used the money to finance their trolley line construction.

From Los Angeles, the route was down Hill Street (from near Temple Street) to Sixteenth Street (Venice Boulevard) and then on a private right-of-way to Beverly Hills. The line, still using its own right-of-way, paralleled Santa Monica Boulevard to Santa Monica, where it turned onto Ocean Avenue. (In 1901, the tracks were extended to Venice via Ocean and Trolleyway.)

By the spring of 1896 the trolley tracks had been extended through the mustard fields which were to become Beverly Hills and Hollywood, past Sawtelle, and to the ocean front at Santa Monica.

"Sherman's March to the Sea" had been completed, and appropriate ceremonies were planned to inaugurate service. When April 1, the day for opening of the line was scheduled, Santa Monicans were well aware of the importance of the occasion. School was dismissed at noon so that the children could witness the historic event and townspeople gathered flowers from their seaside gardens.

Leaving Los Angeles shortly after noon, the first car sped through fields of wildflowers and skirted freshly plowed farms. Families from nearby farms who were unable to go to the ceremonies planned at Santa Monica rode in buggies and side-boards to the tracks to see the spectacle of the electric trolley.

It was at 3:40 p.m. that the first interurban arrived amid frenzied cheering, the explosion of guns and firecrackers, and the blare of the community band. Bouquets of flowers were showered on the arrivals, who included

37

a delegation of tourists from Minneapolis—appropriately serving as harbingers of the wealth of visitors that eventually would make the trolley trip to the seashore and bring more prosperity to the community.

As in the case of the line to Pasadena, the link to Santa Monica became an immediate success and wooed passengers from the slower and less frequent steam passenger service. Sherman and Clark almost immediately began a Pasadena and Pacific extension to Ocean Park, the community adjacent to Santa Monica which was being developed by cigarette manufacturing magnate Abbot Kinney.

The brothers-in-law were to reap a harvest of wealth from their line not only through its operation but in developing major land holdings and as stockholders and directors of banks, water companies, and associated enterprizes. For Santa Monica itself the arrival of the electric interurban provided an inlet for the new population and wealth being attracted to Southern California as the result of its climate and commercial development. Santa Monica's assessed property valuations soared from $1,799,545 in 1896—the year the trolleys arrived—to a three-fold increase of $6,523,086 within a decade.

Similarly, Santa Monica's population of 2,000 was to more than triple within a decade and reach more than 15,000 by 1920, with most of its new residents receiving their first view of the city from the window of an electric interurban.

By the time that General Moses Sherman and Eli Clark completed their lines to Pasadena and Santa Monica, there was no question as to their abilities as builders of interurban systems. However, they had yet

to learn the intricacies of financing. Despite the rising volume of passengers which followed completion of the two lines, Sherman and Clark had been unable to make scheduled payments to bondholders of the Pasadena and Los Angeles Railway because of high costs involved in building the line to Santa Monica.

Bondholders early in 1898 foreclosed on the Pasadena and Los Angeles system. It was acquired by a group of Chicago investors whose principal action was to change the company's name to Los Angeles and Pasadena Railway, reversing the previous order of the cities. Sherman and Clark moved swiftly to retain their ownership in the Santa Monica line by organizing the Los Angeles Pacific Railroad Company to replace their Pasadena and Pacific Railway Company. By this time Southern California was beginning to recover from the burst of the boom and to show signs of substantial although gradual growth.

Cognizant of the area's potential, a group of San Franciscans in the fall of 1898 purchased the Los Angeles Railway Company, the firm formed to operate the Los Angeles Consolidated Electric Railway previously owned by Sherman and Clark. The investors also purchased the Chicago interests in the Pasadena and Los Angeles.

Among the purchasers were Isaias W. Hellman, a banker; Collis P. Huntington, president of the Southern Pacific, and Henry Edwards Huntington, Collis' nephew and heir apparent.

It was through this inauspicious entry that Henry Huntington was to lay the foundations for Southern California's biggest booms and one of America's greatest personal fortunes.

BELOW: Commuters in the outlying areas could enjoy pleasant trips to Los Angeles via the Big Red Cars. This interurban was waiting at the P. E. station on Lake Avenue in Huntington Beach. (Photo by John Lawson)

4. The Man Behind the Millions: What Behind the Man?

In 1869, the year in which the golden spike was driven for completion of America's first transcontinental railway, 19-year-old Henry Edwards Huntington boarded the train in his native upstate New York village of Oneonta to seek his fortune. As the train glided down the Hudson River Valley for New York City, little did he suspect that his journey through the decades would culminate with his fame surpassing that of his Uncle Collis P. Huntington.

Neither did he know that as a railroad builder he was to become a formidable rival of the Southern Pacific that his uncle had founded.

It was Henry Huntington's hands which were to help shape Southern California from farmlands into a metropolis that appeared destined to become the biggest city in the world. Yet the Huntington Library and Art Gallery at San Marino, his endownment of priceless paintings, books, and manuscripts, has transcended in the public's mind the importance of his Pacific Electric Railway.

And the Pacific Electric itself has obscured Henry Huntington's personality.

Like his railroad magnate uncle, Collis, Henry Huntington ruled against a biography which might have mirrored his depths as a man.

"I have been approached regarding a biography," Henry Huntington once said, "but I do not want that. This library will tell the story. It represents the reward of all the work that I have ever done and the realization of much happiness."

There have been few biographical works devoted to his life. Most books pertaining to Huntington deal principally with his acquisition of the famed art and book treasures.

The best know discussion of the magnate was "A Little Known Master of Millions," written in 1914 by Isaac F. Marcosson, at the time an editor of The Saturday Evening Post and until his death in 1961 a highly regarded author of books on famous personalities and international affairs. It has been Marcosson's idealized biography, holding evidence of close cooperation with Huntington in its preparation, which has been widely quoted and has led to a misinterpretation of Huntington as a man.

Yet an understanding of Huntington's motivations can be obtained through an evaluation of Marcosson's volume as compared to the railroad magnate's actions and words.

Marcosson's book initiated the frequently quoted story of the mother who took her little girl for an outing down at the sea. "On the way," the author said, "the child asked:

" 'Whose streetcar are we riding in?'

" 'Mr. Huntington's,' was the reply.

"Passing a park, the little one asked:

" 'What place is that?'

" 'Huntington Park.'

Henry Huntington was approximately fifty years of age and in the prime of life when this picture was taken. His trolley system played a major role in shaping the sprawling City of Southern California. (Pacific Electric)

NEXT TWO PAGES: Trolleys converged at The Triangle at Orange and Citrus streets in downtown Redlands. The large building (right) is the Fisher Block, owned by the family that held interests in the area's trolley systems prior to Huntington. (Redlands Daily Facts)

" 'Where are we going, mother?' continued the girl.

" 'To Huntington Beach.'

"Arriving at the sea, the child, impressed by the sameness of all the replies, ventured one more query:

" 'Mother, does Mr. Huntington own the ocean, or does it still belong to God?' " [1]

The story was not far from the truth, for Henry Huntington amassed a Southern California financial empire of trolley systems, electrical and gas power companies, and land holdings unequaled under single ownership for its day.

In addition he controlled the huge Newport News Shipbuilding Company and served on the board of directors of more than fifty major corporations in which he had large holdings of stock.

Yet he never achieved the position which the evidence shows he sought the most: the presidency of the Southern Pacific Company once held by his famous uncle, Collis.

Henry Huntington was first vice president of the Southern Pacific when Collis died in August, 1900. The way seemed clear to the younger Huntington.

It was Henry's father, Solon, who had assisted Collis Huntington in making his start in California after the gold rush. Collis Huntington never had children of his own. He and his first wife, Elizabeth, had adopted one-year-old Clara Prentice in Sacramento in 1863 after her father had drowned in a flood. He was fond of young people.

The paths of Collis and Henry Huntington became entwined after the nephew arrived in New York City. The uncle had placed Henry Huntington in charge of a saw-mill at St. Albans, West Virginia, where ties were being cut for construction of a new Collis Huntington acquisition, the Chesapeake and Ohio Railroad. Henry Huntington began to climb the ladder of success in his uncle's financial empire and was given successively more important positions.

While visiting his uncle's New York City mansion Henry had met Mary Prentice—older sister of the girl adopted by Collis—and they had fallen in love. Associates said uncle Collis had planned it that way when Henry and Mary were married in 1873.

Collis' first wife died in 1883 and a year later he married a young widow named Arabella D. Worsham. His adoption of her 14-year-old son, Archer, brought no change in the position which seemed evident for Henry Huntington. Archer Huntington was artistically gifted and planned a life as a scholar rather than as a financier.

Henry Huntington's position as Collis' successor became seemingly secure as the years passed. In 1891 he was named second vice president of the Southern Pacific and with his wife and their five children moved to headquarters in San Francisco. Three years later he became the company's vice president and heir apparent for the throne of president.

But even as a special train sped Henry Huntington to New York City for his uncle's funeral the newspapers were speculating as to whether he would become the president of the Southern Pacific. While Collis Huntington had managed to hold the reins of the company while he lived, his death increased the power of financiers who controlled sizeable blocks of its stock and held most of its bonds.

A New York Times account held that Henry Huntington was being opposed for the railway's presidency because "he does not favor paying dividends at once." [2] Collis also had argued for using earnings to expand the company; other major stockholders sought a liberal dividend policy to make its issues attractive in European markets, at the time an important source of American financing.

The discussion over control of the railroad continued for nearly five months after Collis' death. The announcement on February 2, 1901, that Henry Huntington was selling the Southern Pacific stock he had inherited indicated that he had abandoned hope of winning the presidency.

The buyer of the Huntington holdings as well as other substantial blocks of stock assuring control of the Southern Pacific was E. H. Harriman, a New York financier who was in the process of building a railway empire. Harriman had entered the railroad industry following his marriage in 1872. His wife's father was president of a comparatively small railroad line; on associating himself with the company, Harriman began a series of acquisitions which in 1898 gave him control of the Union Pacific Railroad. His railway companies stretched throughout America. The Southern Pacific was to be among the prized possessions of his empire.

The five month delay had been profitable to both Collis' widow and Henry Huntington, joint beneficiaries of the late rail magnate's will. Southern Pacific stock had sold for $32.00 a share when Huntington died; the price had climbed to $50.00 a share by the time it was purchased by Harriman. As a result of the increase, each of the two beneficiaries received an estimated $50 million from the estate.

---

1. Isaac F. Marcosson, "A Little Known Master of Millions," (Boston, 1914), Pp. 23-24.

2. New York Times, September 6, 1900.

Many contemporary observers predicted that Henry Huntington would settle into a relatively slow place of life, devoting his main business activities to the comparatively small local transportation companies he controlled in San Francisco and Los Angeles.

Huntington, however, nurtured no such idyllic ambitions. He had already completed the blueprints for an empire which was to surpass that of his uncle in many respects.

Henry Edwards Huntington appeared on the Southern California scene coincidental with the start of its biggest boom. While he alone did not launch the spectacular growth period, it was Huntington who boosted the boom to its greatest heights through his trolley lines which in turn shaped the nature of the City of Southern California.

During the quarter of a century following his entry into the area, Henry Huntington was to amass one of the nation's great fortunes through his genius and insight in building interurban systems, organizing electrical power and gas utility firms, and gathering mighty land holdings.

Yet there have been motivating forces other than money behind all financial giants. Evident of those behind Henry Huntington was an ambition to emulate many aspects of the life of his uncle, Collis P. Huntington.

Henry Huntington had expected to ascend his uncle's throne as president of the Southern Pacific, a goal thwarted by financiers. The fact that he desired the position even after he was defeated became evident in early 1900 newspaper stories which quoted his associates as predicting that Huntington's "dream" of winning the presidency was imminent.[2] Huntington's affection for his Southern Pacific association waned little through the years. Even after the sale of his major interest in the railroad he retained the office of vice president and as he began retirement he remained a director. He continued to note his Southern Pacific association in listing his major achievements long after the role was eclipsed by the magnitude of his activities in Southern California.

So it was that Henry Huntington cherished a desire of emulating his uncle's life by becoming president of the Southern Pacific. Or, perhaps he thought, better still to create an empire similar to the one which Collis Huntington had built from a standing start.

Henry Huntington's evident admiration for his uncle's way of life was displayed in a variety of ways. He eventually divorced his wife, from whom he had separated the same year that his uncle died, and several years later married Collis' widow, Arabella.

Huntington's desire for a life similar to that of his empire-building uncle was apparent to his biographer, Isaac Marcosson, an excellent reporter and observer of men. After interviewing the interurban magnate, the author noted many parallels between uncle and nephew.

"In short," Marcosson concluded at one point in his narrative, "Henry E. Huntington is a sort of reincarnation of Collis P., with the same thrift, foresight, and constructive energy. . . ."[3]

Huntington's desire for spectacular personal achievement impressed Marcosson so deeply that after their talks he wrote that the electric magnate "was a wealthy man by his own efforts long before the massive figure of Collis P. Huntington yielded to the burden of years."

Henry Huntington's education was basically equal to that of the period's high school, a background essentially extensive for the era. Prior to 1900 he had made wise investments as the result of his association with his uncle's companies, but it was the inheritance which was to lay a foundation for bigger investments.

The vehicle which Henry Huntington selected to carry him to an empire rivaling that of his uncle was the electric interurban, coupled to the Southern California dream of a harbor.

The all-inclusive name of Pacific Electric, designating service beyond the confines of Southern California, indicated the wide horizon he initially set for his railroad system.

The scope of his projected venture became clearer when he engaged Epes Randolph, a highly competent executive from the steam railway industry, to serve as chief engineer in planning and operating his electric railroad.

Huntington evidently had turned his eyes toward Southern California and electric railroads as an alternative to the Southern Pacific's presidency even before his uncle died. In early 1899, Collis Huntington's control of the Southern Pacific wavered briefly and Henry Huntington was ousted briefly from his position as first vice president.[4] A group of investors, including John

2. Los Angeles Times, May 12, 1903.

3. Marcosson, p. 9.

4. Henry Huntington's removal from his position as first vice president of the Southern Pacific, a fact given little consideration in later years, was reported in stories in the Los Angeles Times on April 9 and 14, 1899. The articles quoted financial sources as stating Collis Huntington was forced to "sacrifice" his nephew in order to placate major bondholders and other stockholders of the railroad. When the elder Huntington regained control of the company, he returned Henry Huntington to his vice presidency, according to a story October 29, 1899, in The Times. The incident may well have indicated to Henry Huntington that he would have difficulty in controlling the Southern Pacific after his uncle's death and prompted him to make plans for an extensive electric railroad system.

Bicknell who was associated with Henry Huntington as his attorney, filed articles of incorporation for an electric railroad to be called the Pacific Electric which would build rail lines up the coast of California from Los Angeles. Collis regained control of the company and his nephew was restored to the vice presidency; the early Pacific Electric incorporation subsequently was dropped, although the name was renewed in 1901 in a new move.

Henry Huntington expressed great confidence in Southern California. He said:

I am a foresighted man, and I believe Los Angeles is destined to become the most important city in this country if not in the world. It can extend in any direction as far as you like.

Surveying the area, largely undeveloped on his arrival, and eyeing the technology of the electric railroad, he visualized immense possibilities.

"We will join this whole region into one big family," Marcosson quoted him as saying.

The impression of Henry Huntington that developed over the years was one of a white-moustached and balding individual who was usually smiling but quite austere and moved exclusively in the highest financial circles.

His contemporaries agreed that he most certainly was dignified but also hastened to add recollections of his actions indicating him to be a sociable as well as very human individual.

Born in 1850, Henry Huntington was in the prime of life in 1901 when he began his Southern California electric railroad building program. Behind him was a career with the Southern Pacific that had placed him in the company of laborers as well as financiers. His boyhood in his native Oneonta, New York, gave him a small-town background and his associations with his uncle, Collis, placed him in New York City as well as on the plains of the West.

Serving on the boards of directors of more than fifty of America's biggest corporations, Huntington was welcomed to the intimate councils of the financiers. Yet laborers on his electric railroads found themselves at ease when he stopped to chat with him.

Huntington's sociability was indicated by his membership in numerous clubs in New York and California, including the exclusive California Club and Jonathan Club in Los Angeles. Even so his busy schedule did not keep him from other friendships. William Hertrich, engaged by Huntington in 1904 to landscape his estate at San Marino, recalled planning a trip to San Diego to look at property. Huntington offered to accompany him on the trip. Once aboard the train, the rail magnate produced box lunch for both to eat during the trip.

Huntington did not choose intimate friends indiscrim-

Tycoon E. H. Harriman, head of the Southern Pacific, sought to stop expansion of Huntington's trolleys.

ately. His first impression to strangers was ordinarily one of distance, Hertrich said. When he began to know and trust a person, he was warm and friendly.

To his friends, Henry Edwards Huntington was known as "Ed" or sometimes simply "HEH." Despite the intense anti-liquor campaigns in Southern California during his time, Huntington had a wine cellar at his home. He drank from its contents for social events but did not over-indulge; he also smoked cigarettes occasionally.

Henry Huntington reaped not one but several fortunes in Southern California and through his investments elsewhere. When he died his estate was valued at approximately $40 million—just about the same amount willed to him by his Uncle Collis. An estimated $30 million had gone for the art and book treasures housed at the San Marino estate previously given to a foundation. Considering the value of his land, railroad, public utility company, and other holdings, this amount might well have been more.

One wonders if perhaps the amassing of the great holdings had not been something of a game for Huntington in which the stakes were the ability to create more than merely the money alone.

Even the Los Angeles Record, a newspaper revelling in attacking the magnate, was prompted amidst criticisms of him to admit that money itself was not the only

Hollywood Boulevard was dominated by trolley tracks and overhead wires when this photograph was made in the early twentieth century. Within two decades Hollywood grew into a business district. (Carl Blaubach Collection)

driving force behind Huntington. When his fortunes soared after purchasing immense interests at Redondo Beach, The Record said: [5]

No one can hear Mr. Huntington speak of Los Angeles and not be convinced of his sincere interest in the city and pride in it aside from the money-making possibilities. He is a money maker, of course, but he has pride in his work that doesn't seem to be measured by dollars.

After settling in Los Angeles in 1901, Huntington became associated with many leaders who were notable for their opposition to the Southern Pacific, which was most unusual for a man still serving as a vice president of the company. Typical of those joining Huntington in the Pacific Electric project was George Patton (father of World War II General George S. Patton), who had campaigned unsuccessfully for Congress as an anti-Southern Pacific Democrat.

Furthermore, Henry Huntington was to build his electric system with standard gauge tracks (4'8½") permitting it to inter-change passenger and freight cars with the steam railways, thus competing with those companies. Sherman and Clark, in the general practice of the day for trolley systems, built with narrow gauge tracks (3'6") which confined their use to strictly local passenger service.

That Huntington had hoped eventually to extend his electric railroad lines from San Diego to San Francisco—

stretching the tracks over California along the coast as well as through the San Joaquin Valley—became quite evident to E. H. Harriman, the man who had purchased his interest in the Southern Pacific.

(The railway magnate was the father of the distinguished statesman, W. Averell Harriman, who was born in 1891.)

Edward Henry Harriman and Henry Edwards Huntington had much in common in addition to the similarity of their names. Both were natives of central New York State (Harriman was born in 1848, two years before Huntington), both had entered the railway industry as the result of associations with relatives, both were forceful, intelligent, driving men, and both seemed to be striving for empires.

Despite Senator White's victory for a free harbor at San Pedro, the Southern Pacific under Harriman did not give up hope of dominating rail connections for shipping in Southern California. While retaining its interests at Santa Monica, the S.P. expanded holdings at San Pedro and also acquired control of the Salt Lake Railroad. Harriman thus could expect a rail monopoly as the harbor was dredged. And as Henry Huntington's electric interurban lines expanded, they included Newport Harbor, Huntington Beach, Long Beach, San Pedro, Redondo Beach, and other coastal areas regarded as potential ports—much to Harriman's concern.

Harriman's fears that an efficient electric railroad could devalue his investment were logical and generally known during the era when Henry Huntington's con-

---

5. Los Angeles Record, July 7, 1905.

45

Electric cars en route to Santa Monica stopped at this Los Angeles Pacific station on Hollywood Boulevard and Ivar Street in the early twentieth century. Note the rural nature of the area. (Carl Blaubach Collection)

struction was hitting its peak. It has been the shadow of the years that obscured the battle which developed.

It must be remembered that just seventy years before the start of the twentieth century the first steam locomotive railroads began to operate in America. At first they merely linked cities as did the initial electric interurbans, but they grew to span states and eventually the continent. The stagecoach was relegated to obsolence.

The advent of the electric interurban, which made every car a train, created a dangerous challenge to the steam railroads. Trolleys could run frequently and economically stop at the smallest communities. In an era when competition from busses and automobiles was not a reality electric interurban systems were bringing reduced patronage to the steam railroads they paralleled elsewhere in the nation.

Most trolley systems were slowed in their progress by lack of money. The substantial financial backing of Henry Huntington, together with his personal drive, could produce an electric railroad system with a threat to steam railroads not unlike the danger locomotives had presented the stagecoaches a few years earlier.

A most unusual situation developed as a result of the electric interurban technology, the Southern California opportunity, and the abilities of Henry Huntington.

While the Huntington dream envisioned vast electirc railroad systems, there was no evidence that his ambitions were to parallel steam railways at whatever personal financial costs might be involved.

The Henry Huntington vision had become that of the City of Southern California, the creative goal for which he eventually was to be famed.

When Henry Huntington and his uncle, Collis, had made their initial investments in Los Angeles local streetcar service in September, 1898, area civic leaders shuddered because of the pressure which the Southern Pacific had excercised not only in the selection of the harbor but also in the state's politics in general. Editorialized The Los Angeles Times: [6]

If the usual Huntington methods are pursued—and when haven't they been pursued in the management of Huntington properties? —the foothold which the octopus managers have secured in the street-railway business of Los Angeles will prove to be one of the worse calamities that has ever befallen the community.

The ensuing years during which Henry Huntington built his interurban system were to prove that much the opposite was true.

As his interurban activities were hitting a peak in 1905 he was pressed for information as to the extent of his plans. The Los Angeles Record quoted his reply: "I'm Not Going to Build to the Moon, says Huntington."[7]

If Huntington had lived in the second half of the twentiety century, he undoubtedly would have been building rocket ships for travel to the moon — and beyond.

6. Los Angeles Times, September 17, 1898.

7. Los Angeles Record, July 7, 1905.

5. Trolleys to Long Beach: The P.E. Makes a Story

One pleasant summer evening in 1901 came a proposal for a franchise to construct a high speed electric interurban line linking Long Beach with Los Angeles. It touched off months of debate as to whether the tracks would damage the village's chances to grow and prosper.

Many who favored the Long Beach city council authorizing the construction were most enthusiastic over the estimated $5,000 expected for the franchise, a bonanza which would ease the load on taxpayers in financing needed sewage improvements.

It would have been quite in order, history showed, for Long Beach merchants and property owners not only to have embraced the proposal for a trolley, but even to have helped with the financing because of the bonanza much greater than minor city improvements destined to come to a community with an electric railroad.

Long Beach's population in the 1900 census had been only 2,000; in the ensuing decade its population zoomed of 17,000 — a 610 percent increase which made it the fastest growing city in the United States. The spectacular population increase was generally credited to the convenience of travel afforded by the trolley line from Los Angeles, making readily available the scenic and interesting beach theretofore relatively inacessible.

Fate had it that the Long Beach line, first complete interurban link built by Henry Huntington and one of the most successful in the entire system, was the last to be abandoned.

The beach town had been laid out in 1883 as Willmore City, taking its name from its founder, William Erwin Willmore, an Englishman. Judge Robert Widney, who had a financial interest in the real estate promotion, supervised construction of a horse-drawn car from the Wilmington-to-Los Angeles tracks of the Southern Pacific as an incentive for buyers. Willmore and Widney, with Methodist back-

Horses were tied near the cliffs at Long Beach by visitors during the early twentieth century. The Pacific Electric cars brought crowds to the community and it grew rapidly from a village into a city. (Security Pacific National Bank)

Epes Randolph, regarded as one of America's foremost railroad designers, was chief engineer for the Pacific Electric.

Christian DeGuigne, a San Francisco financier, was among those who incorporated the Pacific Electric Railroad.

grounds, imposed a strong temperance atmosphere on the settlement. Deed restrictions on the lots not only prohibited the sale of alcoholic beverages but even outlawed their consumption on the land. Stringent regulations also provided for "moral" attire for young women at the beach.

Pressed by financial difficulties, Willmore was forced to sell his interest in the project and a syndicate headed by Judge Widney was organized to continue development of the community. Willmore City was given the more expressive — as well as more saleable — name of Long Beach. Widney's car line was purchased by the Southern Pacific, which in 1888 substituted steam trains for the horses. Additional transportation was provided in 1892 when the Los Angeles Terminal Railway, also serving San Pedro and Pasadena, opened a link to Long Beach. Despite its high moral tone, steam railroads and Southern California's general growth during the boom of the 1880's, Long Beach was having a difficult time in achieving the status of a city.

By 1890 the population was only 484 and in 1900 Long Beach appeared relegated to the hole of a small seaside resort for Los Angeles residents. Among the barriers to the city's growth, businessmen said, was inadequate transportation. There were constant pressures for more frequent service than the six to eight trains daily provided by the steam railroads. Railroad officials countered, however, with the argument that they would be happy to provide additional trains — when warranted by an increase in the population.

Yet it was with mixed feelings that the City Council heard the proposal for an electric interurban line at its meeting on June 24, 1901. Speaking on behalf of the line was Colonel Charles R. Drake, a Long Beach settler who previously imported workers from Mexico to work on the tracks of the Southern Pacific.

Colonel Drake requested the council to issue a franchise to permit building a trolley system from Los Angeles to Long Beach, "by a syndicate headed by Henry E. Huntington and I. W. Hellman."[1]

There was no mention of the specific company that would build the line, for the simple fact that Huntington had not unveiled plans for his immense electric railroad empire. As a matter of fact, the Pacific Electric — which was to increase Henry Huntington's fame and fortune and become the model of all trolley lines — wasn't incorporated until November 10, nearly six months later.

His interest in the interurban line, he told the council members, was solely as an investor who expected the resort hotel he planned to build in Long Beach to increase in value as a result of the tourists expected to arrive on the trolley line. Noting the success of the interurban lines built to Santa Monica and Pasadena, the council agreed that such a facility certainly would force the steam railroads to provide additional passenger service. The council also considered that there might be competition in seeking the electric railroad franchise inasmuch as Edwin Spencer Hook, the Illinoisan

---

1. Long Beach Press, June 25, 1901.

John Slauson owned the big Azusa Ranch and wanted good rail transportation. He helped form the Pacific Electric.

John Bicknell, an attorney, helped organize the P. E. so that the Southern Pacific would have more competition.

who had began building streetcar systems in Los Angeles, had entered the interurban field by forming the California Pacific Railway Company to build a line from Los Angeles to San Pedro.

The city fathers decided to offer the franchise to the highest bidder at a council meeting on August 20. Arguments for and against the proposed interurban system immediately erupted.

"There is a strong feeling against allowing any more tracks on the ocean front," the Los Angeles Times correspondent wrote on June 26 from Long Beach.

The franchise proposal called for the tracks to enter Long Beach on American Avenue (later renamed Long Beach Boulevard). Few objected to this proposal since this street was three blocks from the business section of the city. However, the franchise provision for the tracks to turn onto Ocean Park Avenue (later renamed Ocean Boulevard) brought very negative responses from the people whose homes lined the seaside street. Residents already were seeking to have the Los Angeles Terminal Railroad tracks removed from Ocean Park Avenue. They argued that a new set of rails would impede the town's progress.

More opposition came because of Henry Huntington's position as a director and vice president of the Southern Pacific. Huntington's role as an individual investor had not yet been recognized and the public envisioned the electric line being controlled by the Southern Pacific, thus allowing little competition. It was also difficult for the public to

believe that Colonel Drake really had severed his connection with the Southern Pacific and actually intended to develop his Long Beach properties, as he did a short time later.

As the controversy grew, so did Henry Huntington's enthusiasm. He amended the application to provide for a network of local trolley lines. Long Beach newspapers backed the interurban proposal and countered arguments that tracks would reduce property values by predicting that areas bypassed by trolleys would be devalued.

"Wherever the (interurban system) has its center, the town will grow," editorialized the Long Beach Tribune. [2] Merchants and real estate brokers joined in urging approval for the trolley franchise. In an editorial addressed to homeowners The Tribune pointed out benefits of the trolleys: [3]

It is very evident that with the coming of the electric railways the traffic and profits of the (steam) lines will be materially reduced and this is awakening hostility to the innovation. These roads have enjoyed the right of way so long and given the least possible service for the patronage received for so many years that the new era . . . (of electric cars) . . . sets hard upon them. Long Beach has been especially at their mercy.

The controversy became so heated that when the August 20 date arrived for consideration of the franchise, action had to be postponed because, conveniently, the required

2. Long Beach Tribune, August 24, 1901.

3. Long Beach Tribune, August 17, 1901.

quorum of council members was not present. However, The Tribune noted, most of those present at the meeting to voice opposition were only a group of "ladies who own property on the (beach) front." [4]

The matter was no less controversial at the next council session. The city trustees decided to postpone action for three weeks so that "reports" could be gathered on the advisability of awarding the franchise at all. A public session described as a "protest" meeting to discuss construction of an interurban line was called for the evening of September 2 in the Methodist Tabernacle, located in a eucalyptus-forested park between American and Locust Avenues and Third and Fourth Streets. It was the center for the community's activities.

Meanwhile, the Huntington interests began to fear that the controversies would end any hope for an award of the interurban franchise. It was decided for Charles Drake to give a hint of the extensive plans which Henry Huntington was making. A writer for The Tribune reported that during a "pleasant interview with Mr. Drake" plans were unfolded for Huntington's "great system" to include a Long Beach wharf, an idea which appealed greatly to residents who envisioned a harbor which could compete with the one being developed at San Pedro.

The protest meeting in the tabernacle opened with W. W. Lowe, a civic leader whose wife had proposed the new name of Long Beach for the city, giving a talk in which he admitted the plan for a trolley system was "a good idea, but not on the beach front." However, the session adjourned with general agreement that the franchise should be awarded even though the tracks had to be laid on Ocean Park Avenue. Otherwise, speakers said, it was certain that Long Beach would not receive its rightful share of the tourists who came to Southern California.

The fateful night for the council to consider the trolley franchise came on October 30. On hand to represent Huntington was soft-spoken Epes Randolph, a Virginian whose Southern eloquence and accent impressed the beach residents. Randolph had resigned from an important position with the Southern Pacific to direct construction of Henry Huntington's electric railroad system. Seated near him were W. H. Holabird, who also was seeking other interurban franchises, and H. H. Hamilton, unidentified at the time but actually representing Edwin Spencer Hook.

When the council announced it would receive bids for the franchise, W. H. Holabird submitted $1,705 as the first offer. H. H. Hamilton promptly raised the bid to $2,500. Holabird raised his bid to $6,610, after which Epes Randolph stepped forward and offered $7,920 for the franchise. Hamilton countered with an offer of $8,712.

Randolph then entered the winning bid of $9,600. His

competitors shook their heads; it was obvious that the Huntington-Hellman syndicate could not be outbid for the Long Beach line. Randolph was pressed for details of the proposed construction. "It has not yet been decided where the new road will enter the city," Randolph said, "but the direction will be almost as straight to Long Beach from Los Angeles as the crow flies."

There was general rejoicing among Long Beach citizens — not so much because of the promise of an interurban system that was to build a village into a city, but because the $9,600 would balance the municipal budget.

It was becoming obvious to the public that Henry Huntington was making more than casual investments through his purchase of the streetcar lines in Los Angeles the interurban to Pasadena. Shortly after acquiring the Long Beach franchise he started construction of an interurban branch from the Pasadena line to the town of Alhambra. Moreover, he seemed to appear in cities as soon as there was talk of Henry Huntington displayed great wisdom as a railroad organizer in selecting Epes Randolph, previously superintendent of the Southern Pacific's Yuma and Tucson divisions, to design his system. Randolph eventually was hailed as one of the era's outstanding civil engineers specializing in railroad construction at a time when there was much such talent.

Randolph was slender and soft-spoken. He frequently wore a boiled shirt, making him look like the popular idea of a minister. But his language could be violently forceful and expressive when the situation demanded it.

Huntington named him vice president and general manager of the Pacific Electric.

Randolph, drawing the master plan for Henry Huntington's projected trolley empire, strategically placed the lines with such skill that the system would be built according to his proposals long after he departed the scene. Eventually, Southern California's first freeways would parallel his routes. Randolph charted proposed towns both where they logically should develop and where Huntington had acquired land for sub-divisions.

Epes Randolph's immense ability eventually came to the attention of Huntington's rival, E. H. Harriman, who persuaded him to return to the Southern Pacific. In a key S. P. position, he used a private car called Pocahontas — so named because he proudly traced his ancestry back to that Indian princess.

Meanwhile, Huntington rapidly was putting Randolph's plans into operation.

LEFT: Slauson Junction, shown in 1904, was the starting place on the Long Beach line for the route that went to Whittier via Huntington Park and Bell. The community of Watts was three miles south. (Craig Rasmussen Collection)

---

4. Long Beach Tribune, August 20, 1901.

It took a young cub reporter named Harry Carr to unearth the extent of the system which Huntington was planning, and it was quite by accident that he obtained the story. Carr's editor at The Los Angeles Times sent him to interview Huntington, scheduled to board his private car at the Southern Pacific station. The young reporter approached the financier and nervously explained that he had been ordered to get a story but frankly admitted he did not know what questions to ask.

Huntington's blue eyes twinkled and he smiled.

"I'm going to build an interurban system that will cover Southern California," Huntington told Carr. "Would that make a story? Would that make a story?"

Indeed it made a story and communities eagerly began seeking a Huntington line to increase transportation facilities so vital at the time for growth.

Huntington's repetition of his last sentence was habitual and it remained one of his characteristics.

The Los Angeles Record, which continually baited Huntington, said that the rail magnate always repeated his last sentence "for emphasis," although another explanation could have been that he was demonstrating a certain sense of insecurity, particularly under tense situations and penetrating questions from the reporters.

Huntington's utter hatred of newspaper reporters was well known to his friends, and this feeling was undoubtedly sensed by members of the fourth estate. Newspaper stories frequently quoted the repetitions verbatim, sometimes in the interests of accurate reporting and other times in obvious efforts to chastise him for not speaking more freely on confidential matters. The reporters also seemed to enjoy catching Huntington in rare ungrammatical phrases and using them in stories, again probably in revenge for his reluctance to tell them his private plans.

The primary instrument for the big trolley system revealed to Carr was to be the Pacific Electric Railway Company. Its articles of incorporation were signed October 29, 1901—the day before the awarding of the Long Beach franchise. Details of the document, filed two weeks later as a public record, were sufficient to make rival steam locomotive company officials uncomfortable. (See Appendix for a reproduction of the Pacific Electric articles of incorporation.) The new corporation made no secret of the lines to be built parallel to existing steam railroad tracks.

The articles of incorporation provided that the Pacific Electric would absorb the Los Angeles and Pasadena Railroad, and the Pasadena and Mount Lowe Railroad, acquired by Huntington after Professor Lowe met financial problems. The new company also included the Long Beach line.

In addition, however, the Pacific Electric would build, according to its articles of incorporation, a line through Monrovia to Santa Ana via San Bernardino, Redlands, and

This sketch of the pueblo of Los Angeles was made in the early 1850's when the city had barely 2000 residents and was known as the "Queen of the Cow Counties." Fences kept cattle from invading yards. The arrival of railroads and development of the Pacific Electric made Los Angeles grow. (Security Pacific National Bank Collection)

Isaias W. Hellman, the banker who sold the initial bonds to build the Pacific Electric lines, poses in his office. Hellman *was highly regarded by financiers for his conservative management policies. (Security Pacific National Bank)*

Riverside, with branches to Covina, Pomona and Highlands, and another route to Santa Ana via Whittier with a branch going to Pomona. Branches would be built from the Long Beach line to San Pedro and Redondo Beach. The articles also called for line construction from Long Beach to Covina as well as to Santa Ana.

Topping off the extensive plans, the articles provided that a 115-mile line would be built up the coast to Santa Barbara.

The Pacific Electric in effect would establish a new network of rail lines duplicating many portions of the S.P. and Santa Fe systems. Far worse for the Southern Pacific, however, the Pacific Electric would be moving up the coast alongside its recently opened seaside route.

Directors of the new company subscribed to $452,000 of

the $10 million stock authorized for the company. Those named as directors and stockholders were Isaias W. Hellman, Antoine Borel, and Christian De Guigne, who had been associated profitably with Henry Huntington in the Market Street Railway of San Francisco. The trio each took $67,800 or forty-five percent of the total stock issued. The remaining fifty-five percent was subscription by the four other directors: John S. Slauson, owner of the 17,600 acre Azusa Ranch; John Bicknell, attorney for the corporation, and Epes Randolph, engineer for the lines, and, of course, Huntington, whose $98,500 in stock was the biggest piece of the pie. With the corporate groundwork completed, construction of the line to Long Beach and extension of the tracks to Alhambra started.

On February 8, 1902, the directors met in Bicknell's

53

54

office in the Bradbury Block at the southeast corner of Broadway and Third Street.

The group authorized the creation of financing bonds totalling $10 million. Isaias W. Hellman was given the assignment of selling them.

The man Henry Huntington selected to find buyers for the $10 million in bonds to construct the initial lines of the Pacific Electric was a person imminently qualified for the job. Isaias William Hellman's face was distinguished by a rounded black beard and rimless glasses, giving him the appearance of a most conservative banker, which indeed he was. Hellman, fifty-nine years of age when he interurban bond-selling task began in 1902, was respected equally in Los Angeles and San Francisco as a financier.

A native of Bavaria, Hellman immigrated to the United States in 1859 when he was seventeen years old, settling in Los Angeles. Here Hellman spent his first ten years working as a clerk in a dry goods store, investing as much of his earnings as possible in surrounding ranch lands.

In 1868 he had organized a banking house which lead to the formation of the Farmers and Merchants Bank (a forerunner of the Security Pacific National Bank), the Los Angeles Savings Bank, and numerous smaller banks serving outlying communities.

Isaias Hellman was conservative in his financial operations because, as he liked to say, "the man who wants the last drop in the bucket usually gets left."

While the legal reserve for banks was twenty-five percent of its deposits, Hellman varied his reserves at from fifty to seventy-five percent. As a result he was able to meet all demands for withdrawals during the financial crisis of 1875. Consequently depositors who rushed other banks placed their funds in Hellman's banks and the little Bavarian's stature grew in financial circles. Although Hellman was of the Jewish faith, he had a broad outlook and recognized the values of worthy endeavors by other religious groups. He became a generous contributor to Judge Widney's Methodist-supported University of Southern California. Hellman's vision was by no means limited to the immediate Los Angeles area, for he realized that Southern California was destined for growth. When townsites were laid out at Santa Monica, San Fernando, and other outlying areas, Hellman purchased property so that his fortunes could grow with the area.

It was in 1890 that he left for San Francisco to become president of the Nevada Bank, later reorganized as the Wells Fargo Nevada Bank. The following year Henry E. Huntington arrived in San Francisco as vice president of the Southern Pacific. The pair met and were associated in the Market Street Railway Company, sold for a substantial profit in early 1900.

Among the fiction perpetuated over the years was the legend that Henry Huntington used his immense wealth alone to finance construction of the vast Pacific Electric system. On the contrary, Huntington was eager to borrow so that he could spread his funds over investments ranging from land holdings to electrical power firms. Huntington saw Hellman as the individual who could help his plan.

"I could not build railroads without money," Huntington later told Hellman quite frankly. "I wanted you as a partner because you were capable of raising money." [5]

The Huntington proposal of a Southern California trolley system attracted Hellman, who with Borel and De Guigne anticipated a windfall of profits similar to the venture with the Market Street Company.

As matters developed, however, Hellman and his two associates were to become considerably perturbed regarding the turn of events with the Pacific Electric.

5. J. A. Graves, "My Seventy Years in California," (Los Angeles: 1928), p. 104.

Farms dominated Slauson Junction at Huntington Park in the early twentieth century. Tracks at right took cars to Whittier. A vast industrial complex developed around the tracks. (Charles Seims Collection)

This historic photograph shows the arrival of one of the first Big Red Cars in Long Beach after the line was opened in *1902. Most travelers preferred the electric cars to the traditional steam trains. (Craig Rasmussen Collection)*

6. Triumph for Trolleys

As the Pacific Electric tracks neared their Long Beach terminus, citizens of the seaside resort rushed preparations for the crowds and new way of life the trolleys were expected to bring.

The most notable preparations included added safety precautions on the seashore for inlanders who were not accustomed to the rolling surf and city ordinances which sought to protect the dignity of Pine Avenue, the town's main street, by making it illegal to stroll on the sidewalks either in "beach costume" or carrying fishing poles. [1]

"It is to be a big day with the little city by the sea, and a larger crowd is expected than ever was present at a Meth-

odist camp meeting or a Pacific Chautauqua," the Los Angeles Times predicted as the announcement was made that the Pacific Electric service to Long Beach would start on Friday, July 4, 1902.

The mention of Long Beach always had inspired a tongue-in-cheek attitude among the more sophisticated inlanders. Santa Monica made no secret of being a roaring resort, where one could enjoy the seashore with a glass of beer and revel in non-Victorian activities. Long Beach, with its strict

NEXT TWO PAGES: Pine and Ocean in Long Beach was decorated with flags to welcome visitors who rode the high speed Pacific Electric route from Los Angeles for a 1905 holiday celebration. (Security Pacific National Bank)

---

1. Long Beach Press, June 26, 1902.

ban on liquor and Sunday closing of most stores, was regarded as the seaside resort for the more conservative elements.

The arrival of the first Big Red Cars, as small as the trolleys were in 1902, was to awaken Long Beach.

Work on the construction of the tracks from Los Angeles to Long Beach started almost as soon as the franchise was awarded to the Huntington-Hellman syndicate. Gangs of laborers using teams of work horses built the interurban right of way over "The Plains," the name familiarly given to the flat and almost uninhabited area stretching from Los Angeles to the ocean. The biggest town along the way was Compton, which had 452 people. Sheep pastures, farms, and a few cattle ranches stretched over the land.

The land needed for the right of way was obtained by outright gift or through payment of nominal sums to the ranchers and farmers. The task of obtaining the property was fairly easy for it had been established that railroads brought great increases in land values. The property owners, most of whom purchased their land for $5 to $15 an acre, envisioned their immediate areas blossoming into cities. They expected values to climb so that a residential or commercial lot would command a price several times in excess of their cost for a single acre. The farmers and ranchers were correct, of course, and their gift of land for the eighty foot right-of-way was a profitable investment.

The route selected for the Long Beach line by Epes Randolph fulfilled the Huntington promise of a high-speed interurban route. The tracks were built on a private right-of-way uninterrupted by other vehicles for nearly the entire distance. This was in contrast to many electric interurban lines in other sections of the United States which for economy frequently utilized tracks in public streets. The result was slower trolley runs, making the systems less attractive to commuters.

The route from Los Angeles was down East Ninth Street from Main Street to Tennessee Street (later renamed Hooper Avenue), where the electric cars entered a private right-of-way so well engineered that it would do credit to a steam railroad. The interurbans could speed down the line, which had few curves. There were few roads to "invade" the tracks and slow trolleys. Compton was the only settlement of any size between Los Angeles and Long Beach.

The line emerged from its right-of-way at Willow Street in Long Beach. For the approximately three remaining miles to the ocean, the line rode a private right-of-way in the center of American Avenue. Lanes for horse-drawn vehicles and the few automobiles of the era were provided on each side of the tracks. This separation, which enabled the trolleys to roll without concern for other vehicles blocking the way, remained until the 1920's.

Henry Huntington from the start, however, realized that speed would be an asset to his system if it were to compete with the steam railroads. He also was well aware that extensive use of private streets would prevent the use of the tracks by freight cars—a consideration of prime importance in a plan for a mighty rail network.

Real estate promoters, eyeing the results of the trolley on land values at Santa Monica and Pasadena, realized the potential for property long before the tracks reached Long Beach. The Long Beach real estate firm of F. E. Shaw and Co. as early as January, 1902, advertised its Ocean Villa Tract is located "three blocks from the ocean and directly on the Pacific Electric Railroad." [2]

Huntington promised Long Beach residents he would complete the railroad within a year after receiving the franchise, much to the delight of the local boosters. Some midwestern interurban systems of lesser trackage required five years for completion because of financial and right-of-way difficulties. Sherman and Clark took eighteen months to complete their line to Santa Monica even though they used portions of existing track.

As July neared, road gangs were laying 7,800 feet of rails a day on the right-of-way so that the Long Beach line could service the summer traffic to the seashore well before the promised October completion. The speed with which the line was completed evidently exceeded the schedule made by Huntington and Randolph. When it was announced the line would open on July 4 it was disclosed that interurbans from Pasadena and Alhambra lines would be used to launch service pending arrival of new cars on order. The first trial car ran to Long Beach on July 3. The forty-one Pacific Electric officials and other railroad men aboard were greeted by a crowd of enthusiastic Long Beach residents.

But the crowds who would arrive on Independence Day were to deluge Long Beach's 2,000 residents. The Red Cars began running at 6 a.m. July 4 and they continued rolling into the city every fifteen minutes thereafter.

By the afternoon a crowd of 30,000 men, women, and children were swarming over the little village. Most of the visitors came via the new trolley line, but a substantial number of people from nearby farming areas were attracted to view the novelty of electric interurban cars. A count showed that 1,450 buggies and carriages were parked along the beach.

"There were few of the 30,000 visitors who did not cross the trolley tracks at least once," The Los Angeles Times commented.

The bathhouse Charles R. Drake was building as part of his Long Beach investment program was only partially completed but he opened it. Patrons swamped it. "The rush has been so great that because of the lack of dressing room accommodations we have three times had to stop the sale of bath tickets," Drake said happily.

2. Long Beach Press, January 2, 1902.

A youngster awaits for an approaching P. E. car on Long Beach's East Ocean Boulevard in 1904. If you look at the photograph for several minutes, the boy apparently will turn his head — as he did during the time exposure. This trolley line connected downtown Long Beach with the Alamitos Bay area during the early 1900's. (Charles Seims Collection)

The beach and trolleys weren't all that attracted the visitors. The Long Beach Social Club, regarded as a nemesis by the community's "better" people, drew up to 300 customers an hour to cool off with beer placed on sale despite the local prohibition. Officers staged two raids on the club during the day. One raid was thwarted when the patrons destroyed the evidence by drinking it. However, the town marshal managed to seize several kegs of Maier and Zobelein beer.

Numerous inlanders arrived by steam passenger trains to view the arrival of the electric cars. Many were so impressed by the trolleys that they sacrificed the return portion of their tickets so they could return via the wonderful red cars.

When night fell most visitors were exhausted. The town's hotels, whose managements previously would have regarded the arrival of two hundred overnight guests as overwhelming, were bulging at the seams. Several thousand visitors who were too tired to take the trolleys back to Los Angeles simply bedded down on the beach for the night.

The arrival of the Pacific Electric brought an era of spectacular growth for Long Beach after its nearly twenty years of struggling as a sleepy and isolated little seaside resort. On the heels of the trolleys came development of Long Beach Harbor, providing the facilities for the city's transition into an industrial area.

The 1910 census gave Long Beach a population of 17,-809, an increase of eight-fold in a decade; by 1920 the city had 55,593 people. Most of them came by the Pacific Electric.

Shortly after the Long Beach electric line was opened, Henry Huntington made an inspection tour of the facility and pronounced it "the finest road in the world."

Southern California community leaders were inclined to agree with him as they saw Long Beach growing, with the price tags increasing almost daily on property near the Pacific Electric tracks. Quite logically they petitioned Huntington to extend his system to their cities and the interurban magnate was willing to consider the pleas. Huntington, usually clad in a gray suit with spats and carrying a cane, soon became a familiar figure in the farmlands throughout Los Angeles, Orange, San Bernardino and Riverside Counties.

Competing with steam railroads, the Pacific Electric acquired freight cars as well as trolleys. Shippers thus could choose the lowest rates. (Spencer Crump Collection)

He traveled most frequently in a carriage, usually driven by his stenographer, Oscar A. Smith, who years later was to become president of the Pacific Electric Railroad and preside over the demise of the Big Red Cars.

Huntington's instinctive business foresight, not a battery of professional economists frequently used by financial tycoons, was his instrument in choosing the areas where his trolleys—and his investments in substantial land holdings—would go. Climbing a knoll, he would inspect the countryside and visualize the logical course for an area's pattern of developments.

"Mr. Huntington believed each little village would become a city," Oscar Smith recalled, "although he realized that certain areas would have advantages. But he was confident that eventually Southern California would be one big city with homes and stores stretching over the entire area."

After selecting land he wished to purchase, Huntington would delegate employees to negotiate for terms. Then he directed his engineering staff to determine the best route for an electric interurban to the area. By late 1902 Pacific Electric lines were being built to Monrovia, the San Gabriel Valley town where activity lagged since the burst of the boom of the 1880's. A second track was being laid on the Long Beach line, and improvements, including removing some tracks from streets and putting them on private rights-of-ways, were being completed on the Pasadena Short Line.

Huntington's experience as railway executive enabled him to make the Pacific Electric notable for its efficient service. He already had a national reputation as a financier and railroader; the Big Red Cars boosted his prestige. When

he began to construct an extension to San Pedro from the Long Beach line, Huntington found ready cooperation. The Dominguez family, owning a big ranch between San Pedro and Compton, sold him a 120-foot right-of-way covering approximately twelve acres for $20 in 1903. The year before the family demanded — and received — $220 for only two acres sought as a right-of-way for the Los Angeles and Redondo Railway, backed by lesser known names.

In addition Huntington had made an important land acquisition in the San Gabriel Valley by purchasing substantial acreages in South Pasadena and San Marino, on the route of the line being built to Monrovia. Other lines were projected to Santa Ana and Newport Beach. Leaving details of planning additional routes to Epes Randolph, Huntington left in the fall of 1902 in his private railroad car for New York City to look after his eastern business interests.

Meanwhile, others wished to participate in the lucrative trolley revenue from Long Beach. Among them was Edwin Hook, who evidently underestimated the potential during the initial bidding. H. H. Hamilton, his agent, submitted a proposal for a paralleling trolley line but the Long Beach city council rejected it because of Huntington's efficient service and the fact that Hook was experiencing difficulties in building an interurban link to San Pedro.

Henry Huntington, in less than six months, had become the undisputed king of the electric interurban builders.

The year 1903 was to be a momentous and memorable one for Henry Huntington. It was to bring major additions to his land holdings and interurban systems. It also introduced major problems for his empire.

The year began as Huntington returned to Los Angeles from business conferences in New York. He had stopped in San Francisco for conferences with Isaias W. Hellman relative to the progress of selling bonds to finance extensions to the Pacific Electric Railway. Huntington resumed his tours over the Southern California countryside to seek desirable property. His arrival always was greeted enthusiastically by community leaders, obviously envisioning the prosperity to be theirs when an electric interurban line could pour settlers into their areas.

The fact that an interurban line brought prosperity to the communities blessed with a trolley was generally accepted by this time. The frequency and speed of electric interurban service far excelled that of the steam railroads. Commuting to Los Angeles by trolley was becoming a part of the Southern California way of life. Pasadena and Santa Monica, first cities to feel the impact of the interurban, were thriving as the result of the residents who found they could live by the seashore or mountains and take the trolleys to their work in Los Angeles. Similar population booms were starting in Alhambra and Long Beach even though the interurban lines had been in operation for only a few months. Not only was the line to Monrovia, covering important areas of the San Gabriel Valley, nearing completion but the Pacific Electric line to Whittier had been started. Huntington said it would be extended eastward into the citrus areas to cover sections of Southern California eagerly awaiting electric interurban service.

The electric interurbans brought keen competition to the steam railroads, true to the expectations of Long Beach residents. The Salt Lake Railroad and E. H. Harriman's Southern Pacific did not plan to relinquish business to Huntington without a struggle.

The Salt Lake Railroad had been selling ten rides from Long Beach to Los Angeles for $2 but reduced the rate to $1.50 to compete with the new Pacific Electric line. The railroad advertised: [3]

Ride in comfort on trains that make fast time over a smooth track. The Salt Lake Route sells ten ride tickets for $1.50, limit 30 days, for use of anyone.

But the Pacific Electric took advantage of its frequent service and countered with this advertisement: [4]

Remember the electric cars carry you when you are ready to go and bring you back when you are ready to return. Tickets unlimited. Good for anyone at any time.

Then to top it off the Pacific Electric advertisements asked prospective riders:

Why waste time waiting for steam trains when you can take a car at any cross street every fifteen minutes?

Unquestionably travelers preferred to rely on the more than one hundred electric cars to and from Long Beach in comparison to the daily total of eight trains and six trains provided by the Salt Lake Railroad and Southern Pacific respectively.

The growing competition of the electric interurban was highlighted when Los Angeles staged its Festival of Flowers in early May. An estimated 70,000 out-of-town visitors jammed Los Angeles, a city with a population of only slightly more than 100,000 people.

Of the total visitors approximately 47,500 came by electric interurbans and the remaining 35,000 travelers were shared by the three steam railroads. Records showed that the Pacific Electric carried 30,000 of the total on its Long Beach and Pasadena lines while the Los Angeles Pacific provided transportation for 15,000 visitors. The Los Angeles and Redondo Railway, recently electrified from steam railroad status, carried 2,500 visitors. [5]

The Southern Pacific lines carried only 9,000 passengers to the festival and what was worse, used special trains to

Note this early twentieth century interurban's open-air section. (Stephen D. Maguire Collection)

points as far away as Redlands, Riverside, and Whittier to accomplish this volume.

Trolleys even took the spotlight at the festival. A parade of Huntington's electric cars, many decorated as floats, was acclaimed as one of highlights of the event.

President Theodore Roosevelt, stopping briefly in Los Angeles during a western tour, saw the parade and appeared particularly impressed by the role of the trolleys.

"This is marvelous," the President exclaimed during the procession of trolley cars. [6]

The Pacific Electric line was being built to Whittier and the company's articles of incorporation made no secret of the fact that more routes were projected.

Commenting on the situation, the Long Beach Press said. [7]

As intimated recently in The Times, it looks very much as if the fight between the steam railroads and the Huntington electric system is something far more significant than a mere local dispute between railroad magnates. It will not be surprising to learn that Los Angeles has been selected as the battle ground for a sort of "test case" to decide the supremacy between the locomotive and the trolley, which question has been forced to the front of late in many sections of the country.

About a year ago a prominent local steam railroad official expressed the opinion that in ten years from now there would not be a single steam locomotive in the United States.

3. Long Beach Press, August 12, 1902.

4. Long Beach Press, August 12, 1902.

5. Los Angeles Times, May 9, 1903.

6. Los Angeles Times, May 9, 1903.

7. Long Beach Press, April 16, 1903.

Huntington's leadership in the electric railroad revolution was evident. Commented The Los Angeles Herald: [8]

When H. E. Huntington retired a couple of years ago from active participation in the management of the Southern Pacific, it is certain that he became a convert to the revelation of electricity with the clear conviction that this motive power was destined to supersede steam . . . . .

The battle lines were being drawn for a fight between the Harriman and Huntington interests.

The Southern Pacific proposed that the Los Angeles City Council authorize a program providing franchises for a universal 3-cent fare with transfers valid for rides throughout the area. It was obvious that a trolley system could not meet operating expenses under such a liberal plan. The result would be a financial fight to the finish between the transportation interests.

8. Los Angeles Herald, April 1, 1903.

Henry Huntington, knowing that reality was better than a promise, quickly countered with his own program for riders on the Pacific Electric lines. The Huntington plan called for sale of a 500-mile ride book for $6.25. The book would contain 400 coupons, each valued at $1\frac{1}{4}$ cents and good for one mile of travel. Commuters using the book could ride to Compton for thirteen cents, a saving of nearly one-half of the regular fare.

"We think it will be popular," Epes Randolph, general manager of the Pacific Electric, predicted when he announced the plan. "Our rates for this intermediate traffic heretofore have been too high. Mr. Huntington certainly wants to do the square thing by the people." [9]

The universal franchise plan was promptly shelved by the council. Huntington, pleased with his victory, proceeded with his program to expand his various programs on a grand scale.

9. Los Angeles Times, April 21, 1903.

Here is the junction of Main and Spring Streets in the early 1890's when electric streetcars, innovations for the time, shared the road with horse-drawn vehicles. (Title Insurance and Trust Company Collection)

This 1903 photo shows a P. E. car heading to Pasadena through Oneonta Park Junction, at Huntington Drive and *Fair Oaks Avenue in South Pasadena. The junction served the San Gabriel Valley. (Craig Rasmussen Collection)*

7. The Electrics Expand

Henry Huntington's program for expansion was rolling into high gear in the spring of 1903 much to the alarm of the officials of the steam railroads, particularly E. H. Harriman of the Southern Pacific. The Monrovia line, paralleling much of Southern Pacific route through the San Gabriel Valley, had opened amid considerable rejoicing in March 1903 and plans were announced for continuing the trolley tracks onto San Bernardino.

Plans were being made to increase facilities of the Pacific Light and Power Company, formed by Huntington in 1901 to provide electricity for residential usage as well as for his interurbans. An immense power plant would be built on Big Creek in the Sierra Nevada above the city of Fresno.

Huntington's acquisitions of land increased during the early part of 1903. He and associates purchased 2,000 acres of land at Olinda, deep in Orange County. In addition he acquired acreage near Alhambra and south of Pasadena. He

also announced he had purchased the West Coast Land and Water Company which controlled recently-founded Pacific City, shortly thereafter to be renamed Huntington Beach. His plans called for a domestic water plant, pleasure pavilion, and, worst of all as far as the Southern Pacific was concerned, extension of the community's wharf to accommodate larger ships. Huntington's expansions gradually were encircling other areas holding potentials as ports which could compete with Southern Pacific harbor aspirations. An interurban line to Pacific City also would touch Sunset Bay. Lines from Long Beach already were being extended to Alamitos Bay, once planned as the transcontinental terminus of the Los Angeles Terminal Railway, and to adjacent Anaheim Bay, used thirty years before by the settlers of the city of Anaheim. In late April Huntington purchased the San Bernardino Valley Traction Company, facilitating his expansion to the citrus country.

Senator William A. Clark sold his controlling interest in the Salt Lake Railroad to E. H. Harriman and helped fight Henry Huntington's electric railway empire.

Huntington's more alarming acquisitions in early 1903 came with his purchase of the Peninsular Railroad, the Santa Clara County interurban system. It could be pushed northward to San Francisco and southward to Santa Barbara, a proposed terminus of the Pacific Electric. In addition Huntington's purchases in early 1903 included the interurban systems of Stockton and Fresno, ideal for links in a route through the valley to Los Angeles. [1]

The acquisitions would be invaluable for building coastal and interior routes, each paralleling those of the Southern Pacific and linking most of California by electric cars.

Huntington's intentions of participating in the profits which were to come with development of a harbor at San Pedro were even more obvious. After Edwin Spencer Hook's narrow gauge California Pacific interurban route from San Pedro to Los Angeles had been completed in late 1902, Huntington rushed construction of his standard gauge line —which could compete by handling standard freight cars as well as passengers to the port community. Huntington's forces began laying tracks at San Pedro as soon as reports came that the Southern Pacific would seek an injunction to stop him from crossing its right-of-way. Huntington immediately transferred large crews working on the Whittier line and local Long Beach lines to San Pedro. Starting work late one Saturday afternoon, the crews worked throughout the night to lay the interurban tracks. [2]

San Pedrans were amazed on awakening Sunday morning

1. Los Angeles Times, April 24, 1903.

2. Long Beach Press, April 6, 1903.

to find that the Pacific Electric had pushed its track through the community to the harbor's edge.

Increasingly reports came of E. H. Harriman's growing displeasure over the expansion of the Pacific Electric.

"To stop the extension of the broad-gauge trolley lines is the cry of the steam railroads," reported The Los Angeles Times as passengers more and more chose to ride the interurbans. "Clear-sighted railway heads believe that electricity . . . (will) supersede steam as a motive power and many have given up blockading tactics and bowed allegiance and vowed fealty to the electric king."

Henry Huntington as vice president of the steam-operated Southern Pacific while at the same time the president of the competing Pacific Electric was indeed in an unusual position.

Amid the tensions, an announcement was made that the Southern Pacific had purchased Hook's California Pacific Railway for $1.8 million, netting the lanky midwesterner the tidy profit of $1 million for seven years as a builder of electric railways in Los Angeles. Huntington knew the value of the line and offered Hook a higher price. Hook received the Huntington offer an hour after he had sold his holdings to the Southern Pacific.

Commenting on the battle the Los Angeles Times on April 19 editorialized: [3]

What first alarmed the Southern Pacific was Huntington's activity at San Pedro and his reported intentions of building a trolley road through the San Fernando Valley and onto Santa Barbara and San Francisco, thus connecting all of the principal towns of the southern end of the state by interurban lines assuring frequent service.

By this time Huntington, optimistic in his prospects for victory in building a mighty interurban system, threw down a gauntlet for E. H. Harriman. He offered his resignation as the Southern Pacific's vice president, a position he had retained despite his competing activities in the interurban field.

Yet Harriman chose to respond only in silence as though contemplating some other action.

"Mr. Harriman has not yet notified me that my resignation as a vice president and director of the Southern Pacific Company has been accepted," Huntington said. "My resignation was presented in good faith and I see no reason why it should not be accepted.

"Mr. Harriman is prepared to fight the electric roads in Southern California," he continued, "in which I. W. Hellman and myself are interested. On that account it would be

3. An editorial prompted by the announcement of the sale of Hook's interurban route to Senator William A. Clark, organizer of the Salt Lake Railroad, who had joined forces with E. H. Harriman. When Clark announced purchase of the interurban line of April 17, he said it would be used as a "nucleus" for Southern Pacific operations against Henry Huntington.

embarrassing for me longer to continue my connection with the Southern Pacific." [4]

Huntington's challenge to the S. P. was not confined entirely to the Los Angeles basin, but stretched eastward sixty miles into the "Orange Empire" of Riverside and San Bernardino counties. The Southern Pacific and Santa Fe battled in this territory for passengers and freight, and Huntington's activity in the domain meant that his electric lines could be "feeders" for the latter transcontinental railroad.

The trolley king's entry into the Orange Empire came in 1903 with his acquisition of the Riverside and Arlington Railway Company. The firm's principal asset was a six-mile electric railroad from downtown Riverside the community of Arlington (later consolidated into the city of Riverside). The company also had trolley lines serving such diverse places as Fairmount Park and Victoria Hill.

The manager of the Riverside and Arlington was none other than Frank A. Miller, who at the time was achieving fame as the "master" of the Glenwood Mission Inn. The hotel on Main Street between Sixth and Seventh Streets in Riverside incorporated architectural features based on the Spanish missions of California. For more than a quarter century the Mission Inn attracted affluent winter visitors from other sections of America. In the early days, these vacationists rode the Riverside and Arlington, whose carhouse was adjacent to the hotel on Main between Fifth and Sixth. After the Orange Empire and Los Angeles were linked by electric rail lines, they could tour Southern California by trolley. The electric interurbans conveniently rolled down Main Street past the hotel.

Both before and after purchasing the Riverside and Arlington, Henry Huntington was a frequent visitor at the Mission Inn — which he had helped finance. In fact, he frequently used the hotel as a rendezvous for important meetings with the executives of his electric railroads and other companies.

Huntington, already a threat to the Southern Pacific in Los Angeles, triumphantly announced plans for the Riverside and Arlington which would substantially increase his dominance in Southern California. He gleefully said he would extend the electric railroad to Corona and then through Santa Ana Canyon to connect with his Los Angeles area lines, thus taking traffic from the inland territory away from the S. P.

Moreover, Huntington threatened to extend the electric railroad to San Bernardino and Redlands as well as to Escondido and eventually to San Diego.

Huntington never constructed lines through Santa Ana Canyon or to San Diego, but he did extend his holdings in the Orange Empire. In 1907 he won control of the San

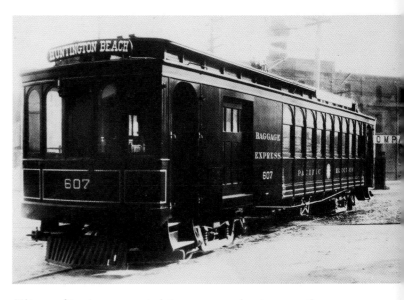

This combination car carried passengers and express on the Pacific Electric line via Huntington Park and Long Beach to Huntington Beach. (Pacific Railroad Publications.)

Bernardino Valley Traction Company, previously owned by local investors. This company owned streetcar lines in San Bernardino and Redlands. It also operated interurban lines from San Bernardino to Highland, noted at the time for its Harlem Springs resort, and from San Bernardino to Redlands. The line to Redlands stretched approximately ten miles, and the route from San Bernardino to Highland covered about fifteen miles.

The opening of the San Bernardino Valley Traction Company's line from San Bernardino to the Arrowhead Springs Hotel in the San Bernardino Mountains in July, 1907, took Huntington trolleys into their second mountain range. His electric cars previously climbed the slopes of Mount Lowe in the San Gabriel range.

Huntington's holdings in the Orange Empire also included the Redlands Central Railway Company, operating a four-mile streetcar line in Redlands. He acquired the company in 1908.

In effect, Huntington controlled the Crescent City Railroad, running approximately nine miles from Riverside to Rialto and built in 1907 by the Riverside Portland Cement Company to carry employees to its plant near Crestmore. The Huntington-controlled Riverside and Arlington leased the

4. *Los Angeles Times*, April 24, 1903.

PICTURE PAGES FOLLOWING:
A Tin-Lizzy turns out of the way as an electric interurban starts to round a curve en route from Pasadena to Los Angeles during the early 1900's. Note the undeveloped countryside. (Security Pacific National Bank)

cement company's line, electrified it, and in 1908 began service on the route.

Huntington's purchase of the San Bernardino Valley Traction Company also gave him control of that firm's wholly-owned subsidiary, the San Bernardino Inter-Urban Railway Company. This firm was formed in 1906 to construct extensions — notably from San Bernardino to Riverside — for its parent company. The trolley magnate was enthusiastic over its goal of connecting his inland electric railroad properties, but the actual construction of linking San Bernardino and Riverside via Colton lagged because of the Huntington-Harriman feud.

The line wasn't to be completed until Henry Huntington had relinquished control of his electric interurban empire.

Henry Huntington had made it clear that he was ready for battle, but little did he suspect the manner in which the foray would come.

Henry E. Huntington's Los Angeles Railway had applied to the Los Angeles City Council for a franchise to lay tracks on Sixth Street from Figueroa Street to the western city limits as part of a plan to build an extension to the Hollywood area. Hollywood, a sleepy hamlet since its founding in 1887, was starting an era of prosperity since being touched by the Los Angeles Pacific tracks as part of the line to Santa Monica.

The council hoped bids for the franchise might reach $10,000, an amount to be welcomed because the municipal budget was substantially in the red.

The day before the franchise hearing had seen the Pacific Electric line to Long Beach jammed with 15,000 passengers who rode to see visiting battleships. A record twenty-six trolleys were placed in service on the line and arrived in Long Beach at four minute intervals. So crowded were the interurbans that passengers actually were clinging to the vestibules.

By contrast, the steam railroads to Long Beach were relegated to second place by the sightseers. The passengers preferred the high speed trolleys.

The day for considering bids was Monday, May 4, 1903 —the day after Huntington's tracks had been laid in San Pedro to the harbor over land claimed by the Southern Pacific.

When the appointed time arrived for opening of the bids City Clerk Wilde could find only one envelope containing offers for the franchise. He opened it and read: [5]

"G. G. Johnson bids $2,500 for the Sixth Street franchise.

"That's the only one I find," he added, noting the surprised railroad men.

Henry E. Huntington sat against the rear wall of the room smiling. He deftly balanced his hat on the head of the cane he held in his right hand. At his right sat J. A. Muir, manager of Huntington's Los Angeles Railway Company; on the other side were William E. Dunn and Samuel Hopkins, attorneys for his companies. Dunn, 42 at the time, was regarded as one of Southern California's most brilliant legal minds. He left his position as Los Angeles city attorney to associate himself with Huntington.

On the west side of the room were seated T. J. Hook, president of the competing Los Angeles Traction Company and brother of Edwin Spencer Hook, and his attorney, Frank J. Thomas.

Across the room alongside the railing before the Board of Public Works was George G. Johnson, a Los Angeles real estate dealer.

Prodded by the transit men the city clerk searched through his papers and produced another bid.

"The Los Angeles Railway Company bids $2,500 for the Sixth Street franchise," he said monotonously, reading the offer submitted by the Huntington-controlled firm. Thomas protested that the right envelope had not been found. The city clerk searched his papers, found another envelope, and as Thomas watched expectantly read:

"For the Sixth Street franchise E. S. Hook bids $5,000."

"Are there any other bids?" asked John Brown, president of the Board of Public Works."

William Dunn walked leisurely over to a newspaper reporter's desk.

"The Los Angeles Railway Company bids $5,500," he said.

"I bid $6,050," said Johnson, seemingly suppressing a smile.

Mr. Huntington smiled. Mr. Hook smiled. In fact, the newspaper reporters noted, everyone smiled for it was amusing to think that a man with the limited assets of George G. Johnson would attempt to build a streetcar line.

Hook raised his bid to $6,655 and Dunn raised the Huntington offer to $7,500.

Johnson, checking figures carefully on a memorandum pad as though he wanted to be sure he could afford such an expenditure, raised his bid to $8,250. The crowd began to sense a drama in the making. City officials from adjacent offices came in to the room to listen.

"I bid $10,000," said Hook in what proved to be his family's last effort at railroad building.

"Make it $20,000," returned Dunn. He walked over to the chair by Henry Huntington side. He looked satisfied.

There was dramatic quietness as Mr. Johnson did more arithmetic on his scratch pad. He offered a bid of $22,000.

Dunn arose and returned to the newspaper reporter's desk alongside the railing in front of the city officials.

"$25,000," he said simply.

Mr. Johnson did more arithmetic on his scratch pad. "$27,500," he said.

5. Details of the $110,000 franchise are based on accounts in the May 5, 1903, editions of the Los Angeles Times, Los Angeles Record, and Los Angeles Herald.

Dunn countered with a bid of $35,000. Johnson topped it with an offer of $38,500. The audience was quiet appeared tense as it listened. Dunn appraisingly eyed the gathering and then, as a man confident that he was to conclude a bargain, announced:

"Bid $50,000 for the franchise."

Dunn walked over and sat down by Henry Huntington, who was still smiling. The newspaper reporters noted that Huntington stopped smiling when Mr. Johnson again began figuring on his scratch pad.

"$55,000," Johnson said calmly. A suppressed exclamation came from the crowd.

Dunn paced the floor and went to a window where he looked out on Broadway. Henry Huntington resumed smiling. Dunn turned from the window and gazed intently at Huntington for a full minute.

The attorney then bid $60,000 for the franchise which had been regarded as worth $10,000 at the most. Proceedings were interrupted at this point for Dunn and Johnson to prove they had ample cash to cover the ten per cent deposit required for a successful bid. Mr. Johnson drew $5,000 out of a large yellow envelope which spectators noted appeared stocked amply with money.

A bid of $66,000 was offered by Mr. Johnson.

"$75,000," cried Dunn instantly, reaching into his pocket and pulling out a large role of $1,000 bills from which to make the deposit.

Mr. Johnson did more arithmetic on his scratch pad, looking inquiringly through his glasses into the yellow envelope as though he wanted to be sure that he did not enter into a project too far above his financial resources.

"I'll make that $82,500," he said simply.

"I'll bid $100,000," countered Dunn, going for a third time to the rear of the room where Henry Huntington was sitting.

All of the spectators turned their eyes towards George G. Johnson. He looked very thoughtful. He paced up and down the room once or twice.

Mr. Johnson walked slowly to the door and looked down the corridor. The spectators concluded that he was quitting because the stakes were too high.

Then the real estate man walked slowly back to the clerk's desk, pulled out his scratch pad, did more arithmetic, and produced an additional $5,000 from the yellow envelope.

He smiled.

"I'll bid $110,000 for the franchise," George Johnson said calmly.

The audience turned expectantly to Huntington and Dunn at the rear of the room.

"That's all as far as we are concerned," Dunn said in most business-like tones, "and we thank you for giving us your time."

A collective sigh of relief ran through the audience.

William Dunn (above) served as attorney for Henry Huntington's companies. George Patton, (below) an anti-S. P. Democrat, served as director in several of the corporations.

This Pacific Electric locomotive, its cabin constructed of wood, pulled freight cars on the company's standard gauge tracks in competition with the steam railroads that once had a monopoly. (Craig Rasmussen Collection)

Henry Huntington and his associates left the room immediately. George Johnson stepped to the clerk's desk to make the necessary deposit for the expensive franchise.

When reporters contacted Huntington later in the day for comments, the interurban magnate was visibly irritated.

"They (the Southern Pacific officials) may deny to the newspapers and the public that they are behind the 3-cent franchise application," Huntington said, "but they have never denied it to me. I say, they have never denied it to me."

Newspaper reporters asked the trolley tycoon why he had continued bidding when the price went so high.

". . . A fellow doesn't like to be beat," he replied. "You know how it is. When a fellow goes into a fight, he likes to stay."

Had he expected the high bidding and would loss of the franchise interfere with his expansion plans?

"I knew that Harriman would bid up for it," Huntington said. "The loss of one franchise need not keep us out of that part of town. There is more than one road to Rome."

Electric cars operating on the $110,000 franchise route would be unable to return so much as minimum interest on the outlay, Huntington said. The reporters pressed him for an explanation as to why he bid $100,000 for the franchise considering its worth.

"Well," Huntington was quoted as saying, "you know how it is at an auction. When a fellow gets to bidding, he don't like to give up. There's a little pride in it. Yes, there's a little pride in it."

For city officials the bidding was a happy occasion. The $110,000 received from the franchise more than balanced the municipal budget.

For Henry Huntington there was a beginning of troubles.

That evening Huntington boarded the Southern Pacific Owl overnight train for San Francisco for a face-to-face meeting with E. H. Harriman to discuss electric railroads.

White poles show the Pacific Electric route to the waterfront at San Pedro in 1903. A P. E. freight car stands on a siding *while a trolley approaches. Tracks at left belong to the Southern Pacific. (Title Insurance and Trust Co.)*

8. Huntington vs. Harriman

While Henry Huntington was enroute to his meeting with E. H. Harriman in San Francisco, newspapers, speculated regarding the meaning of the $110,000 franchise. All of the proposed solutions centered, quite correctly as time proved, around the Southern Pacific's endeavors to stop expansion of the Pacific Electric in general and Huntington in particular.

Clues as to what happened might have been noted in I. W. Hellman's visit to Los Angeles earlier in the year and in the street index to the 1903 edition of the Los Angeles City Directory.

The directory showed that George G. Johnson's real estate office at 145 South Broadway was conveniently across the street from the building housing the offices of Senator

W. A. Clark's Salt Lake Railroad, control of which before was obtained a few days before by Harriman interests. Johnson later sued Senator Clark for $25,000, the amount he claimed was due him for the role he played so successfully in blocking Huntington during the bidding for the franchise. The case was settled out of court. [1]

The dramatic offering of $110,000 for a franchise worth $10,000 was E. H. Harriman's way of notifying Henry Huntington that he had acquired the forty-five per cent interest in the Pacific Electric Railroad owned by I. W. Hellman and his associates, Christian De Guigne and Antoine Borel. These details were not revealed for nearly twenty-five

---

1. Los Angeles Examiner, March 24, 1906.

years. At the time, however, both Huntington and Harriman played their cards close to their chests. Harriman took the role of an innocent by-stander.

Harriman was quoted by reporters: [2]

No, it was no interests of mine which outbid Mr. Huntington for the street railway franchise at Los Angeles . . . Naturally, then, it would seem that this was not what we (he and Henry Huntington) talked about when he called on me . . .

Whoever is doing all this at Los Angeles will have to come to us sooner or later because we own nearly everything down there.

Huntington was less talkative but emphatic.

"There will be no compromise," he told reporters simply. [3]

Popularized reports had it that Henry Huntington was "forced" to share ownership of the Pacific Electric with Harriman in order to placate the railroad baron. The truth of the matter was that Harriman had quite legitimately purchased an interest in the company. The facts were available at the time in Los Angeles county records but apparently were unchecked by those who speculated on the happenings. The situation later was verified by I. W. Hellman, who with Borel and De Guigne joined with Huntington anticipating profits in the electric rail field.

Instead of profits, however, the venture called for more money. A conversation between Hellman and Huntington years later was to clarify the situation. [4]

"When we went into the (Pacific Electric) deal," Hellman had asked Huntington, "did you not fix the amount it would cost us?"

"Yes," Huntington had replied.

"When we had spent that much (the $452,000 paid by the directors) money did I not then sell $10 million worth of Pacific Electric Railway bonds for use of the project?" Hellman continued.

Huntington again agreed and Hellman went on to recall that the interurban magnate added more money of his own and called on the associates to provide additional funds.

"Yes," Huntington agreed, "I could not build railroads without money. And if I had told you what it was going to cost when we began the work you never would have joined me."

Hellman reminded Huntington that he had warned him that he was not going "to break myself" on the interurban system and that Borel and De Guigne were becoming concerned over their finances.

"And did I not beg you," Hellman continued, "to buy our stock . . . and you laughed at me?"

Huntington nodded and said he thought the worrier had no basis.

"You refused to buy our stock," Hellman continued in his talk with Huntington. "Then did I not tell you that I was going to get out and if you did not buy (our stock) I was going to sell it (to other interests)?"

"Yes and I told you to go ahead and sell it," Huntington replied. "I had no idea that you could find anyone on earth who would step into your shoes."

E. H. Harriman was eager to step into the shoes of Hellman and his worried associates. He happily purchased their stock in the spring of 1903, confident that it would give him means to control Huntington's expansion.

In selling Hellman perhaps saw a potential for the interurban system but recalled his frequent saying: "The man who wants the last drop in the bucket usually gets left."

There were reasons for the other stockholders to remain in the Huntington camp. John Bicknell was the attorney for the Pacific Electric and Epes Randolph, long a Huntington friend, was the system's chief engineer and general manager. Jonathan Slauson realized the potential interurbans could bring for his sprawling Azusa Ranch, toward which the Monrovia electric line was pushing.

Harriman, satisfied with his forty-five percent interest, believed he had found a way to stop Huntington. With a sense for the dramatic Harriman had selected the $110,000 franchise to notify Huntington that he meant business.

William Herrin, the Southern Pacific's capable attorney, was named to represent Harriman on the Pacific Electric board of directors.

The Los Angeles Times noted editorially: [5]

Their (Huntington and Harriman) hate for each other was so terrible as to be less intense than only their love for their business interests.

Henry Huntington was smiling and exuding confidence, newspaper reporters observed, when he returned to Los Angeles from the meeting with E. H. Harriman. The latter well could have speculated what projected move put the smile on Huntington's face.

The reporters asked Huntington about his trip.

"I think I made an impression on Mr. Harriman," he said, "to the extent of making him see that the construction

---

2. and 3. Los Angeles Times, May 6, 1903.

4. J. A. Graves, "My Seventy Years in California," (Los Angeles, 1928), Pp. 101-104. The conversation took place in the office of Mr. Graves, president of Hellman's Farmers and Merchants Bank of Los Angeles. Hellman began the discussion by telling Huntington he was disturbed because "your subordinates are reporting that I sold you out." After the conversation Hellman and Huntington shook hands and departed as friends.

5. Los Angeles Times, May 6, 1903.

RIGHT: This trainman posed by his trolley at Covina, a community that received frequent car service after Huntington pushed his lines through the orange grove country east of Los Angeles. (Craig Rasmussen Collection)

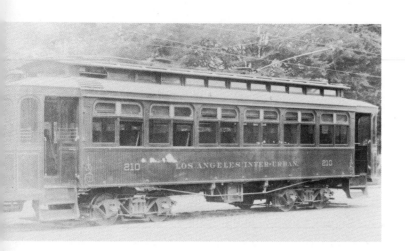

Trolleys carrying the name of the Los Angeles Inter-Urban went into service on Huntington's system in 1903 as he battled the steam railroads. (Charles Seims Collection)

of electric lines would be a benefit rather than a detriment to his steam road. I say I think I made an impression." [6]

Eyes were turning, however, to another Los Angeles streetcar franchise — also valued at $10,000 — for which bids were to be opened on May 11. It was known that Huntington was interested in the franchise and there were speculations that the Southern Pacific might try a repetition of the dramatic $110,000 franchise incident.

Despite the truce Huntington was continuing construction of his Pacific Electric line linking the harbor at San Pedro with the remainder of his system. E. P. Ripley, president of the Santa Fe Railroad, arrived in Los Angeles on May 10 to observe the expected franchise battle. It was an open secret that the Santa Fe was backing Huntington, for through his Pacific Electric tracks it could obtain access to vital areas of the port at San Pedro and compete with the Southern Pacific and Salt Lake Railroad in hauling freight. [7]

William Herrin, attorney for the Southern Pacific, also arrived in Los Angeles for the bidding. The city braced for a return bout between the Huntington and Harriman interests.

As the franchise hearing opened observers noted that William Dunn's pockets seemed to be bulging with cash to be used as a deposit on bidding. It was evident that Huntington planned to be the winner regardless of how high the stakes might go.

But the battle failed to develop.

Huntington submitted the only bid, an offer of $2,500 for the franchise. It was promptly refused by city officials on the basis that the amount was inadequate. The $110,000

franchise battle had spoiled them. Huntington and Harriman undoubtedly had reached an understanding, but the fact that the truce was an uneasy one was obvious because of the cash with which Dunn had armed himself.

Huntington appeared pleased after the hearing even though awarding of the franchise had been continued.

"You seem to have it all your own way this time, Mr. Huntington," a reporter remarked.

The rail magnate smiled non-committingly.

"Oh, you can't sometimes always tell," he said. [8]

Henry Huntington, however, was planning another move in his chess game with E. H. Harriman.

The 1903 battle between the rail barons took a new turn on June 4 when Henry Huntington and a group of his close associates signed the articles of incorporation for the Los Angeles Inter-Urban Railway Company. He described the new corporation as necessary because of Pacific Electric "limitations" which he did not detail.

The limitations obviously were the Southern Pacific's forty-five per cent interest in the Pacific Electric.

"It (the new company) will mean another system of railways in this part of the state," Huntington explained. "The Pacific Electric Railway has all it can look after now. If it were enlarged it might become unwieldy. Therefore for business reasons we organized another company. It's just easier to handle the thing that way, that's all." [9]

The new firm's articles of incorporation were filed with the California secretary of state on June 9, the same day that another Huntington enterprise was officially organized. This corporation was called the Pacific Electric Land Company, a name conveniently similar to that of the Pacific Electric Railway Company in which Harriman's Southern Pacific recently acquired an interest.

Both new companies were notable for a lack of names associated with the Southern Pacific. Among the directors were Epes Randolph, P. E. general manager and still in the Huntington camp at this time; George S. Patton, the anti-S. P. Democrat; George E. Pillsbury, the P. E.'s chief engineer, and Huntington's son, Howard.

Henry Huntington was listed as a director only of the Pacific Electric Land Company, and strangely gave his residence as Oneonta, New York, his birthplace. He had left there years ago and when the Pacific Electric Railway was incorporated less than two years before, he listed San Francisco as his place of residency.

One can only speculate that this was the way one New Yorker, Henry Edwards Huntington, gave another New Yorker, Edward Henry Harriman, the message that he intended to fight.

6. Los Angeles Times, May 12, 1903.

7. Los Angeles Times, May 11, 1903.

8. Los Angeles Times, May 12, 1903.

9. Los Angeles Times, June 10, 1903.

The corporate papers made it clear that both new firms were Henry Huntington companies. The trolley king subscribed virtually all of the stock in both corporations, leaving only token amounts for the directors so they could qualify for their positions. He took $346,500 of the $350,-000 stock issued for the Los Angeles Inter-Urban Railway, and $397,000 of the $400,000 issued for the Pacific Electric Land Company.

Time clouded the role of the two corporations. In subsequent years the firms were described as joint Huntington-Harriman projects or as corporations formed by the Pacific Electric for the purpose of building tracks. When Huntington was planning to retire from the electric railroad field, he did lease the Los Angeles Inter-Urban to the Pacific Electric Railway. After the Southern Pacific eventually acquired his interurban holdings, its P. E. lines used the Pacific Electric Land Company to hold some real estate investments.

But Henry Huntington's initial purpose in organizing the Los Angeles Inter-Urban Railway and the Pacific Electric Land Company obviously was to fight the Southern Pacific by building lines under his exclusive control.

The Los Angeles Inter-Urban's by-laws called for constructing lines to La Habra, Riverside, and Redlands, with branches to Colton, San Bernardino, and Highland. Another line would go from the La Habra line through Santa Ana to Newport Beach. Other proposed routes were from Santa Ana to the Pacific Electric tracks at Watts; from Los Angeles to the San Fernando Valley and Santa Barbara, to Glendale and Burbank, and to Covina and Ontario.

The Pacific Electric Land Company was more general in the goals stated in its by-laws. It would buy land, sub-divide it, produce electric power for interurbans, and "acquire all property of every description necessary" to operate electric railroads."

The Los Angeles Inter-Urban became such a powerful tool for expanding the Huntington trolley empire that soon its tracks stretched for more miles than those of the P. E.

Huntington retained in his own name many of the interurban lines just completed or under construction. When the routes were in operation, he planned to transfer ownership to the Pacific Electric, as he did the Long Beach route. He was thus able to transfer construction rights or completed routes to the Los Angeles Inter-Urban, thus avoiding their control by the Pacific Electric Railway in which he was a reluctant partner with the Southern Pacific.

The Pacific Electric's main interurban lines were the ones to Long Beach, Pasadena, South Pasadena, Alhambra, Whittier, and Monrovia. In addition, it had approximately twenty-five "local" service streetcar lines situated mainly in Long Beach, Pasadena, and Los Angeles. It also owned the line to Altadena and the Mount Lowe incline railway.

The Pacific Electric Building at Sixth and Main takes shape in 1904, symbolizing not only growth for Los Angeles but the importance of electric railroads for Southern California. (Security Pacific National Bank)

By contrast, the Los Angeles Inter-Urban operated lines to Huntington Beach, Newport Beach, Santa Ana, Orange, San Pedro, Glendale, Glendora, Sierra Madre, and La Habra. When the Southern Pacific eventually bought the firm, this one hundred percent Huntington-owned company also had two of the four tracks between Los Angeles and El Molino Junction, a key to service in the San Gabriel Valley, and two of the four tracks stretching from Los Angeles to Long Beach. In addition, this company owned approximately twenty-five "local" service streetcar lines in Los Angeles, Long Beach, Pasadena, and San Pedro.

Aside from constructing new lines, Huntington was expanding his trolley empire by buying existing electric railroads as far away as San Bernardino, Redlands, and Riverside—sixty miles from Los Angeles in the "Orange Empire" agriculture area that promised lucrative passenger and freight revenue.

One acquisition that Huntington's Los Angeles Inter-Urban made closer to his main base was the Los Angeles and Glendale Electric Railroad Company, formed in late 1902 by L. C. Brand, the pioneer Glendale developer. Brand and his associates sold the line to Huntington a few weeks before it was completed in April, 1904. In Glendale, the trolleys entered via a separated right-of-way in the center of Brand Boulevard. Thanks to the passengers arriving on the trolleys,

A Pacific Electric car on Long Beach Boulevard (then American Avenue) prepares to turn onto Ocean Boulevard in this 1904 *photograph. The tracks at far left belonged to the steam Salt Lake Route. (Security Pacific National Bank)*

Brand Boulevard soon became Glendale's main business artery. The line, connecting with other Huntington routes, brought so many people that Glendale was large enough to become a municipality in 1906.

The Los Angeles Inter-Urban had its own trolleys, in the fashion of all self-respecting electric railroads. Some cars were cream-colored and others were green.

But it also provided service with red interurbans carrying the name of the Pacific Electric.

The remainder of 1903 was marked by the various Huntington interests pushing construction of the lines to Huntington Beach, Whitter, Glendale, and Covina. The inevitable booms in land values and sales along the routes by this time were expected with the arrival of the interurbans.

The Whittier line, a Pacific Electric Railway project, was completed in November with a ceremony which, even though impromptu, brought 6,000 spectators into the community of 5,000 residents. Epes Randolph urged people to support the program for pushing the electric line "eastward" by donating the necessary land for the right-of-way. Although residents of most areas were so eager for the convenience and prosperity that usually came with electric railroads, the people along this route apparently failed to recognize the blessings and did not cooperate by giving land.

The right-of-way into Whittier for the last five miles was estimated to have cost Huntington an estimated $50,000

because of the valuable walnut orchards through which it passed and the reluctance of property owners to donate land. The long period of construction of the Whittier route as compared to other lines was due to the high costs of acquiring the land. The unexpected costs undoubtedly had been factors in I. W. Hellman's fears of continuing as a Pacific Electric stockholder.

W. H. Holladay, Huntington's nephew, arranged for a display of fireworks to celebrate opening of the route. Whittier joined the throng of cities blessed with interurban trolleys and the resulting prosperity. The Big Red Cars provided twenty cars daily to and from Los Angeles as compared with daily totals of three by the Southern Pacific and four by the Santa Fe-controlled Southern California Railway.

The Whittier Register happily reported:

Whittier in its matchless location on its hillside now feels the pulsing life of the commercial world in being united to the metropolis of Southern California by the completion of the electric railway on Friday the 6th instant.

It became the accepted hypothesis that the electric interurban was a necessity for a community's prosperity. New routes were built and existing lines were extended to carry the new people settling in Southern California during growth period from 1903 to 1906.

Moses Sherman and Eli Clark extended their Los Angeles Pacific lines from Santa Monica down the coast to

Redondo Beach in late 1903. The competition forced complete electrification of the Los Angeles and Redondo Railroad steam line. Huntington's Los Angeles Inter-Urban Railroad was completed to Santa Ana in the fall of 1905. He purchased a steam line to Orange, converting it to electrical operation as part of the route which appeared headed for Riverside and San Bernardino.

The route to Santa Ana, seat of Orange County, followed a virtually straight course diagonally for thirty-four miles from the Watts junction on the Long Beach line, and allowed speedy travel unequaled on the era's winding roads distinguished mainly by chuck holes. Its private right-of-way emptied the interurbans on Fourth Street, Santa Ana's main business artery. The tracks went down Fourth to the Southern Pacific depot, which was just a stone's throw from the Santa Fe station. Opening of the line brought the subdivision in 1905 of Cypress. Huntington's Pacific Electric Land Company was among the developers of Stanton, also opened in 1905 as a result of the new route. The deep blasts of the interurbans' whistles awakened two sleepy villages fortunate enough to be on the line: Artesia and Garden Grove began to grow into cities with the coming of the trolleys.

Henry Huntington's efficient construction of trolley systems heightened his reputation in the interurban field.

Observing the convenience of the new interurban line into Orange County, the Tustin correspondent of the Santa Ana Blade wrote: [10]

As one resident (of Tustin) forcibly remarked, "We've just got to have it (a trolley), and that's all there is to it. Of course we would like to have Mr. Huntington build a line for us as we think he could do a better job than almost anyone else."

Tustin unfortunately was not to receive the interurban line its residents sought but extensions were being built to La Habra, Glendale, and Covina as Huntington ignored E. H. Harriman's efforts to stop his expansion.

Another Orange County development in 1905 was at Newport Beach, thirty-eight miles from Los Angeles and at the time a village with less than a thousand residents. Its major connection with the outside world was a steam railroad line to Santa Ana, approximately ten miles away. The line was built by entrepreneurs who envisioned developing

10. Santa Ana Blade, June 1, 1906.

This photograph was made as the first Pacific Electric car reached Santa Ana, in the heart of Orange County 40 miles from Los Angeles, in 1905. The trolley is rolling down Fourth Street. (First American Title Insurance Co.)

Newport into Southern California's port in competition with the Southern Pacific's "monopoly" harbor at Santa Monica. The S. P. circuitously managed to buy the railroad and, of course, abandon the harbor project.

Huntington, constantly adding to his domain, bought acreage at Newport and through the Los Angeles Inter-Urban began extending the electric railroad line down the coast from Huntington Beach. Trolleys began running on August 5. After the donation of land and cash from the land developers who would benefit, the electric railroad was extended down the peninsula to Balboa. This route opened July 4, 1906, bringing crowds of sightseers. The convenient access to the nautical community made it easy to commute to Los Angeles office, from Newport and Balboa. Land values skyrocketed, and so did the population. The census four years later gave Newport Beach 4,274 residents, a six fold increase in a decade.

The line, skirting the ocean for approximately fifteen miles from Seal Beach to Balboa, gave passengers magnificent views of the Pacific. The interurbans rolled through Newport and down the peninsula on a separated right-of-way that divided Balboa Boulevard.

Henry Huntington's catalysts for growth were not to be limited to his trolley system and outlying land developments. Not the least of his contributions was the $1.7 million Huntington Building — later known as the Pacific Electric Building — which was opened amid festivities on January 15, 1905.

The building's site at Sixth and Main Streets had been regarded as purely a residential district fringing Los Angeles' central business section, located in the vicinity of First and Spring Streets. The building was opened with a parade of trolleys ranging from the Big Red Cars to Huntington's narrow-gauge streetcars which provided local service in Los Angeles.

The nine-story Huntington Building at the time was the biggest yet for Los Angeles. Its immediate effect was to shift business activity away from the older business section and to pave the way for other major multi-story construction projects.

It appeared that Huntington was satisfied to dominate Riverside, Orange, and San Bernardino Counties and the eastern portion of Los Angeles County, leaving western Los Angeles County including Santa Monica Bay as the realm of Sherman and Clark's Los Angeles Pacific Railway and the independently owned Los Angeles and Redondo Railroad.

The truth of the matter, however, was that Henry Huntington had far from abandoned plans for a spectacular transportation system.

This trolley, serving passengers in Redlands, was decorated for the Fourth of July in 1902. Henry Huntington acquired the Redlands' system for his electric car empire. (Courtesy William G. Moore: Redlands Daily Facts)

The Pacific Electric Building at Sixth and Main in Los Angeles is shown here shortly after its completion in 1905.

Residences still stood near the structure, which was on the outskirts of the established Los Angeles business section.

9. Huntington's Surprise Firecracker

While July 4, 1905, was notable at all Southern California beaches for the thousands of inlanders who arrived at the coastal communities via interurbans, the most spectacular event was on Santa Monica Bay. Independence Day brought the official opening of The Venice of America.

The picturesque development was the brain child of Abbot Kinney, a 55-year-old businessman, scholar, and humanitarian whose extensive education in Europe ranged from economics to the fine arts. He served with Helen Hunt Jackson on the 1883 federal commission which investigated the plight of the Indians in Southern California. Mrs. Jackson subsequently wrote her famous novel, "Ramona," to bring attention to the desperate state of the Indians. Kinney wrote books deploring the spoilage of California's natural resources.

On a tour of Europe, Kinney studied the tobacco industry in Turkey and returned with techniques to popularize cigarettes, previously not highly regarded in America. He became wealthy. Among his acquisitions in Southern California was a large tract of land near Santa Monica. Part of this land he developed into Ocean Park, a prosperous community after completion of the Los Angeles Pacific Railroad.

The remainder of the property was largely marshland and generally regarded as worthless. Recalling the beauty of

Venice, Italy, he decided to turn this land into a real estate development modeled after that city of canals. He appropriately named the project Venice of America. When dredges in the summer of 1904 began carving out what skeptics termed "Kinney's Dream," few people visualized how the marshes could be transformed into a place of beauty.

The public began to appreciate the beauty created in the Venice of America on June 30, 1905, when the canals were flooded with water for the first time and the attractiveness of the development was unveiled as though the curtain of a theatre had been lifted. Quaint concrete bridges spanned canals lined with Italian Renaissance buildings. Gondolas carried visitors through the canals.

The official opening on Independence Day brought an estimated 40,000 visitors to Venice on trolleys of the Los Angeles Pacific Railroad. The potential of Santa Monica Bay for suburban living became more evident than ever. Plans were made to include Venice on trolley sightseeing trips. The project also prompted the construction of a development with similar canals on the marshes by Alamitos Bay at Long Beach, in Pacific Electric territory. The project, called Naples, was opened a year later and provided for the Big Red Cars to run to a quaint Neapolitan hotel.

The potential of Santa Monica Bay had not been overlooked by Henry Huntington, but in order to avoid sharing the spotlight with other beach communities on the Fourth of July he delayed making the announcement of his newest acquisition until July 7.

Then he exploded his firecracker.

Huntington first announced that the purchase of the Redondo Land Company, owning ninety percent of the property at Redondo Beach. The eyes of land speculators turned to the coastal communities. Only July 11 the tycoon made a second announcement: he had purchased the Los Angeles and Redondo Railway Company, the electric railroad whose green trolleys competed with the Los Angeles Pacific in providing service to the area. The news brought reactions in several quarters. The immediate effect was to launch a boom in Redondo Beach land sales reminiscent of the 1887 era because the magical name of Henry Huntington meant progress and growth. The interurban cars of not only the Los Angeles and Redondo Railway but also of the Los Angeles Pacific lines to Redondo Beach were packed with land speculators expecting to reap fortunes.

Individual parcels of land changed hands as many as six times within three days, each time selling for higher prices. One frame building was sold for $4,000 in the morning to a buyer who peddled it for $10,000 at noon; by the evening the second purchaser had sold it for $20,000 during the buying spree which the Los Angeles Record said was "conjured by a name." The newspaper continued: [1]

---

1. Los Angeles Record, July 10, 1905.

Abbot Kinney built the beautiful Venice of America on marshlands at Santa Monica Bay. The community of canals was acclaimed. (Los Angeles Public Library) RIGHT: This official Los Angeles Pacific map shows the Santa Monica Bay areas served.

It is estimated here (in Redondo Beach) that within the past thirty-six hours the entire city has not only changed hands but has been sold again and again at increasing prices.

Ask anyone the reason and there is but one answer—Huntington.

Rumors circulated that the Redondo purchases were only the start of a big Huntington expansion program intended to push his electric interurban lines up the coast to Ventura and Santa Barbara — if not further. The Record reporter pressed Huntington to reveal just how far he intended to extend his tracks

"I am not going to build to the moon," was Huntington's evasive reply. "They seem to think I'm going to build to the moon, but I'm not."

Precisely to whom "they" referred was not discussed, although general reports indicated that the steam railway officials were concerned over Huntington's activity because it threatened more competition. For the time being, however, the interurban and land king was most interested in his Redondo Beach acquisition.

Huntington sold more land in less than two weeks than

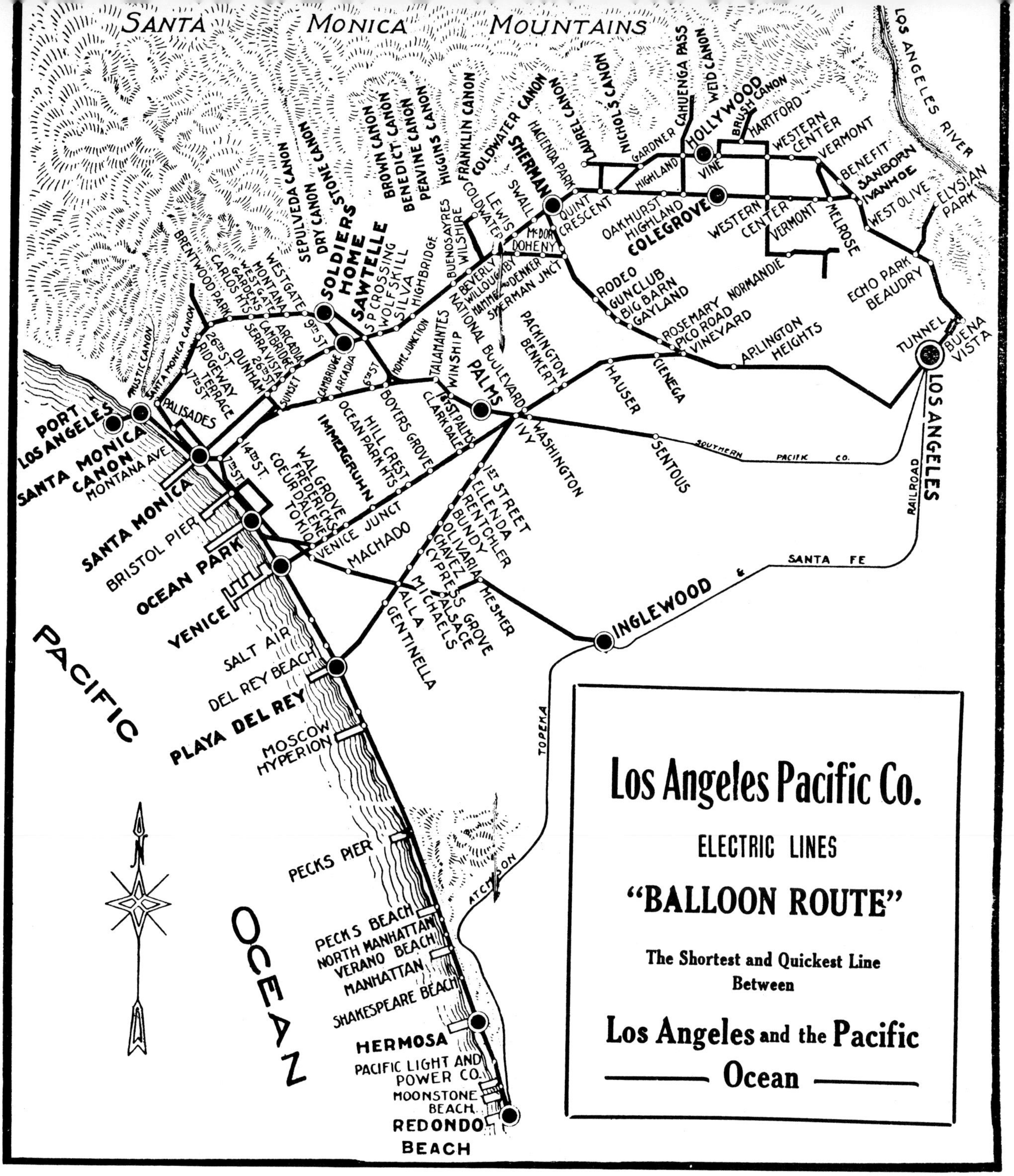
SANTA MONICA MOUNTAINS
LOS ANGELES RIVER
Los Angeles Pacific Co.
ELECTRIC LINES
"BALLOON ROUTE"
The Shortest and Quickest Line Between
Los Angeles and the Pacific Ocean
PACIFIC OCEAN
SEPULVEDA CANON
DRY CANON
STONE CANON
BROWN CANON
BENEDICT CANON
PEAVINE CANON
HIGGINS CANON
FRANKLIN CANON
COLDWATER CANON
SHERMAN CANON
LAUREL CANON
NICHOLS CANON
CAHUENGA PASS
WEID CANON
BRUSH CANON
HOLLYWOOD
HARTFORD
WESTERN
CENTER
VERMONT
BENEFIT
SANBORN
IVANHOE
WEST OLIVE
ELYSIAN PARK
GARDNER
HIGHLAND
VINE
OAKHURST
COLEGROVE
MELROSE
HACIENDA PARK
SHERMAN
QUINT
CRESCENT
McDOR
DOHENY
SWALL
LEWIS
COLDWATER
BUENOSAYRES
WILSHIRE
BEVERLY
WILLOUGHBY
DENKER
SHERMAN JNCT
RODEO
GUNCLUB
BIG BARN
GAYLAND
ROSEMARY
NORMANDIE
PICO ROAD
VINEYARD
ARLINGTON HEIGHTS
ECHO PARK
BEAUDRY
TUNNEL
BUENA VISTA
LOS ANGELES
SOLDIERS HOME
SAWTELLE
S P CROSSING
WOLFSKILL
SILVA
HIGHBRIDGE
HOME JUNCTION
TALAMANTES
WINSHIP
NATIONAL BOULEVARD
PACKINGTON
BENKERT
HAUSER
CIENEGA
PALMS
WASHINGTON
IVY
SENTOUS
SOUTHERN PACIFIC CO.
RAILROAD
SANTA FE
INGLEWOOD
TOPEKA
ATCHISON
WESTGATE
MONTANA
GARDENS
CARLOS HTS
BRENTWOOD PARK
ARCADIA
CAMBRIDGE
SERRA VISTA
9TH ST
26TH ST
RIDGEWAY
TERRACE
DUNHAM
17TH ST
SUNSET
6TH ST
SANTA MONICA CANON
RUSTIC CANON
PALISADES
PORT LOS ANGELES
SANTA MONICA CANON
MONTANA AVE
SANTA MONICA
14TH ST.
7TH ST
BRISTOL PIER
OCEAN PARK
VENICE
BOYERS GROVE
HILL CREST
OCEAN PARK HTS
IMMERGRUHN
WALGROVE
FREDERICKS
COEUR D'ALENE
TOKIO
CLARKDALE
1ST ST. PALMS
VENICE JUNCT
MACHADO
1ST STREET
ELLENDA
RENTCHLER
BUNDY
OLIVARIA
CHAVEZ
CYPRESS GROVE
ALSACE
MICHAELS
ALLA
GENTINELLA
MESMER
SALT AIR
DEL REY BEACH
PLAYA DEL REY
MOSCOW
HYPERION
PECKS PIER
PECKS BEACH
NORTH MANHATTAN
VERANO BEACH
MANHATTAN
SHAKESPEARE BEACH
HERMOSA
PACIFIC LIGHT AND POWER CO.
MOONSTONE BEACH
REDONDO BEACH

had Kinney despite his immense investment in creating the much publicized Venice of America. During ensuing weeks he sold an estimated $3 million worth of Redondo Beach property, regaining most if not all he had paid for the Los Angeles and Redondo Railway and the beach land. Meanwhile, Huntington added to his holdings by purchasing more than 3,000 acres of farmlands adjacent to Redondo Beach.

Interest was heightened when Henry Huntington announced plans to build three wharves for large ships, for such a project revived Redondo's hope of becoming the harbor for Southern California.

Huntington had not forgotten San Pedro, however. After purchasing the Redondo railway he contacted John Gaffney, owner of large property holdings in the area, and obtained a right-of-way permitting him to extend the interurban tracks through the Palos Verdes Hills to San Pedro. Such an extension would have connected with the Pacific Electric tracks at Point Fermin, giving Huntington a second entrance to the harbor at San Pedro, to the additional detriment of E. H. Harriman's Southern Pacific. Huntington also made plans to rebuild the Redondo line's narrow tracks to standard gauge, enabling use of steam railway freight cars.

The Redondo Beach real estate balloon burst almost as quickly as it swelled, and many of the speculators lost heavily when property values returned to lower levels.

Despite the lessened real estate activity, it was becoming evident that the uneasy truce between the electric interurbans and the steam railways was ending.

Following Henry Huntington's expansion into the Santa Monica Bay area in the summer of 1905, it appeared that the rail magnate was becoming more interested than ever in using his electric system to provide the steam railroads as much competition in freight service as he had in the passenger field. Unlike most interurban men of the period, he was adding electric locomotives to his system in order to haul freight.

The situation was evident when a motorman on Huntington's Los Angeles Inter-Urban Railway was charged in February, 1906, with blocking traffic on Third Street in downtown Los Angeles by operating an electric freight train on the streetcar tracks. The growing tension also could be noted in March when A. D. Schindler was removed as general manager of the Pacific Electric because Huntington appointed him to the position without approval of E. H. Harriman, whose Southern Pacific shared ownership of the system. Schindler's ouster reportedly came after he routed freight traffic obtained by the Pacific Electric over the cross-country lines of the Santa Fe Railroad instead of the Southern Pacific. [2]

The bombshell came on March 19 with an announcement that Moses Sherman and Eli Clark were selling their Los Angeles Pacific Railroad to the Southern Pacific. Huntington was particularly angered at the pair because a few days before the sale he had assisted them in obtaining a $12.5 million loan covering their railroad by reportedly providing the lenders a letter stating he did not plan to invade their area with tracks. Huntington declined to detail his feelings publicly but he obviously was infuriated. [3]

"Words that would not look well in print and epithets that are not often resorted to in high financial circles are applied to General M. H. Sherman by Mr. Huntington's associates," a reporter for The Los Angeles Examiner wrote after a visit to the Pacific Electric Building. [4]

News of the railroads, whether steam, electric interurban, or local trolley lines, made headlines in the era. Almost everyone depended on rails for travel or to assure operation of industries, and what affected the companies' operation was widely discussed in every segment of the nation.

Such news became even more important when it involved rail tycoons such as Henry Huntington and E. H. Harriman. The people loved a battle between financial giants.

Moreover, the man named by the Southern Pacific to oversee its Los Angeles Pacific investment was Epes Randolph, formerly chief engineer for Huntington.

Harriman, who was impressed by Randolph's ability as an engineer during a meeting in Los Angeles, personally persuaded him to join his team. Randolph assumed a well-paying position in directing Southern Pacific operations in the Southwest.

Despite Randolph's departure from the Pacific Electric and Southern California, he retained and even expanded his interests in syndicates which invested in land which was so greatly enhanced by the construction of trolley lines. These investments indicated that he retained his faith in the tech-

BELOW: Henry Huntington's purchase of Redondo Beach rail and real estate properties touched off a boom which made this headline in the Los Angeles Record. RIGHT: This map shows the route of the Los Angeles and Redondo Railway.

2. and 3. Los Angeles Examiner, March 29, 1906. Mr. Schindler shortly thereafter became general manager of the Sacramento Northern Railway, an electric railroad which, although not controlled by Huntington, competed with the Southern Pacific in the Sacramento Valley.

4. Los Angeles Examiner, April 3, 1906.

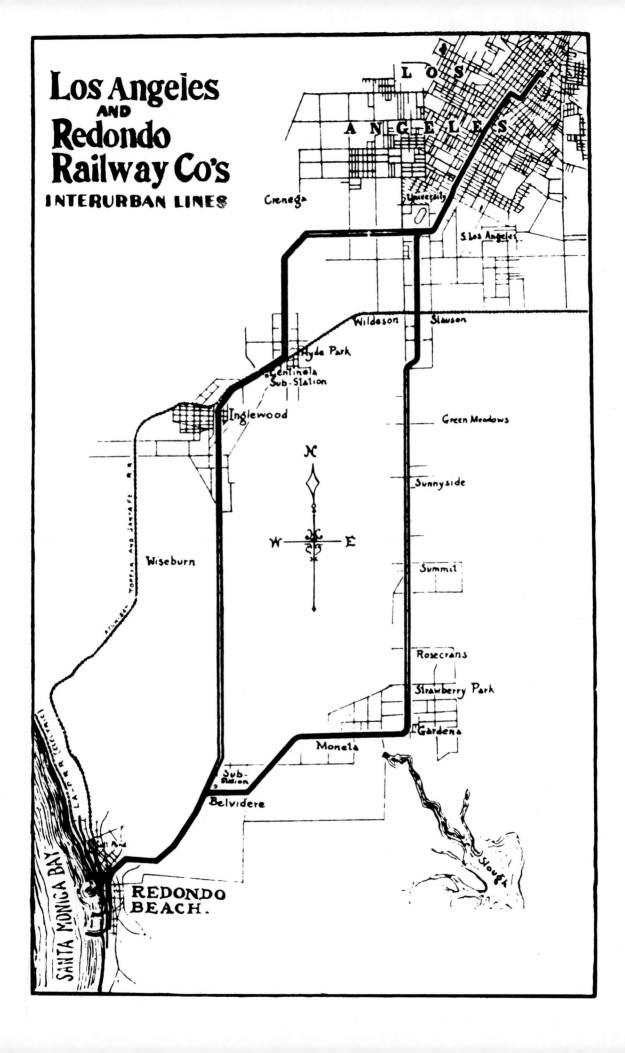

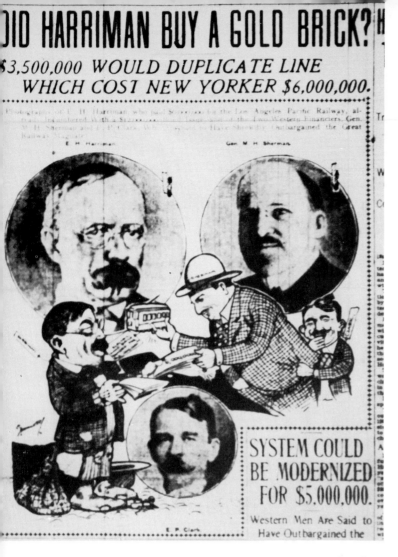

nology of electric cars. Both Randolph and George Pillsbury, who remained with Huntington as chief engineer, were honored by having stops named for them on the P. E. line near La Habra.

Newspapers of the day saw the Southern Pacific acquisition of the Sherman and Clark line as an effort to "curb" Huntington's activities which continued despite the $110,000 franchise.

The Los Angeles Examiner reported: [5]

> The acquisition of the (Los Angeles-Pacific) property greatly strengthens the Southern Pacific transportation interests in and around Los Angeles. It can and undoubtedly will be used, among other things, as a club over the head of Henry E. Huntington to try and prevent him from making extensions of the Pacific Electric Company which will further cut into and divert the local traffic of the steam lines of the Southern Pacific.

> Not withstanding his large interests in the Pacific Electric and his repeated correspondence with Huntington on the subject, Mr. Harriman has never been able to prevent H. E. Huntington from extending his lines as best suited his purpose.

Sherman and Clark received a reported $6 million for the Los Angeles Pacific, and newspapers, maintaining the line was valued at only $3.4 million, cited the price as indicative of E. H. Harriman's determination to stop Huntington.

Henry Huntington busily was planning other attempts to make a reality of his "dream" of a railroad system competing more extensively with the Southern Pacific.

---

5. Los Angeles Examiner, March 21, 1906.

ABOVE: Rail tycoon E. H. Harriman was depicted as having paid too much for the Los Angeles Pacific in this March 23, 1906, panel in the Los Angeles Examiner. BELOW: The name of Henry Huntington brought crowds to speculate on Redondo Beach property. This headline appeared as Redondo real estate prices climbed higher and higher.

10. The Million Dollar Divorce

The spring of 1906 was a time when problems were mounting for Henry E. Huntington. Just two days after the sale of the Los Angeles Pacific Railroad was announced, a second bombshell burst for the general public. Mrs. Mary Prentice Huntington filed a suit for divorce against her husband of thirty-three years, Henry Edwards Huntington.

The news made headlines and stunned America, for the marriage presumably was a happy one. Although Mrs. Huntington maintained her residence in San Francisco, Mr. Huntington frequently traveled there on business trips and it was assumed generally that all was well.

But Mrs. Huntington's divorce petition, filed in San Francisco, revealed that they had been separated since 1900 —the year when his uncle, Collis, had died and immediately prior to launching of his mighty transportation system. [1]

Although the divorce suit came as a surprise, the Los Angeles Examiner immediately began to speculate on the situation. The newspaper reported that "those at all intimate with Huntington affairs do not seem at all surprised at the suit, as they have had an idea for some time that Mr. Huntington was entirely willing to be off with the old love in order to be on with a new one."

While the paper predicted a "new marriage in a year," it did not speculate as to the object of the tycoon's affections.

The big Huntington mansion at the northeast corner of Jackson and Broderick Streets in San Francisco was ablaze with lights the night before the divorce action was scheduled. Mrs. Huntington was preparing for a trip. The divorce hearing was set for 9:30 a.m. and Mrs. Huntington, evidently confident the matter would proceed smoothly, had booked passage for a trip to the Orient on the steamer Korea, scheduled to leave at 1 p.m. the same day. [2]

There was considerable speculation over the causes for the divorce, sought on the technical grounds of mental cruelty. Many newspapers traced the rift back to the controversy that developed when Mrs. Huntington's sister Clara, adopted as a child by C. P. Huntington, had been given $1 million in his will although she expected substantially more.

Clara, who while touring Europe met and married a Prussian officer, Prince Fritz Hatzfeldt-Wildenberg, returned to America while the will was in probate to seek a more generous share of the estate at the cost of Collis' widow, Ara-

bella, and Henry Huntington. Mary sided with her sister, to the displeasure of her husband. Under compromise, the Princess Hatzfeldt settled for an additional $3 million; $2 million was paid by Mrs. Arabella Huntington, and the other $1 million came from Henry Huntington.

Mrs. Clara Prentice, mother of the two girls, verified this speculation in a newspaper interview expressing her strong disapproval of Henry Huntington. [3]

"The difference between Mr. and Mrs. Huntington dates back to the time when the estate of Collis P. Huntington was being settled up," newspapers quoted her saying. "My daughter, the Princess Hatzfeld, came on to California to see that she received her just dues from the estate."

Huntington became angered at the action, she said.

"If Henry Huntington is down on anyone he can be very mean," Mrs. Prentice said. "His uncle was like him in this respect only he was not as bad."

Another reason advanced for the marital break-up was Mrs. Huntington's preference for San Francisco over the Los Angeles area. The Los Angeles Examiner recalled that Henry Huntington had purchased a large tract of land at San Marino with the announced purpose of building a palatial home thereon. Instead of proceeding immediately with the plans he had resided at a Los Angeles hotel.

The San Francisco Examiner saw a third reason in that the divorce suit was filed coincidentally with the purchase by the Southern Pacific of the Los Angeles-Pacific Railroad. Attorneys for the E. H. Harriman interests conferred on

---

3. San Francisco Call, March 22, 1906.

This wooden-sided express car, built in the Pacific Electric shops, was loading freight in Santa Ana when this picture was made. (Carl B. Blaubach Collection)

---

1. According to the petition filed in the Superior Court of the City and County of San Francisco on March 21, 1906, and heard the following day by Presiding Judge Thomas F. Graham.

2. Los Angeles Examiner, March 22, 1906.

Los Angeles Examiner

Stop!
Stop!

THURSDAY   Rain   LOS ANGELES, MARCH 22, 1906   Rain—THURSDAY.   PRICE 5 CENTS

...day law, against
...o petiton, against
...n act.

SMITH RELEASED
SAYS SCOTTY'S
MINE A FAKE.

MRS. HUNTINGTON ASKS DIVORCE

Complaint Filed Yesterday, Case Will Be Heard This
Morning and She Will Sail for Japan This Afternoon

...SS IS
...OR IN
...VANCES.

𝒯HAT in the year 1900, at the city of San Francisco, the defendant, H. E. Huntington,
willfully deserted and abandoned the plaintiff without her fault and against her consent, and ever since that time he has continued separate and apart from the plaintiff.—Ex-
tract from Complaint.

DIVISION OF
PROPERTY I
ALL ARRANG

Another Woman Is
Railway Man's W
Gossip Has It

NO MENTION MADE O
PROPERTY IN COMP

He Is Not Expected
pear When the C
Is Called Today

*This sketch of Mrs. Huntington, along with a headline and
story telling about her demand for a divorce from Henry*
*Huntington, appeared in the Los Angeles Examiner. The
divorce made headlines throughout the nation.*

occasions with Mrs. Mary Huntington before she filed the
suit, the newspapers noted. [4]

The divorce hearing was conducted as scheduled and
took exactly seven minutes. Mrs. Huntington was clad in
an unpretentious pearl gray suit. She wore a stylish hat and
a heavy veil obscured her features. Reciting the legal vital
statistics concerning the marriage, she told the court she
was unable to give a reason for the desertion.

Under the terms of the divorce settlement approved by
the court Mrs. Huntington was to receive $40,000 annually
from a $1 million trust fund.

That afternoon Mrs. Huntington and her daughter,
Marian, sailed aboard the Korea; in doing so she escaped
the horror of the San Francisco earthquake and fire a few
weeks later.

Henry Huntington, on the surface unmoved by the turn
of events, returned to Los Angeles to resume his duel with
the Southern Pacific.

---

4. San Francisco Examiner, March 22, 1906.

86

A trolley waits passengers near Arrowhead Hot Springs, in the San Bernardino mountains above the city of San Bernar- *dino, east of Los Angeles. Huntington's trolleys served diverse areas. (Craig Rasmussen Collection)*

Eagerly awaiting Henry Huntington's return to Los Angeles, the public expected fireworks in the battle between rail tycoons. It would be a spectacle worth watching. Huntington was wealthy and enterprising. E. H. Harriman had achieved a national reputation for his vast rail interests.

Huntington crews were working furiously on the narrow gauge tracks running westward on Sixth Street from downtown Los Angeles. Reports maintained that the interurban magnate planned to convert the line into a standard gauge route to Santa Monica in order to compete with the Los Angeles Pacific under its Southern Pacific ownership. Real estate prices soared in Hollywood, on the logical route of such a line. There was speculation that more frequent service and lower fares would come with a Huntington-Harriman trolley war.

Instead of a competing line to Santa Monica, however, Henry Huntington's next move came where it was least expected and served to verify the reports he wanted to create a system as ambitious as a transcontinental line.

Edward W. Gilmore unexpectedly appeared before the Los Angeles City Council on March 28 with the unusual request for a franchise to use the bottom of the ordinarily dry Los Angeles River as the right-of-way for a transcontinental railroad planned as competition for the existing Southern Pacific, Salt Lake Railroad and Santa Fe routes. Although details never were explained as to precisely how a railroad could be constructed in a river bed covered with water during the rainy season, the franchise was quickly approved by the council.

There were hints that Gilmore represented George Gould, son of the late railroad magnate Jay Gould, whose partially electrified Western Pacific Railroad was being built into the San Francisco Bay area. The Los Angeles City Directory, although evidently not consulted at the time, showed that the paving firm of Fairchild and Gilmore with which Edward Gilmore was associated had offices in Huntington's Pacific Electric Building.

The city council's hasty action in approving the franchise

This combination freight-passenger car, built for San Francisco's Golden Gate and Cliff House Railway in 1886, was acquired in 1902 by the Pacific Electric and used until 1929. (Stephen D. Maguire Collection)

drew heavy criticism from the Los Angeles Examiner. Seeing the deft hand of Henry Huntington in the scheme, the newspaper demanded a recall of the councilmen unless they rescinded the action. The objection to the franchise was based on the fact that it was granted without the formality of bids. The Examiner's publisher, William Randolph Hearst, had been a strong and successful opponent to Collis Huntington's efforts to reduce payments on the federal loans for building the transcontinental railway. His newspaper could see few merits in any activities of Collis' nephew, Henry.

"Another one of the Huntington grabs," The Examiner editorialized angrily. "His attorney, Dunn, is credited with working the deal." [5]

Gilmore denied the charges.

"Believe me, Mr. Huntington is not back of the scheme," Gilmore said, although in a few days Henry Huntington was to be revealed as holder of the franchise.

"I will say that I represent eastern railway interests," Gilmore continued. "These interests are not represented at the present time in this city.

"It is the intention of the interests I represent," he went on, "to build a transcontinental line."

When contacted by The Examiner, George Gould denied that Gilmore represented him.

Newspaper reporters rushed to quiz Henry Huntington, who was leaving for New York City.

"My franchise?" Huntington replied to the questions. "Why I have no franchise." He smiled and reporters pressed him with more questions. "Oh, I see, you mean the river

bed franchise. Why I am as much up a tree as anyone." [6]

Had he talked to George Gould regarding a transcontinental railroad the last time he was in New York City?

"I saw Mr. Gould for we are on friendly terms," Huntington replied, "and we talked over a number of things men talk over when they are friendly."

The reporters pressed Huntington further regarding the franchise.

"If I could," Huntington replied, "I would talk to you about that franchise but I have nothing to say about it. I say I have nothing to say about it."

The next day Mayor Owen McAleer, who had been out of the city when the franchise was granted, returned and promptly vetoed the council's action. The council's mail on the same day brought a letter from Henry E. Huntington notifying the officials that the controversial franchise had been assigned to him.

". . . . Because of the fact that I realize that such a right of way could be utilized by the Pacific Electric Railroad Company greatly to the advantage of said company and equally to the benefit of the people of Southern California . . . . the franchise has been purchased," Huntington's communication said. [7]

His letter then proceeded to request certain revisions in the franchise so that construction could be started on a line.

The councilmen, recalling The Examiner's attacks on Huntington coupled with threats to recall them, hastily upheld Mayor McAleer's veto of the franchise.

Huntington's bid had failed to obtain a vital right of way

5. Los Angeles Examiner, March 29, 1906.

6. Los Angeles Examiner, March 29, 1906.
7. Los Angeles Examiner, April 3, 1906.

ABOVE: A train of four "700 Class" trolleys, built in 1907 and 1908 by the St. Louis Car Company, stopped for a picture at Sherman, which was just east of Beverly Hills. (Carl B. Blaubach Collection) BELOW: San Bernardino Valley Traction Company car 17, built in 1906 by Brill, is shown on Crescent Avenue in Redlands. It continued in service until 1920. (Courtesy William G. Moore: Redlands Daily Facts)

which could have made his electric interurban system part of a transcontinental network.

A few days later in New York City, George Gould was ousted from the Southern Pacific board of directors. But Henry Huntington, whose name was a symbol of prestige and financial power, retained not only his directorship but also the vice presidency he once had sought to vacate.

While Huntington couldn't put a right-of-way in the river, he pushed the tracks of his electric railroad empire to more places in Southern California. Landowners eagerly donated property for right-of-ways, knowing that good transportation would bring prosperity to the area. For construction, the trolley tycoon naturally used the corporations he controlled exclusively, assuring that the lines truly would be competitive with the Southern Pacific.

A branch from the Long Beach line from Dominguez Junction took the Big Red Car tracks to San Pedro in 1905, giving the S. P. additional competition for the lucrative port traffic. Huntington's electric cars reached Santa Ana in 1905, giving farmers in agriculturally rich Orange County a new choice for carrying their produce to market.

The year 1907 brought vast growth to Henry Huntington's trolley empire. He gained control of the San Bernardino Valley Traction Company, with lines in the San Bernardino and Redlands areas; pushed tracks to the citrus and residential community of Azusa, and began construction of two more tracks to Long Beach so that a modern four-track system could efficiently carry the increasing amount of traffic.

A line from San Bernardino in 1907 took the Huntington trolleys to the Arrowhead Springs Hotel in the San Bernardino Mountains. This busy year also found Huntington pushing the Whittier line toward Yorba Linda and presumably to a meeting with his rail properties in San Bernardino and Riverside, completing a line linking Santa Ana to Huntington Beach, another potential port, and successfully negotiating for existing tracks between Riverside and Rialto that could extend this portion of his empire to Los Angeles via Pomona.

Despite the acquisitions, Henry Huntington's interests gradually were turning to other fields: his public utility companies and the great collection of rare paintings and books ultimately destined to overshadow his other accomplishments.

That Huntington would loosen the hold on his trolley empire was an idea that occurred to very few people. His battles to extend his electric railroads through Southern California were well-publicized. The convenient Big Red Cars were becoming an accepted part of the area's life, and Huntington was popular because his trolleys fought the Southern Pacific monopoly by providing freight as well as passenger service. His lines not only paralleled many tracks

"Local" trolley cars also had private right-of-ways. Here is a narrow gauge Los Angeles Railway streetcar operating north of downtown Los Angeles. Huntington acquired control of the company when he relinquished his interest in the Pacific Electric.

of the S. P. and the S. P.-controlled San Pedro, Los Angeles, and Salt Lake Railroad (which later became part of the Union Pacific), but it also reached into areas of Southern California where steam railroads did not operate.

Yet, Henry Huntington, by this time 57 years old, was planning to step out of the trolley scene.

This was the Pacific Electric station at Watts, a busy junction. From here, interurbans continued to Long Beach, San Pedro, and Newport, or switched for Santa Ana, Whittier, or Redondo. (Craig Rasmussen Collection)

11. The Great Merger

The first indications that Huntington was abandoning the interurban field were hidden in announcements made in 1908. One, on June 30, disclosed that Huntington had leased his Los Angeles Inter-Urban, controlling so many key routes, to the Pacific Electric, in which he shared ownership with the Southern Pacific. On the following day, another announcement revealed that James McMillan, P. E. general manager since the 1906 removal of A. D. Schindler, was being given complete authority over management so Huntington could devote his energy to other pursuits.

In 1909 Huntington made additional withdrawals by selling the Southern Pacific several of his interurban properties, notably the Peninsular Railway of Santa Clara County and the Fresno Traction Company. Reports once held that these systems would be key parts of his state-wide electric railroad.

The big news came on November 10, 1910, that Henry Huntington had sold his Southern California interurban interests to the Southern Pacific. Newspapers, reflecting on the efficiency of Huntington operations, speculated as to how the new owners would operate the system. S. P. officials gave assurances that the electric railroad network would not only be retained but expanded.

While the complete details of the financial deal whereby Henry Huntington transferred his electric interurban holdings to the Southern Pacific were never revealed, time made it obvious that the transaction was profitable for him. Huntington and the Southern Pacific held almost equal interests in the Los Angeles Railway Company, the narrow-gauge local streetcar system, and the Pacific Electric Railway which in turn controlled the stock of the Pacific Light and Power Company.

Huntington acquired full control of both the Los Angeles Railway and Pacific Light and Power in transferring to the Southern Pacific his interests in the Pacific Electric and his other interurban properties stretching from Redondo Beach to Redlands. The Pacific Electric shortly began to show operating losses, while the Los Angeles Railway recorded profits for many years. The power company was on the eve of America's great swing to the use of more electrical power. At the

ABOVE: *Hollywood was a farming village between Los Angeles and Santa Monica when this Los Angeles Pacific car operated in the early 1900's. (Security Pacific National*

Bank) RIGHT: *This map depicts the Pacific Electric in 1910, before "The Great Merger" which consolidated LAP and Redondo routes, shown here with lighter lines.*

time, however, the automobile was not regarded as a serious threat to rail transportation and Southern Pacific officials undoubtedly expected great profits from the interurban system as Southern California grew.

The S. P. immediately took over management of the trolley companies, operating them as entities although some joint timetables were issued. It required nearly a year to develop a program for merging the companies. The ultimate program called for the formation of one corporation, a "new" Pacific Electric Railway Company. The names of the other electric railroad companies, including the relatively well-known Los Angeles Pacific, were abandoned in favor of the Pacific Electric that was so popularly acclaimed by the public. The "new" P. E.'s articles of incorporation, signed August 24, 1911, covered fifty-seven pages in a printed book and were so detailed that they included engineering data of the various routes. (See Appendix for a reproduction of the 1911 articles of incorporation.)

The consolidation of the eight companies into the new Pacific Electric subsequently was called "The Great Merger" by historians and P. E. employees.

The new Pacific Electric merged the Los Angeles Pacific Railroad, acquired by the Southern Pacific in 1906 and sub-

sequently rebuilt with standard gauge tracks, along with the Pacific Electric Railway, the Los Angeles Inter-Urban Railroad Company, and the Los Angeles and Redondo Railway Company. In addition it included the other properties previously controlled by Huntington — the San Bernardino Valley Traction, San Bernardino Inter-Urban, Redlands Central, and Riverside and Arlington railroad companies.

Named as president of the new Pacific Electric was William Herrin, the attorney who represented Harriman on the Los Angeles traction scene. He was succeeded in 1912 by Paul Shoup, only thirty-eight years of age at the time but regarded as one of the Southern Pacific's most promising young executives.

Formation of the new Pacific Electric by no means indicated that an end was anticipated for electric interurban construction. On the contrary, the trolley had come to be accepted as a most efficient means of commuter service and the new company's articles of incorporation detailed extensive expansions. Many of the building programs were lines projected by Huntington, indicating the respect with which his activities had been viewed by the Southern Pacific.

Of the twelve major lines proposed for construction, three would have extended the system for statewide service as

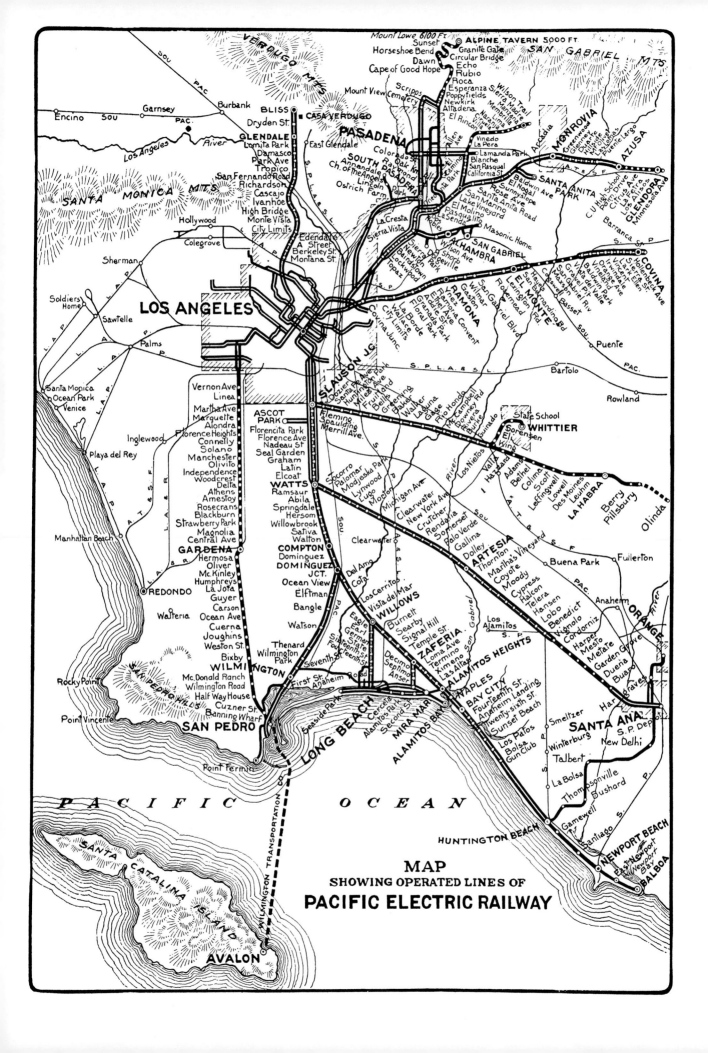

MAP
SHOWING OPERATED LINES OF
PACIFIC ELECTRIC RAILWAY

Attorney William Herrin, who represented E. H. Harriman in the Los Angeles electric railroad field, became the first president of the consolidated Pacific Electric.

projected by Huntington. One line would have taken the tracks from Santa Ana to San Diego, another would have extended from Santa Monica to Ventura, and a third would have gone through the San Fernando Valley to Santa Barbara. Other projected construction provided direct lines between Pomona and Riverside, Long Beach and Covina, from Santa Ana to Corona via the Santa Ana Canyon, and from San Pedro to Redondo Beach over a scenic route in the Palos Verdes Hills. Most of the plans died with the demise of the interurban era.

Regrets expressed by newspapers and civic officials over the exit of efficient Henry Huntington were dispelled by the ambitious program laid down during the merger.

The new company at once became the largest electric interurban railway in the nation. Although its tracks had not reached their peak length, they stretched for over 600 miles. The company's daily schedules provided approximately 1,400 trains, as compared to a combined daily total of 1,200 in Indianapolis, Fort Wayne, Chicago, Springfield, Ill., Detroit, Cleveland, Toledo, Columbus, and Dayton.

The Los Angeles "local" streetcar lines which under The Greater Merger of 1911 became the property of The Los Angeles Railway Corporation, wholly owned by Henry E. Huntington, were by no means the only routes providing city service as differentiated from interurban traffic. On the contrary, on assuming control of the Pacific Electric the

Southern Pacific became a major operator of city streetcar routes not only in Los Angeles but also in principal cities elsewhere in Southern California.

Aside from variations in the types of trolleys used and the frequency of service, the basic difference between the Pacific Electric and Los Angeles Railway system was in the width of the tracks. Huntington's local lines had narrow gauge (3'6"), while the Pacific Electric system, with minor exceptions, was of the standard gauge (4'8½") used on the steam railroads. Those routes with standard gauge track Huntington received under the merger were rebuilt for narrow gauge operation so that his equipment would be interchangeable.

In many portions of Los Angeles tracks were shared by the Pacific Electric and Los Angeles Railway. These instances provided three tracks; the standard gauge Big Red Cars used the two outside rails while the narrow Huntington local cars used one outside track and the inside rail. Maintenance costs were prorated according to proportionate usage.

While the Los Angeles Railway's trolleys, painted green or yellow according to routing, dominated the central Los Angeles area, the Red Cars gave local service in many cities where Huntington had pioneered services. In many areas the Pacific Electric's interurbans and local streetcars shared tracks for portions of their routes. This was particularly true in various cities' downtown areas, traditionally the arrival and departure places of all trolleys. The Pacific Electric's local streetcar service was the heaviest, from the standpoint of individual lines, from 1915 to 1925. During its lifetime as a passenger carrier the company had approximately seventy individual local routes throughout Southern California. Its heaviest-traveled local route was the Hollywood Boulevard line serving Hollywood, one of seventeen local lines in Los Angeles itself.

A drought in 1924 resulted in electric power shortages and provided the excuse to discontinue many local lines suffering from lack of passengers because of the automobile. That year brought abandonment of all five local lines in Pomona as well as routes in San Pedro and Riverside and the only local trolley line in Alhambra.

Outside of Los Angeles, the most individual trolley lines were in Long Beach where Huntington had established streetcar service. They stretched the entire length of Ocean Boulevard from the Los Angeles River to Alamitos Bay. Trolleys ran on Seventh Street from Redondo Avenue westward to Cerritos Slough, the mudflats eventually dredged into Long Beach Harbor. Other lines ran up both Pine and Daisy Avenues to Fourteenth Street, on Magnolia Avenue, Broadway, and Third Streets. Of the twelve lines the city once boasted, the last five were abandoned in 1940.

Pasadena at one time had nine individual local lines and retained its local trolleys well into the sunset of the electric car era. Eli Clark and Moses Sherman had purchased the city's existing horse car lines and electrified them as trolleys. It was usage of major portions of these tracks that enabled them to complete Southern California's premiere interurban link. At one time there were Red Car tracks stretching on Colorado Street, the city's main business artery, a distance of more than six miles from Orange Grove Avenue to Daisy Avenue. Tracks also went up North Fair Oaks Avenue to Mariposa Street in Altadena as well as up North Lake, Lincoln, and Los Robles Avenues, Broadway, and on Columbia, Villa, and Raymond Streets. All trolley service was ended in 1941.

Santa Monica local trolley service came to an end in 1934. The four lines in service at various times ran on Lincoln Boulevard, on Third Street, and to Ocean Park. San Pedro, where Huntington sought to secure rail access to the harbor during the early twentieth century, had six local lines. One line stretched from Sixth Street near the waterfront to Point Firmin while others ran on Beacon and Fourteenth Streets and took trolleys up into the hills as far as Bandini and Santa Cruz Streets.

Trolleys in Santa Ana carried passengers on Fourth Street to the Southern Pacific Depot as well as up North Main Street until 1930.

Other "orange belt" communities also had their share of Red Car service. Although the track did not link Pomona to Los Angeles until 1912, Pomona enjoyed 'local" Pacific Electric service starting in 1907. There were three lines: the Garey Avenue and Park Avenue, the West Second and Park Avenue, and the Holt and East Fifth Street. Service on the lines ended in 1924 and the tracks were removed the following year.

Riverside had local trolleys until 1936. Peak service in the city found four separate lines carrying passengers to the Victoria Country Club, Fairmont Park, down Main Street, and on Arlington Avenue.

Even Redlands, most remote from Los Angeles of the cities served by the Pacific Electric, was blessed with local Red Car service and once had five individual routes. Trolleys ran up to Smiley Heights and also provided service on Orange, Olive, and Citrus Avenues. The last local service was ended in 1936.

The transportation at Mount Lowe, which ranged from the cable incline to sightseeing horse rail cars, was classed as local service and continued until 1936.

Local service continued the longest in San Bernardino, where trolleys rolled until 1942 on two routes. Its service (once totalling three lines) had been highlighted by a line from "D" Street out Third St. to Urbita Springs. Trolleys once traveled on Mount Vernon and Highland Avenues as well as on Eighth Street.

Doom for local trolley service was sounded by the coming of the automobile and the more variable bus routes that

Paul Shoup, who began his railroad career selling tickets for the S. P. in San Bernardino, became P. E. president soon after the merger. He was 38 years old.

also eventually were to spell the end for the electric interurbans.

Los Angeles was an area of major importance for Pacific Electric local service even though the scene was dominated by Huntington's narrow gauge electric cars. Trolley service to Hollywood, essentially "local" in its nature had a heavy passenger volume. There was also much patronage on the Watts local line, which shared the tracks for a portion of the Long Beach route.

Huntington's acquisition of the Los Angeles Railway proved profitable. While the coming of the automobile brought new problems for the Big Red Cars, the Los Angeles Railway prospered as local passenger traffic increased with the city's growth. In 1924, when the Pacific Electric recorded an operating deficit of $592,185, the Los Angeles Railway reported earnings of $2,520,534. The Los Angeles Railway itself was no small operation and continued to expand until the 1920's brought increased automobile competition. Moody's Analyses of Investments (Utilities) reported in 1913 it operated 801 trolley cars over 373 miles of track. By 1925 the system had been extended to 397 miles of track and had a fleet of 1,267 trolleys.

Although in semi-retirement, Henry Huntington remained president of the Los Angeles Railway until his death in 1927. The company was held by the Huntington estate until late 1944 when it was sold to a subsidiary of National City Lines, specializing in passenger bus service. The new own-

The tears painted on this trolley symbolized Los Angeles' feelings when the Metropolitan Transit Authority aban- *doned streetcar service on March 31, 1963, and began using busses exclusively. (Photograph by Gary G. Allen)*

ers subsequently renamed the system Los Angeles Transit Lines and increased the use of busses.

The disadvantage of the local service was that for the most part the tracks were laid in the streets rather than on private rights-of-way. As the number, and sizes, of automobiles increased, it became difficult to navigate the trolleys and schedules were slowed. Fewer people relied on streetcars and the lines lost money.

The story of trolley service vs. automobiles that raged in Southern California was repeated in cities throughout America.

Subways, elevated structures, or other types of private right-of-ways can provide speedy commuter service. Unfortunately, Southern California's trolleys became bogged down on crowded streets. More and more commuters abandoned public transportation and began using automobiles. The result was more jamming of the highways and freeways.

As operating costs continued to mount out of proportion to revenue from passengers, it became apparent that local transportation, like commuter service, no longer held attractions for private capital. Formed as a public agency by the state legislature, the Los Angeles Metropolitan Transit

Authority in 1958 acquired ownership of the Los Angeles local transportation system along with the interurban lines.

The transit authority decided that the few remaining trolleys were too antiquated to provide adequate service and discontinued their operations on March 31, 1963. This decision was a sad one, for the trolleys served South Los Angeles and East Los Angeles — two poverty areas where good public transportation was needed so that residents could travel to jobs.

After the Watts riots of 1965, the official state investigating committee cited the lack of public transportation as one deterrent to residents of the area seeking jobs. (See "Black Riot in Los Angeles: The Story of the Watts Riots," by Spencer Crump; Los Angeles: 1966.)

A face, using the headlight as the nose, was painted on the face of the last trolley operating. Appropriately, the artist painted tears rolling down the face of the faithful streetcar.

Replacing the trolleys were busses, belching smoke, adding to the congestion on streets and freeways, and providing less frequent service at higher fares.

12. A Catalyst for the Cow Counties

The deep blast of the air horns on the Big Red Cars seemed like a signal calling for Southern California to start growing.

When the twentieth century was born, Southern California had been a rolling land unbroken except for farms and a few small villages. A decade later, following arrival of the electric interurbans, the area had passed through its most important growth period and was on its way to destiny as a metropolis.

Henry E. Huntington began his program in 1901 when Los Angeles County had a population of 170,298 and 67,819 resided outside the city of Los Angeles itself. By 1910, as his interurban construction program was drawing to a close, the county had a population of 504,131. The population outside of Los Angeles City had soared to 184,933 residents.

William Garland's prediction of 250,000 people in Los Angeles by 1910 had exceeded itself; what was more the cities were growing at a fantastic rate making the area a single sprawling metropolis instead of a group of isolated towns.

Of the eighteen Southern California cities boasting populations of more than 1,000 in the 1910 census, only two were not located on an electric interurban line.

Of the two, Downey, was the only town suffering a decrease in population. The other was Anaheim, whose prosperity can be credited to the plan of colonization developed by its German settlers.

Among the first communities to grow were Pasadena, South Pasadena, Hollywood, and Santa Monica, all located along the two trolley lines built by Sherman and Clark as they began interurban development. Pasadena's population had been 4,882 in 1900; it reached 9,117 in the 1900 census and zoomed to 30,291 by 1910. The community of South Pasadena had 1,001 residents in 1900 and easy commuting by the Big Red Cars boosted its population to 4,629 residents a decade later. Hollywood, founded in 1887 during the boom following the arrival of the transcontinental railroads, slept until the tracks of the Los Angeles Pacific reached it in 1900.

Santa Monica's growth was spectacular after arrival of the electric interurbans. Its population grew from 1,580 in 1890 to 3,057 in 1900 and 7,847 by the end of the twentieth century's first decade. Long Beach's growth for the ten year span became the greatest in the nation after the Big Red Cars came on the scene. Its 1900 population of 2,252 climbed to 17,809 by 1910—an increase of 690 percent which made it the fastest growing city in the nation.

The electric interurbans nurtured the expansion of the cities close to Los Angeles as well as those distant, for they made it convenient for workers to commute

Operating between Los Angeles and Whittier after the line opened in 1904, this trolley boasted an open section for fresh air aficionados. Whittier service ended in 1938. (Stephen D. Maguire Collection)

NEXT TWO PAGES: Passengers board a P. E. interurban at Baldwin and Sierra Madre in Sierra Madre, linked to Los Angeles by trolley in 1906. Suburban dwellers could commute easily via electric cars. (Pacific Railroad Publications)

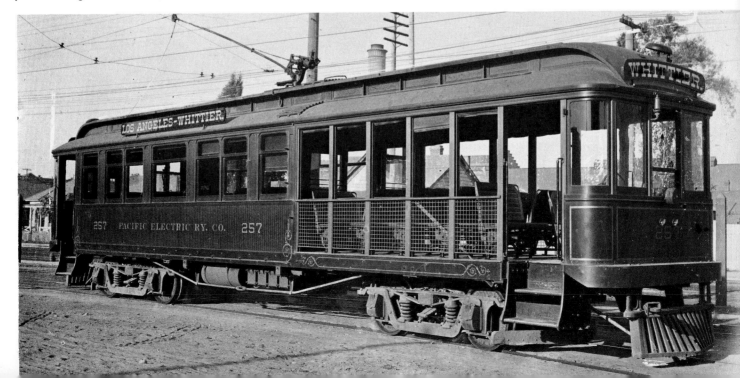

A Los Angeles Pacific trolley travels on Hill Street in downtown Los Angeles in approximately 1909. Note the three tracks to accommodate narrow and standard gauge electric cars. (Carl B. Blaubach Collection)

from a variety of areas. Huntington Park, only farmland at the turn of the century, had 1,299 residents by 1910; in the same period Santa Ana grew from 4,933 to 8,429 residents.

Towns born during the prosperous 1880's only to become sleepy hamlets with the crash were revived by the scores of settlers who, after arrival in Los Angeles via transcontinental trains, boarded interurbans to see the countryside.

"Monrovia's development as a suburban town began with completion of the electric line from Los Angeles in March, 1903," wrote J. M. Guinn, a historian contemporary with the era. A village of 907 in 1890, Monrovia had gained only 298 residents by 1900. By 1910, after arrival of the Big Red Cars, it had become a city of nearly 4,000 residents.

Henry Huntington's touch on Redondo Beach and its railroad had worked magic indeed for the tiny coastal town. Its population in 1910 had tripled in just ten years to 3,000.

Southern California's immense growth cannot be attributed solely to the interurbans. Its climate, start of harbor development, and the almost fanatical zest of its boosters attracted quite naturally investors and settlers. But unquestionably it was the electric interurbans which distributed the population over the countryside and during the century's first decade patterned Southern California as a horizontal city rather than one of skyscrapers and slums.

The interurban era ushered in not only the mere settlement of communities but also the incorporation of

cities along the trolley lines. From 1850 to 1900 there were fourteen cities incorporated in Los Angeles County. During the next decade a total of seventeen cities were incorporated—and all of them were on routes served by the electric interurbans.

Covina was incorporated in 1901, while 1903 brought cityhood to Hollywood, Alhambra, and Arcadia. In 1904 Venice and Wilmington became municipalities. Other cities of the era and their incorporation dates were Vernon, 1905; Sawtelle, Huntington Park, Glendale and La Verne, 1906; Hermosa Beach, Sierra Madre, and Watts, 1907, and Belmont Heights and Inglewood in 1908.

The first decade of the twentieth century in Southern California was the era of the trolley—which brought a rate of growth never before equaled for such an immense area.

The electric interurbans from the very start brought the growth so fanatically sought by Southern California's boosters, but the Big Red Cars became popular with the public immediately for reasons deeper than their obvious economic benefits. People cherished the trolleys for their convenience, for the fellowship of talking with other passengers, and ultimately, because they became the symbols of a period in American life notable for its leisurely pace and lack of sophistication.

New horizons of entertainment opened when the speedy electric cars made travel easy between the communities. Members of the Long Beach Marine Band rode the Red Cars to play at guest concerts throughout the area almost as soon as the line to the seaside city was completed. When the route to Santa Ana was opened, "theatre" schedules were established so that residents could enjoy an evening in Los Angeles and conveniently return to their homes in the orange grove country.

Almost everyone, wealthy or poor, who visited Southern California during the early twentieth century rode the electric interurbans for sightseeing or trips between the individual cities. When Southern Californians traveled to other parts of America, they boasted of the efficient Big Red Cars forming a network in the area. But usually people in other sections of the nations already had heard of the convenient Pacific Electric Railroad, for praise was heaped on the trolley system by a variety of writers and other visitors.

The trolleys were criticized, of course, on many instances. In its first annual report after being created in 1910 the Los Angeles Board of Public Utilities blasted the interurban situation as "abominable" because the interurbans used city streets and urged that the Pacific Electric arrange for private right-of-ways. Crowd-

LIFE IN TOONERVILLE
By Fontaine Fox

THAT NEW EDITOR OF THE TOONERVILLE EVENING APRICOT CERTAINLY 'DON'T KNOW BEANS'

"WOT UV IT! DID YOU SAY! WY YOUNG MAN THET BIRD IS OSWALD, MY PET WOODPECKER, WOT LIVES IN THET HOLE IN THE CAR AN' HIS RETURN FROM THE SOUTH EACH SPRING IS FRONT PAGE STUFF. IN THESE PARTS."

The "Toonerville Trolley," featured in Fontaine Fox's comic panel that flourished through the mid-1930's, indicated the interest and affection in electric cars.

ing of cars during peak travel hours brought criticisms from the riders. But generally, Southern Californians loved the Big Red Cars with an affection mellowing with the years.

I. M. Ingersoll, a popular historian during the early twentieth century, lavished praise on the interurbans, declaring "we cannot question that there is a relation between the mileage of our electric lines . . . and our growing population." George Wharton James, whose books romanticized life in Southern California and did much to attract settlers, cited the variety of interurban lines as among the main ways to enjoy the area he extolled.

Even foreign writers of the early twentieth century praised the electric trolley system. Arthur T. Johnson made many criticisms of the New World in "California, An Englishman's Impressions of the Golden State," published in 1913. At one point he concluded that "there is more oppression dealt out by the plutocrats of the States than there is in any country of Europe—bar Russia" but was forced to admit:

The system of electric "trolley cars," already mentioned, the lines of which radiate like the strands of a spider's web from the heart of the city to the sea on one side and to the summit of Mount Lowe, on the other, is in its scope, management and comfort the best I have ever seen in any land.

The deep meaning of the trolleys for more abundant community life was expressed by a local historian of the era who wrote that the Pacific Electric "brought the entertainment of the metropolis to our doors and gave Monrovia all of the advantages of city life." [1]

Riding the big interurbans over the scenic Southern California countryside was a popular past-time for adults and children. Carl Shoup, son of Paul Shoup who became P.E. president in 1911, recalled that day-long rides on the trolleys were among his memorable childhood experiences.

The affection for electric cars nationally was evident in "Toonerville Trolley," a cartoon series by Fontaine Fox that for years was a popular feature in newspapers. "The Trolley Song" put this meaningful era of American history to music.

The trolleys were fun not only for the passengers but also for their operators and small-fry onlookers. Youngsters were fascinated by the fast interurbans going to far-away places in Southern California. Motormen and conductors expressed pride in their electric cars and frequently had friendly discussions over the pros and cons of various type of rolling stock.

Motormen on the Los Angeles and Redondo trolleys frequently staged good natured races with operators on the Los Angeles Inter-Urban cars on Vermont Avenue between Manchester and Florence Avenues, an area where tracks of the two systems were parallel. It was customary for an operator to idle his car along this section of the track when an interurban of the other company was due. When the trolleys came alongside each other, the wheels clattered as their operators raced.

Passengers on the competing cars waved at each other and cheered; this was part of the fun of the trolley era.

Youngsters did not miss their good times. Boys laid sand, pennies, wire, and pins on the tracks as the speedy electric cars approached, ran for safety, and then gleefully returned for the flattened objects after the interurbans roared past. The bigger boys enjoyed other sports at the expense of the electric cars. It was regarded as great fun to disconnect the trolley arm from the wire and watch, well hidden behind a corner, as the motorman tried vainly to start the car. Another form of amusement was to grease the tracks at hills, thus making the electric car's wheels spin until the operator remedied the situation by absorbing the grease with sand.

Friendships developed among regular commuters, who traditionally had particular seats on the interurbans. Conversations that lapsed when a passenger reached his destination resumed methodically when the next morning the passengers boarded the trolleys en route to work.

The interurbans logically became the symbol of an age cherished, at least in retrospect, for friendliness, lack of sophistication, and good times.

The popularity of the Big Red Cars grew through the years, and in 1926 the Pacific Electric Magazine launched a series of articles dealing with long-time commuters. All of the subjects praised the service. As late as 1958 the affection remained strong for the interurbans. A proposal for voters to authorize funds for civic improvements under the title of "Jobs for Long Beach" was gaining hearty support until it was learned that the plan called for removal of the interurban tracks from Long Beach Boulevard and replacing them with beds of roses. Then, despite pressure from the local newspapers, devotees of the Big Red Cars defeated the proposal at the polls with a few mimeographed handbills and a minimum of newspaper advertisements.

When the interurban era was nearing an end, youngsters (and probably their parents, too!) began to regard trolleys as much fun to ride as something in an amusement park. Author Remi Nadeau, writing in the March, 1960, issue of Westways Magazine, urged readers to ride an electric car from Los Angeles to Long Beach as an experience memorable of the days when the Big Red Cars served many routes.

Scale models of electric interurbans also became popular items. Kits of the Pacific Electric's trolleys (as well as those of other electric railroads) were being produced by E. Suydam and Company in Duarte, California, and William K. Walthers, Inc., of Milwaukee, Wisconsin.

In addition, many fans — some so young that they had never ridden the Big Red Cars — collected a variety of other items relating to interurbans. These items included phonograph records preserving the sounds of the interurbans, spikes torn from old ties and neatly mounted on plaques, and badges once worn by P. E. motormen and conductors. They also collected picture post cards, decals, tie clips, nostalgic books, and a variety of other things bearing representations of the legendary Big Red Cars.

Best of all, trolley museums sprang up throughout the nation when the interurban era was reaching its conclusion. Electric cars of regional systems were carefully preserved as memories of those by-gone times, and frequently trolleys were even operated to give youngsters the opportunity to see how their parents and grandparents once travelled daily.

Several of the Big Red Cars appropriately were preserved as cherished symbols of an important period in Southern California life. These trolleys were being displayed at Travel Town, in Los Angeles' Griffith Park, and at the Orange Empire Trolley Museum, near Perris.

The Orange Empire Trolley Museum, a non-profit or-

---

1. John L. Wiley, "History of Monrovia," (Pasadena, 1927), P. 92.

ganization built by week-end volunteers, deserves a special mention. Cars of the Pacific Electric, as well as of other lines, are being preserved in a park-like atmosphere which is reminiscent of Southern California from 1900 to 1940.

In addition, many fans — some so young that they had never ridden the Big Red Cars — collected a variety of other items relating to interurbans. These items included phonograph records preserving the sounds of the interurbans, spikes torn from old ties and neatly mounted on plaques, and badges once worn by P. E. motormen and conductors. They also collected picture post cards, decals, tie clips, nostalgic books, and a variety of other things bearing representations of the legendary Big Red Cars.

The real interurbans, of course, remained the most fascinating of the memorabilia.

The merged Pacific Electric launched an ambitious program of expansion with enthusiasm matched only in the communities to be blessed with the prosperity traditionally following the start of electric interurban service.

The Southern Pacific, owning the new Pacific Electric, regarded the trolley as a most efficient and economical means of providing interurban service between Southern California cities. There was little serious thought as to competition from automobiles, usually regarded as novelties for the wealthy. It was not until 1914 that the state of California considered automotive registrations as of sufficient importance to retain detailed totals of gas buggies. Roads were poor and Henry Ford's famed Model T, to revolutionize the automotive industry, was in its early stages.

The line from La Habra was extended to Brea and Yorba Linda from 1909 to 1911 while in 1910 interurban service linked San Pedro and Long Beach. In 1912 service reached Torrance, bringing the city industrial development as well as passenger service. Trolleys were heartily accepted as the most convenient way to travel.

The interurban tracks also helped the Southern Pacific provide freight service in an age when there was no competition from motor freight trucks.

Communities eagerly sought electric railroad connections. When the lines were built, elaborate festivities were enthusiastically staged to celebrate the openings — hailed in each case as the beginning of a new era of prosperity for the particular town involved. Crowds cheered the "last spike" ceremony held October 26, 1910, when the extension from Covina to San Dimas went into service. None other than Henry E. Huntington, still a director of the Southern Pacific although in "retirement," rode with the civic leaders on the Pacific Electric interurban officially opening the line to Pomona in September, 1912. Also aboard the trolley was

Paul Shoup, who recently had become the P.E.'s president. He said: [2]

The mission of the Pacific Electric in Southern California is to afford an easy way for the people who are coming in such large numbers to dwell in this Southland to go out and live in suburban territory. It would be the natural thing for them to stop right in Los Angeles but for the work (of the trolleys).

The Pomonans cheered, for like other Southern Californians they had the unquenchable booster spirit thirsting for growth. The Big Red Cars meant growth.

Those cities not touched by the Pacific Electric were heartened a few days later when Shoup announced that the company intended to spend $7 million for track extension programs during the next few years. The first phase of the program, he said, would be to push to San Bernardino.

Although opening of the link was nearly two years away, real estate promoters immediately began advertising property near the proposed route on the strength of the progress expected with the trolleys. Automobiles were becoming more numerous and there were lobbies for more roads, but the Big Red Cars reigned supreme.

Officials of the Southern Pacific were optimistic that the electric railroad lines would become profitable, and it is evident that Pacific Electric executives pressed the parent company for funds to improve the system. Julius Kruttschmitt, chairman of the Southern Pacific, and Paul Shoup, P. E. president, were touring San Bernardino in 1915 after opening of the trolley line to the area. Asked by civic leaders when more improvements were scheduled, Kruttschmitt replied: [3]

On the Southern Pacific and Pacific Electric there are millions of improvements that are being held up. The reason — no return on the investment.

Mr. Shoup has asked for money for various things. In fact, he is a good little asker. But we always keep our little pencils sharpened. However, it is pretty hard to keep the Pacific Electric from growing in a country such as this. It is a prime little property — the best electric line in the world.

The Pacific Electric tracks through the orange grove country to San Bernardino were completed in 1914. So important had the system become to Southern California that the opening of the new link took on the aspects of a Hollywood motion picture premiere.

"Today is the start of a new era for San Bernardino," declared the San Bernardino Sun of July 11, 1914, the day for the route's dedication. It was an obvious prophesy in view of the prosperity that already followed the trolleys to other communities. To add to the festivities,

2. Pomona Progress, September 10, 1912.

3. San Bernardino Sun, April 10, 1915.

none other than John Steven McGroarty, author of the Mission Play, wrote a historical pageant for the event. Thomas Ince, one of the era's leading motion picture producers, brought actors to take the roles of California pioneers in the spectacle. San Bernardino already had a taste of prosperity via the trolleys as a result of the Huntington-owned San Bernardino Valley Traction Company, included in The Great Merger. After the merger the system was operated under the Pacific Electric banner to Redlands, Highland, Colton, and Arrowhead Springs although it was not linked to Los Angeles.

The link between San Bernardino and Los Angeles, built at a cost of $2 million, was hailed for engineering that provided for all roads to pass under or over the tracks between Pomona and its terminus in San Bernardino. Although the remainder of the Pacific Electric operated on a 600-volt electrical system, the San Bernardino route boasted 1,200 volts in its trolley wires so the interurbans could speed over the fifty miles to Los Angeles. As the line opened obvious predictions could be made of the prosperity in store for San Bernardino and Riverside in view of the interurbans' accomplishments in Southern California during the past fifteen years. Estimates were made the San Bernardino's population of 15,000 would treble within a decade because of the new line. The Los Angeles Express forecast "there will be a continuous line of villas" between Los Angeles and San Bernardino. The Los Angeles Times, commenting on the route, envisioned that a solid sea of houses would eventually replace the orange trees on the countryside. The Times editorialized:[4]

The intermediate territory (by the tracks) becomes suburban to the two cities. Not only will the owners of the big tracts and big citrus groves be benefited, but it will promote the little tracts and suburban homes and eventually will cause the entire district to become thickly and prosperously settled.

The opening of the route took on particular local significance because Paul Shoup, president of the Pacific Electric, was born in San Bernardino and started his railroad career there as a ticket agent for the Southern Pacific. A float depicting the ticket booth where he started was a highlight of a parade celebrating completion of the route.

There was wild cheering as the first Big Red Cars from Los Angeles pulled into San Bernardino at 10:00 a.m. In a dramatic ceremony in front of the downtown station on Third Street railroad officials and civic leaders laid the last tie—fashioned, appropriately for the citrus country, from the wood of an orange tree. Mayor H. H.

This tower car was built by the Pacific Electric in 1907 to service trolley wires and continued in operation until 1951. (Photograph by Vernon Sappers)

Rose of Los Angeles and Mayor J. W. Catick of San Bernardino used a silver sledge hammer to drive a silver spike in a ceremony reminiscent of the one celebrating completion of the transcontinental route in the year that Henry Huntington left Oneonta to start his career.

When the Big Red Cars brought their first crowds to San Bernardino's National Orange Show in 1915, Paul Shoup returned for the occasion as the city's leading native son. His speech to the cheering crowds was quite symbolic of Southern California's feeling for the Red Cars. He said:[5]

The Pacific Elecric will bring you, I hope, all that your honest hopes have anticipated; it will do all it can to continue to bring the thousands of strangers that come to California down the main street of your city in daily excursions and events of this kind.

Completion of the line to San Bernardino also connected the existing interurban tracks at Redlands, Riverside, Arlington, and Arrowhead Springs to Los Angeles. The interurban line from Arlington to Corona was completed in 1915, and the Pacific Electric's final extensions, tracks to Fullerton and El Segundo, were opened shortly thereafter.

The Pacific Electric tracks were reaching their virtual peak, stretching from the mountains to the seashore and from the cities to the citrus country.

4. Los Angeles Times, July 10, 1914.

5. San Bernardino Sun, February 6, 1915.

13. Lines to Last

Henry Huntington surprised and pleased Southern Californias with the speed and efficient methods used in constructing his interurban system as soon as a route had been approved. In other sections of the nation, poorly financed electric railway companies after receiving franchises had taken months or in some cases years to lay a few miles of rails. When finished, the road beds were of inferior quality and subject to breakdowns. Many times the builders cluttered public streets with virtually all of the tracks in order to avoid payments for private right-of-way property.

Before Huntington's arrival, William Spencer Hook was regarded as one of the more efficient builders of trolley systems, but he took nearly two years to complete his narrow gauge interurban railway from Los Angeles to San Pedro—a distance of twenty miles. After receiving the franchise for the line to Long Beach in late October, 1901, Huntington started construction almost immediately. In just nine months he completed an electric railway line twenty-two miles long, comparable in its quality to that of a steam railroad!

Interurban promoters, generally inexperienced in railroading, did not find financing their only worry: shortages of ties, rail, material, construction machinery, and labor when most needed slowed their operations as did haggling over the value of property for the right-of-ways.

Although Huntington had been groomed as an executive by his Uncle Collis, his practical education in the down-to-earth construction and operation of railroads had not been neglected. Collis supplemented his nephew's initial experience of cutting railroad ties in West Virginia by assigning him to supervise the laying of track across Arizona.

After winning the Long Beach franchise, Huntington immediately hired W. H. Holabird, an unsuccessful bidder for the line, to serve as his right-of-way agent. Holabird, armed with money and the winning argument that the rail line would increase adjoining property values, was able to obtain the necessary land for the rail corridor stretching down from Los Angeles.

Meanwhile Huntington ordered the ties and rails which arrived by the shipload and were trucked to several points along the proposed trolley line so that construction could proceed at several places rather than merely from the Long Beach and Los Angeles terminals. He established construction camps, each containing from 200 to 300 laborers, along the proposed route. Huntington

could retain the experienced and therefore more productive workers on his payroll because his building and maintenance programs were constant as well as extensive.

When Huntington had completed his Long Beach line so rapidly and opened it in 1902, he had achieved fame as an electric railroad builder almost overnight. Berating William Hook, whose men were still at work on the route to the port, the San Pedro Times said in November, 1902: [1]

His (Hook's) road, if completed, will necessarily be a wretched apology for the magnificent double track, broad-gauge Huntington road to Long Beach.

1. Quoted December 1, 1902, in the Long Beach Press.

A massive trestle on the Pacific Electric route to Glendale takes shape in 1904 during construction of this important line. (Security Pacific National Bank)

Tower cars drawn by horses and mules were used to string the trolley wires when the first electric car lines were built.

Rail tower cars later took over the maintenance. (Security Pacific National Bank Collection)

As construction of the Long Beach Magnolia Avenue local streetcar line started, The Long Beach Press in November, 1902, hailed the building procedures with these words: [2]

As is the custom of the (Pacific Electric) company, they put men and teams enough on the ground to accomplish something and when they went to work this morning it was evident that the road would be completed in a very few days.

The sturdy Pacific Electric roadbeds endured the most strenuous conditions despite the rapid construction Terry Stephenson, Orange County editor and historian, noted that the interurban right-of-way near Garden Grove formed a dam after torrential rains in 1916. It was necessary to dynamite holes in the well-built line in order to permit the water to drain from the area. [3]

The laborers evidently regarded their toil as routine and in many cases even the foremen did not know of

the precise destination of the tracks. In praising the speedy laying of tracks, a reporter for the Long Beach Press noted that "the men in charge are not certain as yet whether the road will continue down Magnolia to the (ocean) front or will turn off on Third Street." The Pacific Electric's engineers appeared in time to give instructions when needed.

Teams of horses and mules pulled construction grading equipment although steam shovels were used in some cases to speed demolition of large embankments. In the later years of the growing line cranes and other equipment were mounted on rail cars for maintenance. Motorized apparatus replaced horses. Hand-powered work cars operated by track repair crews wearing bright red jackets to alert approaching interurbans of their presence manned hand cars, and became a familiar sight along the lines.

Start of construction on the Pacific Electric line to Whittier early in 1903 brought the establishment of the customary work camps along the way to speed operations. Like the route to Long Beach, the Whittier line initially was built

---

2. Long Beach Press, November 24, 1902.

3. Terry Stephenson, "Orange County History Series," (Santa Ana, 1939), Pp. 142-144.

Grease is applied to trolley wire by a work car on the Glendale Line in 1941. The grease kept steel shoes atop trolley *"sticks" from wearing out the overhead soft copper wire. (Stephen D. Maguire Collection)*

with one set of rails so the link could be completed rapidly and placed into service. But Huntington graded his right-of-ways for double tracks, saving himself the expense of more work when passenger volume warranted more rails.

The appearance of the electric railroad construction crews gladdened the hearts of townspeople who could then envision quick completion of lines that would link them to other cities.

"It seems mighty nice to look out through the window from our desk and see the holes being dug, the poles set, the trolley wire strung, and ties and rails being laid for the Pacific Electric line," the editor of the Glendora Gleaner wrote in his edition of December 12, 1907. He added happily that the "line will make Glendora the terminus and connect us with the city of Los Angeles, but twenty-seven miles distant by train and forty minutes by time."

A week later the line officially opened. A brass band played and crowds cheered when the first electric car arrived. Aboard the train were a group of Los Angeles civic leaders headed by Henry Huntington. Speeches praised the trolley tycoon for the well-built line.

Huntington won a reputation for efficiency and quality in the construction of the system not only because of his personal knowledge of railroading but also by retaining engineers who knew how to build lines comparable to those of the steam railways.

The ability of Huntington's engineers to develop techniques for building new lines more rapidly than competing trolley systems gave the Pacific Electric the edge in wooing community cooperation for a proposed route. By 1906 construction methods had progressed so that George Pillsbury, a key official for the Huntington lines, was able to promise residents of La Habra that work on a link to their town could start within ten days after land was donated for a right-of-way. What was more, he assured them that the line stretching nearly ten miles from the Whittier area would be in operation within six months because of the efficient Huntington methods for building.[4]

After the electric railroads acquired by the Southern Pacific were merged in 1911, construction and maintenance operations were consolidated under the Pacific Electric banner. While the P. E. operated as an entity, it was able to obtain the services of engineers and technicians employed by the parent company. With the advent of the automobile, trucks gradually replaced rail work cars as the prime means for transporting repair crews and equipment to the tracks.

When the interurban era came to a close, the gas buggy had the final word. Trucks especially designed for removing tracks uprooted the steel kingdom over which the Big Red Cars once proudly rolled and reigned.

---

4. Santa Ana Blade, January 30, 1906.

ABOVE: Land that was largely undeveloped surrounds the right-of-way used by this three-car Pacific Electric train. The first car, built in 1906 by the St. Louis Car Company, remained in service until 1941. BELOW: This diminutive trolley, used in the early twentieth century for "local" service. (Both Photos: Stephen D. Maguire Collection)

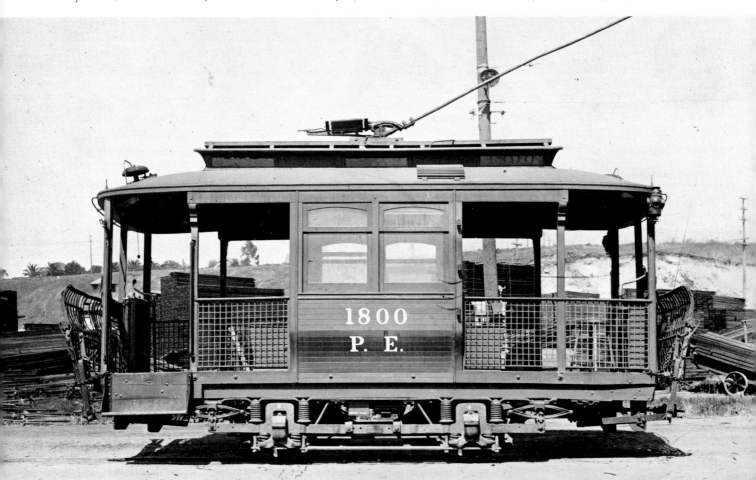

14. The Rails and Real Estate, and Hollywood, Too!

After the railroads pushed across the western United States and subsequently built extensions to key areas during the late nineteenth century it became a well-accepted rule that a town could not thrive unless it had the good fortune of being on a rail route. Many cities prospered and grew only because they stood at strategic points on a railway. This rule prompted the residents of Los Angeles to vote funds in 1872 to finance the Southern Pacific's construction to their city to prevent its permanent relegation to village status.

The arrival of the electric interurban in Southern California made the same rule applicable for area community developments. Trolley lines brought growth beyond expectations to Long Beach, Pasadena, Santa Monica, and points on the tracks between the cities. Few people considered purchasing homes unless assured of the convenience of trolley service. Subdivisions and towns grew on land whose greatest promise for livability was its proximity to the railway tracks. Farms—if adjacent to rail lines—became cities and real estate promoters became wealthy.

Where the Big Red Cars went, the real estate developers followed and the City of Southern California was created.

The land closest to the trolley tracks became the most valuable. The Tichenor Tract, near the Los Angeles Inter-Urban Railway's Newport line in eastern Long Beach, in 1905 advertised lots "by the tracks" for $350. Identical lots three blocks from the tracks were only $250. Many farms adjacent to interurban lines were subdivided for homes. The property was lower in price than real estate near downtown Los Angeles and convenient trolley service placed the homes only a few minutes from offices and stores. Thousands of migrants arriving in Los Angeles eagerly purchased surburban sites for their homes. Editorialized The Long Beach Press: [1]

One of the striking features of the real estate situation just now is, not only here but in other cities, the influence of electric roads upon the value of residence property. This influence is two-fold. It largely increases the value of suburban property within a short distance of a city while at the same time it tends to act as a shock upon unreasonably high prices for inside residence lots. When a person can buy an acre half an hour's ride from the business center for $500 he is likely to hesitate about paying $1,500 for a fifty foot lot that is only about ten minutes nearer to his office.

Unquestionably the electric cars made suburban living attractive to the average family. At the turn of the century such people could not afford an automobile and would have been forced into cramped city apartment dwellings destined to become slums. The real estate activity churned by the electric interurbans undoubtedly surprised most landowners, although hints of the prosperous era that was to blossom shortly came as early as 1901 when Henry Huntington was disposing of his interests in the Southern Pacific. At that time Frank Wiggins, who as manager of the Los Angeles Chamber of Commerce directed the area's boosters, informed a newspaper reporter: [2]

Another (real estate broker) told me . . . if you have any Los Angeles property, hold onto it or mark it up twenty-five percent. . . for a big boom is coming this way and property is going to be more valuable than ever . . . there seems to be an impression that Southern California is on the eve of the greatest development it has ever seen. The railway deals (between Huntington and Harriman over the Southern Pacific) going on at the present are expected to play a prominent part.

While the communities touched by the interurban lines prospered generally, the individuals and companies specializing in real estate developed reaped the greatest profits. Among the first to gain from trolley construction were Moses H. Sherman and Eli Clark, who received direct profits when property owners along the line to Santa Monica encouraged the builders by the gift of 225 acres of ranchland—knowing well that the remaining acreage would gain in value with improved transportation. Sherman and Clark also owned portions of the Beach Land Company, developer of Playa del Rey in a then isolated area. The investment of $200,000 in streets and surveys plus the extension of the Los Angeles Pacific tracks to the development produced a residential area favored by settlers and profitable to the company's investors. The presence of the Los Angeles Pacific's tracks also helped to bring success for Abbot Kinney's Venice of America which, as beautiful as it was, would have otherwise been remote for visitors and property buyers in the pre-automobile era.

The greatest individual profits were reaped, of course, by none other than Henry Huntington, who on his entry into Southern California recognized the potential riches in land adjacent to electric interurban tracks. Despite his evident interest in expanding his electric

---

1. Long Beach Press, April 1, 1903.

2. Los Angeles Times, February 4, 1901.

railroad system beyond the confines of Southern California, his program capitalized on the rule that communities grew alongside rails. Huntington purchased immense amounts of land near Alhambra just as he extended lines to that city. His early real estate acquisitions also included vast acreages in what became the Oak Knoll district and the town of San Marino, both in the San Gabriel Valley where his interurban network was the thickest.

Huntington's share of the profits came from several directions. He made money selling land purchased at comparatively low prices and subsequently made more desirable when the trolley tracks were built. A second source of income obviously was through fares paid by the commuters after they purchased his property. In some areas he gleaned additional profits because his electric power and domestic gas companies served the tracts. He formed the Huntington Land Company to consolidate real estate sprawling throughout Southern California and acquired the controlling stock in numerous other companies owning property stretching from the mountains to the seashore. Huntington's real estate holding covered land in Glendale, Seal Beach, Huntington Beach, Olinda, and the San Fernando Valley as well as in downtown

Los Angeles where values soared despite the settlement of suburban areas.

But no one had a monopoly on the profits so lucrative in the sale of real estate made more valuable by electric railroads. Real estate men thrived in Long Beach following its awakening by the trolley. Land three blocks from the ocean sold for $300 an acre prior to completion of the Pacific Electric line. Six months after the Big Red Cars arrived real estate broker F. E. Shaw advertised Long Beach land a mile from the seashore for $700 an acre with the triumphic notation that "the Pacific Electric line has been constructed through and around our property." [3] The technology of the interurban itself was magical enough to attract buyers. Start of construction of a Pacific Electric local line in Long Beach brought forth "The Electric Tract" on adjoining property. After the line reached Santa Ana, a barley field was subdivided and advertised as "The Pacific Electric Tract" so that buyers would note its proximity to transportation.[4]

Special interurban excursions sponsored by real estate

3. Long Beach Tribune, March 22, 1903.

4. Santa Ana Blade, January 30, 1906.

This 1925 view at Huntington Beach shows how the trolley tracks dominated the ocean front between the coast and strand. More autos were going into use at this time. (Security Pacific National Bank Collection)

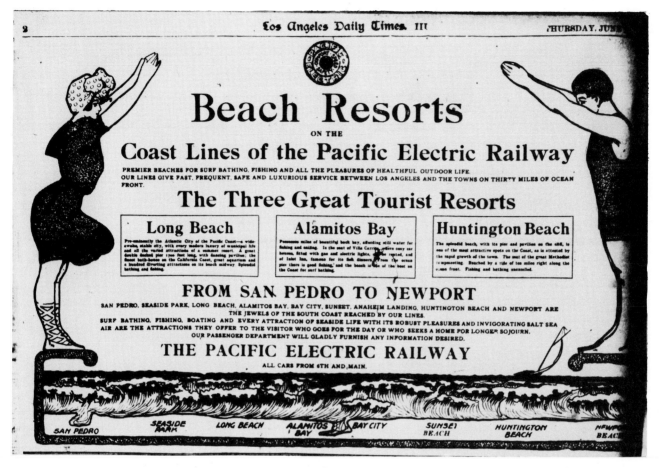

promoters became tools of the trade not only to carry prospects to inspect the property but also to demonstrate the ease and speed of transportation. After Sunset Beach was opened in 1904 its promoters lured buyers with a round-trip from Los Angeles for twenty-five cents, including lunch.[5] The developers of Seal Beach (initially named Bay City) proudly advertised that the town was "on the line of the Pacific Electric Railway only forty-five minutes from Los Angeles;" seaside lots were offered for $350 each.

Sightseeing trips via trolleys provided a general impetus to the sale of property along the interurban lines, for once visitors saw the variety of towns and attractions their inclination to settle in Southern California increased. It became the common-place for the interurban railways to offer free rides on the sightseeing trips, before the practice was stopped by federal and state regulations, when it appeared a scheduled car would

leave with substantially less than its capacity.[6] Involved in the area's growth on a variety of fronts, both the Los Angeles Pacific and Pacific Electric regarded the practice as a sure way to lure permanent residents.

Delighted investors told their success stories: shrewd property transactions were made possible by the existence of the interurbans. After completion of the line to Huntington Beach and increased real estate sales, an investor identified only as T. G. Harriman was quoted as follows: [7]

That corner lot with a frontage of 110 feet on Main Street and 50 feet on Ocean Avenue sold last April for $5,600 to the Union Investment Company. In less than six weeks I bought it

---

5. Los Angeles Examiner, June 29, 1905.

6. Harry O. Marler, formerly general passenger agent of the Pacific Electric, reported in a 1962 interview with the author that when it appeared a sightseeing trolley would leave with only a few fare-paying passengers, free trips were offered guests at various hotels. Many such riders were prompted to purchase property and reside in the area as the result of such tours.

7. Los Angeles Times, June 29, 1905.

Frequent service by the Los Angeles Pacific and Los Angeles and Redondo lines was used by a real estate developer to lure buyers in a 1906 ad in the Los Angeles Examiner. Note that the lots were priced at $90 each.

for $10,000. That was on May 19 and on June 19 I sold it for $16,000.

Is it worth it? Well, the man who bought it off me has subdivided it into eight plats and gets $20 per month ground rent for each plat, which means six percent on an investment of $32,000 or twelve percent on his actual cash investment—whichever way you choose to figure it.

Many people who expected to make quick profits on real estate transactions were doomed, however, to disappointment. Completion of an electric railroad line frequently brought intensive speculation on adjacent property. Prices skyrocketed to many times the pre-trolley values only to collapse when the novelty of the line ended or interest switched to another community where a new route had opened. The investors who bought prudently and retained property for several years generally made the more durable profits.

After completion of interurban routes, construction of local service trolley lines brought growth to areas in cities previously without public transportation. Opening of the East Seventh Street line of Long Beach in 1910 prompted contractor Marcus Campbell to tell a newspaper reporter happily: [8]

Within a radius of two blocks in this section there are ten new houses building. This is a good illustration of the rapidity with which this section has been improved since the (trolley) car line has been extended over Seventh Street.

Promoters of housing tracts near downtown Los Angeles also boarded the trolley bandwagon to attract buyers. Vacant lots described as "close in" were advertised at Watts with the claim that "low fares and quick service downtown in only fifteen minutes" made the lots,

priced at $50 each and up, most desirable.[9] The advertisements added that as well as being suitable for residences the lots could grow the "finest celery, peas, cauliflower, lettuce and other garden truck," alluding, no doubt, to the usage of the property immediately prior to its subdivision. The advertisements neglected to point out that the narrow lots—averaging only twenty-five feet in width—were so small that they were not conducive to quality housing. Real estate promoters in many areas, anxious for profits from land near the trolleys, placed seemingly competitive prices on lots so tiny that they encouraged the erection of substandard housing.

For the budding community unfortunate enough to be by-passed by the electric railroads there was, at least temporarily, death. Thomas B. Talbert, founder of Talbert (later Fountain Valley), recalled in his "My Sixty Years in California" (Huntington Beach News Press, Huntington Beach, 1952) that he moved his real estate office from his fledgling community to Huntington Beach when the Big Red Car tracks approached in 1903. He and other property owners moved buildings from nearby towns to the beach community, anticipating the customary prosperity which arrived with the trolleys.

Talbert and fifty-one other real estate agents were in full operation in the little town of less than a thousand people by the time the Red Cars made their inaugural trips on July 4, 1904. The real estate men were not disappointed: the trolleys brought more than 50,000 visitors the first day and land prices skyrocketed as speculators sought to climb aboard the boom.

For nearly thirty years following the advent of the

8. Long Beach Press, December 27, 1910.

9. Los Angeles Examiner, March 23, 1906.

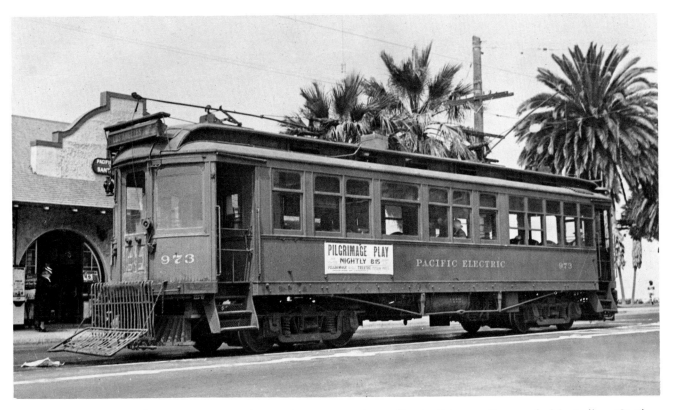

An interurban waits at the P. E. station on Ocean Avenue in Santa Monica during the 1930's. Note the ad for the Pil-grimage Play in Cahuenga Pass, reached by trolley. (Stephen D. Maguire Collection)

electric interurban in Southern California, real estate promoters capitalized on the proximity of their land to trolley lines in their advertisements and, before automobiles became numerous, usually directed the public to the particular cars to board in order to reach the subdivisions. In 1902 the Carson Investment Company urged prospective buyers to "take the Alhambra electric cars from Spring and Fourth" to view its Pasadena Villa Tract where one-fourth acre residential tracts sold for $350. This company was able to offer the ultimate in an endorsement for its property: advertisements hailed the fact that none other than "H. E. Huntington bought twenty-two blocks for $16,000." [10]

Without a doubt the name of Huntington alone was a glowing testimony to the profits available in Southern California real estate during the early twentieth century. Judge Robert M. Widney, among the most ardent of the real estate brokers, reported in an advertisement that Huntington lost $900,000 in a steel company stock investment made at the urging of J. P. Morgan, the New York financier.

"Mr. Huntington's Southern California investments, however, make him a big winner for the year," continued Judge Widney's advertisement.[11] "Moral: look to Southern California, not New York, for profitable speculation." The booster proceeded to remind buyers that he had many properties from which to select.

William M. Garland, who was the sales agent for many Huntington properties, lived up to his "booster" reputation by his enthusiasm over the electric railroad tycoon when he purchased full page newspaper advertisements proclaiming: [12]

Mr. Huntington's advent into Los Angeles placed our city ten years ahead of its natural growth.

As usual, Garland's advertisements contained more truth than fiction. Those who indicated concern over Huntington's acquisition of the area's electric lines in

---

10. Los Angeles Times, July 7, 1906.

11. Los Angeles Record, October 17, 1903.

12. The advertisements appeared in Los Angeles newspapers July 9-10, 1905, when Henry Huntington's purchase of large property holdings at Redondo Beach as well as the Los Angeles and Redondo Railway launched a land-buying spree.

A steam shovel cuts the right-of-way for the Pacific Electric through Cahuenga Pass in 1910 as construction was starting *on the line linking the San Fernando Valley with Los Angeles. (Title Insurance and Trust Company Collection)*

1898 had swiftly changed their minds. People spoke of Southern California's immediate and future growth and in the same breath praised Henry Huntington.

Just as real estate developments followed the interurban routes, so did the very nature of the trolley lines shape individual cities. Patterns to be noted for years began in the early twentieth century when retail shopping centers inevitably hugged the rails for the convenience of patrons. Among the most notable examples of this influence was Glendale's downtown business section: business structures lined Brand Boulevard, traversed for more than two miles by interurbans, but residential developments predominated only two blocks on either side of the tracks. Major shopping areas thrived on Long Beach's Pine Avenue, Pasadena's Colorado Street, San Bernardino's Third Street, Santa Ana's Fourth Street, and Pomona's Second Street because the arteries were served by trolleys.

The influence of the trolley reigned over real estate promotions well into the 1920's. Developers of Oneonta Park in the South Pasadena area proudly advertised in 1922 that "750 Pacific Electric cars daily" passed the subdivision.[13] Advertisements with maps showing the routes of the Venice Short Line as well as the Beverly Hills-Santa Monica Line made it clear to prospective buyers in the Pico Boulevard Heights Tract in western Los Angeles that no commuter problem was involved for those who purchased homes.[14] The trolley lines were extended on a limited basis to spur land sales even in the 1920's, when the automobile was accepted as competition. D. W. Temple, founder of Temple City, drove a silver spike in 1924 to celebrate extension of the San Gabriel line to the new community. In the same year

13. Los Angeles Times, March 19, 1922.
14. Los Angeles Examiner, March 19, 1905.

A new building rises in Long Beach during the growth of the 1920's. A San Pedro-bound Red Car pulls onto Ocean from Pine and another trolley approaches from Los Angeles.

At the right, a Salt Lake and Los Angeles steam train, using the south side of Ocean, is receiving passengers. (Security Pacific National Bank Collection)

the developers of the Belmont Shore area of Long Beach paid the Pacific Electric $63,000 to extend tracks for two miles into the subdivision.

When the highways were built, they followed the travel routes already formed by the electric railroad lines—further shaping the nature of the City of Southern California. In many cases the principal automobile arteries directly paralleled the electric tracks.

Yet the role of the trolleys in shaping the City of Southern California was not limited to real estate developments. As the electric interurban era drew to a close, not the least of its contributions to the nature of the city was its part in the selection of a site for the University of California at Los Angeles. Fullerton, Burbank, Sierra Madre, and Ocean Park sought the campus, but one of the principal reasons for selection of the site in West Los Angeles was its proximity to the Pacific

Electric tracks once part of the Los Angeles Pacific system. In recommending the site the seventeen-man selection committee (whose members included William E. Dunn and William M. Garland), reported: [15]

The many avenues of approach to the Beverly Hills district for vehicular traffic and the proximity of the site to present electric railway transportation which can be brought direct to the (West Los Angeles site) site at a relatively small cost convince us that this locality does offer the greatest saving of traveling time and expense to thousands of students.

When the Big Red Cars finally rolled into the realm of history, they left a sprawling City of Southern Cali-

15. James R. Martin, "The University of California in Los Angeles: a Resume of the Selection and Acquisition of the Westwood Site," (Los Angeles, 1925), Pp. 84-85. The rail line was never built because of the approaching end of the trolley age. The university was served by busses.

A Pacific Electric car pauses on the seaside tracks near tourist cottages at Newport Beach. Service started in 1906 and *encouraged commuting between the port and Los Angeles. (First American Title Insurance and Trust Co.)*

fornia built precisely as it was because the rail lines had encouraged just that development.

Interurban lines through the Los Angeles coastal basin and San Gabriel Valley opened the way for profitable housing tracts, but perhaps the biggest single real estate development to roll to success on the electric cars was that of the San Fernando Valley.

Although comparatively isolated from other · sections of Los Angeles by mountains, the valley was an obvious area for the eventual overflow of population. The two things needed to help develop the area were water and adequate transportation. The boosters were to be quite competent in dealing with these minor inadequacies.

The San Fernando Valley had its first taste of prosperity, mild and brief though it was, when the Southern Pacific passed through the area as it built its line to Los Angeles in 1874. The townsite of San Fernando was established and

the Maclay School of Theology was founded with the financial assistance of George Maclay, one of the Valley's principal landowners, and Judge Robert M. Widney, noted for his many talents. The infrequent service of the steam railroad failed to churn the town's development. In 1893 the theology school was moved to the University of Southern California in Los Angeles and its Valley property was sold.

A mild beginning for the population boom eventually to fill the valley basin with homes and commercial centers came in 1904 when Leslie C. Brand, a real estate developer, organized the San Fernando Mission Land Company. Associated with him in the company were a group of men whose interests could profit not only from the sale of land but also in its subsequent use. The group included, of course, Henry E. Huntington, whose magic name and trolley cars would help develop Glendale, on the valley's fringe. The project was a success and Glendale became a thriving bedroom community for Los Angeles. Much of the adjoining San Fernando Valley remained as ranches and fruit orchards.

The valley was dry and desert-like and it appeared it would remain so because of the lack of water. The boosters, aided by the ingenuity of engineer William Mulholland, devised a solution for the water problem. In 1908 construction was approved for the Los Angeles aqueduct from the Owens Valley, well-watered by the melting snows of the Sierra Nevada range.

In September, 1909, an option to purchase 47,500 acres of land in the San Fernando Valley was taken by Harry Chandler, general manager of the Los Angeles Times. The price tag on land was $2.5 million, or slightly more than $45 an acre. A year later, water was assured and the option was exercised by the Los Angeles Suburban Homes Company, a thirty-man syndicate including Chandler and his father-in-law, Harrison Gray Otis, publisher of The Times; Moses H. Sherman, then serving as president of the Los Angeles Metropolitan Water District, the agency authorizing the vital aqueduct, and Henry E. Huntington, along with other key Los Angeles financial leaders.

The members of the syndicate reaped immense profits.

The backing of the real estate venture by such prominent men in a position to influence construction of the aqueduct —coupled with the fact that the terminus of the facility was near their big land holdings and substantially removed from central Los Angeles — drew criticisms in subsequent years. Sherman, at the time a director of the merged Pacific Electric, was attacked for his dual role as an investor in the syndicate and a member of the Los Angeles Board of Water Commissioners, the agency building the aqueduct. However, the voters authorized bonds for the project in 1907—nearly two years before Chandler obtained the option. In retrospect it was evident that the Valley was destined for eventual development and obviously with profits. The syndicate envisioning and executing the big project no doubt committed its greatest crime in seeing the area's potential and proceeding to act.

Even with the abundant supply of water promised by Owens Valley the community needed closer ties with central Los Angeles in order to succeed. The development program therefore called for extension of the Pacific Electric tracks into the San Fernando Valley. The interurban project started in 1911. The tracks led from the Hollywood line and were laid in Cahuenga Pass, the gap between the Hollywood Hills and Santa Monica Mountains where hardly more than sixty years before the Americans met the Mexicans in a battle for California. Cheers from the enthusiastic public and shouts of potential bargains for those who would buy land from

This 1912 ad heralded the opening of the Pacific Electric line to the San Fernando Valley, biggest of all real estate developments relying on trolleys for a boost. BELOW: A 1916 scene shows Van Nuys Boulevard, dominated by trolley tracks. (Security Pacific National Bank)

real estate agents greeted the official opening of the interurban link on December 7, 1912. A massive program to sell lots in the new town sites was launched although the first water from the Owens Valley project would not arrive for a year.

Even before the tracks were completed, the trolley line was heralded as a factor destined to make San Fernando Valley property highly desirable.

"The new electric double track railway is nearly completed," W. P. Whitsett, sales manager for the tract, announced in a newspaper advertisement three months before its opening. "This means that prices will advance soon. Get in at once."[16]

The Los Angeles Aqueduct, bringing water 215 miles from the Owens Valley, was completed in 1913 at a cost of $24.6 million. As the first water churned into the facility's

16. Los Angeles Times, January 21, 1910.

Valley terminus, William Mulholland made a speech famed for its brevity:

"There it is. Take it."

Surveyor V. J. Rowan divided the land into lots of varying sizes, many suited for small farms and others desirable for commuter homes.

Tract 1,000 was the official designation given to the giant subdivision that shamed all others in its magnitude when Rowan recorded the venture on March 14, 1911.

Advertising its San Fernando Valley property, the Los Angeles Suburban Homes Company proudly pointed out that it had "paid a substantial sum to the Pacific Electric" to assure extension of the tracks. The need of interurban service to assure success for a real estate development was well known. As a matter of fact, rails were regarded as nearing the water in importance for saleable land. The land developers incorporated the Los Angeles and San Fernando Valley Railway Company when

Two venturesome bicyclists use a dirt road from Hollywood into Cahuenga Pass in the early twentieth century. Trolleys *ended this rural flavor and brought Hollywood its first growth. (Security Pacific National Bank)*

A trolley speeds through Cahuenga Pass, gateway between the central Los Angeles area and the San Fernando Valley. *in this 1920 picture. This rail artery later was covered by a freeway. (Security Pacific National Bank)*

they started operations. The railway company including right-of-way for tracks became part of the Pacific Electric, which actually built the line.

When the extension was completed, the subdividers of Tract 1,000 beckoned buyers to the Valley in advertisements proclaiming that the P. E. "has laid its tracks on a perfect roadbed of crushed rock and established one of the best operated branches of their entire system."[17]

The main trolley right-of-way was located in the center of Sherman Way, itself subsequently becoming a principal artery for automobiles through the Valley.

As housing tracts replaced ranchlands most of the San Fernando Valley annexed to Los Angeles in 1915 so that it could utilize the Owens Valley water coming so conveniently to its very door.

17. Los Angeles Times, August 11, 1912.

The abundant supply of water was coupled with the blessing of an electric railroad to attract buyers of property in Tract 1,000.

The value of electric railway service remained important to sales of land in the San Fernando Valley until the end of the trolley era in the 1920's. The Big Red Cars carried commuters to the valley on its heavily traveled tracks until the line's abandonment in 1950. During less than forty years the San Fernando Valley's

PICTURE PAGES FOLLOWING: Pacific Electric cars frequently were used by the Hollywood movie makers in filming hilarious comedies. This scene is from "Harold Lloyd's World of Comedy." (© by Harold Lloyd; Used by Permission)

population skyrocketed beyond most predictions made even for Los Angeles itself as it existed in the early twentieth century.

When the transcontinental railroad completed the last leg of its cross-country stretch to Los Angeles, many small villages blossomed with the subsequent prosperity. Among them was a tiny community laid out in 1887 west of Los Angeles on ranchlands regarded as highly desirable for suburban living. The settlement, a generous label for the cluster of few houses and orange groves, was named Hollywood.

The end of the real estate boom was cruel to Hollywood and even by 1900, after thirteen years of existence, the town was hardly more than a crossroads. Deer often strolled down from the nearby hills and wandered on the streets. The principle passenger service to the community was via the narrow gauge, steam-power Cahuenga Valley Railroad. Its schedules were infrequent.

It was the electric interurban rather than motion pictures which gave Hollywood its first injection of hope. Sherman and Clark, building their Los Angeles Pacific trolley line to Santa Monica, passed near the settlement. In 1900 they finished a branch route to the Hollywood area. The extension gave encouragement to Hollywood and in 1903 its residents voted to incorporate as a city. The town had a population of only 600 but it began to grow as electric cars brought crowds to look at subdivisions promoted largely on the strength of the trolley service. By 1910, when residents voted to annex to Los Angeles in order to assure an adequate water supply, Hollywood was a thriving community of 10,000 people.

In 1911 Hollywood's first motion picture, "The Law of the Range," was made by the Nestor Film Company in a barn at the corner of Sunset Boulevard and Gower Street. Other film producers quickly made the westward trek and Hollywood began to take its place as the

Here is another trolley scene from "Harold Lloyd's World of Comedy." The comedian used tracks on Hollywood and Sunset Boulevards for filming movies using electric cars. (© by Harold Lloyd; Used by Permission)

A Red Car speeds through the San Fernando Valley during the late 1930's. For more than four decades, Valley residents *were served by the trolleys which made Los Angeles only minutes away. (Security Pacific National Bank)*

entertainment center of the world. The attractions were many: the area was near the Mexican border where producers could flee if accused of patent infringements; the territory was diverse in its scenic attractions for use in the pictures, and the mild, sunny climate allowed year-around production.

During the ensuing years the Big Red Cars were to play important parts in the film industry not only in bringing film hopefuls to the studios via the Hollywood trolley line but also in the productions themselves. The Pacific Electric was acclaimed in the motion picture industry for its cooperation with the studios.

The Big Red Cars were useful "props" in countless comedy chase scenes. Many of those featuring Harold Lloyd

and the team of Oliver Hardy and Stanley Laurel became classics.

The terrain travelled by the trolleys in those wonderful movies has changed so much with development that it is difficult to pin-point the locale of the electric car antics. Curious as to just where the movie-makers went for the scenes, I contacted Harold Lloyd while writing this book. Most of the scenes were made near downtown Hollywood itself. Among the favorite lines for filming was on Franklin Avenue. Lloyd's studio also used streetcars on Hollywood Boulevard between Western and Vine Avenues and on Sunset Boulevard near Gardener's Junction.

Needless to say, in that era of silent movies, there were relatively few automobiles to interfere with the activity.

For the convenience of the movie makers, the P.E. detoured passenger cars so that steam locomotives could be filmed on the tracks. The interurban station at Palms was regarded as typical, at least for screen purposes, of a depot in a small town and appeared in many motion pictures.

Harry O. Marler, later general passenger agent for the system, made many arrangements for use of the Big Red Cars in scenes ranging from depictions of trolleys crashing into autos (a special attachment was used on interurbans to avoid damage) to simple scenes of the leading players catching a streetcar. The Red Cars,

becoming nationally known, were ideal backgrounds for identifying a picture's locale as Los Angeles without the need of explanatory dialogue or titles.

When the Hollywood Subway was completed, it was used during slow hours for motion pictures localed in the New York subway system.

After sound was added to motion pictures, the first "talkie" on a moving streetcar was made by Paramount Pictures in 1929 at Twelfth and Hill Streets in downtown Los Angeles. Clara Bow was the star of the picture, "The Saturday Night Kid."

Comic Buster Keaton achieved a record for using

This picture from a 1929 issue of the Pacific Electric Magazine showed actor George O'Brien playing the role of a motorman on a trolley trucked to the Fox Studios. The P. E. cooperated frequently with movie producers.

124

ABOVE: *The Pacific Electric's Beverly Hills station was surrounded by few other buildings in the 1920's, but con-* *venient trolleys were giving impetus to growth. Cars contin-* *ued to Santa Monica. (Security Pacific National Bank)*

the equipment when he purchased twelve obsolete Red Cars in 1926, had them remodeled to resemble Civil War vintage rail equipment, and employed them in a "wreck" at Truckee while filming "The General."

Among the more sophisticated uses of the Big Red Cars by the film-makers was told by Bosley Crowther in his biography of producer Irving Thalberg, "Hollywood Rajah." During the early sound era, one of the few theaters with adequate equipment for previewing motion pictures was in San Bernardino, fifty miles east of Los Angeles. Thalberg's studio, Metro-Goldwyn-Mayer, chartered a Pacific Electric interurban, stocked it with food, and had it pick up its load of dignitaries. M-G-M was conveniently situated in Culver City, a community served by the Pacific Electric. The studio executives responsible for the film could enjoy eating and playing cards while the trolley carried them to the theater.

Aside from service to commuters and use as "props," the Big Red Cars also were the heart of a system that carried freight to the very doors of the studios, most of which were adjacent to the Pacific Electric tracks.

Trolley tracks stretched through Hollywood.

For commuters, there was trolley service on Franklin Avenue, Hollywood Boulevard, Western Avenue, Sunset Boulevard, Santa Monica Boulevard, Argyle Avenue, Vine Street, and even part of the way into Laurel Canyon. Sections of the track were on private rights-of-way, but much of the track was in the street — creating the battle with automobiles that plagued trolleys throughout America.

As the years passed the motion picture studios recognized that the trolley age was nearing an end and made numerous purchases of retired Big Red Cars for use in giving authenticity to future "period" pictures.

125

ECHO MOUNTAIN
3200 FT. ABOVE SEA LEVEL

PACIFIC ELECT
RAILWAY
3

LEFT: *Posing for pictures on cable cars was part of the Mount Lowe excursion. This 1932 photo included this book's author: the youngster in the center row; to the left is his mother, Mrs. Jessie Person Crump.*

Sightseers bound for the famous Orange Empire Trolley Trip board a P. E. interurban in about 1920. when the tours were reaching a peak. The trip went to San Bernardino and Riverside. (Craig Ramussen Collection)

15. A Day for a Dollar

For nearly three decades tourists placed the sightseeing excursions well at the top of their lists of things to do and see during a Southern California visit.[1] Local residents, too, could not resist the enchanting lure of the tours covering a variety of scenery. Trolley systems in other areas provided sightseeing trips, but none could compare with the tours on the biggest electric railroad in the world.

The immense interurban system was built primarily to carry passengers between the cities for work, shopping, or social visits, but it was inevitable that rail links to scenic points of interest in Southern California, noted for its variety of scenery and a favored place for tourists, would be used for the worthy purpose of excursion trips.

Few people during the early twentieth century owned automobiles and sightseeing in horse-drawn carriages over the few existing roads was hardly a pleasure. Riding the Big Red Cars over relatively distant routes to the sea-

---

1. Much material for this chapter was provided the author in interviews with C. M. Pierce, who managed the Balloon Trolley Trip shortly after the turn of the century, and Harry O. Marler, manager of sightseeing trips for the Pacific Electric before becoming the company's general passenger agent.

THE PACIFIC ELECTRIC MAGAZINE

Pacific Electric Magazine covers picture the attractions of visiting Mount Lowe. A 1928 issue (above) shows the cable cars on The Great Incline. Trolleys at three levels on the trip from the cable cars to the tavern are pictured on a 1928 issue. The tour was immensely popular.

shore, mountains, or citrus groves made memorable family outings. The electric interurban excursions began almost with the advent of the system and continued, although on varying scales, until its doom.

In the early era the Sherman and Clark Los Angeles Pacific and Henry Huntington's Pacific Electric each offered tours to compete for the sightseer's dollar. The most famous and longest lasting excursion was the Mount Lowe trip, designed particularly for sightseers. Its builder, Professor Lowe, encountered financial difficulties and the line was acquired in 1901 by Huntington for consolidation into his Pacific Electric Railway. Residents of Southern California enjoyed the mountain trip because it contrasted to the flat plains on which most cities were situated. Out-of-state visitors found it an attraction because it demonstrated the area's boast of both orange groves and alpine regions within short distances.

The Mount Lowe trip must take all superlatives: it was the most famous, most widely visited, most unusual, and longest lasting of year-around tours exclusively for pleasure seekers.

The cable railroad carrying passengers approximately 1,500 feet from a pavilion in Rubio Canyon up a sixty percent grade to Echo Mountain was the line's outstanding feature. From Echo Mountain, travelers rode narrow gauge (3'6") trolley cars around 127 curves and eighteen trestles to the base of Mount Lowe, 5,000 feet above sea level. There visitors could enjoy dining and a hotel and cabins.

In those pre-smog days, visitors could look down on the communities of Southern California and see the buildings, fields, roads, and railroad tracks. Catalina Island, more than forty miles away, was visible on many days.

The nineteen-mile trolley trip from Los Angeles through Pasadena and Altadena to Rubio Canyon required approximately seventy-five minutes. It took just ten minutes to ride the cable car to Echo Mountain, but it required a half hour for the 3.57 mile ride around the curves and over trestles to the Alpine Tavern on Mount Lowe.

The ride was scenic and the curves were fun. Passengers never complained about the time required for the trip.

Besides the Balloon Route and Mount Lowe, the best-known excursions were the Old Mission Trolley Trip, Triangle Trolley Trip, and Orange Empire Trolley Trip.

The Old Mission trip took visitors to Mission San Gabriel and the Ostrich Farm in South Pasadena. The Triangle trip, taking its name from the shape of its route, went from Los Angeles to Santa Ana, Huntington Beach, Long Beach, Point Firmin, and return. Visitors stopped for lunch at the Naples Hotel, a quaint structure on a canal at the Long Beach development.

Although not connected to Los Angeles by trolley tracks until 1914, San Bernardino had its own electric car tours for visitors and residents. The best-known trip was the

This narrow-gauge trolley rolls through the snow on the winding Mount Lowe route, illustrating the scenic and cli- *matic contrasts of the terrain served by the 1,164-mile Pacific Electric system. (Craig Rasmussen Collection)*

"Poinsettia Route" tour, which took travelers from San Bernardino to Colton, Urbita Hot Springs, Base Line, Highland, and Redlands.

Huntington's Pacific Electric provided tours to Long Beach and the Naples development inspired by Abbot Kinney's Venice of America as well as to Mission San Gabriel, romanticized in tourist guidebooks and novels popular at the time.

Vying for the place as the most famed tour of the era was the Los Angeles Pacific's Balloon Trolley Trip, so named because its route from Los Angeles to Santa Monica and back to Los Angeles via Venice was shaped on a map like a giant balloon. Ornate illustrations depicting the balloon-shaped route became familiar on posters as well as in newspapers and magazines. The trip reached its greatest popularity under the management of C. M. Pierce, who at the age of 96 in 1962 observed that the tours were successful "because they showed people the beauties of Southern California."

Incidentally, while Pierce and I were discussing the trolley era, the nonagenarian paused to demonstrate a back-ex-

ercising board for which he was sales agent. His vigor and enthusiasm did credit to a man a fourth of his age.

Pierce rented the interurban cars for $10 each, including a motorman. On peak days he used as many as thirty trolleys to take the throngs of visitors over the Balloon Route. The riders stopped at the Hollywood home of artist Paul De Longpres, noted for his paintings of flowers, and then went on to the ocean at Santa Monica, stopped for lunch at Playa del Rey, and saw the canals of Venice before returning to Los Angeles. On special occasions, Pierce dressed in a costume tailored like the uniform of an army general to make his direction of the tours more flavorable.

The fare for the trolley sightseeing trips was $1.00. The tours, all of them jammed with a variety of scenic attractions over a fairly large area, promptly were labeled "A Day for a Dollar."

"A Day for a Dollar" became a popular tag line attached to advertising for the tours. For the price, there were few sightseeing trips in the world that could equal that Southern California "Day for a Dollar."

129

This group of sightseers posed for a picture before boarding "special" Big Red Cars waiting to take them on sightseeing trips. The time was the late 1910's; roads were poor. (Stephen D. Maguire Collection)

The Poppy Car was another trolley excursion trip started early in the century. Visitors boarded the deluxe interurban for a day-long trip allowing for stops to tour communities served by the Pacific Electric.

The people in the small communities, eager for growth, welcomed the visitors arriving on the trolleys. When The Poppy Car excursions to Monrovia began in 1905, the city's Chamber of Commerce appropriated $150 monthly to entertain guests and a local historian remarked:[2]

So popular did this car become that Monrovia handled a thousand people a week during part of the time, and many of the "Poppy Car" excursionists are now Monrovians.

As the trolley excursionists saw and enjoyed Southern California's little towns they settled in the communities. The towns became cities.

Special interurbans also were scheduled to carry the immense number of tourists arriving in Los Angeles via the transcontinental railways directly from the depot to hotels in the outlying communities. The Virginia Hotel, built in Long Beach by Colonel Charles Drake as part

of his investment program, was highly popular with wealthy vacationers and boasted special parlor car service to carry its guests from Los Angeles.

After The Great Merger of 1911, the Pacific Electric emphasized excursions as the flow of tourists to Southern California continued, although the company itself, rather than Pierce, managed the trips. Harry O. Marler, who started his rail career with the Los Angeles Pacific and became general passenger agent of the Pacific Electric, directed the program. Marler, in 1962 recalling activities during the peak days of the excursions, told of soliciting excursion riders at stations with this chant:

The Famed Balloon Route Excursion,
A Pleasant Diversion,
Not Up in the Air,
But on the Earth,
Visit Eight Beaches and Ten Cities

The Pacific Electric sent Marler to major eastern and midwestern cities providing most of Southern California's tourists to promote the excursions as highlights of western vacations.

2. John L. Wiley, "History of Monrovia," (Pasadena, 1927), P. 97.

The organized excursion trips were by no means limited to Mount Lowe or the Balloon route. The Old Mission Trolley Trip took visitors to Pasadena, Glendora, and Mission San Gabriel, while the Triangle Trolley Trip carried sightseers from Los Angeles to Santa Ana, Huntington Beach, Long Beach, Point Firmin at San Pedro, and back to Los Angeles.

Completion of the line to San Bernardino brought the start of the Orange Empire Trolley Trip on January 3, 1915. The all-day trip took passengers through the beautiful orange grove country stretching eastward from Pomona and Covina to San Bernardino. Travelers stopped for lunch at the ornate Mission Inn.

Other trolley trips carried passengers to Redondo Beach's plunge and dance hall, both owned by the Pacific Electric, as well as to Casa Verdugo, a company operated Spanish restaurant in Glendale.

San Bernardino's Urbita Springs Park (later called Pickering Park) was also owned by the Pacific Electric and proved a major attraction even before the area's trolley lines were linked to Los Angeles. In 1912, when San Bernardino's population was approximately 13,000, a crowd of 15,000 was expected for the Fourth of July but an estimated 20,000 people packed the park. The San Bernardino Sun reported in its July 5 account:

Even this is but a crude guess, for exact figures were not available for the cars were still carrying passengers at midnight.

The park, incidentally, eventually became the site of Inland Center, a major shopping development.

The Big Red Cars rolled for service at many special and annual trips established from time to time.

The biggest special event served almost exclusively by the Pacific Electric was America's first international air meeting, held January 1 through 20, 1910, on table-like Dominguez Hill near Dominguez Junction where the San Pedro route branched from the Long Beach line. The meeting was the first to emphasize to Americans the potentials of airplanes as opposed to balloons and provided national publicity to a young aviator named Glenn Curtiss, later the founder of a major aircraft manufacturing company.

The Pacific Electric established special service and on the meeting's first day transported most of the 20,000 spectators lured by the curiosity of airplanes. Attendance increased daily and trains composed of three interurbans each sped to the area, arriving at the rate of one train every ten minutes. By the time the twenty-day event ended, it had been viewed by more than 500,000 people—most of whom traveled by Pacific Electric.[2]

---

3. Los Angeles Times, January 21, 1910.

This ad depicted the attractions of the "Poinsettia Route" tour, which took sightseers to points of interest near San Bernardino. (San Bernardino Public Library)

During the early years of the tours, the price of a ticket was $1.00 and passengers travelled approximately 100 miles. Advertisements heralded that the trolleys offered "100 miles for 100 cents."

Many trolley systems in America operated parks, hopefully making money not only from the concessions but also from the fares paid by people to reach the places. The Pacific Electric operated several such facilities.

The Magnolia Avenue line in Riverside carried visitors to Chemawa Park, just north of the Sherman Institute for Indians, and trolleys also served Riverside's Fairmount Park, once owned by the P. E. The company also owned the plunge and dance hall at Redondo Beach and Casa Verdugo, a popular Spanish restaurant in Glendale.

Special cars carried spectators and participants to the X Olympic shell races in 1932 at Long Beach's Marine Stadium, adjacent to the right-of-way to Newport Beach. As a boy, the author resided nearby the stadium. His mother gave him an Olympic souvenir cap (still one of his cherished possessions), and wearing it he watched the Big Red Cars bring passengers to the events.

Annual events in Southern California, where diversified community events were staged with pride and in quantity, received special attention from the Pacific Electric.

The first and most famous of the attractions served with special cars was the Tournament of Roses in Pasadena. The Big Red Cars traveled from almost every community to the New Year's day parade. Special trolleys also went to San Gabriel for the annual presentations of The Mission Play, a highly-romanticized version of life in early California written by the prolific John Stephen McGroarty, the state's poet laureate, a Los Angeles Times columnist, and one-time Democratic member of the United States House of Representatives.

When the Pomona line was completed in 1912, special cars began annual trips to the Los Angeles County Fair. Opening of the San Bernardino line in 1914 brought interurban service to the National Orange Show held each year in the city. As in the case of the fairgrounds at Pomona, rail service went directly to the gates of the show. Attendance at both events soared when they were served by trolley lines.

The production of low-priced automobiles popularized the family automobile trip. This, together with the production of better motion pictures and the invention of radio as attractions for leisure time, doomed the trolley excursions.

An attempt was made in 1928 to boost passenger volume by encouraging the pleasant tradition of family sightseeing trips through the Sunday Pass. Priced at $1.00, the "passes" permitted a passenger to ride an entire Sunday on the Big Red Car interurban lines. The program continued through most of the Depression, but the family automobile prevented its success.

World War II brought a new twist for sightseeing. The All-Year Club of Southern California, the advertising organization which helped bring the people that have jammed

A 1914 photograph shows a trolley navigating the sharp curves and steep grades on the Mount Lowe Railway.

the area, produced a series of pamphlets giving directions for using the regularly scheduled busses and electric interurbans for sightseeing. The pamphlets were distributed to the great influx of servicemen, few of whom had ever seen Southern California and, because of limited funds, might not have been able to visit points of interest.

Among the last special trips discontinued were those of the interurbans carrying passengers to the Catalina Island ship terminal in Los Angeles Harbor. The service was abandoned by the Metropolitan Transit Authority after it assumed control of interurban traffic in 1958.

The Balloon and Old Mission Trolley Trips fell victims to changing times in 1923 and the Orange Empire Trolley Trip was abandoned in 1929 after several years of existence on a weekly schedule. The famed Mount

A trolley rounds The Circular Bridge, one of the thrilling highlights of the Mount Lowe trip, in 1915. Pasadena, Al- *tadena, and surrounding communities stretch in the then-smogless distance. Note right-of-way to the left.*

Lowe trips ended after a 1936 fire destroyed most of the resort. The trolleys made their final special trips to the county fairgrounds at Pomona in 1950 even though regular passenger service on the route ended three years earlier. The interurbans took their last passengers to the biggest event of all, the Rose Parade, on New Year's Day of 1951—the year when passenger service to Pasadena was ended.

As the passenger routes of the Pacific Electric were discontinued during the years, members of various rail fan associations chartered interurban for nostalgic "good-byes" to the lines.

The last trip for the Big Red Cars was, appropriately, an excursion. In the early morning hours of April 9, 1961, the day after service officially ended on the Long Beach line, a two-car train chartered by the Electric Railway Historical Association carried rail fans from Long Beach to the Pacific Electric Building in Los Angeles and back down to Long Beach on the right-of-way once so heavily traveled by sightseers.

ABOVE: Passengers board the Big Red Cars at the Glendale station in 1910. The Glendale high-speed line was heavily-travelled during the years; commuters hailed its convenience.

(Craig Rasmussen Collection) BELOW: A trolleyman relaxes by a wooden-framed interurban on the Venice line in the 1940's. (Photograph by John Lawson)

16. The Trolleymen: My Red Coat, My Red Flag

The working hours for the conductors, motormen, mechanics, and other personnel who operated the Big Red Cars were long ones during the early days of trolleys and they remained long in comparison to other industries until shortly before the end of the interurban era.

Yet over the years the Pacific Electric employees developed an affection and enthusiasm for the system matched only by the passengers.

Many books of the early twentieth century extolling the virtues of Southern California living warned prospective migrants to assure themselves that they had saleable trades or professions before making the westward trek. Otherwise, some authors warned, men might be forced to take jobs as conductors on the trolleys. Gradually there were substantial increases not only in the prestige of working the Pacific Electric but also in the pay scales.

In 1901 the starting wage for motormen and conductors was eighteen cents an hour, with a pay scale increasing at the rate of one cent per hour annually until reaching top pay of twenty-two cents an hour. The pay was generally the same as that on trolley systems in other sections of the nation, but nevertheless the labor turnover was great as the men sought and found other occupations.[1]

The beginning pay was increased in 1903 to twenty-two cents an hour—a bonanza prompting the trolley workers to stage a fete at the Los Angeles car barns honoring Henry E. Huntington and his son, Howard, for their generosity. All employees evidently were not happy, for a union was organized under the impressive name of the Los Angeles Division of the Almagamated Association of Street Railway Employees of America. Leading the group was Lem Biddle, described by the Los Angeles Times on May 8, 1903, as a member of the "council of mischief makers."

An attempt at a strike proved futile and Henry Huntington summed up his feelings as follows:[2]

We have no quarrel with any unions and care little what such bodies are doing so long as they do not interfere with our work. If our workmen would organize a mutual benefit union, they would meet with no opposition from the railway companies. The trouble is that the unions are not organized for benefit but for trouble. This is well illustrated by the present instance . . .

1. Periodic studies by the United States Bureau of Labor Statistics reported the average wages for employees of electric streetcar systems in major cities.

2. Los Angeles Herald, April 25, 1903.

I object to unions because they are harmful to the men themselves. No one man who joins a union does so of his own volition. They are driven to it through fear, and trouble follows.

The low hourly wages did not necessarily mean low take home pay in contract to other sections of the nation. Most Red Car workers put in at least ten hours, six days a week. Time and a half for over forty hours was unheard of. This gave the average conductor or motor-

A 1931 issue of the Pacific Electric Magazine pictured a P. E. motorman, so familiar to commuters of the era, at the controls of a trolley in downtown Los Angeles.

Hail the Motorman! He of Good Judgment; Quick Eye; Steady Nerve.

I object to unions because they are harmful to the men themselves. No one man who joins a union does so of his own volition. They are driven to it through fear, and trouble follows.

The low hourly wages did not necessarily mean low take home pay in contract to other sections of the nation. Most Red Car workers put in at least ten hours, six days a week. Time and a half for over forty hours was unheard of. This gave the average conductor or motorman $13.20 weekly or an annual $686.40, approximately $100 more than the national average.

The Great Merger of 1911 and the subsequent influence of the Southern Pacific resulted in company policies designed to keep employees contented under the leadership of Paul Shoup, president of the new Pacific Electric. Previously an editor of Sunset Magazine when published by the Southern Pacific, in 1916 he initiated the Pacific Electric Magazine, a periodical which became popular with employees.

Shortly thereafter the Pacific Electric Club was formed. It served to develop fellowship within the system and to stage a variety of social activities. It was not designed to help negotiate for wage increases.

Pacific Electric conductors and operators in 1914 were receiving hourly pay starting at twenty-five and reaching thirty cents after five years on the job. This pay was for the actual working time; conductors and operators received fifteen cents an hour while waiting at a streetcar barn for an assignment.

The average Los Angeles trolley conductor or motorman was receiving $988 annually in 1914, according to a study by the United States Bureau of Labor Statistics. Despite the healthy increase in total pay since 1903, there was a turnover that year of thirty-one percent of the motormen and forty-four percent conductors who left for other employment. The Chicago elevated railroad, with comparable pay, had a turnover of only three percent for motormen and six percent for conductors. Nationally, however, the turnover in the labor force was much heavier, averaging ninety-four percent for motormen and conductors. Pay scales for trolley operators dipped to as low as fifteen cents an hour in Chattanooga, Tennessee.[3]

Part of the Southern California turnover in electric railroad employment undoubtedly came from the increasing range of other work opportunities developing as the area grew.

The turnover was a factor in the Pacific Electric's raising pay scales in 1917 to a starting wage of forty-one cents an hour and pay of forty-seven cents hourly after

three years with the company. This gave motormen and conductors nearly $1,500 annually for the six day week of sixty hours ordinarily worked.

By 1919 Los Angeles had achieved a reputation as a "no unions" city destined to continue for many years and the atmosphere was anything but conducive to Pacific Electric employees organizing for collective bargaining, even though the union brotherhoods had been formed by workers on the steam railroads. The P.E. conductors and motormen had formed, however, what they termed a "committee" to seek goals similar to those of unions. In the summer of 1919 the committee decided to call a strike.

The walkout started on August 15. The company contended that only 1,500 of its 5,000 employees left their jobs; the committee claimed the support was much greater. Members of the railroad brotherhood unions walked off their jobs in sympathy, stalling transcontinental train service. A court injunction eventually ordered them back to work.

The effect of the Pacific Electric strike was felt in varying degrees throughout Southern California. Approximately 5,000 beach-goers were stranded at Venice because of inadequate personnel to operate trolleys. Twenty-seven citrus packing plants at Redlands were forced to suspend operations because of the lack of Pacific Electric freight service.[4]

The company offered a twenty percent bonus over regular pay to personnel who would operate its cars.

As strike-breakers operated the Big Red Cars, P.E. Vice President H. B. Titcomb told a luncheon of Los Angeles businessmen:[5]

We were an open shop, we are an open shop today, and we are going to remain an open shop.

An so it was to be for years.

The strike committee's support dwindled and by mid-September Red Car service was back to normal.

The prosperous 1920's brought high morale to the system. Fringe benefits were increased. The Pacific Electric Club with dues of only twenty-five cents a month provided a wide range of activities for the employees. Within the club were separate organizations for bowling, baseball tournaments, rod and gun enthusiasts and musicians. In addition the club staged frequent dances and gave holiday parties. There was even a club auxiliary for the wives of Pacific Electric employees.

Employee benefits in 1928 included free transportation to work and reduced fares for other travel, $500

---

3. Reported in 1916 by the United States Bureau of Labor Statistics.

4. and 5. Los Angeles Examiner, August 19, 1919.

ABOVE: Technicians perform the maintenance work on an interurban during the 1950's at the P. E. yards near Seventh at the Los Angeles River in Long Beach. (Photo by Maxine Reams) RIGHT: Frank Nixon, father of President Nixon, posed for this picture while serving as a P. E. motorman on the Whittier line. (Nixon Family Collection) BELOW: Crewmen pose by "The Commodore," luxurious officers' car boasting a kitchen. The public could ride the car (for extra fare) in the 1940's for daily round-trip between Los Angeles and Newport Beach, where O. A. Smith, P. E. president, resided. (Carl B. Blaubach Collection)

1100 Designs Are Used in Punches

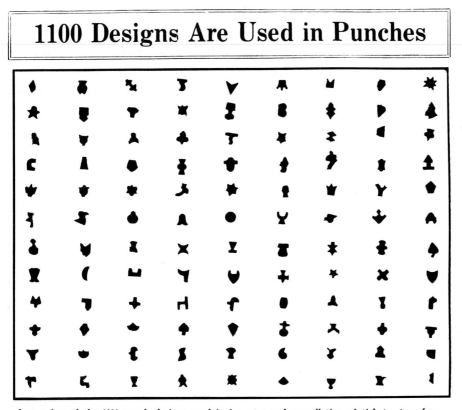

Just a few of the 1100 punch designs used in issuance and cancellation of tickets, transfers, etc., by our Conductors. Note the distinctive characteristics of each and imagine about a thousand more as equally dissimilar.

This illustration depicting the variety of punch designs that helped distinguish conductors appeared in the Pacific Electric Magazine. Designs provided a code to determine who issued tickets or transfers.

in group life insurance after a year's service a medical department treating employees for fifty cents to $1 monthly, and two weeks vacation after a year's service.[6]

The company also maintained the Pacific Electric Camp in the San Bernardino Mountains, where employees and their families could vacation at minimum costs. It offered study courses in subjects ranging from stenography to electrical engineering under the supervision of educators.

The columns of the Pacific Electric Magazine were filled with letters from passengers and quotations from newspapers attesting to the courteous and efficient service of the conductors and motormen.

The ultimate contribution to the employees' program was the four-story Pacific Electric Club Building, a $500,000 structure completed in 1929 on Los Angeles Street, adjacent to the Pacific Electric Building. The building soon became a center of company social activities, boasting a theatre for sound motion pictures, a ballroom, game rooms, and lounges furnished for women employees.

---

6. Pacific Electric Magazine, April 10, 1928.

Many trainmen found varying forms of achievement after leaving the company.

Frank Nixon worked as a motorman on the Whittier to Los Angeles line in 1907 and 1908. He met his future wife, Hannah Milhous, at a taffy pull in Whittier. They were married in 1908, and their son — Richard Milhous Nixon, a future President of the United States — was born in 1912 at Yorba Linda. The Nixon home was a short walk from the town's Pacific Electric station.

The Nixon family, its members informed the author, made occasional trips to Los Angeles via the Pacific Electric and rode the Big Red Cars from Yorba Linda to Whittier to visit the Milhous family. They alighted from the interurbans at Laurel Avenue and walked the half mile north to Whittier Boulevard, where the Milhous home was situated.

Richard Nixon, as a Whittier student and then attorney prior to entering public life, never commuted via the Red Cars. However, he did use the Motor Transit busses on Whittier Boulevard after the P. E. launched this service in the late 1920's and early 1930's.

Other Pacific Electric employees also won recognition.

Willard Wright, once a ticket seller in the main Los Angeles station, became a newspaper literary critic and subsequently famed under the pen name of S. S. Van Dyne as creator of the fictional detective Philo Vance. Joel Ogle, serving as a conductor on the Santa Ana Line while attending law school, liked the area and after passing the bar examination became the legal counsel for Orange County.

Issues of the Pacific Electric Magazine were filled with accounts of conductors and motormen who became doctors, lawyers, engineers, artists, and writers as the result of part-time studies.

Although the trainmen wore black uniforms, the men themselves were far from non-entities to the commuting public. Regular riders and the conductors exchanged pleasantries and in many cases were on first-name terms.

The company rules permitted conductors and motormen to choose their routes on a seniority basis. Thus an employee with seniority wanting a particular line could "bump" a newer man to obtain a route he wanted. The company itself could identify conductors by their ticket and transfer punchers. Each of the 1,100 conductors working at the peak of the Pacific Electric's operation had a puncher making a distinctive and identifying perforation on tickets.

The profile of the typical Pacific Electric employee from the start paralleled that of the average migrant to Southern California. The American Midwest, contributing most of Southern California's settlers, also provided the bulk of the Pacific Electric employees. The South and Northeast contributed employees in proportion to the general migration from those areas. There were also employees of mid-European derivation who, because of language difficulties, found a comfortable life in the mechanical departments.

In the early days the typical trolley employee was in his early twenties and frequently chose the work because it was readily available. As the years passed, the Pacific Electric offered security, better wages, and added fringe benefits, all helping to make a decline in the labor turnover. As the Red Car era neared its end, the average employee was a middle-aged person who counted many years of service with the line. He was safety conscious, loyal to the company, and knew most of his regular passengers by their names.

One of the highlights of employment with the Pacific Electric was the annual picnic at Redondo Beach where activities centered around the company-owned plunge. For those occasions, special trains of Red Cars took employees and their families to the fun. The Depression of the 1930's killed the company picnic and caused personnel cutbacks and wage reductions as passenger patronage declined. Pressures to form a union increased.

The Pacific Electric MAGAZINE

ISSUED MONTHLY BY THE EMPLOYES OF THE PACIFIC ELECTRIC RAILWAY

VOL. 1. LOS ANGELES, CALIFORNIA, JUNE 10, 1916. NO. 1

OUR FAMILY ROUND TABLE

The Pacific Electric Magazine is the family round table.

The employees of the Pacific Electric are one large family with many ties and many common interests. We work for a common purpose. Out of the community result thus achieved, we get individually our livelihood. Our common interest is and should be deep and earnest.

Team work is essential in this our common interest. It is best done when the members of the team know and appreciate each other; know and appreciate each other's efforts; know and appreciate the family problems as a whole.

With our prosperity as a family, comes our individual prosperity; never otherwise. Beyond this material gain through more closely knit ties, comes something else worth while. Our life lies largely in our work. It can be made more interesting, more enjoyable, if the horizon of every employee can be widened to a fuller view of the activities of all.

We cannot accomplish these views by the good family way of sitting down at dinner together and talking things over. But we can make a family round table out of this Magazine, and in spirit get together once a month.

Enliven this round table as you like with good stories, items of family interest, anecdotes and personal notes, and with well considered suggestions, concisely expressed, in behalf of our common cause.

The editor will need the help of the whole Pacific Electric family. He may censor our literary gems, or sidetrack our finest efforts, but have in mind that he has only eight pages to reflect all our views and news. And go on helping him. It won't do any good to obliterate the editor; perhaps we couldn't get another.

The round table is ready; you are invited to fall to!

Paul Shoup

First issue of the Pacific Electric Magazine on June 10, 1916, carried P. E. president Paul Shoup's message hailing the publication as "Our Family Roundtable."

Amendments to the Federal Railway Labor Act in 1934, among the long-overdue social reforms guided by President Franklin Roosevelt, cleared the way for a union. After passage of the act, P.E. president David W. Pontius called a mass meeting of employees at the Olympic Auditorium in Los Angeles where he dramatically told the cheering trainmen that the law permitted them, if they choose, to form a union.

The Pacific Electric Brotherhood of Railroad Trainmen was formed as an outgrowth of the law.

The most effective strike on the Pacific Electric

system started on May 24, 1946, as the union sought wage adjustments. The Big Red Cars were quietly placed in barns as 2,700 conductors and operators along with 4,500 other employees stopped work. A report that trolleys were left standing in the streets at the strike hour was denied indignantly by P.E. president O. A. Smith, who retorted:

Our men are not of that type.

Traffic in Los Angeles, still relying heavily on the Red Cars, came to a standstill. The 500,000 commuters who used the Pacific Electric turned to car pools, hitch-hiking, and chartered busses. Automobile traffic in Los Angeles was seventy-five percent above normal and parking lots were so crowded that motorists happily paid the $2.00 fine to park all day on streets. During the crisis, Pacific Electric employees obligingly agreed to operate two garbage trains daily from Los Angeles to hog farms near Fontana to avert a health menace.

The strike was settled on May 26 with a pay raise of 18½ cents an hour, and labor peace reigned for eleven years.

Most of the Big Red Cars had been retired in favor of busses when the next strike came on December 1, 1957. This time the employer was Metropolitan Coach Lines, the company that acquired the commuter service from the Pacific Electric in 1953 and increased emphasis on busses.

By the time the strike ended on January 24, 1958, it was obvious that commuters no longer relied heavily on public transportation. Estimates showed that only 250,000 riders were affected—less than half the number eleven years before. The automobile was being so widely used by commuters that while the strike crowded downtown Los Angeles parking facilities, the lots by this time were so numerous that they could accommodate the cars.

The union wanted a thirty-five cent an hour wage increase and a forty-hour week. Metropolitan Coach Lines countered with an offer of twenty-one cents an hour more over a period of a year and continuation of the forty-eight hour work week traditional in the transportation field.

The settlement approved by a vote of 511 to 490, a narrow margin of twenty-one votes, accepted the twenty-one cents an hour coupled with the forty hour week that had been prevalent for years in other industries.

In a sense the issue of hours really no longer mattered to private enterprise, for the Los Angeles Metropolitan Transportation Authority, a recently-formed state agency, was to assume operation of the commuter system in just forty days.

But to the drivers, it probably meant much more

than showed on the surface. Touching the controls of a Big Red Car was one thing, but forty-eight hours of wrestling the steering wheel of the large busses replacing the interurbans was an entirely different ordeal.

However, we must remember that the conductors, motormen, and mechanics were only part of the team that kept the interurbans rolling.

The other part of the team were laborers that kept the right-of-ways in a safe condition for the cars.

In the summer of 1943 Mexican-American youths clashed in street fights with Anglo-Saxon servicemen in a series of riots accentuating a long-standing black mark on ethnic relations in Southern California. These tensions so apparent in the 1940's were spawned a half century before when laborers were imported from Mexico to build electric and steam railroad tracks as well as to work in the area's farms and citrus groves. It is from these workers that the majority of Mexican-Americans of twentieth century Los Angeles are descended. Contrary to popular opinion, few are descendants of the Mission Indians (who were virtually extinct by the late nineteenth century) or the Spanish who first settled California.

As for the Mexican railway laborers, few newcomers who arrived enthusiastically in a nation heralded for its freedoms and opportunities received harsher receptions at the hands of their hosts. There have been few instances in the United States where a longer period has been required to heal the misunderstandings among Americans of different backgrounds.

A similar problem developed when Chinese were brought to America to build the Central Pacific. Hanging from the sides of precarious cliffs in the Sierra Nevada range, they hewed from solid rock the right-of-ways to hold the transcontinental tracks. Their pay for this work was so low that it introduced the idiom "coolie wages" into the English language. The tracks were built eastward by Irish laborers, who also were poorly paid by standards of the day. Other workers were angered at their willingness to accept low pay, but by the start of the twentieth century both groups of immigrants were being accepted into other phases of American community life.

It remained for the Mexican to provide the low-priced labor for construction of Southern California's interurban lines. Clad in a red jacket to alert approaching interurbans of his presence and propping a red flag on

RIGHT: This feature in a 1926 issue of the Pacific Electric Magazine showed how P. E. employees helped the company's Mexican-American workers, but it did not deal with effective means for helping the people.

140

SANTA FREELY CARES FOR MEXICAN KIDDIES

Conductors' Accounts' Bureau young ladies again did their bit in providing Santa with gifts to Mexican children. During spare moments they made several hundred weird and amusing species of stocking cats. From left to right are seen: Irene Brundige, Jean Cochrane, Esther Craig, Edith Simeon, Helen Spafford, Josephine Livingston, Gertrude Hiles, Esther Quast, Winnie Littlefield and Blanche DeVore.
Below is seen Miss Peterson gladdening the hearts of a host of young folks.

ENGINES and cars and wagons; balls and marbles and dolls; games and books and candies— and—

Swarthy little innocent faces, five hundred or more, abeam with joy that would make your heart glad to behold.

Such, thanks to the generous response of Pacific Electric employees, was the Christmas which gladdened and made joyous the lives of young Mexican Kiddies living in the Camps of the Company throughout the system.

Following quickly Club Manager Vickrey's appeal for toys and clothing for these young worthies came liberal and worthwhile donations from all points of the system. Within only a few days the amount received assured the best visit from old Santa yet experienced by these young people. Following the Company's practice candies, nuts and fruits were also distributed along with donated gifts.

As usual the bulk of the work of distributing fell to the lot of the Misses Karr and Peterson, and for days these ladies, who devote their entire time throughout the year looking to the comfort, health and well-being of Mexican families, were busily engaged in getting ready for the task of distribution. Through their thorough knowledge of the status of every family, number of children, ages, etc., the gifts were all distributed by Christmas day to the best advantage, just as any wise old Santa would do.

He knew that she would thank him not,
He cared not for her scorn;
He offered her his street car seat,
To keep her off his corn.

So you are lost? Why didn't you hold on to your mother's skirt?"
"I couldn't reach it," sobbed the child.

HEIGHT OF WAVES

We often heard exaggerated stories of towering waves during sea storms. Frequently we hear stories of waves having reached almost impossible heights. Speaking generally, these tales are just about as authentic as those told by Mr. City Fisherman as to the exact size of his catch.

As a matter of fact, it is extraordinary for a wave to attain a height of 70 feet, while the average size is considerably less. The mountainous waves encountered in the North Atlantic usually measure 40 feet, although the upward-shooting, quick-falling ones attain greater altitudes. The big waves of the North Pacific rarely measure more than 30 feet. The highest waves ever met in the South Pacific did not exceed 50 feet. Those in the Mediterranean seldom reach a height of 20 feet.—Exchange.

Trolleyman Dewey Tingler waits for an approaching car in Southern Pasadena during the 1920's. P. E. trolleymen came from many backgrounds. (Jeannie Boggs Collection)

the right-of-way for extra protection, the Mexican soon became a familiar person at work on the area's railroad tracks.

Just as hoards of materials were assembled to expedite building of the railroads, gangs of Mexican laborers paid "coolie wages" were brought to the scene to do the work. Mexico teemed with men eager for new opportunities. The nation at this time was convulsed in the throes of revolutions and political upheavals as its people struggled against the regime of dictator Porfirio Diaz. Labor recruitment was easy for companies in Los Angeles specializing in bringing men from Mexico for work on the railroad lines.

The procedure was for the labor recruiter, called a "rustler" because his task was to herd men to America, to be sent from Los Angeles to northern Mexico, an area where living conditions at the time were particularly difficult. Studies conducted by the graduate school of the University of Southern California during the peak of migration and continuing through the 1940's detailed the treatment and plight of the Mexicans.[7]

The recruiters promised wages truthfully more than double those a man could receive in Mexico—although this was only half of the usual pay for comparable work by non-railway employers in Southern California. Contracts

provided transportation to Los Angeles and, if the men worked for a stipulated period of one or two years, the return trip to Mexico. The studies showed that approximately half who came to the United States worked their full terms and returned to Mexico, where they used their savings to invest in farms or businesses. The others remained on the railroads or took different jobs in Southern California.

Wages in Mexico at the time ranged from twenty-five cents to fifty cents daily. By 1910 the Pacific Electric was paying laborers $1.50 to $1.75 for a work day of approximately ten hours. The pay included quarters in a trackside camp which in the early days ordinarily consisted of barracks or tents for single men. Later, small frame cottages were provided for families. The pay scale, not including quarters, for similar labor at the time was $2.50 to $3.00 daily. The Mexicans who came to Southern California in complete innocence of local standards quickly were tagged "scale cutters" and were disliked by other workers.

Criticism was leveled at the railroad for its inclusion of living quarters in its pay scale. By 1913 the Mexican laboring on a non-rail job was paying approximately $5.50 monthly for a tiny family cottage. The U.S.C. studies showed the Pacific Electric laborers actually were paying $13.50 monthly for their "free" quarters in company camps. The "bargain" accommodations accounted for the lower pay scale.

"It is clear from these facts why the railroads prefer to furnish houses for their employees," one U.S.C. study concluded.

"All other races meet the Mexicans with an attitude of contempt and scorn (because of their willingness to accept the company housing and wages)," another U.S.C. study observed. "The Mexicans respond to this attitude with one of defiance, pride, hate, and extreme dislike. They are clannish . . . consequently the spread of American customs among them is very slow and their amalgamation and assimilation does not proceed rapidly."

A solution to the problem proposed in one university study was "abolition of the system of stimulating immigration (by the recruiters) now employed by the railroad labor agencies."

"Until this is done," the study concluded, "the normal forces of supply and demand cannot operate to give the Mexicans a living wage. Only when the Mexican laborer is enabled to demand and receive an adequate wage will it be possible for him to raise his plane of living."

A defense presented to the practice of employing the Mexicans was that the railroads did provide regular jobs while work in many other fields was on a casual basis.

---

7. The U.S.C. studies quoted in this chapter are principally "A Survey of the Mexicans in Los Angeles," a thesis presented by William Wilson McEuen in 1914 to the Department of Economics and Sociology, and "Second Generation Mexicans in Belvedere," a thesis prepared by Mary Lanigan in 1932 for the Department of Sociology.

To Huntington's credit, the policy initiated when his first lines were built was to pay more than the prevailing wage for railroad laborers. The public expressed surprise at his payment of $1.85 daily, nearly a third more than the going rate, when construction of the Alhambra line started in 1901.[8] Two years later wages fell to $1.00 daily and the Mexican laborers attempted to form a union. In April, 1903, approximately 500 struck and left their jobs; 300 refused to join the walkout. Huntington broke the strike by hiring unemployed laborers desperate for jobs.[9]

While the Pacific Electric refused to meet the scales of non-railway employers, it could and apparently did pay more than other railroads, all of which followed the practice of using Mexican laborers. When Henry Huntington rushed to lay his tracks at San Pedro in 1903, a Southern Pacific official expressed amazement at the availability of so many workers to complete the job in record time.

"The Southern Pacific brings 155 Mexicans in," joked a Pacific Electric official, "and we hire 156 of them."[10]

Critics, mainly social workers and anti-railway newspapers, fired verbal volleys against both Huntington and his contemporaries because of conditions in the railroad camps. Editorialized The Los Angeles Record:[11]

The paternalism of Huntington, proudly acclaimed as the fairest kind of treatment of the ignorant Mexicans who are brought from the south to build the electric lines, is being scrutinized by public officials.

Dr. J. Powers, a public health official, and a county health inspector identified by the newspapers only as Mr. Quierola, then visited the Pacific Electric camp near Compton and expressed indignation over sanitary conditions.

"These people are not living like civilized beings," the doctor angrily told a reporter. "I counted over 100 people who live in these shacks, of which there were not over eight." Quierola added that "the conditions would not be tolerable in a stable."

After public and official pressure had been exerted, the Pacific Electric began to upgrade the facilities. By 1925 the company had established twenty-two "model" section camps throughout Southern California. The July 28, 1928 issue of the Pacific Electric Magazine, published for California employees, gave this description of the company's program:

8. Alhambra Advocate, October 9, 1901.

9. Los Angeles Herald, April 25, 1903.

10. Los Angeles Herald, April 6, 1903.

11. Los Angeles Record, April 6, 1904.

Laborers "recruited" from Mexico work on the streetcar tracks in downtown Los Angeles during the early rail construction era. Most railroads in Southern California relied on the Latin-Americans as a source of cheap labor.

Thriving communities did not look favorably upon the housing of these (Mexican) people within their city confines, and citizens of many communities exercised much effort to prevent their becoming established.

During recent years, however, due to the great thought and effort made in making these camps models of modern community living, the agitation has subsided.

Today, due solely to the intelligence that was employed in building, maintaining, and supervising these camps they are no longer looked upon with disfavor but on the contrary are pointed out as an achievement . . . truly, the passer-by today sees in the 22 Mexican camps of the Pacific Electric both neatness and orderliness among lawn, shrub and trees surrounding the buildings.

Despite the pride the company took in its camps, concern was expressed over the people themselves in a 1927 article in the Pacific Electric Magazine. Referring to the Mexican railway laborers as the "humble and conscientious foreigner," the article reported that "after careful investigation to learn the truth . . . it was realized that careful supervision (of the Mexican employees) was necessary. The big task of the Pacific Electric was to educate these immigrants in cleanliness and right living."

While the camps with their careful supervision were considered "models" (at least by the P. E.), the rented housing chosen by Mexican laborers in preference to the company's facilities were a far cry from model dwellings. In fact, one U.S.C. study described such a home "of the better class" in these words:

These habitations are built of rough one by twelve (inch) pine boards . . . on end and the cracks battened. Only a thin board partition divides one habitation from another and privacy is therefore lacking. This sacrificing of privacy with the resulting tendencies toward crime and immorality is one of the worst features of these barrack-like habitations . . . the kitchens are six by ten feet and have as a permanent fixture a small cook stove in one corner which was ordinarily in fair condition . . . the other room, which served as a sleeping and living room, was ordinarily furnished with one bed and one or two chairs . . . there were four toilets for twenty-six (family) units.

Even the average Pacific Electric employee with an Anglo-Saxon background failed to understand the plight of the Latin-American laborers. For example, the January 10, 1926, issue of the Pacific Electric Magazine carried an illustrated article telling how P. E. employees gathered and distributed toys for "... swarthy little innocent faces, five hundred or more, abeam with joy that would make your heart glad to behold.... Such, thanks to the generous response of Pacific Electric employees, was the Christmas which gladdened and made joyous the lives of young Mexican Kiddies living in the Camps of the Company throughout the system...."

The article failed to mention that a drive for adequate wages for these laborers, many of whom had difficulty speaking English, would have given them funds so that they would not need to face the humiliation of accepting charity to make Christmas pleasant for their children.

The great problem—not recognized either by the university researchers or the railroads—was that an attempt was being made to impose Anglo-Saxon standards of morality and living onto a foreign culture without giving its people the full participation in the various phases of society. By isolating the Mexicans in camps or substandard sections of the city, yet expecting the people to conform to unfamiliar patterns, a volcanic situation was created and would boil, below the surface, until the inevitable confrontations to demand the social and economic rights that they should have been receiving through the years.

As the California-born children of the Mexican immigrants matured, the youngsters naturally sought living standards enjoyed by their Anglo-Saxon schoolmates and depicted in the motion pictures. This craving for the American way of life played an immense part in sowing the seeds of dissatisfaction.

Not until the 1960's did the Mexican-Americans actively demand their rights, and ironically this movement of the

A viaduct carried autos over the Pacific Electric's private right-of-way near Vineyard Junction, in West Los Angeles. (Stephen D. Maguire Collection)

Chicanos began under the leadership of Cesar Chavez in the predominantly agricultural San Joaquin Valley. Such organized action more logically should have begun in Los Angeles, with its immense population of Mexican-Americans. It is also strange that such a movement did not begin earlier, since it was logical that as the California-born children of the Mexican immigrants matured, they would naturally seek living standards enjoyed by Anglo-Saxon schoolmates and depicted in motion pictures.

The years between the building of the Pacific Electric and the beginning of the Chicano era brought many changes, including many Anglo-Saxons who were wiser and more tolerant after observing the need for understanding in a world shaken by racial and international tensions.

As the Big Red Car era neared its end, the group which had helped to build the line was recognized as part of the "family." A column in the Pacific Electric Magazine during the 1950's, "Senior Employees Fellowship," was written by a Latin-American. A Mexican laborer, retiring after long years of service, told the publication's editor that he would:

Treasure in my heart every kind smile and handshake of every chief of mine, and it is gratifying to look back and see only smiling faces. May God bless them! I only wish that my heart could be a sort of mirror where they could see the reflection of their kind souls!

Another retiring Latin-American jokingly told the editor that his plans included writing the pleasant memories of his association with the Pacific Electric under the title of "My Red Jacket, a Red Flag, and My Shovel."

An Alhambra-San Gabriel interurban is pictured in 1941. Cars turned at Sierra Vista Junction to Alhambra, or could *continue to San Marino, where tracks went to the Huntington estate. (Stephen D. Maguire Collection)*

17. A Bride for the Builder

Huntington's palatial home at San Marino, started in 1906, was completed in 1910. Into it flooded priceless books, paintings and other art treasurers purchased throughout the world by his agents. Surveying his 200-acre estate, crowned by a Georgian-Colonial manse amidst rare plants, he announced his retirement. Henry Huntington then entered onto one of the most active retirements in the financial world.

Although he had abandoned the interurban field, he retained his land companies, the Los Angeles Railway, and the Pacific Light and Power Company. He also served on the board of directors of nearly fifty leading corporations, including the Southern Pacific, Hammond Lumber Company, Minneapolis and Saint Louis Railway Company, the Chesapeake and Ohio Railway Company, and the Newport News Shipbuilding and Drydock Company. Huntington shared the controlling interest in the latter company with his uncle's widow, Arabella.

This is the way Henry Huntington's estate at San Marino appeared shortly after its completion in 1910.

While the Pacific Electric struggled with rising costs and automobile competition, Huntington's holdings were in companies that paid dividends.[1]

A day in 1913 would find early riser Huntington usually breakfasting at 7:00 a.m. after which he rode from his estate in his private electric interurban car, the Alabama, built in 1904 and named for Arabella Huntington's native state. After reaching the Pacific Electric Building he would direct the destinies of his companies.[2]

New York City found him a frequent visitor for meetings of the boards of directors of various companies demanding his presence. After a business trip in April of 1913 he sailed for Europe. Newspapers considered the trip a vacation. It proved to be a honeymoon.

Word was flashed from Paris on July 17 that Henry Huntington had married his Uncle Collis' widow, Arabella. The New York Times' headline on the story reported "Mrs. C. P. Huntington Weds in the Family." [3]

A small group of friends attended a reception and saw the happy Huntingtons off on an automobile tour through the south of France. At the time of their marriage Henry Huntington was 63 years old and Arabella (who had been 32 years younger than Collis) was 60 years of age. The marriage was hailed in the newspapers as ideal, for the pair had much in common: both collected fine are works and their business interests were parallel. In addition to their large holdings in several companies, the pair had joined forces in 1901 to give the Princess Hatzfeld, sister of Henry Huntington's first wife, a total of $3 million to drop her claim for a larger share of the Collis Huntington estate. During the rail magnate's divorce proceedings several years before, newspapers speculated that the 1900 separation stemmed from a family dispute over the estate.

The marriage of Henry and Arabella came as no surprise in Los Angeles. Their engagement was rumored as early as two weeks after the divorce when Huntington visited New York City for the Southern Pacific board of directors meeting following his futile attempt to secure the Los Angeles River franchise.

At the time Arabella Huntington had vigorously denied the rumor of an impending marriage.

"Why as you can see, I am still in mourning for my husband," she told newspaper reporters, who described her as wearing a "magnificent" black lace gown and a pendant of pearls and small diamonds when they called on her. "My thoughts naturally are far removed from matrimony, and besides, Mr. Henry E. Huntington is my late husband's nephew . . ." [4]

Reporters who quizzed Huntington at his Jonathan Club residence (atop the Pacific Electric Building in Los Angeles) also received a denial. So vigorously did Huntington deny the rumor, wrote reporters, that his glasses fell off.[5]

On their return from Europe early in 1914 Henry and Arabella began to divide their time between San Marino, which he preferred, and New York City, her favorite. Directed by William Hetrich, a young Bavarian horticulturist retained in 1904, a host of laborers created a lavish oriental garden in a ravine in time for her arrival.

To facilitate traveling the Huntingtons acquired two private railroad cars, the San Marino No. 1 and the San Marino No. 2. These were housed on the grounds of the San Marino estate and reached transcontinental lines over a private spur connecting to the Pacific Electric tracks in San Marino. One car was equipped for the comfort of Mr. and Mrs. Huntington; the other was

1. According to listings of his holdings as reported in "Walker's Manual of California Securities and Directory of Directors" and other financial journals of the period.

2. A typical day for Huntington was described in "The Trolley Man and The Angel Hosts," in the April, 1913, issue of Sunset Magazine. The article by Frances A. Goff was based on an interview with Huntington at San Marino.

3. New York Times, July 17, 1913.

4. and 5. Los Angeles Examiner, April 6, 1906.

outfitted for their servants and had kitchen facilities.

Mrs. Huntington was described as a gracious hostess at San Marino, and her charm added to the natural beauty and architectural grandeur of the estate. As her hearing became impaired, she learned to read lips and put the art to good use at receptions. When guests arrived, intimates at a distance would mouth the names of the arrivals so that she could give a personal greeting even to those she had met only once before.

In 1915 Huntington's health began to fail and he delegated more authority to others in managing his properties. At the same time his energies turned more and more to the acquisition of books and masterpieces.

Many wealthy men collected books and paintings. Henry Edwards Huntington collected libraries and art galleries.

An interurban pulls onto Fair Oaks Avenue in Pasadena for service on the Los Angeles via Oak Knoll Route in 1941. Cars went in Fair Oaks to the right-of-way in Huntington Drive. (Stephen D. Maguire Collection)

KILLED, 72.	VICTIMS OF STREET CARS *In Los Angeles and Its Immediate Vicinity* IN THE PAST 27 MONTHS.	INJURED, 614.

DEATH DEALING CARS ROUSE CITIZENS' IRÉ.

MAN THROWN THIRTY FEET THROUGH THE AIR.

Photo-diagram showing the manner in which Bohmil Hadacek was hurled thirty feet to his death by a Santa Ana car near Watts Station. The lower picture is a photograph of the unfortunate young man.

Bohmil Hadacek.

TOO HIGH SPEED, PEOPLE PROTEST.

Three People Killed Near Watts During Past Few Weeks by Huge Cars.

EMPLOYES CHARGED WITH CARELESSNESS.

Bohmil Hadacek of Latin station

'NOTHING TO THESE

SOCIETY FAVORITE'S DUAL LIFE IS REVEALED.

Former Actor and Entertainer of New York's "400" Is in Jail on Charge of Stealing Costly Clothing.

[Special by Leased Wire, the Longest in the World.]
NEW YORK, March 25.—Revelations of a daring dual life of five years' standing have followed the arrest and imprisonment of John Wilmer Martine, ex-actor, linguist, man about town, member of the Y. M. C. A., and the friend and entertainer of noted society people, both in this country and

18. When Death Rode the Rails

The immense size of the interurbans and their speed combined for spectacular and disastrous crashes when accidents did occur. With the inception of the trolleys, collisions involving them became a popular topic of public conversation and a major source of newspaper headlines. The novelty of the interurban, the principal means for travel between the communities, naturally attracted attention in an age when bicycles and horses dominated the streets.

The initial problem of shock to horses was apparent in this account of a trolley's arrival shortly after completion of the extension to Alhambra: [1]

There was a little excitement in front of Crow and Drake's store Monday evening. As the electric car approached, James Montgomery's horse did a circus act, turning almost a back somersalt, his head being caught under the shafts of the buggy. He was loosened and there was no damage to anything.

When the Pacific Electric opened its Long Beach route in 1902 a trolley car managed to crash into a tally-ho and further enliven that busy Independence Day. Its driver, Robert Carpenter, escaped with minor injuries.

On being formed in 1910 the Los Angeles Board of Public Utilities initiated a practice of tallying streetcar accidents within the city limits. Before it discontinued the compilations as automobile accidents became of greater frequency and concern in ensuing years, it recorded some interesting facts concerning trolley mishaps.

Other electric interurban car victims were not so fortunate, however. The newspapers reported the tragedies in great detail, much to the pleasure of the reading public which in most cases had few other exciting events in that less tense age.

The Big Red Cars, because of their size and speed, were much more deadly than the slower local trolleys, the board noted. In 1915 the local streetcars were involved in accidents injuring 5,668 people and killing twelve people but the interurbans, with less trackage in Los Angeles, were comparatively more lethal by hurting 659 and taking eleven lives. Compared to other cities of America, however, Los Angeles was relatively safe for trolley passengers. New York City, Boston, and San Francisco averaged one death for every 6.8 million to 7.9 million passengers carried. The rate for Los Angeles was one death for every 30 million passengers.

After studies in 1913, the board's engineers concluded that "men deliberately take greater chances than women" in boarding trolleys. They reported that seventy-six percent of those injured while climbing aboard trolleys were men. They found, however, that women accounted for sixty per-

cent of those injured while alighting from electric cars. The engineers suggested that the feminine accident rate might be reduced if women "exercised due care in alighting, holding the car . . . with their left hands . . . and facing backwards" as they made their departure

A board study showed that in 1913 forty-three percent of those killed by trolleys were pedestrians. Twenty percent who died were attempting to board or leave a car, while twenty-four percent were riding in automobiles or horse-drawn wagons when fatally injured. The remaining percentage represented victims of miscellaneous accidents, including on-the-job mishaps to trolley employees.

As the number of horseless carriages increased, they became involved in a proportionately greater number of accidents, the Los Angeles board discovered. Studies showed that in 1912 automobiles were involved in forty-four percent of the accidents. A year later gas buggies figured in fifty-five percent of the accidents. In 1912, horse-drawn vehicles were involved in fifteen percent of the trolley collisions but by 1914 they were connected with only six percent of the mishaps.

Many tragic accidents occurred when pedestrians decided to use the Pacific Electric tracks for shortcuts. The right-of-ways were attractive for walking since sidewalks were few. A typical such accident occurred in early 1906 and involved Bohmil Hadacer, 20, strolling on the tracks near Watts when a Big Red Car came out of the darkness and hit him.

"The man was thrown thirty feet," The Los Angeles Examiner reported, "falling on his head with such force that his neck was broken." [2]

Newspaper accounts usually gave minute and frequently gruesome details of the accidents because of the public's immense interest. Newspaper crusades against railroads in general, highly popular in the trust-busting era of President Theodore Roosevelt, also called for accentuating interurban accidents. The pro-labor Los Angeles Record based many attacks against interurbans on its contention that company owners forced employees to operate the trolleys at excessive speed and were interested primarily in profits instead of human lives. William Randolph Hearst's Los Angeles Examiner conducted a campaign against electric interurbans on its general policy of opposing the railroads. Hearst was a violent enemy of the Southern Pacific in general and Collis P. Huntington in particular. The Examiner frequently reminded readers of the uncle-nephew relationship between Collis and Henry Huntington when it criticized the Pacific Electric during its early years.

---

1. Alhambra Advocate, July 19, 1902.

2. Los Angeles Examiner, March 26, 1906

In reporting the death of a man who had been walking along the electric interurban tracks near Compton, The Examiner complained that "31 persons have been killed by the electric cars . . . and 231 injured since January 1, 1902" [3] As part of criticisms of both the Pacific Electric and the Los Angeles Pacific, the anti-railroad newspapers frequently ran box scores on accidents. However, the journalists seldom felt obligated to note when the accidents involved negligence on the part of the victims.

On the other hand, coroner's juries in many fatal accident cases found that comparatively inexperienced men operated the big electric cars at high rates of speed.

It became an assumption with the motormen on the speeding interurbans that pedestrians knew the danger of the trolleys. On the contrary, the public maintained its faith in the motormen and the wonderful technology of the interurban and thought the big cars could grind to a stop with a minimum of notice.

Nila J. Knagenhjelm, 61, paused late one afternoon in 1905 on the tracks of the Redondo line of the Los Angeles Pacific to tie a shoe string. The motorman of an approaching car rang his bell as a warning. Apparently preoccupied with his shoe or believing that the car was on the opposite track, Knagenhjelm failed to move. The motorman applied the brakes, but it was too late. The trolley hurled the victim twenty-five feet through the air to his death. [4]

Faith in the motorman's ability to stop his trolley in time to avoid an accident paid off in at least one incident. One evening in 1906, T. E. Taylor, his pockets bulging with $300, was walking near the Monrovia line tracks as he returned to work at the Lucky Baldwin Ranch at Santa Anita. A man approached him in the darkness and displayed a gun.

"Put your money on the ground or I'll blow a hole through you," the unwelcome stranger informed Mr. Taylor. The ranch hand paused a moment, mulling over the chances of saving his money as well as his life. He saw the welcome headlight of an approaching interurban.

Taylor promptly stepped between the tracks pointing out to the bandit that if he carried out his threat it would certainly cause the trolley to stop. The bandit then would be arrested for murder, he argued, when the curious crowd swarmed off the interurban. The bandit made a quick decision and disappeared into the darkness. The motorman, sighting the man on the track, screeched to a halt. Mr. Taylor boarded the interurban and rode it to safety. [5]

An electric interurban made a spectacular and gory end in 1915 for a man who jumped in front of a speeding trolley near Redlands. An investigation showed that the victim had financial problems and for an unknown reason chose a most unconventional means to make his exit from the world. [6]

At least one accident resulted in improved hospital attention for the injured after the victim of an unusual electric interurban mishap received medical care only after considerable delay. Thomas Smiley, identified by the Long Beach Press only as "one of the best known characters in town," had been quietly enjoying a night-time trip on the trolley from Los Angeles. As the interurban car neared Sixth Street and American Avenue, he arose from his seat, walked leisurely down the aisle to the vestibule, and stepped from the speeding car as though he thought it had stopped. The alarmed conductor vainly tried to grab him.

The interurban screeched to a stop. The horrified trolley crewmen and passengers raced back to the lifeless heap on the ground. Smiley was severely injured not only from the fall but also from the impact of hitting an electric power pole after his unexplained exit. The ribs on his left side were broken and his lung was punctured.

There were "great fears," The Press reported, that he would not recover.

The accident stirred a campaign for more efficient procedures at the county hospital, when after being rushed for treatment to Los Angeles on an interurban, Smiley was refused admission to the facility because of the late hour. He was forced to spend the night on a cot in the police station.

The victim, returned to Long Beach two weeks later, was described as "not entirely recovered but out of danger" despite his ordeal. Meanwhile, authorities at the hospital pledged improved emergency service as a result of the incident. [7]

The technology of reproducing photographs in newspapers was not sufficiently advanced during the early part of the twentieth century to permit wide use of pictures of the accidents. Editors remedied the situation by utilizing artists' sketches of the most spectacular crashes. Cartoons and editorials in the anti-railway newspapers shifted the blame for accidents onto the executives of the interurban companies. Trolley operators were treated as helpless tools of the magnates, who were pictured as threatening employees with the loss of their jobs if they did not run the electric cars at top speed in order to maintain schedules and thus assure passenger revenue.

Much blame for accidents actually was traced to the companies' willingness, as well as necessity because of the newness of the technology of the trolley, to hire inexperienced interurban operators and trust them at the throttles before

3. Los Angeles Examiner, March 22, 1903.

4. Los Angeles Examiner, July 6, 1905.

5. Los Angeles Examiner, April 6, 1906.

6. San Bernardino Sun, March 20, 1915.

7. Long Beach Press, December 13 and 27, 1902.

adequate training. Typical of such accidents was one in which a Pacific Electric interurban crashed into a Salt Lake Railroad work train, killing one passenger. Blame was placed on the interurban operator, and J. L. Loweman, foreman of a coroner's jury, added in a report of findings: [8]

We further censure the Pacific Electric Railway Co. for placing two new and inexperienced men in charge of that car.

Many of the accidents resulted from tragic misunderstandings. Typical of such incidents was one in early 1906 at Long Beach which occurred as Mrs. F. C. Smith and Miss Mary Griswold started to cross Third Street at Cedar Avenue as a trolley approached. The electric car paused as though to stop and the women hesitated. The trolley resumed speed as the operator assumed the women recognized the danger. Miss Griswold, however, thought the car was stopping and walked onto the tracks. Even though the motorman jammed on the brakes, the car hit the woman and killed her instantly. [9]

The general public was not the only group involved in accidents as a result of the coming of the interurban. As with any type of equipment distinguished by weight and moving parts, there were many dangers to employees. Despite company safety campaigns there were many injuries and some deaths. A 1907 accident took the life of W. D. Holliday, a Pacific Electric track foreman who, preoccupied with his work, stepped in front of a speeding interurban.[10] Motorman Houston Sellers was fortunate enough to survive a 1906 accident that occurred when his head struck an electric power pole as he was leaning out of his moving interurban near Compton. [11]

Safety education campaigns were intensified annually, but accidents involving employees continued virtually until the demise of the Big Red Cars. While many injuries came from moving equipment, others resulted from the basic technology of the interurban, electricity. Arthur L. Hatch, operator of an electric sub-station on the Long Beach line and a veteran of thirty-four years on the job, touched a 15,-000 volt line in 1953. He died thirty-seven hours later .

The accidents that came with arrival of the horseless carriage eventually dwarfed those of the electric interurban both in frequency and severity. The growing number of collisions involving automobiles exclusively forced newspapers to relegate trolley accidents to second place. However, autos compounded the problems of crashes for the trolleys. The Southern California countryside was being covered by

more and more roads, many of them invading the Pacific Electric's right-of-way.

The unexpected meetings of speeding automobiles and fast interurbans at these grade crossings resulted in many tragic accidents. A typical grade crossing accident occurred in May, 1927, when an automobile driven by a Chino minister, the Rev. S. F. Heilman, 56, was struck by an interurban on the Monrovia line. The automobile was described as "ground to pieces" after being hurled 150 feet. The minister was killed as were his three passengers. [13]

Miss Eudelia Holden faired better when her car collided with an interurban at San Dimas in 1926. Although her automobile was hurled through the air, it landed on its tires and she managed to walk away with only minor injuries. [14]

Summer week-ends traditionally summoned thousands of inlanders to the Southern California beaches to escape the inland heat and at the same time enjoy surf-bathing, dancing, and fun in the amusement zones. When the day drew to an end there were mad dashes for seats on the homeward-bound Big Red Cars. Although additional interurbans were pressed into service for the crowds, there never seemed to be enough seats and sometimes there was not even standing room.

The fun of a day at the beach, however, was always worth even the ride home on the packed interurbans.

Just such a day in 1913 resulted in the accident that took its place as the worst and most tragic on Southern California interurban lines. It also brought the installation of mechanized safety equipment previously sadly neglected.

The accident also unfolded a drama of assorted displays of human courage.

It was on July 13, a Sunday evening, that the traditional crowds were returning inland from the beaches. All coastal areas served by the trolleys were popular in the summer but Venice, because of its picturesque setting and proximity to the central Los Angeles area, commanded particularly large crowds. Extra interurbans went into service.

One three-car interurban train stalled at Vineyard, the junction near Hollywood and Beverly Hills where the Venice Short Line joined the main Santa Monica Line to share tracks for the last few miles into downtown Los Angeles. It was 9:20 p.m. Emil Bartholomew, conductor on a second train forced to halt behind the stalled cars, began walking back to erect danger flags to warn other approaching trolleys. The Pacific Electric's operating rules provided that, in event of a breakdown,

8. Los Angeles Times, June 1, 1904.

9. Santa Ana Blade, January 20, 1906.

10. Los Angeles Record, July 8, 1907.

11. Los Angeles Examiner, January 15, 1906.

12. Pacific Electric Magazine.

13. Los Angeles Examiner, May 23, 1927.

14. Pomona Progress, September 15, 1926.

ABOVE: *Virtually the entire front page of the Los Angeles Examiner was devoted to the 1913 Venice line crash, the Pacific Electric's worst accident. BELOW: This 1905 headline appeared in the Los Angeles Record, which charged trolley firms were lax in safety standards.*

the conductor was to walk back 300 feet and place a torpedo on the tracks so that it would explode as a warning under the wheels of an approaching train. The rules instructed the conductor then to walk back another 300 feet and lay two more torpedos on the track for extra precaution. This procedure for a warning 600 feet from stopped cars was prescribed because there was no system of lighted automatic block signals to alert motormen of trains on the tracks ahead.

Bartholomew, an employee of the interurban system for only two weeks, placed the first torpedo on the track in accordance with the rules. He made his way back approximately 200 feet of the second 300 feet when he saw the headlight of a three-car interurban approaching. He stepped onto the track and waved his flag. Two short blasts from the oncoming train would indicate the warning was noted.

The cars sped towards him.

Bartholomew, frantically waving the flag, listened for the assuring sound of two short blasts of the train's air horn.

There were no such blasts.

Bartholomew continued to wave the flag desperately until the cars were almost upon him. Then he jumped to safety. As the cars sped past, the conductor heard the two short blasts, but they were too late.

"A few seconds later there was a deafening crash, the sound of rending metal, splintering wood, the crash of broken glass, combined with shrieks of terror and cries of pain," one newspaper account reported.[15]

The impact of the crash was so powerful that the front of the approaching car was forced well into the rear of the stalled interurban. Passengers trapped in the wreckage screamed with cries of pain and fear. Those able to free themselves from the crushed cars ran to a nearby electric power house, grabbing crowbars and axes to break into the interurbans and rescue the injured. Red flares illuminated the darkness and gave a ghastly hue to the scene as rescue workers went into action.

The fact that the interurban cars had wooden bodies made the crash all the more tragic. The newer steel cars, used on some lines, would have formed shells to give the passengers more protection from the impact.

Nurses Henrietta Chittenden and Martha Nylander, given an unexpected day off from duties at Clara Barton Hospital, spent it at the beach and had boarded one of the ill-fated interurbans.

"I got more experience in those three hours than I

15. The Los Angeles Examiner, July 14, 1913. Information regarding this tragedy is based on accounts appearing July 14 and 15 in The Examiner, Los Angeles Times, Los Angeles Herald, Los Angeles Record, and Long Beach Press.

Traffic was snarled on Ninth Street in Los Angeles when this interurban was derailed in a 1943 accident. The size *of the Big Red Cars made accidents involving them spectacular. (Stephen D. Maguire Collection)*

expect to get again in a life time," Miss Nylander told reporters. She and Miss Chittenden both uninjured, gave first aid to the screaming victims.

"I began to need bandages by this time," Miss Nylander said, "and I guess you know how I got them. Many women slipped off their petticoats and tore them up in strips for me. Many of them (the passengers) were as heroic as you read about in novels. But there were others who crowded around screaming and shutting off the air from those who needed it badly. It's worth being a nurse, just to have helped that night."

Dazed but unhurt, passenger Oscar Rannert from San Bernardino sat among the wreckage and regarded himself as among the luckiest of men. At the start of the trip he started to take a seat at the rear of a car. Two men rushed for the seat and Rannert, observing

a woman with them, yielded and stood in the aisle. A few minutes later the accident occurred. The man who took the seat he relinquished was crushed to death.

Another passenger, Charles Hoffman, his arm broken, dragged twelve injured persons to safety and then fainted. Although injured, rider Eugene Friedman made his way from a wrecked car to get water for a man who cried out his thirst. When he returned, the man was dead.

The next day a count showed twelve persons killed. An estimated 200 people were injured.

Joseph Foster, motorman on the interurban that hit the standing train, at first was believed dead but later was found nearby in a dazed condition. The car brakes failed, he said, and he leaped from a window moments before the impact.

Paul Shoup, president of the Pacific Electric, issued

153

Despite its size, a Pacific Electric interurban was overturned in a 1944 accident on the Glendora line. The passenger car that it struck was virtually demolished by the impact of the crash. (Los Angeles Times)

a statement placing the responsibility for the accident jointly on Bartholomew and Foster. He also noted the high costs of installing the automatic signals that would have reduced the human error.[16]

"The Pacific Electric is yet in a pioneer stage," he told newspaper reporters. "Its revenues are not on a dividend basis."

But the coroner's jury which considered evidence in the tragedy held a different viewpoint. Instead of blaming the two employees, it criticized the Pacific Electric for hiring inexperienced men and not installing adequate safety equipment.

The next day Paul Shoup bowed to the verdict and announced that automatic block signals would be installed on the interurban system.[17] The action was a major movement in an intensive program eventually making the Pacific Electric one of the world's safety interurban railroads and a leader in the use of automatic signalling.

16. Long Beach Press, July 16, 1913.

17. Los Angeles Times, July 17, 1913.

As Southern California grew, more roads invaded the interurban right-of-ways. There were also more people in Southern California. Accidents increased as the result of the two factors. In the early days of the interurban, damage suits were filed only in the worst accidents. As people became more sophisticated damages were claimed for the smallest accidents, ranging from such minor incidents as vague foot injuries presumably suffered after misjudging the height of the steps into a trolley.

From 1910 to 1920 the Pacific Electric was named as defendant in less than 300 law suits in Los Angeles County. During the period from 1921 to 1930 approximately 1,200 individuals named the company in suits, while from 1931 to 1940 nearly 1,800 named the firm in complaints. While many of the legal actions concerned matters other than accidents, the increasing ratio can be noted as the result of more automobiles and the vast gain in population. Many law suits were baseless while others had merit. Most in the latter class were settled out of court.

The Pacific Electric management's answer to the accident problem was safety education. These efforts, along with the fact that the passing years seasoned the interurban operators, resulted in major reductions in the accident rate. A company report showed for 1926 that accidents of all types totalled 7,270, a decrease of 4.1% from 1925. The safety campaign was so successful by 1931 only 441 accidents of all types were reported even though approximately the same amount of traffic was being handled as five years before.

Crashes involving the Big Red Cars were both terrifying and spectacular from the beginning of the trolley era until its end. The author's experience with collisions involving Pacific Electric interurbans included covering the tragedies as a journalist and on one occasion being a passenger aboard an interurban which struck a car.

This crash occurred in 1951 while riding a Los Angeles-to-Newport interurban, which hit a passenger car crossing the right-of-way across Seventh Street just west of Ximeno Avenue in Long Beach. So sturdy was the interurban that the passengers were hardly shaken, but the automobile was crushed. Its driver, trapped in the twisted steel of his car, screamed, "kill me, kill me, so I won't suffer!" The driver was removed alive from the wreckage, but died shortly thereafter.

The wreck and suffering was typical of interurban-auto crashes over the years.

The wrecks this author observed as a newspaper reporter minutes after they occurred left most of the automobiles completely demolished and those inside of the cars critically injured or killed instantly. The impact of the Big Red Cars was as though the autos had been thrown through the air like toys.

The fast-moving interurbans remained a source of menace until they stopped running, but the relative danger decreased as both trolley operators and automobile drivers became more cautious.

Statistics were never compiled on the number of accidents reported per mile of trolley operation. However, as big as the menace of the interurbans appeared in the early 1900's, that danger was small as compared to the proportionate toll of lives the automobiles soon took annually.

During the early part of the century, anti-railway newspapers frequently charged (but did not prove) that the companies were in league with traffic officers to "look the other way" when trolleys violated a law. As the twentieth century passed its midpoint, the operators as employees of a public agency, the Los Angeles Metropolitan Transportation Authority, and officers were, in effect, members of one family. Traffic citations — when infrequently given to public transportation drivers — merely added to the delays and subsequent costs of operating the system.

Severe damage to one of the trolleys involved in the Vineyard Junction accident of 1913 is shown in this photograph taken after the crash of the cars from Venice. (Craig Rasmussen Collection)

The Big Red Cars had few problems with autos until roads cut into the right-of-ways. *ABOVE:* A 1907 photo shows a P. E. car waiting at the Semi-Tropical Park terminus of the Edendale line. (Title Insurance and Trust Co.) *BELOW LEFT:* An interurban on the Newport Beach line crosses the Santa Ana River during the late 1930's. (Photo by John Lawson) *BELOW RIGHT:* The cover of a 1929 issue of the Pacific Electric Magazine, saluting a Shriners convention, showed a Big Red Car going through the traffic on Hill Street in downtown Los Angeles.

19. Invasion of the Tracks

As the twentieth century's second decade drew to a close, Southern California could look back at growth rivaling that of the first ten years. The bulk of this could be traced again to the influence of the Pacific Electric, expanded under control of the Southern Pacific, more efficient, and an accepted part of life in Southern

A population boom had swept toward the West in general and California in particular. While the 1920 census showed that the population of the United States gained nearly twenty percent during ten years, the population of California had increased forty-five percent during the decade.

The Pacific Electric territory, embracing the counties of Los Angeles, San Bernardino, Orange, and Riverside, absorbed more than its share. The four counties, had a total of 629,969 residents in 1910, and 1,211,528 people in 1920—a gain of ninety-four percent or about double the rate for the state in general. Los Angeles, commercial center of the southern area as well as hub of the region's interurban operations, had fared well. The 1920 census showed the Queen of the Cow Counties had passed its traditional rival, San Francisco, in the population count. Angelenos could proudly boast in 1920 that they numbered 576,673, exactly 70,003 more persons than resided in San Francisco. Just ten years before, the census gave 319,000 residents to Los Angeles and 416,000 for San Francisco. Communities linked to Los Angeles by the electric interurbans grew proportionately.

Southern California's population growth during the decade hinged on many factors. The mild climate was a strong drawing force, and the construction of the harbor at San Pedro increased economic opportunities for those who otherwise might have been unable to reside in the area.

The efficiency and convenience of the Big Red Car interurban system, whisking people to the contrasts of the orange groves, seashore, mountains, villages and cities, and showing them the opportunities, encouraged visitors to vacation permanently in Southern California. As the interurbans spread the settlers, the existing communities reached adolescence and more cities were born. Of the thirteen cities incorporated in Los Angeles County during the decade which ended in 1919, all but one was located on a Pacific Electric line. This single exception was San Fernando, incorporated in 1911 in anticipation of the boom expected for the San Fernando Valley following the announcement that the Red Car was coming to the area.

The decade brought prosperity to those who owned city-destined farmlands and for merchants whose village stores became merchandise marts serving a vastly increased population.

Pasadena, the first city blessed by the arrival of an interurban, continued to grow. Its 1920 population was 45,354, a fifty percent increase in ten years. Long Beach, a seaside village of barely 2,000 residents when the Big Red Cars arrived in 1902 and the nation's fastest growing city during the next eight years, also sustained its growth rate. The 1920 census gave it 55,593 residents, more than triple its population of 17,809 only ten years before. Santa Monica, reached by a myriad of electric interurban lines that encouraged commuting residents, by 1920 had 15,252 residents, a nearly two-fold increase in a decade.

Commuter cities grew throughout the Los Angeles area as a result of the convenient Big Red Car system. The 1910 census gave Glendale 13,536 residents, an

The 1920's, with more automobiles, brought many accidents involving cars racing trains to crossings. The Los Angeles Examiner commented with this cartoon.

increase of more than 10,000 in ten years, and Alhambra's population reached 9,096, a gain of 4,000 residents since 1910. Huntington Park's 1920 population was 4,513, an increase of 3,000 since 1910, while Monrovia could boast 5,480, a gain of nearly 2,000 residents during the decade.

The more distant cities which were linked to Los Angeles by the Big Red Cars also prospered. Santa Ana's 1920 population was 15,485, an increase of 7,000 residents in ten years, while San Bernardino had 18,721 residents, a gain of 6,000 since 1910. The population of Ontario in 1920 was 7,280, an increase of 3,000 in ten years. The city of Orange, which had 2,920 residents in 1910, had a population of 4,884 only ten years later.

But a problem was developing for the Big Red Cars as a result of the very population boom they had nurtured.

This problem was the automobile, eventually to sentence the electric interurban to death.

The automobile itself was not the real villain in the interurban story: this role was played by the roads and highways demanded for the growing number of private vehicles.

In 1905, as the electric interurban construction neared its peak, there were only 6,428 horseless carriages throughout California. Automobiles were distinctly luxury items, and the few people owning them found travel arduous over the limited number of roads suitable for such vehicles.

However, by 1919 the four counties served by the Pacific Electric had 170,915 automobiles, of which 140,967 were in Los Angeles County alone. Automobile owners had pressured state and local authorities for road building programs. Only a few thousand dollars were spent to build roads in 1909, but by 1916 appropriations for road construction throughout California approached $10 million and expenditures in the state for 1922 alone hit $25 million. Paved highways began to form a network over the Southern California countryside.

While automobiles initially were considered as mild competition for the trolleys, the destruction of the interurban rights-of-way by invading roads was beginning to concern officials of the Big Red Car line. Interurban schedules slowed as the trolleys were forced to reduce speed for automobiles moving across the rights-of-way which a few years before had been open countryside. The accident rate soared as motorists attempted to race trains to the crossings.

By 1923 there were 481,543 automobiles registered in the four county area. Registrations reached 580,451 by 1925 and zoomed to 693,175 automobiles in 1927. More automobiles increased the demand for more and

wider highways, and to build the highways as cheaply as possible more arteries were cut across the interurban tracks, causing trains to increase running time. Had underpasses been constructed and the rights-of-way guarded as zealously as the freeways of mid-century California, the Big Red Car tracks undoubtedly would have remained economically useful for many years.

Motorists defied grade crossings with their faith in the speed of their automobiles. Motormen on the interurbans similarly appeared confident that automobiles would yield to them because of the obvious dangers as well as laws giving trains the right-of-way. A spokesman for a national automobile association predicted the trend of the decade that doomed the interurbans in November, 1921, when he issued a warning to motorists ignoring the dangers of grade crossings. During the nine months prior to his plea, 586 automobiles were destroyed throughout the nation at grade crossings.[1]

The Pacific Electric launched a fight to maintain its system by resisting efforts to permit automotive traffic over its right-of-ways. Attempts were made to remedy the damage by the construction, through joint public and railroad financing, of overpasses and underpasses at points where automotive traffic was the heaviest.

In most cases there were too few viaducts and they were built too late. Road construction hit new peaks as the pressure to place all available funds into pavements came from car manufacturers, automobile owners, and various other elements throughout Southern California which benefited from such construction.

When the Pacific Electric line to San Bernardino opened in 1914, the company boasted that the route had no grade crossings from near Pomona for twenty-five miles to its terminus in the orange grove country because of adequate viaducts. The increased automobile traffic soon brought pressures for roads in the area and the high-speed route was "invaded" by crossings.

Construction of the line to Long Beach in 1902 included laying the tracks down American Avenue (Long Beach Boulevard) in a private right-of-way with the public thoroughfare on either side so that vehicles would not interfere with the electric cars.

Eyeing the prosperous times of the 1920's property owners demanded that the street be widened by abolishing the private right-of-way and paving around the rails. David W. Pontius, then general manager of the Pacific Electric, correctly prophesied that the action "would mean congestion like in Los Angeles."

"If the tracks were paved in on all American Avenue between Anaheim Street and North Long Beach,"

---

1. New York Times, November 13, 1921.

he told the Long Beach City Council in 1925, "there would be no reason why all the tracks between Los Angeles and Long Beach should not be paved in as the country settles up along the line. It would only be a matter of time until the tracks of the Pacific Electric would be of little use to the public and of no value to the owners (the Southern Pacific) of the property." [2]

Pontius' prophetic words were of no avail, for the pressures in Long Beach, as elsewhere, were for street improvement programs. The right-of-way was paved and the result, duplicated on other interurban lines throughout Southern California, was a thirty percent increase in the traveling time for trolleys in the area involved because of automotive traffic on the tracks.

The reduction in traveling time was the main excuse for commuters to abandon interurbans in favor of automobiles, a situation which eventually compounded a difficult traffic problem.

Among those turning to horseless carriages was Henry Huntington, who after retiring purchased an automobile for use in San Marino. Huntington's car was powered, appropriately, by an electric battery.

During ensuing years the "invasion" of the tracks permitted in Southern California was to be cited as a national example of how to destroy an efficient transportation system. In a 1960 survey of America's commuter problems, Time Magazine noted the situation by saying: [3]

The penalty for failing to snap life into the nation's public transportation is to see many U.S. cities share the fate of Los Angeles.

The rail commuter system that once operated 6,200 trains daily . . . was a hit-and-run victim of cars. Since then, at a cost of $1.6 billion, the city has built 271 miles of freeways and 266 miles of expressways to accommodate some 2,000,000 motorists — and is furiously working on 107 more. But, says Edward T. Telford, engineer in charge of construction, "it will be years before we can catch up to the need—if we ever can."

The Los Angeles Board of Public Utilities in its 1913 report expressed alarm over the existence of nine automobile grade crossings over the Pacific Electric tracks. By 1925 there were 1,200 grade crossings over the Red Car lines throughout Southern California, and as the population increase demanded more highways the tracks retreated in the face of new invasions. Even after more tracks were abandoned, there were 1,834 grade crossings in 1947.

When the last Big Red Car made the final run over the Long Beach line in 1961, there were forty grade crossings on the route 1902 had seen arrow-straight and virtually uninterrupted by roads so that the trolleys could achieve speed.

2. Long Beach Press-Telegram, June 19, 1925.

3. Time Magazine, January 18, 1960, P. 72. Copyright 1960 by TIME, Inc. Used by permission.

A speeding car moves across a Pacific Electric right-of-way near Covina. Operators of the interurbans were forced to slow their trains to avoid accidents, thus substantially increasing the length of the trips.

In the 1920's it was becoming increasingly obvious that the electric interurbans would be doomed unless steps were taken to go over— or under—the automobile traffic.

An immense subway carrying trolleys beneath downtown Los Angeles streets until they reached the countryside was among the improvements proposed by the Southern Pacific's E. H. Harriman following his 1906 purchase of the Los Angeles Pacific Railway.

The project actually called for twin subways, each containing two tracks and running from Hill Street in downtown Los Angeles beneath Fourth Street to Vermont Avenue. From here the tracks would surface and continue to Venice and Santa Monica. Harriman's plan was praised as an ideal means for the trolleys to circumvent traffic, even then growing heavier as Los Angeles swelled and automobiles became popular. The Los Angeles City Council issued

THE PACIFIC ELECTRIC MAGAZINE

Vol. 12   LOS ANGELES, CAL., NOVEMBER 10, 1927   No. 6

Pico Grade Separation, Now Nearing Completion

A bridge for trolleys over Pico Avenue in West Los Angeles was pictured in this 1927 Pacific Electric Magazine cover. The structure was typical of the company's efforts to avoid the automobiles which were increasing operating schedules.

a permit for the construction and preliminary work started in 1907 only to be stopped by a business recession.

Subsequent efforts to shorten interurban running time were reduced to construction of two tunnels through Bunker Hill by the Los Angeles Pacific for cars traveling to the western area. One tunnel extended nearly 550 feet from First to Temple Streets and the other, almost 1,000 feet long, carried cars from Temple Street to Sunset Boulevard. The tunnels, opened in 1909, were lauded not only for eliminating the longer route around the hill but also for avoiding vehicular traffic.

As road construction invaded more right-of-ways and the ever-increasing numbers of automobiles slowed schedules, Pacific Electric officials turned to Harriman's 1907 plan as a means to maintain, or perhaps even build, passenger travel volume. London went underground with its transportation system in 1908, and New York had opened its subway system in 1904. The subterranean arteries ignoring intersections, pedestrians, and automobiles were regarded as well suited for the Los Angeles traffic picture, becoming tangled and difficult as the 1920's grew older.

Part of the decision to build a subway was based on a California Railroad Commission order in 1922 granting the Pacific Electric certain fare increases on condition that the underground facility would be constructed. The company also expected to save more than $50,000 annually in costs ranging from salaries and electrical power to maintenance and injury claims. The Pacific Electric hoped that if the subway was successful, extensions could ferret throughout Southern California to attract passengers by providing speedy schedules.

Harriman's proposed four-track subway covered a distance of more than four miles. The project that became a reality under the name of the Hollywood Subway was of considerably less magnitude, stretching approximately four-fifths of a mile from Hill Street between Fourth and Fifth Streets to a point near First Street and Glendale Boulevard. There its two tracks surfaced and sent trolleys to Western Los Angeles County. The public enthusiastically hailed the subway as the start of an answer for the transportation problem and envisioned extensions to points throughout Southern California.

Ground was broken early in May, 1924, at the tunnel's Glendale Boulevard terminus. Construction methods were quite different than for the Manhattan subways, where workmen blasted through solid granite rock. The material in the path of the Hollywood Subway was primarily soft shale, loosened by dynamite and air drills. The tunnel was lined with reinforced concrete. The downtown Los Angeles terminus sat on the site of the Pacific Electric's Hill Street Station, removed when construction started. A basement terminal was constructed with a foundation strong enough to support a major building. The rights for erecting this structure were sold to a group of Los Angeles investors who formed the Subway Terminal Corporation to construct a twelve story office building.

Construction of the underground terminal started in May, 1925, a year after crews began work on the tunnel. Erection of the office building commenced immediately after completion of the terminal's foundations. The facility was by no means an inexpensive project: the cost of the land, tunnel, terminal, and building was estimated at $5 million.

On November 30, 1925 — seventeen months after ground breaking—the Hollywood Subway was officially opened in dazzling ceremonies with civic dignataries proclaiming the project the seed of a vast subterranean system that would solve Los Angeles' travel problems for all times.

There was no champagne to celebrate the opening because of the Great Experiment called Prohibition. However, a bottle of ginger ale provided by David W. Pontius, general manager of the Pacific Electric, was smashed against a Big Red Car to herald the official start of service. The subway was a success. Interurbans and local trolleys serving Santa Monica, Hollywood, Venice, Glendale, Burbank, Beverly Hills, and the San Fernando Valley as well as other western areas used the tube. Each train saved up to fifteen minutes, thanks to the direct route and lack of interference from automobiles.

The underground station became a busy center of life: there were rushing passengers, news stands, and lunch counters. The Subway Terminal Building itself was profitable. And popular, too, for the commuter fortunate enough to be employed at an office in the structure could merely alight from his train and take an elevator to the proper floor.

After the Hollywood Subway was termed a success, there were considered discussions by both Pacific Electric and public officials as well as civic groups for extensions rivaling the underground systems of New York and London. Proposals called for subway arteries stretching from downtown Los Angeles into the general directions of the San Gabriel Valley, Long Beach Harbor, the heart of the Hollywood section, and towards Glendale. But construction of subways, requiring excavation and re-enforcement, was an expensive proposition. Costs were estimated at approximately $20 million for an extension to Santa Monica and up to $40 million for a two track subway all the way to the Long Beach area.

Some solution was needed, however, for the increasing automobile traffic slowing the interurbans and robbing them of passengers who could not tolerate the time consuming trips.

It was early in 1926 that the construction of elevated tracks for the Pacific Electric means of surmounting the traffic problem was proposed. The very idea touched off one of the bitterest campaigns in the history of the City of the Angels.

Stepping forward promptly to oppose the elevated railroad plan was Harry Chandler's Los Angeles Times, long an advocate of improving the decaying Plaza area. The newspaper backing construction of a union railway passenger terminal adjacent to this section where the city had started during the Spanish era. The railroads had opposed the construction of a new terminal in any section of the city.

On January 7, 1926, the Southern Pacific, Union Pacific, Santa Fe, and Pacific Electric jointly unveiled a plan for building a union terminal at Fourth and Central Streets—near the central business section but

The Subway Terminal Building was photographed soon after it opened in 1925. BELOW: Here is the first electric car to roll through the Bunker Hill tunnel, opened in 1909 in an earlier effort to avoid delays in surface traffic. (Both Photos: Security Pacific National Bank)

LOS ANGELES—PASADENA—via OAK KNOLL

NORTH

STATIONS	Miles																												
		*	*	*	†	*	†	*	*	*	*	*	*	*	*	*	*	*	*	*	*	*	*	*	*	*	*	*	*
Los Angeles......	.00	6 20	7 20	7 35	7 50	8 05	8 25	8 55	9 10	9 45	10 10	10 45	11 15	11 45	12 15	12 45	1 15	1 45	2 15	2 45	3 15
Covina Jct.......	3.13	6 37	7 37	7 52	8 07	8 22	8 42	9 12	9 27	10 02	10 32	11 02	11 32	12 02	12 32	1 02	1 32	2 02	2 32	3 02	3 32
Sierra Vista.....	7.42	6 44	7 44	7 59	8 14	8 29	8 49	9 19	9 34	10 09	10 39	11 09	11 39	12 09	12 39	1 09	1 39	2 09	2 39	3 09	3 39
Oneonta Park....	8.31	6 46	7 46	8 01	8 16	8 31	8 51	9 21	9 36	10 11	10 41	11 11	11 41	12 11	12 41	1 11	1 41	2 11	2 41	3 11	3 41
El Molino........	10.04	6 49	7 49	8 04	8 19	8 34	8 54	9 24	9 39	10 14	10 44	11 14	11 44	12 14	12 44	1 14	1 44	2 14	2 44	3 14	3 44
Pasadena........	13.00	7 05	8 05	8 20	8 35	8 50	9 10	9 40	9 55	10 30	11 00	11 30	12 00	12 30	1 00	1 30	2 00	2 30	3 00	3 30	4 00

STATIONS	Miles																							
		*	*	*	*	*	*	*	*	*	*	*	*	*	*	*	*	*	*	*	*	*	*
Los Angeles......	.00	3 45	4 15	4 45	5 02	5 17	5 32	5 45	6 00	6 15	6 45	7 15	7 45	8 15	8 45	9 15	9 45	10 15	10 45	11 15	12 00
Covina Jct.......	3.13	4 02	4 32	5 02	5 19	5 34	5 49	6 02	6 17	6 32	7 02	7 32	8 02	8 32	9 02	9 32	10 02	10 32	11 02	11 32	12 17
Sierra Vista.....	7.42	4 09	4 39	5 09	5 26	5 41	5 56	6 09	6 24	6 39	7 09	7 39	8 09	8 39	9 09	9 39	10 09	10 39	11 09	11 39	12 24
Oneonta Park....	8.31	4 11	4 41	5 11	5 28	5 43	5 58	6 11	6 26	6 41	7 11	7 41	8 11	8 41	9 11	9 41	10 11	10 41	11 11	11 41	12 26
El Molino........	10.04	4 14	4 44	5 14	5 31	5 46	6 01	6 14	6 29	6 44	7 14	7 44	8 14	8 44	9 14	9 44	10 14	10 44	11 14	11 44	12 29
Pasadena........	13.00	4 30	5 00	5 30	5 47	6 02	6 17	6 30	6 45	7 00	7 30	8 00	8 30	9 00	9 30	10 00	10 30	11 00	11 30	12 00	12 45

PASADENA—LOS ANGELES—via OAK KNOLL

SOUTH

STATIONS	Miles																										
		*	*	*	*	*	*	*	*	*	*	*	*	*	*	*	*	*	*	*	*	*	*	*	*	*
Pasadena........	.00	5 30	6 30	6 50	7 05	7 20	7 35	7 50	8 10	8 25	8 55	9 25	9 55	10 25	10 55	11 25	11 55	12 25	12 55	1 25	1 55
El Molino........	2.96	5 44	6 44	7 04	7 19	7 34	7 49	8 04	8 24	8 39	9 09	9 39	10 09	10 39	11 09	11 39	12 09	12 39	1 09	1 39	2 09
Oneonta Park....	4.69	5 47	6 47	7 07	7 22	7 37	7 52	8 07	8 27	8 42	9 12	9 42	10 12	10 42	11 12	11 42	12 12	12 42	1 12	1 42	2 12
Sierra Vista.....	5.58	5 49	6 49	7 09	7 24	7 39	7 54	8 09	8 29	8 44	9 14	9 44	10 14	10 44	11 14	11 44	12 14	12 44	1 14	1 44	2 14
Covina Jct.......	9.87	5 56	6 56	7 16	7 31	7 46	8 01	8 16	8 36	8 51	9 21	9 51	10 21	10 51	11 21	11 51	12 21	12 51	1 21	1 51	2 21
Los Angeles......	13.00	6 13	7 13	7 33	7 48	8 03	8 18	8 33	8 53	9 08	9 38	10 08	10 38	11 08	11 38	12 08	12 38	1 08	1 38	2 08	2 38

STATIONS	Miles																							
		*	*	*	*	*	*	*	*	*	*	*	*	*	*	*	*	*	*	*	*	*	*
Pasadena........	.00	2 25	3 00	3 30	4 00	4 15	4 30	4 45	5 00	5 30	5 55	6 25	6 55	7 30	8 00	8 30	9 00	9 30	10 00	10 30	11 10
El Molino........	2.96	2 39	3 14	3 44	4 14	4 29	4 44	4 59	5 14	5 44	6 09	6 39	7 09	7 44	8 14	8 44	9 14	9 44	10 14	10 44	11 24
Oneonta Park....	4.69	2 42	3 17	3 47	4 17	4 32	4 47	5 02	5 17	5 47	6 12	6 42	7 12	7 47	8 17	8 47	9 17	9 47	10 17	10 47	11 27
Sierra Vista.....	5.58	2 44	3 19	3 49	4 19	4 34	4 49	5 04	5 19	5 49	6 14	6 44	7 14	7 49	8 19	8 49	9 19	9 49	10 19	10 49	11 29
Covina Jct.......	9.87	2 51	3 26	3 56	4 26	4 41	4 56	5 11	5 26	5 56	6 21	6 51	7 21	7 56	8 26	8 56	9 26	9 56	10 26	10 56	11 36
Los Angeles......	13.00	3 08	3 43	4 13	4 43	4 58	5 13	5 28	5 43	6 13	6 38	7 08	7 38	8 13	8 43	9 13	9 43	10 13	10 43	11 13	11 53	...

* Daily. † Daily except Sunday. X Express. Light figures A. M. Dark figures P. M. Extra service Sundays and Holidays according to requirements of travel.

ANNANDALE LINE

THROUGH CARS LEAVE SIXTH STREET FOR ANNANDALE			THROUGH CARS LEAVE ANNANDALE FOR LOS ANGELES		
6 10	7 50	4 40	6 40	8 20	4 50
†6 30	8 25	5 20	7 00	8 40	5 30
6 50	9 10	5 40	†7 20	9 20	5 50
†7 10	3 30	6 00	7 40	3 50	6 10
7 30	4 00	6 20	8 00	4 20	6 30
....	....	....	....	....	6 50

Cars leave Avenue 64 for Annandale 9:50 A. M., 10:15 A. M. and every 30 minutes until 3:15 P. M., 3:40 P. M., then 7:00 P. M., 7:20 P. M., 7:45 P. M., and every 30 minutes until 12:15 A. M.

Local cars leave Annandale for Avenue 64, 10:00 A. M., and every 30 minutes until 3:30 P. M., then 7:10 P. M., 7:30 P. M., and every 30 minutes until 12:30 A. M.

—† Daily except Sunday.

Classified

EDENDALE LINE

Runs between Edendale and Arcade Depot. First car leaves Arcade at 6:00 A. M., then every 7 minutes until 10:05 A. M., then every 9 minutes until 3:29 P. M., then every 7 minutes until 7:06 P. M., then every 8 minutes until 7:46 P. M., then every 10 minutes until 8:16 P. M., then every 10 minutes until last car at 12:30 A. M. First car leaves Edendale at 5:20 A. M., then 5:40, 6:04, then every 7 minutes until 10:37 A. M., then every 9 minutes until 4:01 P. M., then every 7 minutes until 7:38 P. M., then every 10 minutes until last through car at 12:00 midnight. Cars leaving Edendale at 12:30, 12:40, 12:50 and 1:00 A. M. go to Car House.

WATTS LINE

Runs between Los Angeles and Commercial Sts., and Watts. First car leaves Watts at 4:50 A. M., then 5:20, 5:30, 5:40, 5:48, then every 6 minutes until 9:00 A. M., then every 10 minutes until 4:40 P. M., then every 7 minutes to 5:20 P. M., then every 5 minutes until 5:40 P. M., then every 7 minutes until 7:30 P. M., then every 15 minutes until last car at 1:30 A. M. First car leaves Los Angeles and Commercial Sts., at 5:45 A. M., next car at 6:00 A. M., then 6:15, then every 6 minutes until 9:45 A. M., then every 10 minutes until 3:45 P. M., then every 7 and 8 minutes until 4:30 P. M., then every 5 minutes until 6:15 P. M., then every 7 minutes until 6:45 P. M., then every 15 minutes until last car at 12:45 A. M.

LOS ANGELES—CATALINA ISLAND

Outbound from Los Angeles	Miles	Daily	Daily ex. Sun.	Sat. Only	Inbound from Avalon	Miles	Daily	Daily ex. Sun.	Sun Only
Los Angeles	.00	9 15	2 15	5 00	Avalon, C. I.......	.00	7 00	3 45	6 30
San Pedro........	22.00	10 00	3 00	6 00	San Pedro......	27.08	9 30	6 00	8 45
Avalon, C. I......	49.08	12 15	5 20	8 15	Los Angeles......	49.08	10 15	6 45	9 30

Light figures A.M. Dark figures P.M. For Schedule of cars between Los Angeles and San Pedro, see San Pedro via Dominguez card.

This page from a 1911 P. E. timetable shows the frequency of service, including at night. Note that the Big Red Cars carried riders from downtown Los Angeles to the heart of Pasadena in 45 minutes, even during rush hours.

162

LOS ANGELES to REDONDO BEACH via INGLEWOOD and GARDENA—Second Street Station

Stations: Los Angeles, Inglewood (10.2), Hawthorne (13.2), Lawndale (14.7), Gardena (12.5), Moneta (13.7), Belvidere (16.7), Redondo Beach (20.2), Cliffton (22.0)

*Daily. † Daily except Sunday. F Flyer. I Via Inglewood. G Via Gardena. S Via Sunnyside. Light figures A. M. Black figures P. M.

REDONDO BEACH via INGLEWOOD

NOTE.—In making the trip to Redondo Beach via Inglewood we advise you to pay the TEN CENTS EXTRA—stop off at Slauson Ave. and see Angeles Mesa. You will find the view of the city from this beautiful plateau the finest to be had. This subdivision of 440 acres is offered in large homesites, including complete high class improvements at from $600 up. Sold on very easy terms. Values absolutely will double in two years. See the agent or call at downtown office—sixth floor—640 South Broadway. Angeles Mesa Land Co.

REDONDO BEACH to LOS ANGELES via INGLEWOOD AND GARDENA

Stations: Cliffton (0), Redondo Beach (1.4), Belvidere (4.5), Lawndale (6.8), Hawthorne (8.3), Inglewood (11.3), Moneta (7.6), Gardena (8.7), Los Angeles (22.0)

*Daily. † Daily except Sunday. F Flyer. I Via Inglewood. G Via Gardena. Light figures A. M. Black figures P. M.

LOS ANGELES—Hill St. Station—REDONDO BEACH
Via Playa Del Rey, Manhattan and Hermosa

LEAVE LOS ANGELES, HILL ST. STA.				LEAVE REDONDO BEACH			
6 30	10 00	2 00	5 30	†6 15	9 45	1 45	5 45
a7 00	10 30	2 30	a6 00	†6 45	10 15	2 15	6 15
7 30	11 00	3 00	6 30	†7 15	10 45	2 45	7 15
8 00	11 30	3 30	7 30	†7 45	11 15	3 15	8 30
8 30	12 00	4 00	8 30	8 15	11 45	3 45	9 30
9 00	12 30	4 30	9 30	8 45	12 15	4 15	10 30
9 30	1 00	5 00	10 30	9 15	12 45	4 45	11 30
	1 30				1 15	5 15	

Extra service on Sundays and Holidays.
Light figures A. M. Black figures P. M. Connections made at Playa del Rey for Venice, Ocean Park and Santa Monica. Running every 30 minutes, 6:12 A. M., until 7:12 P. M. From 9:05 P. M. until 12:05 A. M., connections irregular.
a Connect at Ivy Park for Santa Monica and Port Los Angeles, via Air Line.
† Cars do no local work between Hill St. Station and Vineyard, except Sundays.
Running Time—Los Angeles to Vineyard 23, Ivy Park 29, Playa del Rey 43, Manhattan (Center St.) 53, Redondo Beach 1.03. Redondo Beach to Playa del Rey 20, Ivy Park 34, Vineyard 40 minutes.
Distance Los Angeles to Playa del Rey 15.01, Redondo Beach 24 miles.

SANTA MONICA (Montana and 7th)—PLAYA DEL REY

Leave Montana Ave. 6:10 A. M., and every 30 minutes until 9:40 P. M.; then 10:40 and 11:40 P. M.; then 12:40 A. M. to Ocean Park car barn.

Leave Playa del Rey 6:14 A. M., and every 30 minutes until 10:14 P. M.; then 11:14 P. M., and 12:14 A. M. Connections made at Playa del Rey with trains from and to Los Angeles and Redondo, up to 8:14 P. M. From 8:14 P. M. until 12:14 A. M., connections from Redondo and to Los Angeles irregular.

This 1911 timetable shows the frequency of trips between Redondo Beach and Los Angeles via Hawthorne and Inglewood. Road at the time were poor, and the travel time was considerably longer via relatively slow autos.

163

The first passengers, a group of P. E. and city officials, to ride through the Hollywood Subway, cheer the occasion. The subway was regarded as the ideal way to avoid street congestion. (Title Insurance and Trust Co.)

substantially romoved from the Plaza. Aside from its location, the distinguishing feature of the plan was its incorporation of extensive elevated track connections enabling the Pacific Electric to exchange passengers at the proposed facility. Unlike the elevated systems of Chicago, New York, and Philadelphia that occupied public streets, the "El" tracks initially suggested for Los Angeles were to be on a private right-of-way stretching from the Pacific Electric Building at Sixth and Main

Streets to the proposed union terminal and then to the Los Angeles River. From here the tracks would have joined existing rights-of-way on the heavily traveled lines to the San Gabriel Valley and the harbor area.

The Pacific Electric's general manager, David W. Pontius, lauded the plan for elevating the tracks because it would "remove 1,200 trains daily from the streets and eliminate 18,000 (individual) grade crossings daily" thus cutting from seven to twenty minutes from the traveling

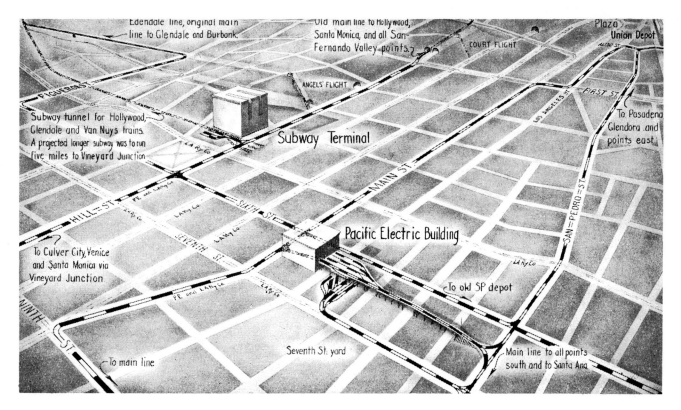

Edendale line, original main line to Glendale and Burbank.

Old main line to Hollywood, Santa Monica, and all San Fernando Valley points.

COURT FLIGHT

Plaza Union Depot

ANGELS' FLIGHT

Subway Terminal

Subway tunnel for Hollywood, Glendale and Van Nuys trains. A projected longer subway was to run five miles to Vineyard Junction

To Pasadena Glendora and points east

Pacific Electric Building

To Culver City, Venice and Santa Monica via Vineyard Junction

To old SP depot

To main line

Seventh St. yard

Main line to all points south and to Santa Ana

ABOVE: Operation of the Hollywood Subway, starting beneath the Subway Terminal Building, is depicted in this drawing from Trains Magazine. The drawing also shows the elevated approach to the P. E.'s Sixth and Main station and surface tracks. (Trains Magazine; Used by Permission) BE-

LOW LEFT: Glendale and Hollywood cars emerge from the subway. (Pacific Railroad Publications) BELOW LEFT: This drawing shows the route on Glendale Boulevard after cars emerged from the subway. Electric cars saved up to fifteen minutes by using the subway route.

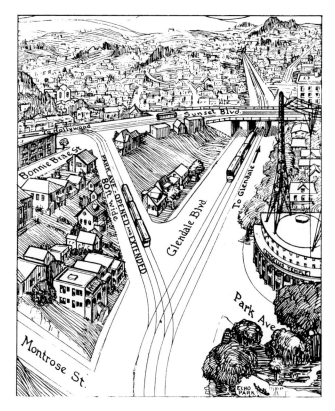

ABOVE: Sir Thomas Lawrence's "Pinkie" was among the art treasures which Huntington acquired for his collection. (© The Huntington Library: Used by Permission) BELOW: Henry Huntington was born in this house at Oneonta, New York. Before his death, he presented it to the city for use as a public library (Photograph by the Author)

time on various lines. William Randolph Hearst's Los Angeles Examiner agreed that elevated tracks were a logical answer to the transportation problem, as did four of the city's five other daily newspapers. Pledging support for the plan were The Herald, The Illustrated Daily News, The Evening Express, and The Record.

The Los Angeles Times stood alone in its opposition, blasting the proposal as one not only ending all hopes for a union passenger terminal but threatening great hazards for the city.

The Times commented editorially:

Elevateds are the most dangerous of all railroads because of their lofty swaying structures, impossible to make rigid and constantly exposed to the deteriorating influence of sun, wind and rain. They are dirty, deafening, hideous. They depreciate appallingly the section of the city through which they run.

The merits of an elevated railroad system rapidly developed into a battle of newspapers, with The Times aligned against its five competitors.

A Los Angeles city charter provision requiring a master plan for rapid transit developments quickly was noted by The Times. Proponents of the Pacific Electric plan commissioned such a report, which dutifully detailed the pressing need for adequate transportation but made the tactical error of recommending eventual construction of elevated systems in the public streets, including a portion of Sunset Boulevard.

The Times pounced on proposals to extend the elevated tracks as evidence that countless unsightly structures would be built throughout the city. It also argued that the elevated plan was only a scheme of the railroads to circumvent rulings from both the Interstate Commerce Commission and the State Railroad Commission favoring the Plaza location for the passenger terminal.

The battle decided the pattern of Southern California interurban transportation for many years.

The Los Angeles City Council, torn between the power of The Times on one hand and, on the other, the voices of the city's five other newspapers and the railroads, decided to toss the problem into the people's laps. May 2 was set as the date for a straw vote to decide on the two proposals. The elevated became the hottest issue of the ballot, previously scheduled to decide municipal issues ranging from zoning regulations to construction of a new city hall. During the weeks prior to the election, the pros and cons of an elevated railroad system became the subject of editorials in the newspapers as well as for countless discussions between commuters on the electric interurban cars.

The ballot did not provide for voting directly on the proposal of an elevated system but, obtusely, on issues relating to the matter. Proposition No. 8, favored by those advocating an "El," actually called for construction of a union passenger terminal at an under-termined location. Proposition No. 9, backed by The Times, provided for the terminal near the Plaza.

The Times argued that the strategy of the railroads was to defeat construction of a terminal at any location, and noted editorially that Prosposition No. 8 called for "additional study" before action.

Typical of the arguments against Proposition No. 9 was that of the liberal Los Angeles Record, which maintained that the Plaza site was backed by the conservative-minded Times as a "pet project of Harry Chandler and his big real estate speculating friends" to boost the value of land in the area. The extent to which ownership of property near the Plaza was concentrated was not detailed during the campaign. It was obvious, of course, that wherever the terminal was located, adjacent property would be benefited. Land ownership throughout Los Angeles by the time was considerably diversified.

In striking back at the opponents, The Times concentrated on the danger that the plan would open the way for a web of elevated systems in the streets, bringing clattering electric cars speeding past the windows of offices and apartments. The newspaper contended that although the basic system proposed three miles of over-head track on privately owned land, the master plan provided for eventual construction of sixty-one miles of elevated tracks in the downtown area alone.

The railroads told their story in double page news-paper advertisements contending that "elevated trains will take the passengers swiftly into and out of Los Angeles on overhead structures of modern design. The effect will be to annex to Los Angeles in 1927 a wide area in four counties (Los Angeles, Orange, Riverside, and San Bernardino) through the quickened service that will bring their people into and out of Los Angeles."

The promise of better service envisioned with the elevated system promptly resulted in real estate brokers advertising the proximity of their particular housing tracks to the "rapid transit system of the Pacific Electric."

As the battle progressed individuals and groups throughout Southern California chose sides in the controversy. It was obvious that the elevated system was highly favored by most organizations. Downtown Los Angeles viewed the "El" as a way to increase retail volume and property values by making travel easy. Outlying communities favored the overhead system because they expected it to boost their desirability as commuter cities and thus enhance land values. William Wrigley, the chewing gum magnate and owner of Catalina Island in announcing he opposed the Plaza site, said he favored an elevated railroad to facilitate Southern California's development. The Los Angeles Chamber of Commerce

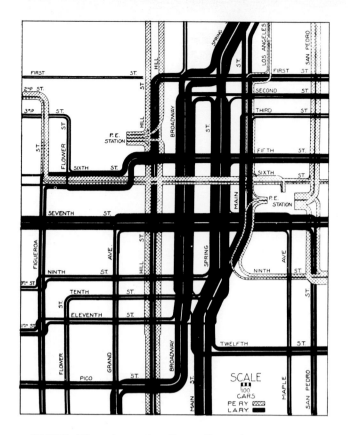

ABOVE: The volume of trolley traffic on downtown Los Angeles streets during the mid-1920's is depicted in this map, prepared by advocates of elevated tracks. Thicker lines indicate heavier traffic. BELOW: This map shows proposed plans for building a system of elevated tracks.

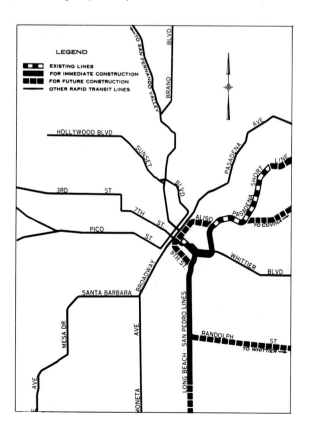

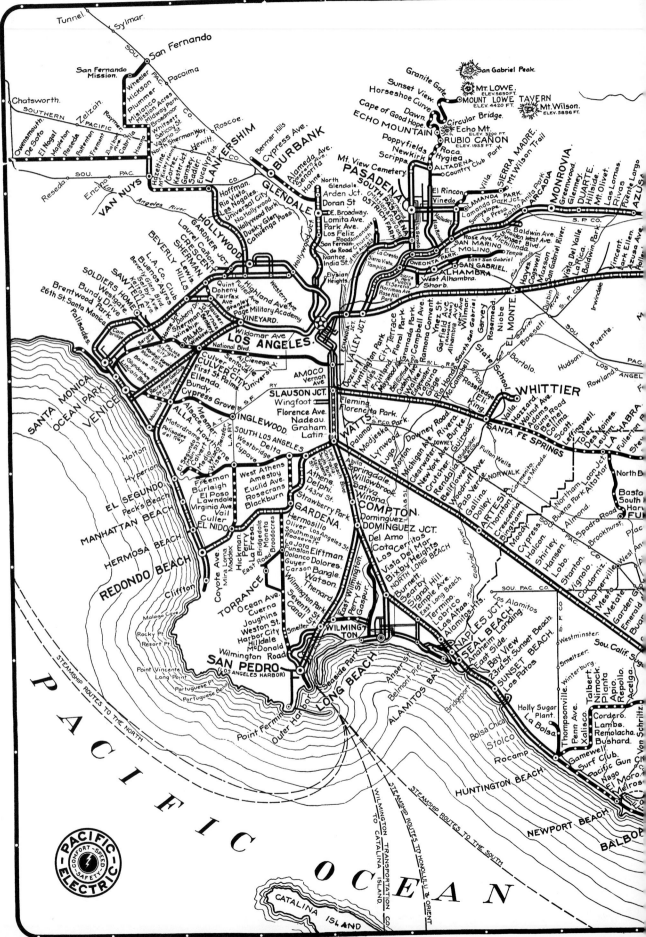

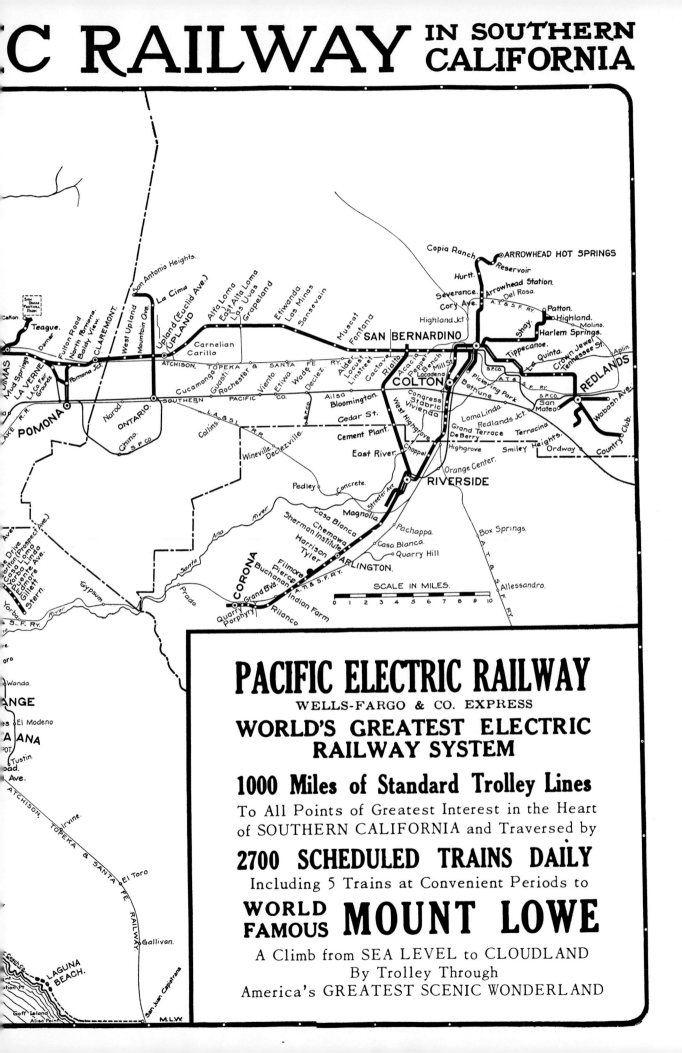

Asleep at the Switch?

also joined in opposing the Plaza plan. Chambers in communities throughout Southern California endorsed the proposal for an elevated railroad, anticipating more growth for their areas.

Almost alone in its opposition to the overhead railroad, The Times emphasized dangers of defacing the city with such a system and citing efforts of other cities with overhead to remove the "Els."

When the ballots were counted, they showed that The Times was a most potent voice in Los Angeles' civic life. Citizens demonstrated their alarm at the danger of an elevated system defacing the City of the Angels by defeating the overhead plan by a substantial margin. The union passenger terminal at the Plaza location was endorsed by a narrow margin despite opposition by the other newspapers. The final tally of votes showed Proposition No. 8, permitting the "El" construction, defeated by 115,493 to 72,714. Proposition 9, for the Plaza station, was endorsed by 94,404 and opposed by 90,464 voters.

Cost of the elevated system to the Pacific Electric at the time was estimated at $2 million because of its usage of facilities the transcontinental railroads planned as part of the project. If the "El" had been constructed by the Pacific Electric alone, its estimated cost would have been a prohibitive $25 million. The P.E. plan, if voters endorsed the initial project, was to extend the tracks from the elevated's termination by the Los Angeles River along the banks to Glendale. The tracks also would have been built along the river banks by Long Beach to avoid traffic on the streets.

The union passenger terminal at the Plaza became a reality in 1936. An elevated system spanning the ever-increasing traffic problem had become a dream. But the inevitable nightmare of clattering, bulky elevateds that might have solved the problem never developed.

Traffic in downtown Los Angeles was becoming increasingly heavy during the 1920's, creating congestion and slowing the interurbans. LEFT: This 1924 scene was made at Broadway near Second Street. It was possible to park on downtown streets, and there were few patrons for parking lots. RIGHT: Arrows in the artist's drawing indicate the Pacific Electric's proposed elevated tracks.

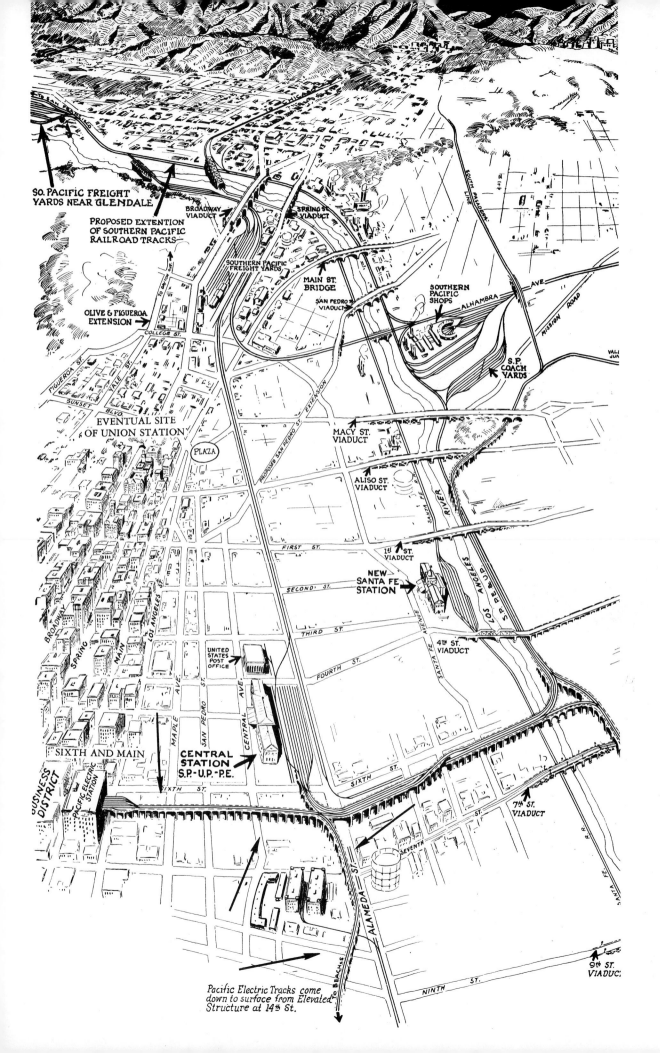

SO. PACIFIC FREIGHT
YARDS NEAR GLENDALE

PROPOSED EXTENTION
OF SOUTHERN PACIFIC
RAILROAD TRACKS

OLIVE & FIGUEROA
EXTENSION

TO SAN PEDRO AVE.

COLLEGE ST.

BROADWAY
VIADUCT

SPRING ST.
VIADUCT

SOUTHERN PACIFIC
FREIGHT YARDS

MAIN ST.
BRIDGE

SAN PEDRO
VIADUCT

SOUTHERN
PACIFIC
SHOPS

ALHAMBRA AVE.

MISSION ROAD

SOUTH PASADENA

S.P.
COACH
YARDS

VAL.
JUN.

FIGUEROA ST.
YALE ST.

SUNSET BLVD.

EVENTUAL SITE
OF UNION STATION

PLAZA

PROPOSED SAN PEDRO ST. EXTENSION

MACY ST.
VIADUCT

ALISO ST.
VIADUCT

SANTA FE RY.

RIVER

LOS ANGELES

FIRST ST.

1ST ST.
VIADUCT

NEW
SANTA FE
STATION

S.P.E. U.P.

SECOND ST.

BROADWAY

SPRING

MAIN

LOS ANGELES

THIRD ST.

4TH ST.
VIADUCT

UNITED
STATES
POST
OFFICE

FOURTH ST.

MAPLE AVE.

SAN PEDRO ST.

CENTRAL AVE.

SANTA FE AVE.

SIXTH AND MAIN

CENTRAL
STATION
S.P.-U.P.-P.E.

SIXTH ST.

ST.

7TH ST.
VIADUCT

BUSINESS
DISTRICT

PACIFIC
ELECTRIC
STATION

SEVENTH

R. R.

SANTA FE

ALAMEDA ST.

BRANCH

9TH ST.
VIADUCT

NINTH ST.

Pacific Electric Tracks come
down to surface from Elevated
Structure at 14th St.

ABOVE: Covers of these Pacific Electric Magazines saluted beach areas served by the trolleys. The two-car train was on the P.E. right-of-way hugging the coast between Redondo

Beach and Playa del Rey. BELOW: An interurban train leaves its car barn to make the trip from Venice to Los Angeles. (Photograph by John Lawson)

20. The P. E. Hits the Peak:

The Roaring Twenties, carrying the American economy to new heights, also brought the peak of operations for the Pacific Electric. The era was a logical time for the greatest activity of the Big Red Cars because the national prosperity nurtured intensive western growth centering in Southern California.

More than four decades of aggressive boosting for Southern California's mild climate, varied scenic attractions, and economic opportunities, coupled with the world wide impact of Hollywood motion pictures, were bearing fruit.

The population of Los Angeles as well as its surrounding territory more than doubled from 1920 to 1930. Los Angeles, given 576,673 residents in the 1920 census, had 1,238,648 people a decade later. The rate of growth was far outpacing the fondest dreams of those boosters who hardly more than a half century before sought a transcontinental railroad link as a helping hand for the city of barely 5,000 residents.

The 1920's continued the growth in the outlying areas. The counties of Los Angeles, Orange, Riverside, and San Bernardino started the decade with a total of 1,121,528 people; the 1930 census gave the four counties a total of 2,542,090 residents. Farms were giving way to new communities, and the existing cities were growing as the Big Red Cars made commuting easy.

The peak of the Pacific Electric's rail service has been placed variously at points between 1923 and 1927 by differing students of the system. However, it was in 1923 that the highest number of individual interurban and local streetcar lines—115—were in operation and in 1924 that the Big Red Cars carried their record number of riders, a total of 109,185,650 passengers. (The exceptions for 1924 as a peak passenger year came only during World War II and immediately thereafter as a result initially of troop movement and war workers and subsequently with a tremendous population increase).

The system reached its maximum extension in 1926 when its tracks stretched for 1,164 miles, an increase of thirty-five miles from 1923, sixty-four from 1920, and nearly double the track mileage existing when the

It was during this era that the Pacific Electric played an important role on the social and economic life of Southern California. The extensive service, backed by the catching advertising slogan of "Ride the Big Red Cars," made deep impressions on local residents as well as tourists. The time produced memories that were cherished long after the trolleys sped into history.

The tracks stretched from San Fernando to Redlands as well as from atop Mount Lowe to the Pacific Ocean. The diverse operation used over 800 passenger cars ranging from the mule-powered vehicles for sightseers at Mount Lowe to the high-speed interurbans running from Los Angeles out to San Bernardino and Redlands. There were 6,000 scheduled cars daily as compared to only 1,400 in 1911.

A commuter could board a Big Red Car in Long Beach and arrive in Los Angeles fifty mintues later. It took only forty-five minutes to ride from Pasadena or Glendale to downtown Los Angeles. Commuters from Santa Monica could reach Los Angeles in approximately an hour.

The interurban lines not only radiated from Los Angeles but also ran between individual cities. There were scheduled trips from San Pedro to Balboa via Long Beach, from Pomona to Upland, from Pasadena to the Catalina Island steamship terminal in Wilmington, and from Upland to San Antonio Heights. In the orange grove country, there were routes from San Bernardino to Redlands, Highland, and Patton as well as into the mountains to Arrowhead Springs.

The Pacific Electric Building at Sixth and Main Streets was the nerve center of the system. The terminal was busy with passengers hurrying to catch interurbans leaving almost every minute of the day. Its news stands and lunch counters did a lucrative business, and a host of coin-operated amusement and vending machines were kept active by passengers awaiting trains.

The basic contributor to trolley patronage was the person commuting from his suburban home to a Los Angeles office. There was also substantial traffic from shoppers from outlying areas (the major regional shopping center was not yet even a dream) and from tourists, numerous and prosperous with the times.

Automobiles, although bothersome to the operation of the trolleys, were only on the verge of making important inroads on commuter traffic and busses had not yet become a competitive factor. Veteran residents relied almost completely on the Pacific Electric. The volume of passengers encouraged the company to make plans for its Hollywood Subway, completed in 1925, and to propose an elevated railroad system in order to retain patronage.

As the Pacific Electric system reached its peak, its lines radiated in five basic directions. A line stretched to Glendale and Burbank, while another went out to

The bus influence of the 1940's is symbolized in this picture at the Main Street Station in Los Angeles.

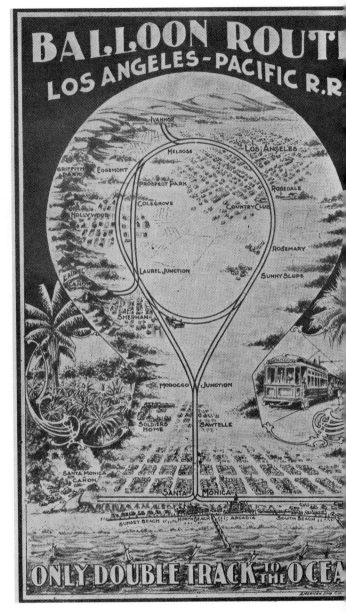

The famous Balloon Trolley Trip, so named because of the shape of its route, was depicted in a 1903 advertisement.

the San Fernando Valley through Hollywood. A third line pushed westward to Santa Monica, a fourth went south to Long Beach, and a fifth reached eastward through the San Gabriel Valley.

The westward line to Santa Monica had extensions branching off to Venice and Redondo Beach as well as tracks serving Culver City, Beverly Hills, and Torrance.

On the Long Beach line, a branch switched from Slauson Junction for Huntington Park, Whittier, and Yorba Linda; at Watts, on line left for Santa Ana and another went to Gardena, Torrance, and Redondo Beach; tracks at Dominguez Junction led to San Pedro, and in Long Beach itself a line branched off for Newport Harbor.

This 1918 photo was taken at Colorado and Raymond in Pasadena. Note the policeman directing traffic; this was an *innovation at the time because of the increasing number of automobiles. (Craig Rasmussen Collection)*

The San Gabriel Valley could boast the heaviest concentration of lines. Pasadena received excellent service. Routes went to Sierra Madre and through Arcadia and Monrovia to Glendora. Another route stretched through the valley to San Bernardino and provided branches to San Dimas, Pomona, and Ontario.

In San Bernardino itself, another group of lines stretched to Riverside and Corona, up to Arrowhead Hot Springs, and over to Redlands.

Southern Californians well could agree with the words of David W. Pontius, extremely popular with both employees and the public as general manager of the Pacific Electric and eventually its president, as he hailed the system in the December 10, 1929 issue of the Pacific Electric Magazine:

It has been definitely proven that there is not now, and probably will never be, any other agency that can so well handle mass transportation as the electric trolley.

In our own section, this railway has been the greatest reliance of and greatest single element in promoting the growth and progress of over forty-five cities and their adjacent territory. It was not only the pioneer, but the permanent resident.

The optimism of the times also prompted the company to build many new passenger stations in the communities it served. Dedications of the buildings were marked by enthusiastic ceremonies and townspeople pointed with pride to the structures.

The Big Red Cars did more than merely serve commuters who had jobs in Los Angeles. They became popular for travel to the New Year's Day Rose Parade in Pasadena, the National Orange Show in San Ber-

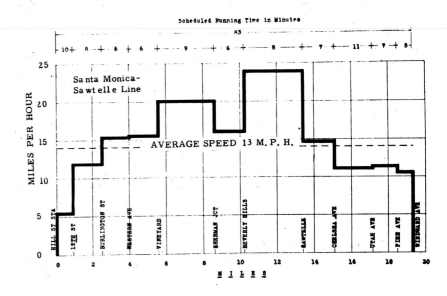

This chart, prepared during the 1920's by the California Public Utilities Commission, showed average speeds at various points on the Santa Monica line. Street traffic and roads cutting into the rights-of-way reduced speed to an average of thirteen miles an hour. Other P. E. lines also were slowed by traffic.

nardino, the Los Angeles County Fair at Pomona, and the Mission Play in San Gabriel.

Operating in Southern California where superlatives were expected, the Pacific Electric out-boasted all other interurban systems by truthfully billing itself as the "world's greatest electric railway system." The actual operation of the immense railroad was divided into four "districts:" the Southern, Northern, Western, and Eastern. Each of these districts was bigger than practically any other interurban system in America.

The Southern District included the lines operating down the Southern "corridor" through Watts to Long Beach, Redondo Beach, San Pedro, Torrance, Huntington Beach, Newport Beach, Santa Ana, Whittier, Fullerton, Yorba Linda, and El Segundo.

The Northern District encompassed lines to Pasadena, South Pasadena, Alhambra, Mount Lowe, Arcadia, Glendora, El Monte, Pomona, Uplands, Ontario, and San Dimas.

The Western District covered lines to Santa Monica, West Los Angeles, Playa del Rey, Venice, Manhattan Beach, Hermosa Beach, Inglewood, Beverly Hills, Hollywood, Glendale, Burbank, and the San Fernando Valley. The latter three areas were included in the district because their cars operated through the Hollywood Subway, common starting point for most interurbans serving communities west of Los Angeles. Despite its proximity to Santa Monica, the El Segundo line was excluded from this division and placed in the Southern District because it operated through the Southern "corridor."

The Eastern District covered all operations east of Upland. Among the communities in this district were San Bernardino

Redlands, Colton, Bloomington, Rialto, Fontana, Riverside, Arlington, and Corona.

Each district had its own supervisors, assigned employees and work schedules, specific electric cars, and repair facilities.

In 1928 the Pacific Electric initiated its Sunday Pass, an institution for sightseeing through most of the depression for those without automobiles. A "pass" costing $1.00 permitted its buyer to unlimited riding for a Sunday over all of the Pacific Electric system except Mount Lowe and the area beyond Pomona. A $2.50 "pass" enabled the passengers to ride the Big Red Cars out to San Bernardino and Redlands as well as up to Mount Lowe. A total of 975 "passes" were purchased on April 29, first Sunday when they were offered; by July 15 more than 2,500 "passes" were being sold every Sunday.

Lee Shippey, columnist for the Los Angeles Times, praised the "passes" with these words: [1]

Yesterday we had a friend from New York to show around and, as habitual, were short of money. So we set out to see how much of the beauty, charm, romance, and variety of this territory and autoless man can see for one lone dollar . . . We traveled a total of 127 miles, about the city, through several interesting beach resorts . . . Los Angeles Harbor . . . into the fringes of the orange empire, to one historic mission, and halfway up a noble mountain.

Topping his praise of the Sunday Pass, however, was a letter to the Long Beach Press-Telegram from George

1. Quoted in the Pacific Electric Magazine, June 10, 1928.

176

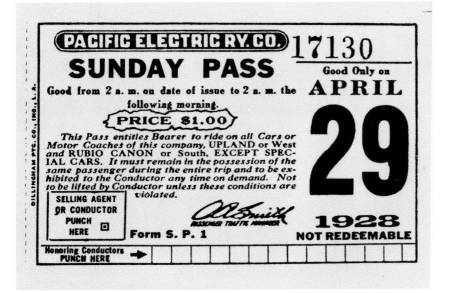

The famous "Sunday Pass," launched in 1928, permitted passengers to ride all day.

Livesey, reporting that he logged 334 miles during one Sunday of riding the Big Red Cars.[2]

Despite the praises, the trend had started toward automobiles. In 1925 the total number of passengers using the Pacific Electric dropped to 102,921,794, a decline from 1924's record 109,185,650 riders. The company began to substitute bus routes for the trolley lines.

The effect of more automobiles and lengthened running time between destinations for the interurbans because of automotive interference reduced the Pacific Electric's total passenger volume in 1928 to 103,417,260 persons, of which 16,556,079 rode by busses.

A study prepared by Laurence R. Veysey as a 1953 bachelor's thesis for Yale University and later published as "Passenger Service of the Pacific Electric" (Interurbans, Los Angeles: 1958) showed that during its lifetime the merged Red Car system had a total of 143 separately scheduled interurban and local streetcar lines. (Four of the lines were created from 1930 to 1942 through use of existing trackage.)

In 1920 as the Pacific Electric was reaching its greatest heights, only twenty-one of the lines (fourteen of them marginal local routes) had been abandoned. Approximately thirty-five scheduled lines were discontinued during the Roaring Twenties as the Big Red Cars passed their peak of service.

When the Motor Transit Company, initial name of the rail company's bus affiliate, moved its headquarters to the Pacific Electric Building, the Pacific Electric

Magazine of February 10, 1931 greeted employees with these words:

. . . Contrary to the wish we sometime inwardly hold when relatives "move in," we hope they prolong their stay . . . We repeat, "Welcome, Motor Transit: make yourselves right t'home."

The busses not only were to stay, but they were to crowd out the Big Red Cars.

David W. Pontius was vice president and general manager of the Pacific Electric during most of the 1920's. He became president in 1929. (Los Angeles Times Photo)

---

2. Pacific Electric Magazine, May 10, 1928.

Pacific Electric Magazine

Vol. 14 LOS ANGELES, CAL., AUGUST 10, 1929 No. 3

21. "Ride the Big Red Cars"

Shortly after the Pacific Electric line to Long Beach was completed, George B. Kelly, garnished with the title of assistant passenger agent of the new company, visited newspapers in the area, launching what was to become an extensive and eventually famous advertising program.

The title "assistant passenger agent" was the nomenclature for the individual that handled advertising.

"Mr. Kelly is an old time newspaperman, a jolly, jovial good fellow." The Long Beach Press reported after one of his visits, "and a hustler for the company he represents." [1]

In launching his electric interurban system, Henry Huntington recognized that building the lines and providing the service alone would not be enough; he would need to tell the public when his cars ran and otherwise encourage patronage. Transportation at the turn of the century was a highly competition business; the convenience of departure and arrival times were immense selling points to the public. The rail lines providing the most attractive schedules from a time standpoint stood to obtain patronage.

The early advertising of both the Pacific Electric and Los Angeles Pacific systems followed the patterns established by the transcontinental railroads. Small "box" advertisements listed destinations along with departure and arrival times. [2]

Southern California's tourist economy called for certain variations however. Most tourists during the early part of the century came during the winter months to escape the colder climates. In addition to enjoying the mild climate, tourists expected to see Southern California's orange groves, mountains, and beaches. The winter season, therefore became a time when "schedule" advertisements were supplemented with suggestions for trips on the various trolley lines to the beaches, Mount Lowe, or into the orange grove country.

The Great Merger uniting the electric lines under Southern Pacific ownership consolidated advertising programs. Advertising was not confined to the newspapers alone either before or after the consolidation of the companies. Colorful folders featuring communities served by the electric railroads were distributed not only from racks in the trolley stations but also were placed in the steam railroad depots in Southern California and sent eastward to lure tourists westward. Many of the folders were in full color and depicted the waxy green orange groves, inviting beaches, and palm-lined residential streets of the cities.

1. Long Beach Press, October 14, 1902.

2. Such advertisements appeared regularly in most area daily and weekly newspapers.

Posters advertising the scenic points of interest served by the interurbans also were placed in train depots and hotels. The advertising program ordinarily was handled by an individual assigned to the task by the company.

The growing competition of the automobile altered the situation. As part of a general program to retain its leadership in the interurban field, the Pacific Electric in 1917 engaged the national advertising agency of Lord and Thomas

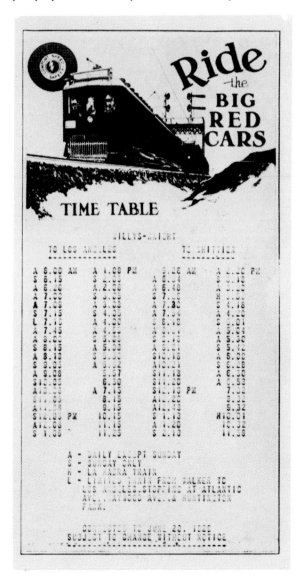

This 1929 timetable, designed for posting in stations, carried the famous "Ride the Big Red Cars" ad theme which helped perpetuate the Pacific Electric in history.

PUBLIC SHOWN RIGHT WAY ON HIGHWAY

Three of the more recent bill-board displays now appearing adjacent to heavily traveled highways as an aid to selling the public on idea of riding the Big Red Cars.

adopted the policy of filling that need so that there can be no reasonable criticism from the viewpoint of lack of service because of lack of electric

CONTINUING to tell the public of the economy and desirability of travel over P. E. lines, the bill-board advertising campaign is to be continued throughout the present year.

DISCARDED CLOTHES WAN

In the many Mexican camps tered throughout the system the

ABOVE: Photos of billboards urging commuters to "Ride the Big Red Cars" instead of using autos were shown in a 1926 issue of the Pacific Electric Magazine. RIGHT: There were fewer commuters when employment dropped during the Depression. This ad, widely used in 1930, featured the drastic reduction in Big Red Car fares.

—later reorganized as the Foote, Cone and Belding Advertising Agency—to plan its campaigns. Assigned as account executive to the campaign was Don Belding, heading a team that switched the direction of the advertising program from one of "destinations" to one seeking to popularize riding the Pacific Electric cars throughout the area.

"What we tried to do was to increase the number of riders 'in between' (the major travel points)," Belding recalled. [3] "At that time most of the shopping was done in downtown Los Angeles and the suburban shopping center, as we know it (in 1962), was completely unknown. The best way to get downtown was by the Red Cars. But even then people were starting to use their autos more than the Red Cars. The goal was for an increase in Red Car passengers."

---

3. In a 1962 contact with the author.

The slogan "Ride the Big Red Cars" became famous as the nucleus for an extensive advertising campaign launched in 1925, midpoint in the era when the Pacific Electric was fighting the battle to retain the commuters who were turning to automobiles.

Billboards throughout Southern California carried the slogan, as did timetables distributed to riders and banners tied to the trolleys. When downtown Los Angeles stores had sales, their advertisements included reminders for shoppers to "Ride the Big Red Cars" when coming to eye the bargains. Similarly, posters and advertisements for the Mission Play, the National Orange Show, the Los Angeles County Fair, and other events tied in the suggestion that the attractions could be easily reached if one would "Ride the Big Red Cars."

"The slogan worked," Belding recalled. "We knew that

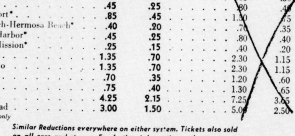

by the response to some of the events when traffic materially increase."

So intensively and effectively was the "Ride the Big Red Car" theme used that years later many persons once intimately associated with the Pacific Electric assumed that the slogan has been concocted for the campaign started in 1925. Actually the interurbans were popularly called "Big Red Cars" shortly after they began service and the slogan "Ride the Big Red Cars" was used in Pacific Electric "box" ads as early as 1910. [4]

Who should be given the credit for reviving the slogan and making it famous?

Belding maintained no single individual deserved complete credit for the extensive use of the slogan inasmuch as the program was a "team effort" utilizing many skilled writers, artists, and technicians.

A companion slogan developed concurrently was "Safe, Fast and Comfortable," incorporated into the official emblem on the Pacific Electric cars and also used on time tables and various advertising.

The "Ride the Big Cars" campaign was among the most effective advertising programs in any field. As ambitious and effective as it was, however, the advertising was unable to stem the tide of the times. Pacific Electric commuter traffic continued to decline, following the nation-wide pattern of a shift to automobiles.

---

4. A typical example was in the January 2, 1910, issue of the Los Angeles Examiner.

ABOVE: Oscar A. Smith, one-time secretary to Henry Huntington, discusses transit problems while serving as P. E. president in the 1940's (Los Angeles Times) BELOW: A Pasadena-bound car leaves the Sixth and Main station. (Pacific Railroad Publications)

Henry Huntington's palatial San Marino home is pictured at the mid-point of the twentieth century when it served as a gallery for a priceless collection of paintings. It attracted visitors from throughout the world.

22. The Huntington Heritage

After Henry Huntington's marriage to Arabella Huntington in 1913, he continued an active "retirement" in managing his financial empire but he was gradually retreating from the business world and devoting more and more time to collecting what became a priceless collection of art objects, rare books, and manuscripts.

His fame as an interurban builder had earned Huntington the title of "The Trolley Man;" [1] it would have

been more appropriate if he had been called "The Electric Man," for it was the growing field of electrical power generation and distribution which built his fortune to a degree that was not widely realized.

Huntington formed the Pacific Light and Power Company early in the century to provide gas and electric power for householders as well as his interurban system. Among the immense tasks which the company undertook after Huntington's 1910 "retirement" was the construction of the Big Creek hydroelectric project, an engineering feat for its day. Electricity generated from the

---

1. The title of "The Trolley Man" was used in numerous magazine and newspaper articles devoted to Huntington after his retirement.

Typical of folders issued by the P. E. to help promote passenger traffic was this one detailing points of interest for hikers near interurban routes. It was issued in approximately 1915. (John Packard Collection)

facility in the Sierra Nevada near Fresno was carried 240 miles to the company's service area stretching from Los Angeles to San Bernardino.

Despite his ownership of the company, Huntington demonstrated that he retained his ideas of economy by excusing himself from guests in his home to extinguish unneeded electric lights in a hallway.[2]

A subsidiary of the Pacific Power and Light, the Southern California Gas Company, became an entity and a major utility organization in its own right.

Seeking less responsibility as the years moved on, Huntington in 1917 agreed for a merger of Pacific Power and Light Company with the Southern California Edison Company. Until the merger, Pacific had been the dominating firm in the electrical supply field. Formed in 1901 with assets of $5 million, its value by 1916 reached nearly $60 million as compared to $38 million for the Edison unit with which it merged.[3]

Other Huntington interests included the Huntington Land and Improvement Company, organized in 1902 with capital of $100,000. By 1917 its assets were "conservatively appraised at $15 million," an increase of $5 million from an appraisal in 1912. In addition, Huntington controlled the Newport News Shipbuilding Company and had vast blocks of stocks in eastern and midwestern railroads. He also retained ownership of the Los Angeles Railway Company, dominating local street-car service. The competition of automobiles did not reduce travel on local passenger lines as much as it did on the interurban routes. In 1914, the Pacific Electric reported a deficit, but Huntington's company made nearly $1 million.

Huntington gradually delegated more responsibility of operating his empire to his son, Howard E. Huntington, and trusted attorney, William Dunn.

Henry Huntington increased his interest in the collection of art works and books. When the rare book collection of E. Dwight Church of Brooklyn was placed on sale early in 1911, Huntington purchased the entire library for an estimated $1 million.

Two weeks later a fine vellum copy of the Gutenberg Bible, first book printed with movable type was offered in the sale of another collection. The first bid was only $10,000. After spirited bidding the Bible was sold for a record $50,000 to book dealer George D. Smith, who announced that he represented Henry Huntington — seated beside him on the occasion in the auction room.

2. William Hertrich in an interview with the author.

3. Growth of the two companies can be noted in reports recorded in the annual editions of "Walker's Manual of California Securities and Directory of Directories," published starting in 1908 by H. D. Walker Company, San Francisco.

Perhaps as Huntington sat in the room his mind went back to the day of the $110,000 franchise.

"There's a little pride in it," he had said. "Yes, there's a little pride in it."

Huntington continued his purchase of rare books and manuscripts. His library was to house a first folio of Shakespeare's plays and the manuscript of Benjamin Franklin's autobiography. The library could boast that it had forty percent of the 26,143 books published in England or the English language prior to 1641. The rare art works amassed by Huntington included Gainsborough's "Blue Boy" and Lawrence's "Pinkie."[4]

The art and book treasures were housed at his San Marino estate, beautifully landscaped over a period of years with rare plants under the direction of William Hertrich. In 1919 Huntington executed a deed of trust whereby his San Marino estate and its priceless treasures would be administered as a non-profit foundation so that the public could admire the collections and scholars could utilize the facilities for study.

It has been suggested that Henry Huntington amassed his collections and dedicated them to the public with the hope that he would be remembered well, recalling the stories composing the harsh legend of Collis P. Huntington.

A possibility, perhaps, but hardly believable for a man with the creative ability of Henry Huntington who was so positive in the forcefulness of his development of Southern California. It is more logical to suppose that as Huntington matured he developed a desire to assist culturally the area which he had helped build. He did this by collecting in one place the treasures which otherwise would have been scattered throughout the world.

Shortly after he announced plans for his library and art gallery he spoke of the scholars who would some day visit the facility:

I perhaps shall not live to welcome them, but . . . when they come . . . it is my desire to make their goal worthwhile.

Considerable influence in his decision to dedicate the treasure-laden Henry E. Huntington Library and Art Gallery to the public was provided by Archer Huntington, son of Arabella Huntington by her first marriage. Archer won considerable acclaim as a scholar early in his life and was a patron of the arts. When the institution, long contemplated by the magnate, was created by a deed of trust in

---

4. An excellent description of the collection and how Huntington assembled it is contained in "Henry Edwards Huntington: The Founder and The Library," (San Marino, 1948) by Robert O. Schad.

These portraits of Mrs. Arabella Huntington and Henry E. Huntington, painted by Oswald Birley, were hung in the main exhibit hall of the Huntington Library in San Marino. (© The Huntington Library: Used by Permission)

1919, Archer Huntington was named a member of its board of trustees. [5]

Just how much the magnate spent on his collections was never revealed. Some estimates placed the expenditures as high as $50 million. At the mid-point of the twentieth century, the collection was priceless.

Before his death, Collis Huntington had built a $250,000 mausoleum at his Connecticut estate. In 1926 Henry Huntington commissioned plans for a Grecian-style masoleum located on the highest point of the San Marino estate. Huntington spared no cost in building the structure; it was there that he and Arabella would be entombed.

The electric magnate's philanthropies were not confined to his San Marino estate. He provided an endowment for the Collis P. and Howard Huntington Memorial Hospital in Pasadena as a tribute to his uncle and son. The memory of his parents was honored by dedication of the family home at Oneonta, New York, as a library and public park.

As the years passed, Huntington found his circle of intimates dwindling. His son, Howard, had been in ill health for years and died in 1922 and in 1925 William Dunn suffered a fatal heart attack.

Arabella Huntington died in 1924 at her New York City home at Fifth and Fifty-seventh Streets. Behind her she left a record of considerable personal acclaim for her assistance to a variety of cultural and educational organizations.

---

[5] According to information supplied to the author by Mrs. Anna Huntington.

Despite the personal losses Huntington remained active and enthusiastic, although he was himself ailing. He kept his seat on the board of directors of the Southern Pacific, and traveled on his private cars between New York and Los Angeles in the interests of business and his art collection.

Early in 1927 he boarded the private cars in San Marino for medical treatment in the East. He jovially assured his friends that he expected to live for many more years.

It was ironic that Henry Huntington, a symbol of the rail age, died on May 23, 1927, just as the newspaper headlines were heralding Charles A. Lindbergh's accomplishment of flying across the Atlantic Ocean.

Immediately after Huntington's death in Philadelphia, newspapers speculated that his lavish expenditures for art treasures must have depleted his vast fortune. On the contrary, when his will was filed for probate his estate was valued at more than $40 million despite the millions he had spent.

A special train took his private cars, carrying Huntington's body, to the Pacific Coast. When it approached Los Angeles, the funeral car, draped in black crepe, was attached to a Pacific Electric locomotive. The way was lined with mourners and the locomotive, its bell tolling, pulled the car through the streets to the San Marino estate. There Henry Huntington was placed in the magnificent masoleum where Arabella Huntington previously was entombed.

The front and back covers of this Pacific Electric Magazine showed employees meeting in the auditorium of the P. E. *Club, adjoining the Sixth and Main station. Many activities were held for employees.*

23. The Rolling Stock, Fares, and Finances

When a horse-drawn wagon carried Southern California's first electric interurban up Fairoaks Avenue into Pasadena on February 19, 1895, it attracted crowds of curious spectators who gathered around the vehicle that went into operation ten weeks later when the tracks to Los Angeles were completed.

As the new trolleys stood ready for their first trip from Pasadena to Los Angeles, a newspaper reporter described them enthusiastically: [1]

They (the electric cars) are finished even to the pretty ground bordered mirrors set across tables. The broad reversible seats are in red plush, and are very soft and easy.

They are 35 feet long and 8½ feet high. Twenty-one feet of the length is the enclosure where two rows of seats, eight on a side, are placed for those who prefer the interior. Ten feet of one end, the rear, are given over to the smoker, where smokers and people preferring to ride outside may ride.

From that day until well past the demise of the interurban system in 1961 the trolleys proved immensely interesting to young and old alike. Official and unofficial fraternities of trolley enthusiasts became experts in the histories of individual cars, the particular interurbans assigned to specific routes, and numerous specialized areas pertaining to the rolling stock.

The means of identifying various trolleys became the merged Pacific Electric's numbering system dating from 1911. It began with number "1," an antiquated horsecar, and continued through streetcars for local service as well as the big interurbans to number "1975," a rail work car. Trolleys with basic similarities were classified in groups, each owning a specific range of 100 numbers thus enabling the enthusiasts to refer to cars as the "400" class or "1200" class.

During its lifetime the Red Car line used nearly 2,000 separate cars, although the most in operation at a single time was approximately 880 in 1924. In addition the Pacific Electric owned many freight cars.

The fastest and most ornate trolley ever to roll on the system was Henry Huntington's private car, capable of moving ninety miles an hour. A variety of cars for the average traveler on the Pacific Electric were placed into service over the years.

The fastest passenger interurbans for the system, a State Railroad Commission report of 1939 showed, were the big

50 Cars for Pacific Electric

All Steel

Included among recent shipments of cars from our Philadelphia Plant was a lot of fifty center-entrance front-exit type for the Pacific Electric Railway, Los Angeles.

These cars are of all-steel construction according to the railway's standard design

and measure 52 ft. 2 in. over bumpers, 8 ft. 10 in. wide over posts and accommodate 65 seated passengers.

This type car weighs less than 23 tons complete, ready for operation which is comparatively light for this class of high-speed service.

This manufacturer, knowing the prestige of selling cars to the P. E., featured the news in an ad.

steel trolleys of the "1200" class which could hit sixty miles an hour and were used on the lines to Long Beach, Santa Monica, and San Bernardino.

The slowest were the tiny four-wheeled Birney streetcars used for local service which were capable of up to twenty-five miles an hour but never needed the speed because of the stop-and-go nature of their service. The Birneys, with thirty-two seats, had the smallest capacity of any of the cars. The big "1200's" took the honors of providing the most space; they provided sixty-five seats and the state's studies showed that another sixty-five people easily could find standing room in them.

The trolleys of all types became familiar throughout

---

1. Pasadena Evening Star, April 30, 1895. Reports of the California Railroad Commission (later the California Public Utilities Commission) and the Interstate Commerce Commission also described the interurban cars. Various issues of Interurbans (Los Angeles, 1943-Present) discussed the trolleys.

The "catcher" on this Big Red Car was intended to serve as a cushion to reduce impact if the trolley hit an auto or pedestrian (Charles Seims Collection)

Southern California and their fame was perpetuated by their eye-catching red color, which with their ordinarily immense size and frequency of service helped to develop the Pacific Electric's famous slogan, "Ride the Big Red Cars."

Why Henry Huntington decided upon red for the cars of his electric interurban line is a matter he never felt called upon to discuss with his intimates, at least those who survived the midway mark of the twentieth century. Red was not one of his favorite colors. Nor was the red inherited from the Los Angeles and Pasadena Railroad which he acquired as his initial venture in the Southern California interurban field; its coaches were olive trimmed in yellow.

The color may have been inspired by the red plush seats in the initial Pasadena interurbans or he may have been prompted to use the distinctive marking because of his familiarity with the traditional red cabooses of the steam

railroads. Oscar A. Smith, his one-time stenographer, and William Hertrich, associated with him in 1904 as horticulturist for his San Marino estate, have suggested more expedient and practical motivations. They speculated that the color was chosen for its visibility and because it distinguished the interurbans from those of competing lines.

The red trolley cars made their appearance early in 1899 when Huntington used the designation "Pacific Electric" on a local Los Angeles trolley line he had purchased. The Pasadena cars eventually were painted red, and soon after the line to Long Beach opened in 1902 the Red Cars were becoming famous in Southern California.

So renowned were the cars by early 1904 when the system was extended to Whittier that completion of the line was celebrated by the Whittier Register by publishing a "Red Car" edition with red letters across the newspaper's front page.

As the years passed, new interurbans became larger and faster. While the rolling stock of many transit systems was limited to a few models of interurbans, the Pacific Electric increased its diversity of electric cars. Many types of trolleys catered to different needs ranging from local transportation to lines stretching up to fifty miles from Los Angeles. And, too, after The Great Merger of 1911, the parent Southern Pacific could transfer equipment from its electric interurban systems on other sections of the Pacific Coast.

The innovation of the "California Car" came with opening of the Los Angeles and Pasadena Railway. The name was bestowed because one section of the trolley was protected by windows but a second section opened to the air for the convenience of smokers and the pleasure of mild-climate enthusiasts.

The opening of the line to Long Beach in 1902 followed by Huntington's concentrated activity at building his basic system brought the arrival of thirty "California Car" interurbans built by the St. Louis Car Company, at the time the leading firm in the electric car construction industry. The cars, each seating forty-eight persons, were the basic equipment for Huntington's service to Pasadena and Alhambra as well as to Long Beach. As new routes opened, trolley car technological improvements developed and types of service varied, with many models of electric trolleys placed into service. A tally of operating records showed that during the system's more than half century of operation, more than 1,600 separate pieces of interurban equipment transported passengers. In addition, the Pacific Electric operated electric locomotives, box cars, gondolas, flat cars, and cabooses for its freight service.

RIGHT: The process of spray-painting the "red" on the Big Red Cars to keep them attractive was described in a 1928 article in the Pacific Electric Magazine. Painters used brushes on the cars in the earlier days.

Adding Red to 'Big Red Cars'

A PCC interurban, most modern used by the P. E., rolls on the Glendale route after being acquired in 1940. The cars eventually were sold to nations which still relied on trolley systems. (Pacific Railroad Publications)

The building of electric trolley cars grew into big business with the development of traction lines throughout the nation. Among the major car builders were the American Car Company of St. Louis, Barney and Smith Car Company of Dayton, Ohio, J. G. Brill Company of Philadelphia, the Cincinnati Car Company of Cincinnati, Ohio, the Jewett Car Company of Newark, Ohio, the Pullman-Standard Car Company, and the St. Louis Car Company. All of the companies were represented by equipment on the Pacific Electric system. In addition, prior to The Great Merger the Los Angeles and Redondo Railway maintained its own car building shops. Its craftsmen produced interurbans acclaimed as the pride of the line and the envy of other interurban operators.

While emphasizing service trolleys, the interurban lines did not neglect "deluxe" cars. The greatest of this class was The Alabama, the private car of Henry Huntington. The St. Louis Car Company built the car for the railroad magnate in 1904 and without a doubt it was the most spectacular trolley ever constructed. It was sixty-three feet long and weighed 103,000 pounds, making it twice as long and three times as heavy as typical interurbans of the day.

The Alabama, named for the home state of the rail magnate's second wife, whisked Huntington on tours throughout his interurban empire. The greatest problem in its operation lay in navigating the sharp curves of tracks in downtown Los Angeles, a task accomplished only when its motorman operated it at two miles per hour. After relinquishing control of the Pacific Electric in 1910, Huntington placed his private car in storage on his San Marino estate. It remained there until 1920 when it was sold to the Sacramento Northern Railroad for use as a parlor car; its motors went into a Pacific Electric locomotive.

A most unusual type of trolley was the funeral car which served its purpose in the pre-automobile era on the Los Angeles and Redondo line. Later converted into a passenger car with fifty-two seats, it saw use in interurban service until the 1930's.

The typical interurban familiar in Pacific Electric service was the wood-framed trolley with square windows for the motorman. At its front was a metal device popularly called a "cow catcher;" in reality it served to push brush or large rocks from the track and softened the impact when collisions occurred. The cars varied in width from eight to nine feet and seated from forty to sixty passengers, depending on the model.

The Big Red Cars were large even from the start; they grew more massive as the years passed and there were needs for greater seating capacities in order to reduce operating deficits. The interurbans placed into service for Pasadena in 1895 weighed approximately 33,000 pounds, were 11½ feet tall, thirty-three feet long and carried thirty-two passengers. The cars purchased by Huntington when the Long

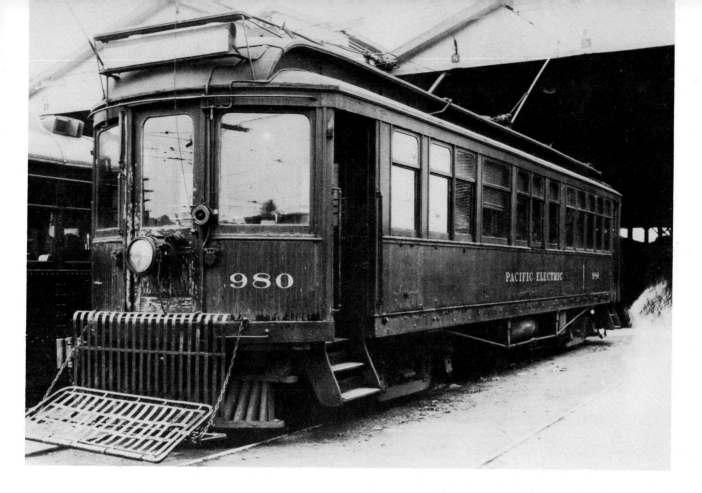

ABOVE: *This interurban, built in the early twentieth century and distinguished by wooden sides and rounded front, was typical of cars on the Venice line until its end in 1950.*

(Charles Seims Collection) BELOW: Equipment included electric locomotives and tower cars to repair wire. (Craig Rasmussem Collection)

Beach line opened had a weight of 56,000 pounds. They were nearly twelve feet tall, forty-three feet long, and provided seats for forty-eight passengers.

By 1910 the "work-horse" and most typical car of the Pacific Electric system had become a 58,000 pound interurban built by the St. Louis Car Company. Towering slightly more than twelve feet above the tracks, it was forty-three feet long and could seat fifty-six people. Two, three, and even four of the trolleys were linked to form trains for heavy service. Heavy duty interurbans weighing approximately 85,000 pounds and capable of seating up to sixty passengers were purchased by the Pacific Electric in 1913 from the Jewett Car Company. They could operate on 600-volts, standard on the existing interurban system, as well as on the high-speed 1,200 volt line built to San Bernardino.

The last interurbans built especially for Pacific Electric service proved to be the heaviest and tallest of the Red Car System. Constructed by the Standard Steel Car Company in 1925, each of the fifty cars weighed 96,000 pounds, were 9½ feet wide, and were 13½ feet high. Although used primarily for service in the San Gabriel Valley, they also were used on other sections of the system.

The ultimate in interurban cars came in 1934 with de-

velopment of the President's Conference Committee cars as the result of research into needs for rolling stock by the heads of electric railroads throughout America. In a sense the PCC cars, as they were called, represented a return to the lightness of interurbans at the turn-of-the-century in an effort to reduce operating costs. Although the sleek interurbans provided fifty-nine seats, they weighed only 41,000 pounds and were but ten feet high—a substantial reduction in size from the bulky cars being used in Pacific Electric service. The company purchased thirty of the cars in 1940 for service to Burbank and Glendale in an effort to speed travel and control costs. While riders loved the PCC cars, no move was made to acquire others for the system because it was obvious that a switch to bus service was inevitable.

The freight cars grew increasingly important as the years passed and the Pacific Electric attempted to find means to offset passenger service losses. In 1911 the company listed 972 freight cars on its rolls. Financial reports in 1923 showed the P. E. had 1,662 freight cars and their types indicated the diversity of service. The rolling stock that year included 323 box cars, 444 flat cars, 67 gondolas, 10 stock cars, and 23 tank cars. By 1928 the company listed 2,628 freight cars among its assets. Even by the depression year of 1932, when fewer interurbans were in service, there were 2,256 freight cars in operation.

The Pacific Electric also had cabooses used in the freight operations and tower cars utilized to repair trolley wires. The company's operating facilities included, of course, electrical power sub-stations located throughout the area and, to house the trolleys not in use, car barns in the principle communities.

Repair operations for the Big Red Cars were concentrated at the Macy Street Yard in Los Angeles. Other mechanical work on the interurbans was performed at the Morgan Street Yard in Long Beach and smaller yards at other large cities.

Drinking fountains and toilet facilities were missing on most of the Big Red Cars because of the comparatively short nature of their routes. These facilities were provided, however, on the interurbans assigned to the lengthy trips to San Bernardino and Riverside.

In the realm of local streetcar service, the Pacific Electric used trolleys designed for that specialized need. The most widely used vehicle was the Birney car, named for their designer, engineer Charles O. Birney, and first produced in 1916. The cars were only twenty-eight feet long but could seat twenty-eight passengers. They were economical not only because of size but because they could be operated by one man serving as both motorman and conductor. The dimi-

LEFT: There were many contrasts in P. E.'s cars. Equipment ranged from this interurban to the cable cars that climbed The Great Incline on the Mount Lowe trip.

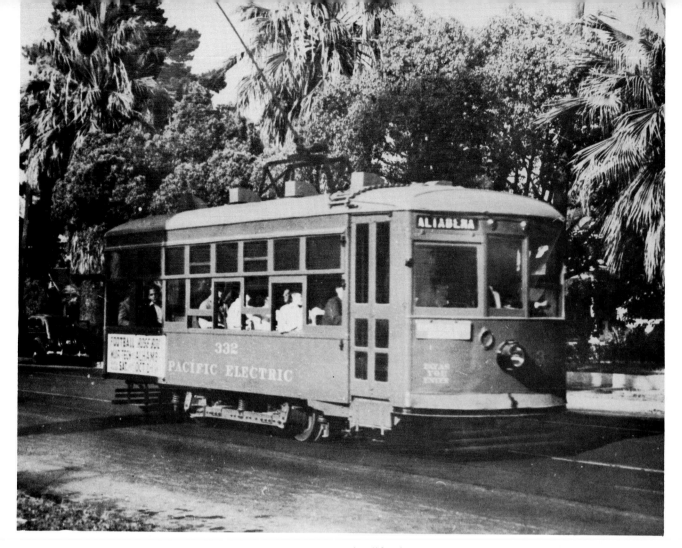

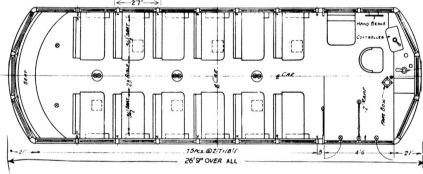

The Birney streetcars, smallest of the P. E. trolleys, seated just thirty-two people and could be operated by a motorman who did double duty as a conductor. These cars were used on "local" lines where traffic was light. (John Lawson Collection)

The Alabama, twice as long and three times as heavy as most interurbans, was built in 1904 as Henry Huntington's private car, which he owned personally. The car was painted green instead of the red he favored for his trolley system. Huntington used the luxurious car for inspection tours of the P. E. (John Adair Collection)

nutive Birney cars became popular for short-haul traffic in Los Angeles as well as on the Pacific Electric's local lines in San Bernardino, Riverside, Redlands, Pasadena, Long Beach, San Pedro, Santa Monica, and Venice.

A second type of trolley widely used for local traffic was a low-slung electric car introduced in 1920 providing an entrance near the motorman and exit through sliding doors in the center of the vehicle. The trolleys, forty-five feet long and highly maneuverable in traffic, seated sixty-five passengers. They journeyed the heavily-traveled lines to Hollywood and the San Fernando Valley as well as on routes in Long Beach and Pasadena.

The company was proud of its famous red color and kept the trolleys sparkling. In 1927 the Pacific Electric spent $100,000 in repainting cars, spraying the lacquer in a technique borrowed from the growing automobile manufacturing industry. Crews of cleaners and window washers, usually women, went to work on the trolleys after they completed a day's operations to keep the cars sparkling and bright.

The number of Big Red Cars operating varied during the years as equipment was sold or junked, new cars purchased, or trolleys transferred to the system from other Southern Pacific interurban properties. The Pacific Electric

reported in 1913 that it was operating 608 passenger cars, including nineteen cars capable of handling freight as well as riders. A year later in that pre-automobile era it owned 623 passenger trolleys.

By 1923, as passenger volume swelled, 748 Big Red Cars took to the rails. A record 880 interurban and local trolleys resided in the car barns of the Pacific Electric at the start of 1925 as the system reached peak service. The depression, with its reduction in travel and incipient shift to bus service, brought cutbacks in the numbers of trolleys. By 1932 just 721 electric passenger cars cruised the routes.

Not only did trolleys retire as rail service on various lines came to an end, but there was no new rolling stock for the surviving routes. The fifty interurbans ordered from the Standard Steel Car Company in 1925 were the last built specifically for the Red Car line; the thirty modern PCC cars purchased in 1940 were the last new electric cars acquired by the Pacific Electric. Replacement interurban cars brought in from parched Southern Pacific electric systems in other areas. Nineteen aluminum cars built in 1929 for the Northwestern Pacific system of the San Francisco Bay area went into service during World War II to meet the growing need for transportation. More reenforcements came

ABOVE: Heavy construction equipment begins excavation of the underground area for the downtown Los Angeles terminus of the Hollywood Subway. BELOW: Gondolas carry cement to re-enforce walls of the tunnel where interurbans entered Glendale Boulvard. (Both Photos: Security Pacific National Bank)

195

during the war with transfer to the Big Red Car line of fifty-two interurbans from the Southern Pacific's abandoned commuter lines in the Oakland area. The electric cars were on the verge of being scrapped when the war dictated their need to carry the influx of workers to shipyards and to transport military personnel.

The problem of rising costs for construction of interurbans coupled with the continuing deficits of the Pacific Electric forced the extended use of the cars. The trolleys for the initial interurban line to Pasadena cost an estimated $3,500 each. When Henry Huntington paid approximately $7,000 for the then deluxe cars to use on his new line to Long Beach, the thrifty-minded raised their eyebrows at such an outlandish expenditure. By 1910 the price of a full-sized interurban had soared to nearly $15,000 and within a decade a price tag of $20,000 on an interurban car was common. As the trolley era neared an end, the PCC cars cost more than $30,000 each, which was beyond the budget limitations of a company already losing money.

During the early part of the century, anti-railway newspapers frequently charged that the trolley companies were in league with traffic officers to "look the other way" when trolleys violated a law. As the twentieth century passed its midpoint, the Los Angeles Metropolitan Transportation Authority and its successor, the Southern California Rapid Transit

District, and police officers were, in effect, members of one family. While officers gave traffic citations, so difficult for average motorists to fight in court, to passenger car drivers, such "tickets" seldom were given to bus drivers. When infrequently given to bus operators, traffic citations merely added to the delays and the mounting costs of operating the system.

Reports by the State Railroad Commission and its successor agency, the State Public Utilities Commission, were critical of the Pacific Electric for resisting replacement of its antiquated equipment with modern electric cars. A commission report in 1939 placed an average value of $700 on the majority of the interurban cars and recommended replacing of most of the equipment. The company's retort was its ailing financial condition. As late as 1938 the system used 196 interurban cars with wooden bodies, according to the 1939 state report, despite the fact that steel body construction had long been standard. Several interurbans purchased by Huntington in 1902 remained in service as late as 1940. Electric cars placed into service by the Los Angeles Pacific in the pre-Huntington era before 1900 faithfully continued hauling passengers until 1948.

The ranks of the Red Cars sank as the busses replaced electric lines. Company reports showed that the number of

A two-car Pacific Electric train moves down Fourth Street in Santa Ana in the early 1940's, beginning the 34-mile trip to Los Angeles. The P. E. had a private right-of-way for most of this line. (Photo by Robert McVay)

The scene is on Ocean west of Magnolia in Long Beach during the 1920's. The white building (right) a grocery store *owned by the author's parents. County offices later occupied the site. (Charles Seims Collection)*

trolleys in operation had dwindled to 721 by 1932, to 648 in 1936, and 546 by 1939. After heavy abandonments of lines in 1940 there were only 409 Red Cars in operation, but World War II saved trolleys from the scrap heap. The Pacific Electric reported 431 electric cars in operation during 1943 and 454 in service in 1945. Resumption of the emphasis on busses after the war brought retirement for more trolleys. By 1950 there were 311 electric cars in operation and by 1952, the year before the Pacific Electric sold its passenger service to Metropolitan Coach lines, there were only 170 trolleys in use. Metropolitan began to retire the remaining cars in favor of busses.

Problems of maintaining the electric interurbans developed as the Red Car era neared its end. It became evident that maintenance of the electric cars was an art as well as a technical skill as the handful of specialist mechanics continued to service the trolleys.

The companies that once thrived manufacturing trolleys had diversified into new fields or quit business. Parts for the antiquated cars were becoming difficult or in many cases impossible to obtain. The answer to this problem became "cannibalizing," a term the interurban mechanics applied to the practice of retiring a trolley but retaining it so they could remove vital parts to replace those required for operating cars. [2]

The Pacific Electric emblem was dropped from the Big Red Cars in 1953 when the passenger service was sold to Metropolitan Coach Lines. A few cars remained in 1958

2. According to Ted Huemerich, superintendent of maintenance for the cars, in a 1959 interview with the author.

when the Los Angeles Metropolitan Transit Authority was formed by the state legislature in 1958 to provide public transportation where private enterprise had failed. They were adorned with a new emblem, "L.A.M.T.A." There were discussions relative to repainting the cars the light green adopted by the transit authority, and one interurban even was given the new color as an experiment.

But it was obvious that the interurban era was ending for Southern California, and the few remaining trolleys were allowed the dignity of rolling along in their final days garbed in the distinctive red which Mr. Huntington somehow selected for his system.

While the competition of automobiles and "invasion" of the right-of-ways caused the ultimate demise of the Big Red Cars, the burden of the Pacific Electric's huge bonded indebtedness and the reluctance of the commuting public to pay increased fares were major contributing factors to the fatal illness.

The fact that most trolley systems in the United States encountered financial problems in their early stages and had to reduce operations for lack of initial capital and subsequent high interest payments on their debts was pointed out in the Stanford University Press book "The Electric Interurban Railways in America," in which authors George W. Hilton and John F. Due analyzed the national electric car era. Undoubtedly the Big Red Cars ran as long and as efficiently as they did because of the Pacific Electric's well-heeled owners: in its early stages, Henry Huntington who made fortunes in electrical power and real estate, and after 1910, in the powerful Southern Pacific. Other electric inter-

197

urban systems had neither such financial backers nor did their service areas hold the potential of ultimate return on the investment which appeared in Southern California.

The annual profits or losses of the system while controlled by Huntington could not be determined because of the lack of state of federal laws at the time requiring such statements. However, it was evident that he realized a profit —although slight — from the Pacific Electric's operations. The limited reports available (through the National Archives) noted P. E. profits of $290,280 and $363,364 in 1908 and 1909, just prior to Huntington's sale of his interest.

Financial reports after 1911, however, showed that the Pacific Electric made a profit for only eight of the forty-two years during which rail passenger service was its business.[3] The system showed the modest, yet promising, profit of

ing the prosperous 1920's losses were well over $1 million almost every year.

The growing popularity of the automobile after 1912 caused many interurbans to operate at well below their seating capacity during all except peak service hours. Operating costs soared because, logically, employees wanted wages comparable to those in profitable industries. The Pacific Electric sought financial remedies in applications for fare increases, against which a variety of interests lobbied. When upward adjustments in far schedules were approved, the increases inevitably forced more people into the more economical usages of automobiles. Pacific Electric deficits continued to develop as part of the vicious circle.

The interest on the company bonds, at their onset in 1911 almost equal to the value of the entire traction system on

Fare Re-Adjustment Application is Made

Failure of Passenger Traffic to Keep Pace with Community Growth Responsible. Auto Increase a Large Factor

APPLICATION for a readjustment of passenger fares was filed by the Company on January 11th with the California State Railroad Commission, in which body is vested the legal power to grant or reject the plea after a determination of the facts involved.

A seven and twelve cent cash local

its operating expenses and fixed charges.

"The last adjustment of fares made by the Railroad Commission went into effect January 1, 1921, and it did not at that time, and has not since, provided a fair return upon the value of the property. The Company has continued upon such unsatisfactory return

application, "that in order to secure the necessary new money to be invested in the public service, the interest charges and taxes should be earned on the new investment, as well as on the money already expended. It is therefore proper, and the request is reasonable, that the passenger rates should be so increased as within a

PACIFIC ELECTRIC MAGAZINE

$477,816 at the end of its first year of operation in 1912. All hopes for profit bonanzas from normal rail passenger service after that time were doomed. Profits fell to $71,204 in 1913 and annual deficits were reported until 1923, one of the peak years of operations, when the company had an operating surplus of $330,915. World War II, bringing heavy troop and freight movements on the Pacific Electric and a new emphasis on commuter travel as the result of gasoline rationing and high industrial employment, gave the line its most profitable years. Profits hit $1,546,807 in 1942 a record $5,602,315 in 1943, $1,922,194 in 1944, and $356,264 in 1945. Despite high post-war employment, deficits of $218,879 and $1,760,073 were reported for 1946 and 1947 respectively. The eighth profitable year was 1948, when the company had a surplus of $33,180.

Operating deficits for other years ranged to as high as $2,779,322 during the Depression year of 1933. Even dur-

the basis of national averages, almost perennially eliminated profits.

The company's balance sheet in 1912 showed a bonded debt of $52,200,000, or more than $52,000 for each of the 988 miles of track then in operation. Surveys at the time indicated that the average value of American interurban systems, including cars, buildings, and electric generating equipment, was $60,000 a mile. The Pacific Electric was valued, at least on paper, at even more. When incorporating the merged company, the Southern Pacific set the Pacific Electric's capital stock at $100 million, which would have made the system worth $100,000 a mile. The fog of confidential merger negotiations between the P.E. and S.P. obscured the real value, for no one knew whether the system was actually worth this amount or whether the valuation was raised to provide a wedge for future concessions in fares.

A strong argument that a substantial part of the large indebtedness came about through Henry Huntington's shrewd dickering in selling his interests may be made by noting that, prior to the merger, the individual interurban

---

3. According to reports filed with the California Railroad Commission and its successor, the California Public Utilities Commission.

A Bellflower-bound interurban speeds down the four-track southern rail artery after leaving Los Angeles. A "local" trol-ley headed for Watts rolls on the outside track. (Pacific Railroad Publications)

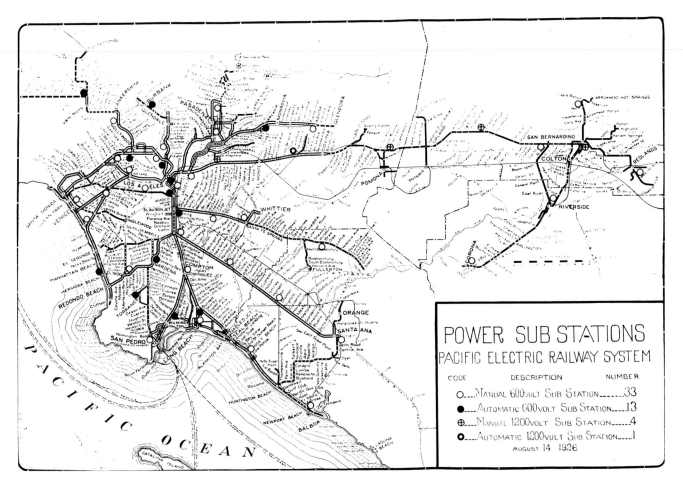

This map shows the distribution of electric power stations in the P. E. system during the 1920's. The power units, each *a substantial structure, were well-known landmarks in their areas and helped provide efficient service.*

lines consolidated into the Pacific Electric were mortgaged by bonds totalling approximately $17 million. The owners had relatively small amounts of cash equities invested in the lines. The newly-formed company's action in mortgaging itself for three times the value of the previous bonds may well have resulted from the price paid by the Southern Pacific.

Pacific Electric officials in subsequent years acknowledged that the system was worth substantially less than $100 million and was, indeed over-mortgaged. In discussing the company's financial predicament during 1919 labor troubles, H. B. Titcomb, then vice president, told a businessmen's luncheon that the Pacific Electric was valued at only $50 million and was burdened by a mortgage which had reached $57 million.[4] The Pacific Electric properties were valued by a State Railroad Commission report at $88 million in

1928, at a time when bonds of $54.6 million were outstanding.[5]

Except for certain years during the Depression of the 1930's the Pacific Electric made a profit before payment of the interest on its mortgage. In 1914, despite the fact that there were more automobiles and operating costs had increased, the company reported a net income of $2,446,000. After paying $3 million in interest on its bonds, however, it showed a deficit of $610,101.

Property taxes on its cars, right-of-ways, stations, and other facilities also added to the financial burdens of the years.

When the Pacific Electric attempted to balance its books by decreasing frequency of its cars or raising fares, strong opposition from the riders occurred. Joining the passengers in the opposition were merchants and real estate developers

---

4. Los Angeles Examiner, August 29, 1919.

5. Pacific Electric Magazine, February 10, 1927.

ordinarily champions of the profit system. They knew well that low fares and frequent service brought shoppers to their downtown stores and buyers to homes in their subdivisions. The Pacific Electric management itself realized that low fares and frequent service were major factors in maintaining passenger volume. Attempts at balancing the financial books consequently ranged from experiments at increasing service as well as to reducing it and at "bargain" as well as higher basic fares.

Revenue from passenger traffic varied sharply through the years, and usually on a curve similar to that for general business activity. Annual passenger revenues hovered at $10 million annually during most of the prosperous 1920's and hit a peak of $12,324,394 in 1926. The money from riders dipped to a low of $6,259,966 in 1934 and climbed to a record $21,134,222 in 1944.

In launching the Red Car system, Henry Huntington had realized the need for price competition with the existing steam passenger trains. While the Salt Lake Railroad charged $2 for ten rides to Long Beach, he offered ten rides for $1.50 on his competing electric lines. When competition sprang up in 1903, he offered prices so low that interurban riders could travel for as little as 1¼ cents per mile as compared to a previous two cents a mile. The base fares which he established even after upward adjustments were well below two cents a mile and remained standard for years after The Great Merger.

Fare adjustments authorized by the State Railroad Commission in 1918 established interurban fares at 3 cents a mile on one way tickets and 2½ cents a mile for round-trips, although 30-ride "family" commutation booklets sold for 1½ cents a mile. An experiment launched in 1929 made use of "unlimited passes" designed to develop the Red Car "habit" for commuters. The cost of the monthly passes were $6 to Alhambra or Glendale, $12 to Long Beach or San Pedro, $11.50 to Van Nuys, $7.50 to Compton, $11.50 to

Sources of the Pacific Electric's revenue were shown in this chart of operation from 1916 to 1937 prepared for the California Railroad Commission. The relative importance of freight revenue became greater through the years.

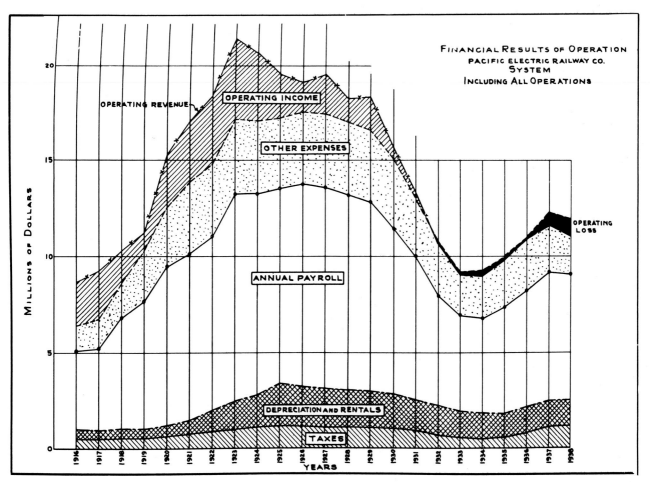

Pedro, $11.50 to Van Nuys, $7.50 to Compton, $11.50 to Redondo, Hermosa, or Manhattan Beaches, $9.50 to Santa Monica and Venice, and $7.50 to Pasadena. The passes were popular with the public and brought mild increases in travel volume, but were discontinued because of the substantial decreases in revenue suffered by the company.

The Depression of the 1930's brought more financial problems. The general recession resulted in a tremendous drop in patronage, for there were few jobs to which to commute. Employees' wages were reduced and service was cut back, but the interest payments remained. Pacific Electric operating losses hit $1.9 million in 1930 and by 1932 had. soared to $2.5 million. Allocation of money to replace aging equipment became out of the question for the financially ailing system.

While the bonds of many trolley companies became worthless, those of the Pacific Electric continued to receive good ratings by financial services because the securities were guaranteed by the Southern Pacific.

As it petitioned to reduce service or increase fares, the Pacific Electric pointed to its mounting losses. Critics responded by pointing out that the parent company, Southern Pacific, owned a substantial amount of the bonds contributing to the deficits and therefore profited from the interest payments. It was also argued that the parent company benefited from freight the Pacific Electric initiated for its transcontinental lines. The railroad's defenders countered by noting that the Southern Pacific could have earned a return on its money in other channels and that electric service was not needed for cross-country freight.

The weight of the Pacific Electric's immense bonded debt remained a burden through 1953, when the Big Red Car passenger service was purchased by Metropolitan Coach Lines. The Pacific Electric's deficit for 1952, last full year in which it provided passenger service, was $435,897. The year would have been a profitable one had it not been for a payment of $922,633 in interest on the bonded debt.

The Big Red Cars never were able to fight their way completely out of the red.

A tile roof graced the Pacific Electric station at Corona, reached via Riverside and one of the most distant points on the sprawling interurban system. Cars reached Corona by going through Arlington. (Charles Seims Collection)

A train of six interurbans speeds down the Long Beach line to the Catalina Island ship terminal at Wilmington in the 1930's. *The Big Red Car ride was the first lap for the journey. (Pacific Railroad Publications)*

24. The Thrifty Thirties: Toward the End of the Line

As the Depression of the Thirties sent the country into the doldrums, Will Rogers remarked that America was having "all the distinction of being the only nation in the history of the world that ever went to the poor house in an automobile."

It was certain that Southern Californians, despite the hard times, were not planning to ride to the poor house on the Big Red Cars. The 107,180,838 passengers carried by the Pacific Electric in 1929 had sunk to a total of 67,695,532 riders on busses and trolleys by 1934. The one-third reduction in volume hit the company with greater operating deficits and struck the long-time riders by the elimination of more unprofitable lines and crowding of cars. Automobiles once regarded as luxuries became necessities. Many families found it more economical to operate an auto than to use public transportation, particularly when extensive mileage was involved. Gasoline ranged in price from 11 to 14 cents a gallon. Since actual operation costs of an automobile were as low as two cents a mile, the gasoline buggy proved cheaper transportation for family outings than tickets on the interurbans. Those persons fortunate enough to have jobs often organized car pools to save money.

The Depression brought gloom along with its sharp reduction in trolley travel and an emphasis on economies.

David W. Pontius, president of the P. E. told employees: [1]

> This is not the time for indulging in the glooms or becoming hysterical, but rather it is opportune to buckle down cheerfully, facing boldly facts and issues as they confront us . . . .
>
> Save everything possible in the way of materials and time; light and power; water, gas, and telephone use; and of anything else that necessitates the expenditure of money. Every employee can help. And do not repeat idle gossip—business depressions are as much a state of mind as they are the state of conditions.

A survey by the Los Angeles City Street Engineering Department showed that on a typical day in 1931 visitors to the downtown area totalled 697,000, an increase of fifteen percent since 1923. But of the total travelers, 435,-000 used automobiles as compared to only 290,000 eight years before. A total of 315,000 persons traveled by interurbans into the downtown area on the 1923 survey day; only 250,000 used the electric cars to reach the central section eight years later.

The Pacific Electric began the twentieth century's third decade with approximately fifty interurban routes and thirty local streetcar lines. Despite the company's officials expressing hopes that controls on operating costs and "temporary" elimination of unprofitable routes would inject new line into the system, the Pacific Electric ended the decade with less than thirty interurban lines and approximately twenty local service routes.

By this time the Big Red Cars were an integral part of community life and the generation took them for granted. There were frequent criticisms of crowded trolleys, reductions in the frequency of schedules, and increased running time the result of automobile traffic. All things considered, however, people still loved the trolleys, the magnets pulling the suburbs close to the city, available when there were no automobiles, and creators of camaradie among commuters never duplicated in a motor car. To serve this group, an organization named the Commuters' School of Southern California was organized by J. Gustin White, educational director of the Los Angeles Young Men's Christian Association. The purpose of helping people to improve their minds by studying during their daily trips failed: people preferred to chat and enjoy the countryside despite the long trips. A more acceptable innovation was the introduction of boards for playing bridge on several of the longer routes. [2]

The initial trolley services to die during the decade were local streetcar lines in many outlying cities. Few objected when interurban service halted on such lightly traveled lines as from San Bernardino to Arrowhead Springs, Highland, and even Redlands. The basic lines serving Los Angeles, however, also were beginning to fall because their revenue did not underwrite operating costs.

---

1. Pacific Electric Magazine, July 10, 1930.

2. Pacific Electric Magazine, March 10, 1931.

In 1933 the Central Business District Association spurred a last effort to build a rapid transportation service. Its members correctly feared that the end of adequate transportation into downtown Los Angeles would shift retail sales and property values elsewhere. Prepared by consulting engineer Donald N. Baker, the report entitled "A Rapid Transit System for Los Angeles" made its bow on November 15, 1933. The report recommended extending the Hollywood Subway to Glendale and building two more subways, each with four tracks; one would go to Pasadena and the other would serve Santa Monica. It also proposed an elevated railroad to Long Beach. The massive system would have been leased to the Pacific Electric to operate. The tab of this ambitious system was estimated at $37 million, of which the federal government would give $10 million in order to provide jobs for the unemployed. Financing the plan through bonds was proposed.

But 1933 was a depression year and despite their fears more drops in property values because of inadequate transportation, land owners had greater fears of more taxes. The proposed system died on paper.

The Pacific Electric in desperation turned more and more to bus routes in an effort to find the elusive profit which had fled the rails. Busses could be operated by a driver instead of the motorman and conductor required for the interurbans, their smaller capacity permitted the frequent schedules which commuters seemed to demand, and there could be variances in routes from the expensive rail right-of-ways.

Oscar A. Smith, the man who presided over the slow death of the rail cars was the one-time stenographer for Henry Huntington. The magnate had noted Smith's abilities and advised him to seek a position with greater opportunities. Smith went to work with the Southern Pacific, and after The Great Merger of 1911 was assigned to the Pacific Electric. After serving in various capacities, he became president of the electric interurban system in 1937.

The big move to kill major interurban lines came in 1939 after a State Railroad Commission report advising the Pacific Electric to attract passengers by launching an extensive modernization program. The company, wearied after years of deficits, argued against the commission's urging that rail service be retained when possible and sought to substitute the more economical busses on major routes. The year of 1938 had already seen the stifling of interurban service to basic portions of the Whittier line, which included Yorba Linda and Huntington Park, as well as for the line to the city of San Fernando although cars continued to run as far as Van Nuys in the San Fernando Valley.

Increased emphasis on busses to replace trolleys was indicated in this 1930 article in the Pacific Electric Magazine. The story dealt with the Motor Transit Company, acquired for the P. E.'s entry into bus service.

BUILDING OF GREAT MOTOR TRANSIT SYSTEM

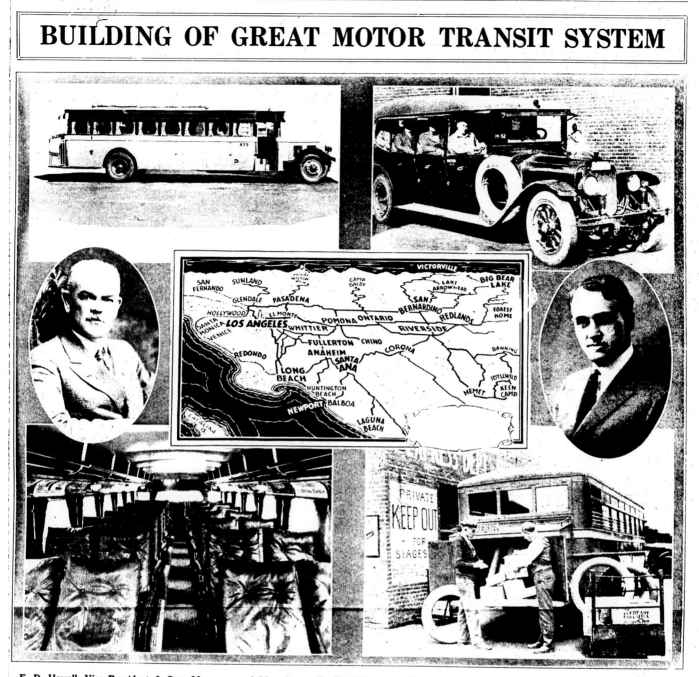

F. D. Howell, Vice President & Gen. Manager, and Max Green, Traffic Manager, who have figured prominently in the development of the system. With the Pacific Electric's acquirement of a large interest in the Company Mr. Pontius became Chairman of the Board of Directors.

THE history and development of the Motor Transit Company, of which the Pacific Electric Railway now owns controlling interest, is practically a true parallel of the romantic and rapid growth of highway transportation in general in the State of California.

The early motor stages of California were merely an outgrowth of the "jitneys" or private touring cars running hither and thither without any regular schedules or routes, charging whatever fares their passengers would stand without responsibility and going wherever their passengers desired.

Along in 1915 when the so-called motor bus business was mostly a "free-for-all" so far as routes and methods of obtaining business were concerned, O. R. Fuller was practically forced into the picture. At

IN ORDER to acquaint employees with the scope of operations, improvement in transportation that will result through Southern California, and the mutual benefits to be derived by the coordination of the Motor Transit Company into our system the accompanying article tells the historical background and development of this splendid motor coach system.

Another article will follow in the September issue detailing present methods of operation, equipment, passenger, freight and express service.

the time, he was local distributor for White Trucks and had sold a few trucks upon which bus bodies had been built and operated under the fictitious name of "P & E Bus Line" (Passenger & Express) and doing business between Los Angeles and Whittier.

Naturally, through the lax methods of operating busses in those hectic days most operations at that time were more or less "fly-by-night" attempts without capital or business experience.

So when the "P & E" suspended operations in November, 1916, as did many in those days, Mr. Fuller was obliged to take back

(Continued on Page 12)

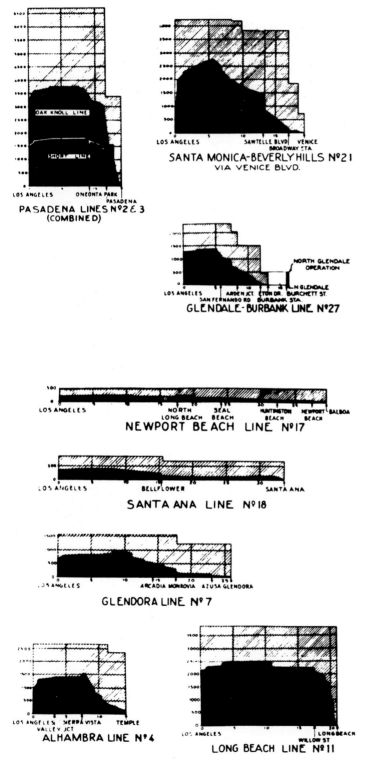

The problem of empty seats on the Pacific Electric inter-urban routes was depicted in this 1938 study by the California Railroad Commission. Shaded areas show available seats; dark portions indicate occupancy.

PASADENA LINES Nº 2 & 3
(COMBINED)

SANTA MONICA-BEVERLY HILLS Nº 21
VIA VENICE BLVD.

GLENDALE-BURBANK LINE Nº 27

NEWPORT BEACH LINE Nº 17

SANTA ANA LINE Nº 18

GLENDORA LINE Nº 7

ALHAMBRA LINE Nº 4

LONG BEACH LINE Nº 11

In 1940, electric interurban service stopped from Los Angeles to Fullerton and Riverside as well as on two routes to Santa Monica although the fast "air line" direct route was maintained. That year also brought an end for service to Redondo, Hermosa, and Manhattan Beaches, and to Torrance. In late 1941 bus service was substituted for rail service to Alhambra.

It appeared to be the era of the bus, and more abandonment of rail service would have been made had not World War II, with its immense demands for transportation, occurred.

World War II drew thousands of workers into Southern California to man the aircraft factories and other war plants. The influx of newcomers, coupled with the fact that rationing of gasoline and tires greatly reduced the use of automobiles, brought record demands on the Pacific Electric system.

Pending plans to abandon the interurban lines were shelved when the war started and the Big Red Cars began to carry loads of passengers. The indication that the public habit of using trolleys was returning, along with the vast numbers of new residents, gave hope to Pacific Electric officials that the system was turning to the profit column. [3]

The Pacific Electric had transported 79 million passengers in 1940; in 1945 it carried nearly 180 million riders. The revived glory was short lived for the post-war era brought increased traffic problems. The new automobiles were even bigger, and the Big Red Cars were bulky, moving with difficulty through the streets of cities more jammed than ever with traffic.

The last major effort of the Pacific Electric to transform itself into a modern rapid transportation system was in July, 1947. The company sought state and city funds to help finance construction of a Red Car right-of-way in the center of the Hollywood Freeway, at the time in the planning stage.

P. E. President Oscar Smith, in discussing the plan, predicted that the running time from Los Angeles to Hollywood could be cut by fifteen minutes as a result of the proposed no-grade crossing right-of-way. He foresaw a solution to the ever-present commuter problem by noting that an existing two-track Pacific Electric system in the center of the freeway through Cahuenga Pass could handle twice as many people per hour as the eight lanes for automobiles. If the proposed Hollywood Freeway-interurban line became successful, the principle could be extended to the other freeway systems being planned. Cost of the railroad system in the freeway was estimated at nearly $20 million; public officials frowned at such an expenditure. Tremendous freeway construction programs, highly popular with a public flustered by traffic problems, were earmarked for available funds.

The combination of freeways with an electric car right-

---

3. Oscar A. Smith in a 1962 interview with the author.

A trolley from the San Fernando Valley speeds over a right-of-way in Cahuenga Pass Freeway during the late 1940's. The P. E. contended the tracks could carry far more passengers than autos in the adjacent highway. Tracks in all freeways would have helped solve the area's critical travel problem. (Pacific Railroad Publications)

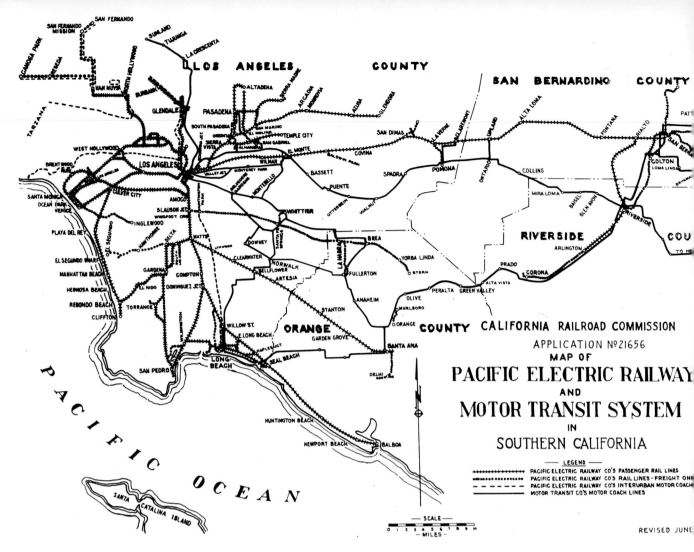

This map shows the Pacific Electric system in the late 1930's when busses were replacing electric cars. BELOW: An article *from the Pacific Electric Magazine indicated how the Depression of the 1930's affected employees.*

of-way to solve the transportation problem was placed on a shelf with the previous proposals of elevated and subway systems.

It was obvious that the bell was tolling for the end of the Big Red Cars.

Coincident with the rejected freeway proposal, the State Public Utilities Commission (which had succeeded the State Railroad Commission) issued its 1947 "Case No. 4863: Report on Engineering Survey of Operations and Facilities of Pacific Electric Railway Company."

The report may well have been the death knell of the Big Red Cars, for it recommended expenditures for improvements which — even though needed — would have been prohibitive for a financially ailing company operating at a deficit for years. The study urged the Pacific Electric to spend $4,922,125 within five years to bring the system's tracks up to "adequate standards." The ultimate cost of

Decide to Forego Annual Employees' Picnic

D. W. PONTIUS, President, decided late last month that due to present economic conditions it would be necessary to forego our annual outing.

"Decision not to hold the picnic was made with great reluctance" said Mr. Pontius. "Due to depression existing all over the country, as a result of which our passenger and freight revenues have been very materially reduced, it is essential that we forego some of our pleasures and conserve resources for necessary expenditures.

"Please express, through the Magazine, my very great regret, with the hope that present conditions will improve and that with another year we will be able to hold the picnic again, as usual."

rehabilitating the operation was estimated as more than $8 million, not including expenditures for new electric interurban cars to replace the aging trolleys.

Additional outlays for an unprofitable rail system were out of the question to the Pacific Electric's parent company. Already the Southern Pacific itself was moving into a diversified program based on the closing of the rail era: its future operations were to include interests in bus systems, trucking companies, and even oil pipelines. Pointing to the increasing deficit, the Pacific Electric filed petitions seeking authority from the State Public Utilities Commission to substitute busses on more rail lines. Cities, community organizations, and commuters pressured for continuance of rail operations. Pacific Electric officials presented winning arguments as they noted the operating deficits that were history.

When abandonment of rail service began, it proceeded rapidly. Among the first rail routes to end were those to the San Gabriel Valley, where the Big Red Car lines once were so numerous it was difficult to be away from the sound of their distinctive horns. Service to Pomona was discontinued in the fall of 1950 immediately following the close of the Los Angeles County Fair. Service on the popular Pasadena Oak Knoll line also came to an end in last 1950. Other 1950 rail abandonments ended service to Huntington Beach, Venice, surface lines to Hollywood, and the route to Santa Ana.

Commuters hoped that the last existing electric line to Pasadena could be salvaged and petitions were widely circulated in efforts to retain service. The route was doomed when key portions of the right-of-way were condemned for construction of the San Bernardino Freeway. The Pacific Electric, faced with huge expenditures to relocate the tracks, was successful in its plea to substitute busses on the line. The Pasadena Short Line, once a key link in the vast interurban system, consequently came to an end in the fall of 1951, when rail service to Glendora and Monrovia also stopped.

By this time it was obvious that the interurban system was to be a bus operation. Long circulated rumors that the Pacific Electric banner was to disappear from the Southern California commuter service scene came true with an announcement that effective October 1, 1953 the company's passenger facilities were being sold to Metropolitan Coach Lines, a company concentrating on bus operations.

Despite its basic bus complexion, Metropolitan Coach Lines found itself operating trolleys to Bellflower, Long Beach, and San Pedro as well as through the Hollywood Subway to Glendale and Hollywood. It moved to replace these services with busses but was successful only in abandoning the Big Red Car lines to Glendale and Hollywood, ending the routes via the Hollywood Subway in the summer of 1955.

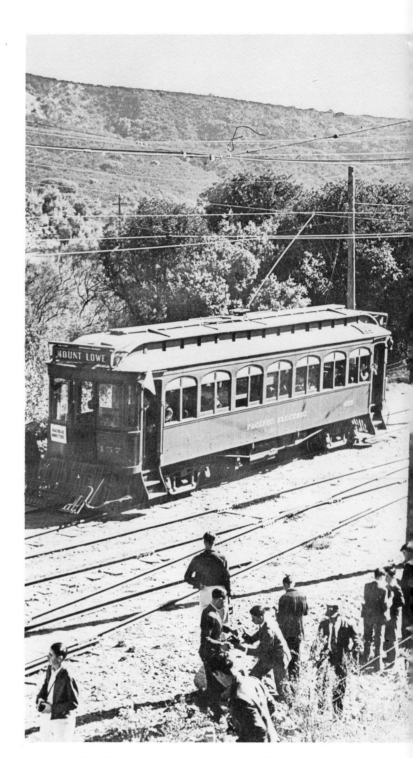

A group of trolley fans enjoyed an excursion aboard an interurban with ornate arched windows as service to Rubio Canyon, at the start of the Mount Lowe cable railway, was ending in 1937. (Craig Rasmussen Collection)

As Southern California's interurban age came to an end, these Big Red Cars awaited loading onto ships that would *take them to other nations where trolleys still were economically useful to carry commuters. (Los Angeles Times)*

If the Pacific Electric had found it difficult to please the commuting public, Metropolitan Coach Lines found it impossible. There were growing pressures even in the most conservative circles for the formation of a public agency to provide transportation. The years had proved that public transportation was not attractive for a free enterprise organization whose obligations included providing dividends for stockholders as well as service for the riders. Amid the clamor of complaints and cries for a solution to the public transportation problem growing worse with the years, the Metropolitan Transit Authority was formed by the state legislature to operate a transit system over the area once served by the Pacific Electric. The authority succeeded Met-ropolitan Coach Lines on March 3, 1958.

The new authority found its bondholders as demanding as stockholders in expecting operating revenue to cover expenses. While studies were launched for new methods to conquer the commuter problem, busses were regarded for the time being as more economical than trolleys. Pressures were renewed to discontinue the three remaining trolley routes. Rail service to Bellflower ended in 1958 and the following year trolley service to San Pedro halted.

As the twentieth century started its third decade, the only remaining Big Red Car route was the one to Long Beach, once had been praised by Henry Huntington as the "finest road in the world."

Freeways of the twentieth century paralleled routes of the Big Red Cars, which helped establish travel and growth pat- *terns. Here is the Long Beach Freeway, alongside the Pacific Electric's Long Beach line. (Photo by the Author)*

25. The Legacy of the Big Red Cars

As the Big Red Cars moved into the shadows of history, Southern Californians looked from crowded freeways and never-ending fields of houses at the tapestry of city development, sociological viewpoints, and economic progress that came with the electric interurbans.

For other sections of the United States the invention of the trolley provided little more than another mode of transportation: the framework of cities was formed prior to building of the electric lines that only supplemented the existing railroads.

But the technology of the electric interurban came at that important time when Southern California was on the verge of its greatest growth period.

It was the trolley lines built by Henry Huntington, William Hook, Moses Sherman, Eli Clark — and even the

diminutive horsecar line constructed by Judge Robert Widney that started it all — which set the stage for the development of the City of Southern California in areas that otherwise would have remained grazing land for years. By making it easy for new residents to reach these areas, the City of Southern California became a horizontal city where slums were at a minimum and patio living in suburban homes was a tradition.

It was noteworthy that not until well past the mid-point of the twentieth century, as the interurban era came to an end, did construction trends turn to the erection of structures exceeding by far the ten-story heighth of Henry Huntington's Pacific Electric Building. Then, as the commuter problem became more acute, there were cries for taller buildings for more compact living.

This trolley operated from Sierra Vista (near Alhambra)
to Watts, carrying "local" stop passengers. The photograph
was taken in 1942 during a pause at Echandia Junction.
(Carl B. Blaubach Collection)

The greatest failure, probably, came in the slowness of the public and public officials to grasp the fact that the role of providing transportation could not be filled by private enterprise. The unprofitable situation of commuter traffic was obvious for at least forty years. If a state authority had been created as late as 1945 to utilize public funds to maintain the Red Car right-of-ways and purchase modern equipment, millions of dollars spent on freeway construction might have been saved.

What would the second half of the twentieth century hold for commuters in the City of Southern California?

Surveys and reports were compiled by business groups and governmental agencies, but it was difficult to decide on the most efficient and economical pattern for a new rapid transit system.

Southern Californians had become different from people in other sections of America in their commuting habits. It was obvious they would be most demanding in the extent of a rapid transit system's routing and its frequency of service. The extreme to which Southern Californians relied on their own automobiles to eliminate walking and waiting time for public transportation was shown in a 1954 report for the Metropolitan Transit Authority. The report stated that while the average number of occupants for each automobile in New York City was 7.03 and 5.95 in Philadelphia, it was but 2.76 persons in Los Angeles.

The members of a society so orientated to automobiles would not be likely to drive miles to a rapid transit artery near their homes or walk blocks from it to offices. Whatever transit system was to be devised would certainly need to consider the impelling factor of the automobile that helped to stop the Red Cars.

For many years there were discussions of a monorail system, sharing right-of-ways with the freeway in many areas

The Pacific Electric Building at Sixth and Main was pictured on the cover of this booklet, issued in 1945 to tell the public about the system so vital for commuters.

Laborers impassionately remove the rails and ties of the Pacific Electric's once busy Monrovia line, over which trolleys carried commuters fast and comfortably to points in the San Gabriel Valley. (Photograph by the Author)

The author and his children, John Spencer and Victoria Elizabeth Margaret, enjoy the Orange Empire Trolley Museum, where cars are preserved for future generations. (Photograph by Mary Dalgarno Crump)

but otherwise almost certainly defacing many business and residential areas as surely as the elevated railroad Los Angeles voters rejected in 1926. Discussions turned to a subway system, obviously an expensive proposal but one eliminating the need for costly right-of-ways.

As the pros and cons were discussed, thoughts turned to another factor dooming the Big Red Cars: cost of operation. It was obvious that any future system would find its greatest usage during the peak travel hours to and from work in the morning and evening. Yet its employees would expect, quite correctly, continuous work shifts.

New York City, with its immense population density of 25,000 people per square mile, was unable to operate its transportation system at a profit. How did Los Angeles, with only 5,500 residents per square mile, expect to provide adequate service without an overhead so huge that even its cost of construction could not be paid?

Perhaps that answer was to be in the fields of automation and electronics . . . perhaps in the model train layout permitting one person to operate several locomotives.

Block signals, an innovation in the early twentieth century, were soon to be accepted by all railroads. An electronic

system incorporating the ultimate in safety features could provide means to open and close rapid transit car doors automatically as well as to start and stop equipment.

The problem of building an adequate rapid transportation system seemed a major one for the last half of the twentieth century, but so did building a metropolis appear big to the men who decided in 1900 that there would be a City of Southern California.

The twentieth century's first five decades, when the Big Red Cars reigned with speed, efficiency, and friendliness, brought immense changes to Southern California. The years left a heritage of growth for the area and personal achievements for the men who had led the development.

For the City of Southern California, labeled the "cow country" a century before, there appeared no end for the growth and the future buildings were to be skyscrapers.

For Judge Robert Widney, the man who had started what became a metropolitan interurban system so that he could ride home, the pleasure came of seeing his village grow into a city before his death in 1932.

Abbot Kinney, the man who preferred the title of philosopher to financier and made his dream of the Venice of America come true, died in 1922, ten years before oil derricks were to cover the development and the famous canals were to be filled. Only at mid-century had action been taken to restore marina development in the area.

Eli Clark and Moses Sherman went on to develop vast real estate holdings as well as to serve as directors of the merged Pacific Electric, enjoying active lives until Sherman's death in 1932 and Clark's passing in 1933.

Edwin Spencer Hook's enjoyment of the immense profit he made on the sale of his traction company was to be of short duration. He died in 1904, just a year after the transaction.

Edward Henry Harriman, who battled the construction of electric railroads, died in 1909 amidst a new campaign to shape a world-wide railroad system. He never saw the fruit of the merged Pacific Electric.

For Henry Huntington, of course, came achievements equaling those of his uncle. He won fame as a builder of Southern California as well as founder of one of the world's great libraries and art galleries.

Archer Huntington, who preferred the life of a scholar to that of a railroad magnate and helped inspire Henry

Goodbye, Big Red Cars

PICTURE PAGES FOLLOWING: *These Big Red Cars, which once moved commuters so comfortably and efficiently were being scrapped on Terminal Island in the 1950's. (Photo by Maxine Reams)*

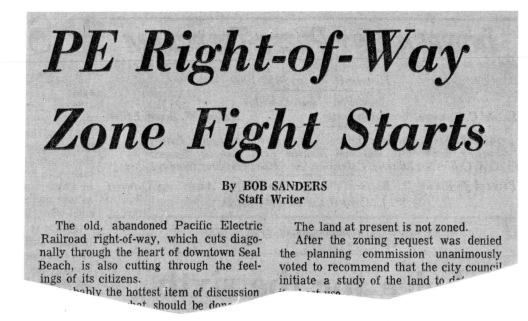

PE Right-of-Way Zone Fight Starts

By BOB SANDERS
Staff Writer

The old, abandoned Pacific Electric Railroad right-of-way, which cuts diagonally through the heart of downtown Seal Beach, is also cutting through the feelings of its citizens.

Probably the hottest item of discussion ... what should be don...

The land at present is not zoned.

After the zoning request was denied the planning commission unanimously voted to recommend that the city council initiate a study of the land to d...

ABOVE: The Pacific Electric remained a factor in the area's development long after the Red Cars quit running. This story appeared in the Long Beach Independent in 1970 during an attempt to zone a right-of-way for apartments.

BELOW: A two-car train crosses the Santa Ana River en route to Los Angeles. The P.E. had its own right-of-way for most of the forty-mile trip from Santa Ana. (Carl B. Blaubach Collection)

Southern California as well as founder of one of the world's great libraries and art galleries.

Archer Huntington, who preferred the life of a scholar to that of a railroad magnate and helped inspire Henry Huntington to build his great library, died at the age of 85 in 1955. He was interred near his step-father, Collis P. Huntington.

Professor Thaddeus Lowe lost control of his mountain railroad and died, heavily in debt, in 1913. His creation of a pleasant mountain retreat reached via rails came to an end in 1938 when a forest fire destroyed the tracks and tavern at Mount Lowe.

The Angel's Flight Railway continued to operate as a reminder of Los Angeles' early days until 1969, when it was dismantled as part of an urban renewal project centered on Bunker Hill.

Horace Dobkins, the young man who envisioned a bicycle freeway to Los Angeles, dismantled his dream and sold the lumber at a substantial profit. He moved on for other business successes, served as mayor of Pasadena, and in 1962 at the age of 96 recalled the era happily as he enjoyed life in his home atop a hill at San Pedro.

Charles H. Howland, the man who first attempted to operate an electric streetcar in Los Angeles, died almost penniless a few years after his 1887 experiment failed.

After his perfection of a successful electric railroad system, Frank J. Sprague went on to achieve more fame by inventing apparatus for high-speed elevators and submarines. By the time he died in 1934 he was acclaimed as one of the world's greatest engineers.

Isaias W. Hellman, the man who helped Henry Huntington finance the Red Car lines, died in 1920 after seeing the village where he started as a banker grow into a major

Epes Randolph, first chief engineer for the Pacific Electric, went on to serve the Southern Pacific and was assigned by the company to stop the flood waters of the Colorado River threatening to cover the Imperial Valley of California in 1906. He died in 1921.

Death came to George Patton, retired for many years, a few weeks after Henry Huntington died in 1927.

Stephen Mallory White, who won the battle for a harbor at San Pedro, never lived to see the great development he fathered. He died in 1901 of an ailment produced by the mighty work he accomplished in one short term in the U. S. Senate. His statue in the Los Angeles Civic Center was one of the few erected in Southern California, an area distinguished by its lack of statuary.

For the railroads, gone were the bountiful profits of the days when the trust-busters fought for reforms. Legislators were looking mercifully at the rail carriers as they looked favorably on mergers of the companies to restore profits and even considered subsidies to encourage passenger service.

Charles M. Pierce, who came to Southern California in the early twentieth century hoping the mild climate would give him a few more years of life and stayed to develop sightseeing in trolleys, died in 1964 at the age of 97.

Paul Shoup, who became president of the merged Pacific Electric, when only 38 years of age, went on to achieve the Henry Huntington dream, the presidency of the Southern Pacific. After his retirement from that position he remained active in civic life until his death in 1946.

William Garland continued to make his predictions of spectacular population increases for Los Angeles, but after 1910 his forecasts drew respectful consideration instead of doubtful smiles. Just before he died in 1948, he made his final prediction — that Los Angeles' population would reach three million by 1960. For once the prediction failed to come true, but only because the sprawling City of Southern California had come into being. Although more new residents continued to settle in the area and total population increased, the 1950's gave birth to many new cities. In many cases they were created only because of local "pride" and could be distinguished as separate cities solely by legal boundaries.

Cities and small communities had a reason to exist in the early twentieth century, when miles of fields and unpopulated areas separated them. The numerous little cities, fitting together like pieces of a jig-saw puzzle, were frivolous and wasteful for the 1970's. Mr. and Mrs. Average realized little from being the residents of such cities except the dubious honor of providing money for city officials to take junkets attended only by their carbon copies from other cities.

The Big Red Cars helped create the City of Southern California in virtually every way except the actual incorporation of such a municipality. It seemed inevitable that eventually all municipalities in Southern California would merge into a borough form of government to save taxes and improve efficiency. Such a merger would include, of course, the merger of the ports of Los Angeles and Long Beach, which, although adjacent to each other, were actually competing and had dual managements!

Such a consolidated City of Southern California could solve many mutual problems — including that of commuter transportation.

Landowners, correctly concluding that the arrival of trolleys would enhance the value of their remaining property, donated right-of-ways for the Pacific Electric. When the interurbans stopped running, these right-of-ways, ranging from twenty to two hundred feet wide, were regarded as virtually worthless.

The continuing growth of the City of Southern California made even these strips of land potentially valuable by the 1970's.

220

For example, few people could visualize use except as a parkway for the relatively wide right-of-way dividing Electric Avenue in Seal Beach when Red Car service ended in 1950. Yet, in 1970 developers proposed putting apartment buildings on the strip.

Value of the land was estimated at $100,000 an acre!

Despite the lack of a rapid transit system, Southern California's cities continued to grow, but that growth brought problems — particularly when suburban shopping centers antiquated traditional "downtown" districts. Seeking to modernize these downtown areas, malls were constructed on Pomona's Second Street and Riverside's Main Street. The tree-shaded walkways made contrasts to the era when trolleys rolled down these streets. Long Beach's Pine Avenue, where trolleys also once ran, was lacking in a modernization program and was distinguished by aging buildings, many of them vacant. "Progress" even took its toll of the city's once beautiful beach, noted for its big ocean breakers and view. The breakwater of the city's commercial harbor reduced the giant breakers to small waves, and artificial islands for oil drilling marred the marine view.

Vestiges of the Pacific Electric were rapidly disappearing in the 1970's.

Rubio Canyon, starting place for the Mount Lowe incline railway and once symbolic of primitive mountain areas, was being engulfed in the 1970's by a residential development that in a sense symbolized the over-development of Southern California through the use of all land areas.

The 1970's began with an emphasis on bus transportation, which made the clogged freeways even more difficult for motorists to navigate.

No longer was the Pacific Electric Building at Sixth and Main alive with the bustle of commuters and the clicking of interurban wheels.

The great Hollywood Subway, once busy with crowded interurbans, was sealed as useless. The Subway Terminal, at one time the hub for rushing crowds, was deserted.

The Big Red Cars were gone.

The destiny of many trolleys was to be piled into big stacks, like toy trains, as they awaited scrapping. Other interurbans were ingloriously dumped into the ocean as experimental havens for marine life.

The destinations of other interurbans were happier, and many trolleys still had opportunities for glory. They had been taken to Mexico, Argentina, and other nations which hoped that the trolleys could help develop their sparsely settled areas with the effectiveness demonstrated in Southern California.

Memories of the P. E.'s Big Red Cars remain at the Orange Empire Trolley Museum at Perris. The facility is maintained by a non-profit group to preserve picturesque equipment of the interurban era. (Photograph by Jim Walker)

Youngsters enjoy the thrill of a rare ride "up front" with the motorman on April 8, 1961, the last day of service for the Big Red Cars. Many children took their first — and last — trolley rides on that day. (Photo by the Author)

26. Goodbye, Red Cars

It was April 8, 1961, the last day for operation of the Big Red Cars to Long Beach, the only surviving line of the electric interurban system once covering Southern California.

Throughout the day extra cars, pressed into service, accommodated crowds of people seeking last rides on the interurbans.

There were white-haired oldsters reminiscing over the glory of that Fourth of July back in 1902 when the trolleys majestically rolled into sleepy seaside village of Long Beach and linked it to the hub of Southern California.

There were retired Pacific Electric employees proudly recalling the polite word of greeting from the ever-smiling Henry Huntington who had given them a polite word of greeting as he boarded their trolleys as he went about his business.

There were commuters who had ridden the interurbans for years and wondered if modern-day engineers could ever devise a rapid transit system with the efficiency of the Pacific Electric.

And there were youngsters being taken for their first— and final — rides on the Big Red Cars because this would be their last opportunity for such fun.

ABOVE: *An interurban from Pasadena rolls into the P. E. station at Sixth and Main in 1942. (Carl B. Blaubach Collection) BELOW: This Big Red Car was lettered "Metro-* *politan Coach Lines" after that bus-oriented firm bought the system. The scene was at Bellflower in 1957. (Stephen D. Maguire Collection)*

In the 1920's, the Hollywood Subway teemed with activity. At mid-century, the facility was deserted, useless, and only *a reminder of the days when electric interurbans proudly carried commuters. (Photograph by the Author)*

223

A combination freight-passenger car built in 1915 heads two passenger cars once used in the Portland, Oregon, *traction system. The 1943 scene was on Long Beach Avenue in Los Angeles. (Carl Blaubach Collection)*

The motormen eased the rules a bit against the long-standing rule forbidding passengers in the operator's compartment and let some of the children ride up front with them.

Shortly after midnight the curtain rose on the last "all aboard." People gathered at the Long Beach station on Ocean Boulevard at Pacific Avenue where for nearly six decades beach-goers, service men, tourists, and commuters had begun and ended many trips.

The interurbans called forth the usual deep enthusiasm and affection from the crowd of less than 200 who stood sadly by. The demise of the old Red Cars was attended by these few friends, a far cry from the 30,000 cheering and curious folk who had swarmed to thrill at the birth.

An attractive young lady escorted by a midget smoking a cigar glided by. On other occasions she might have been the highlight of the evening. But this time the Big Red Cars had the spotlight.

Unwilling to believe that the Red Cars could die, there were people circulating petitions asking the Metropolitan Transit Authority to breath life into this symbol of growth. One young man circulated a brochure headed "A Last Day Inquiry," detailing reasons why the public agency should not abandon the rail service.

There were amateur and professional photographers taking the last pictures of the interurbans with their red paint now fading. Throngs boarded the last train, composed of two cars, and waved as it rolled to Los Angeles.

A few minutes later a special two-car train chartered by the Electric Railway Historical Association of Southern California rolled up, loaded its passengers, and began following the other train to Los Angeles.

There were deep, almost mournful blasts of the interurban's air horn, once so familiar, when the trolleys sped over the countryside, helping to make life pleasant and building the City of Southern California.

And there were tears. . . .

Goodbye, Big Red Cars.

THE APPENDIX

A. Where the Trolleys Ran — When and How Often

The major interurban lines operated by the Pacific Electric are listed here, along with the details, when available, of (1) where the tracks were situated; (2) mileages between points; (3) frequency of service, and (4) running times between major stations.

For most of the first half of the twentieth century, the Big Red Cars, along with their tracks and schedules, were among the most familiar of things to Southern Californians. With the departure of the trolleys, however, it became virtually impossible to determine the routes or other data without accurate records.

The author has compiled this information for those not familiar with the system, but who may wish to retrace the routes and schedules followed by the Red Cars. It must be emphasized that some routes were combined or used in part to form other lines over the years; the compilations here represent only the major lines of the Pacific Electric. Note also should be made that changes in residential developments and work patterns also varied running times and the relative importance of various lines.

The Pacific Electric's main enemy was the auto-mobile, which attacked the trolley system in two major ways. Automobiles cut across rights-of-way and crowded streets once dominated by electric cars, slowing schedules. The increasing number of automobiles also resulted in better roads, which carried commuters faster and more directly between their homes and places of employment. The technology of the automobile and its highways progressed fantastically from 1900 to 1950. Only minor changes were made in the technology of the electric cars during these years; virtually no improvements were made in railroad right-of-ways.

The distance between points on the lines are based on official Pacific Electric timetables and other records. The frequency of schedules and representative running times also were obtained from timetables and have been included to show how people traveled when the Pacific Electric served the Los Angeles area.

In regard to running times, it should be noted that those from 1925 onward usually represent *scheduled* travel time rather than *actual* timing. The increasing volume of automobile traffic starting in the 1920's played a great role in slowing the electric cars.

SOUTHERN DISTRICT

The Pacific Electric's Southern District embraced all of the lines in Orange County, plus those in southeastern Los Angeles County. For the purpose of these listings, the author has divided the lines into those connected to Los Angeles by the southern "corridor," and those operating between district cities.

Southern "Corridor" Route

The lines of the Pacific Electric Southern District connected to Los Angeles followed a common route to Slauson Junction. Use of the route began July 4, 1902, with opening of the Long Beach Line. At that time the tracks went from Sixth and Main Streets in Los Angeles east on Ninth (which became Olympic Boulevard in the 1,000 block) to Tennessee Street (later renamed Hooper Street), and then turned south onto a private right-of-way. After opening of the elevated tracks from the Pacific Electric Building at Sixth and Main in 1910, the route was on these tracks to San Pedro Street, and south on San Pedro to Ninth, where it connected to Hooper. The private right-of-way from this point divided Long Beach Avenue to Slauson Junction, situated one block south of Slauson Avenue.

MILEAGES:

Los Angeles	0.00
Slauson Junction	4.27

LONG BEACH LINE

Passenger service on the Long Beach Line began July 4, 1902, and ended April 8, 1961. *Route:* the line followed the Southern "Corridor" Route to Slauson Junction and from there went south on a private right-of-way through Watts. This right-of-way divided Willowbrook Avenue from 108th Street in Watts to Greenleaf Drive in Compton, continued south through Dominguez Junction (at approximately Alameda Street and Santa Fe Avenue), crossed the Los Angeles River via a private bridge, and in Long Beach at Willow Street ("North Long Beach") divided American Avenue (later renamed Long Beach Boulevard) to Anaheim Street. From Anaheim, the tracks continued in American to Ocean Boulevard, and west on Ocean to P. E. storage yards adjacent to the Los Angeles River at Ocean Boulevard and Loma Vista Drive. There were P. E. car barns on the east side of American between Fifth and Sixth Streets until the late 1910's, and a depot on the south side of Ocean at Pacific until 1961.

MILEAGES:

Slauson Junction	4.27
Watts	7.45
Willowbrook	9.39
Compton	10.92
Dominguez Junction	13.31
Cota	14.96
North Long Beach (Willow Street)	17.52
Long Beach (Pacific and Ocean)	20.37

FREQUENCY OF SERVICE — 1911: every 30 minutes (54 round trips daily); 1920: every 20 minutes; 1934: every 30 minutes; 1946: every 15 minutes between 8 a.m. and 8:30 p.m.

RUNNING TIME — 1911: 40 minutes on locals and 36 minutes on limiteds; 1913: 48 minutes outbound and 50 minutes inbound for locals and 42 minutes outbound and 46 minutes inbound for limiteds; 1926: 51 minutes for limiteds; 1944: 54 minutes for limiteds; 1954: 60 minutes for limiteds.

SAN PEDRO VIA DOMINGUEZ LINE

Passenger service on the San Pedro via Dominguez Line began November 24, 1904, to Wilmington and on July 5, 1905, to San Pedro. *Route:* the line followed the one to Long Beach to Dominguez Junction, where the tracks turned southwesterly on a private right-of-way adjacent to Alameda Street, continuing to Lomita Boulevard; from here, the private right-of-way cut south diagonally, paralleling Drumm Avenue between Cruces and Young Streets. From "B" Street and Island Avenue the private right-of-way paralleled portions of Neptune Avenue and then entered San Pedro on a right-of-way adjacent to Front Street to Harbor Boulevard and then parallel to Harbor Boulevard. The depot was on the east side of Harbor at Fifth Street.

MILEAGES:

Dominguez Junction	13.31
Watson	17.19
Wilmington (Canal Street)	20.06
San Pedro (5th Street)	22.68

FREQUENCY OF SERVICE — 1911: every 30 to 60 minutes (23 round trips daily); 1946: every 20 to 30 minutes (approximately 55 round trips daily).
RUNNING TIME — 1911: 40 minutes to Wilmington and 45 minutes to San Pedro, 1946: approximately 60 minutes to Wilmington and 70 minutes to San Pedro.

HUNTINGTON BEACH-BALBOA LINE

Passenger service started July 4, 1904, to Huntington Beach, August 5, 1905, to Newport Beach, and July 4, 1906, to Balboa. Passenger service ended June 9, 1940, to Balboa, and on June 30, 1950, to Huntington Beach and Newport Beach. *Route:* the line followed the one to Long Beach to approximately a block north of Willow Street, where at 27th Street and Long Beach Boulevard the tracks cut southeasterly over a private right-of-way forming the boundary from Olive Avenue to Pacific Coast Highway between the cities of Long Beach and Signal Hill.

This right-of-way paralleled Appian Way (by the Marine Stadium) from Nieto Avenue to the San Gabriel River in Long Beach, and used private bridges to cross Alamitos Bay and the river. The right-of-way through Seal Beach (originally known as Bay City) was in the center of Electric Avenue and, until 1942, across Anaheim Bay to Sunset Beach. In 1942, construction of the U. S. Naval Ammunition and Net Depot caused the line to be re-routed from Electric Avenue at Seventeenth Street north to Coast Highway. The tracks followed a private right-of-way south of Coast Highway to Phillips Street and then turned onto a private right-of-way dividing Pacific Avenue in Sunset Beach. After leaving this community, the line followed a private right-of-way between Coast Highway and the ocean to the Pacific Electric station on the south side of Ocean Avenue at Main Street in Huntington Beach. From here, the line continued on a private right-of-way south of Coast Highway to approximately Fifty-ninth Street in Newport Beach, where the line entered a private right-of-way dividing Seashore Drive. At Thirty-second Street the tracks curved to Newport Boulevard and at McFadden Place entered a private right-of-way dividing Balboa Boulevard. It continued on Balboa to the line's terminus at Main Street.

MILEAGES:

North Long Beach (Willow Street)	17.52
Zaferia	20.11
Naples	23.00
Bay City (Seal Beach)	24.11
Anaheim Landing	24.83
Sunset Beach	26.70
Huntington Beach	32.46
Newport Beach	37.82
East Newport	39.66
Balboa	40.00

FREQUENCY OF SERVICE — 1911: approximately every 60 minutes (19 round trips daily; 1940: 9 round trips daily.
RUNNING TIME — 1911: 47 minutes to Seal Beach (Bay City); 62 minutes to Huntington Beach; 74 minutes to Newport Beach, and 80 minutes to Balboa.

SANTA ANA LINE

Passenger service to Santa Ana began November 6, 1905, and was discontinued to points between Bellflower and Santa Ana on July 2, 1950, and to Bellflower on May 25, 1958. *Route:* the line followed the one to Long Beach to Watts, where it cut southeasterly over a private right-of-way dividing Santa Ana Boulevard to Mona Boulevard and dividing Fernwood Avenue (a continuation of Santa Ana) in Lynwood to Wright Road. The tracks then continued on a private right-of-way southeasterly, cutting diagonally through Clearwater (later renamed Paramount) and dividing Flora Vista Street in Bellflower (originally called Somerset). The Pacific Electric station was at the northeast corner of Bellflower Boulevard and Flora Vista in Bellflower. The private right-of-way continued through Artesia (later renamed Dairy Valley), Cypress, Stanton, and Garden Grove. The tracks paralleled the northern boundary of Willowick Golf Course, crossed the Santa Ana River, and then turned eastward, emerging at Artesia Street from the private right-of-way onto Fourth Street in Santa Ana. The tracks continued down Fourth to the Pacific Electric station at 424 East Fourth Street.

MILEAGES:

Watts	7.45
Lynwood	9.70
Clearwater (Paramount)	13.06
Somerset (Bellflower)	15.40
Artesia	18.43
Cypress	21.65
Stanton	24.69
Benedict	24.77
Garden Grove	28.51
Santa Ana	34.00

FREQUENCY OF SERVICE — 1911: every 30 to 55 minutes (20 round trips daily); 1935: 9 round trips daily; 1940: 13 round trips daily; 1946: 22 round trips daily.
RUNNING TIME — 1911: 34 minutes to Bellflower, 61 minutes to Garden Grove, and 75 minutes to Santa Ana; 1941: 83 minutes to Santa Ana; 1943: 50 minutes to Bellflower, 78 minutes to Garden Grove, and 96 minutes to Santa Ana; 1946: 97 minutes to Santa Ana.

WHITTIER LINE

Passenger service to Whittier began November 7, 1903, and was discontinued south of Walker on January 22, 1938, and over the remainder of the line on March 6, 1938. *Route:* the line followed the one to Long Beach to Slauson Junction, where it turned east in a private right-of-way dividing Randolph Street in Huntington Park. After leaving Randolph Street at Greenwood Avenue in Downey, the private right-of-way continued in a southeasterly direction to Los Nietos, where it shortly after crossing Norwalk Boulevard it turned northward. The right-of-way was approximately midway between Gretna and Lynalan Avenues from approximately Mines Boulevard to Whittier Boulevard. The tracks then turned onto Whittier, continuing to Philadelphia Avenue, and went down Philadelphia to the Southern Pacific-Pacific Electric station at Comstock Avenue. The tracks continued one block eastward to Greenleaf Avenue.

MILEAGES:

Slauson Junction	4.27
Huntington Park	5.42
Maywood Avenue	6.73
Bell	7.19
Baker	7.66
Laguna	10.07
Rio Hondo	11.40
Rivera	12.39
Los Nietos	14.50
State School	16.68
Whittier	17.35

FREQUENCY OF SERVICE — 1911: every 15 to 60 minutes (33 outbound and 31 inbound trips daily); 1935: 1 round trip daily.
RUNNING TIME — 1911: 16 minutes to Huntington Park, 31 minutes to Rivera, 35 minutes to Los Nietos, and 47 minutes to Whittier.

LA HABRA-YORBA LINDA LINE

Passenger service began in 1906 to La Habra and in 1911 to Yorba Linda. *Route:* the line followed the one to Whittier to Los Nietos, from where the private right-of-way continued paralleling Lambert Road from approximately Hommage Avenue to Leffingwell Road, and the Union Pacific right-of-way from approximately Mills Avenue to Walnut Street in La Habra. The Pacific Electric station was between Second and Electric Avenue at Hiatt Street. The tracks paralleled Superior Avenue between Alpine and Fonda Streets. The private right-of-way went southeasterly to Puente Street in Brea, and then headed easterly. The Pacific Electric station was at the right-of-way's intersection with Pomona Avenue. After leaving Brea, the right-of-way turned southeasterly and shortly after crossing Valencia Avenue paralleled the south side of Imperial Highway to Lemon Drive in Yorba Linda. The right-of-way paralleled Park Drive to Yorba Linda Boulevard and ended at Lakeview Avenue.

MILEAGES:

Los Nietos	14.50
Leffingwell	19.39
Des Moines	20.92
La Habra	22.19
Randolph (Brea)	25.00
Oleo	26.00
Loftus	27.20
Yorba Linda	29.75

FREQUENCY OF SERVICE — 1911: 7 trains daily.

RUNNING TIME — 1911: 14 minutes to Huntington Park, 27 minutes to Rivera, 30 minutes to Los Nietos, 48 minutes to La Habra, and 66 minutes to Yorba Linda.

FULLERTON LINE

Passenger service to Fullerton started in 1917 and ended on January 22, 1938. *Route:* the line followed the one to La Habra and after leaving the Pacific Electric station there continued on Electric Avenue to Laon Junction (at approximately Bright Avenue). The line then went southward on a private right-of-way which at approximately Valley View Drive turned eastward and crossed Spadra Avenue via an overpass between Hillcrest Park and Glenwood Avenue. The private right-of-way continued east to Harvard Avenue and then curved south, cutting throught what became Fullerton College and south of Chapman Avenue paralleling Lawrence Avenue to Santa Fe Avenue. The private right-of-way paralleled Santa Fe to Pomona Avenue, crossed Pomona, and ended at the Pacific Electric station on the south side of Commonwealth Avenue between Spadra Road and Pomona Avenue.

MILEAGES:

La Habra	22.19
Laon Junction	22.54
Bastanchury	25.11
Sunny Hills	25.22
Fullerton	27.60

FREQUENCY OF SERVICE — 1917: 9 round trips daily; 1937: 1 round trip daily.

RUNNING TIME — 1917: 74 minutes.

REDONDO BEACH VIA GARDENA LINE

Passenger service on this line began November 12, 1911, and ended January 15, 1940. *Route:* the line followed the one to Long Beach to Watts, from where the track headed southwesterly over a private right-of-way paralleling 110th Street from Compton Avenue to Central Avenue, and Lanzit Avenue from Central Avenue to Broadway. The tracks curved southward in a private right-of-way dividing Athens Way to approximately 134th Street and continued south, curving southwesterly and paralleling 149th Street from approximately Figueroa Street to Orchard Street and continuing to Vermont Street. At approximately Compton Boulevard, the private right-of-way turned south and divided Vermont, continuing to Gardena Boule-

vard where it curved onto 166th Street, dividing 166th from Berendo Avenue to approximately Raymond Avenue. The private right-of-way turned southward approximately one block and headed eastward, paralleling 168th Street. The tracks entered Redondo Beach on Diamond Street. The tracks paralleled the ocean to Clifton.

MILEAGES:

Watts	7.45
South Los Angeles	9.88
Athens	10.31
Strawberry Park	12.75
Gardena	13.57
Hermosillo	14.13
Moneta	14.74
El Nido	17.84
Redondo Beach	20.89
Clifton	22.26

FREQUENCY OF SERVICE — 1911: every 30 minutes (27 round trips daily); 1927: 17 round trips daily.

RUNNING TIME — 1911: 62 minutes; 1922: 64 minutes.

SAN PEDRO VIA TORRANCE LINE

Passenger service began on March 19, 1912, and ended January 15, 1940. *Route:* the line followed the one to Redondo Beach via Gardena to Hermosillo (approximately 166th Street and Raymond Avenue), and followed a private right-of-way curving south to Normandie and then dividing Normandie from approximately 170th Street to 226th Streets. Tracks left the main route at Dolanco Junction (204th Street) and in a private right-of-way dividing Torrance Boulevard to 212th Street went to the Pacific Electric shops in Torrance. The tracks returned to the main line near 226th Street via Plaza del Amo. From 226th Street, the tracks paralleled Normandie Avenue until just before reaching Leonardo Avenue, where the private right-of-way curved southeasterly across Normandie Avenue and Anaheim Street. The private right-of-way went south adjacent to Gaffey Street to Pacific Avenue, and on Pacific to Front Street. The private right-of-way continued until again meeting Front Street, and the tracks then went on Front to First Street in San Pedro. From here, the tracks followed a private right-of-way adjacent to Front Street to First Street, and parallel to Harbor Boulevard from First Street to Fifth Street.

MILEAGES:

Hermosillo	14.70
Humphreys	16.90
Torrance (Ocean Ave.)	18.90
Weston Street	20.40
San Pedro	25.10

FREQUENCY OF SERVICE — 1922: every 60 minutes; 1924: every 70 minutes.

RUNNING TIME — 1922: 76 minutes outbound and 73 minutes inbound.

EL SEGUNDO LINE

Passenger service to El Segundo began August 10, 1914, and ended October 31, 1930. *Route:* the line followed the one to Redondo via Gardena to South Los Angeles, where at 116th Place and Broadway the private right-of-way continued eastward midway between 116th and 117th Streets to Vermont Avenue. From here, the private right-of-way went southeasterly parlelling Broadway from Crenshaw Boulevard to Inglewood Avenue in Hawthorne and then curving southeasterly into El Segundo. The private right-of-way then curved northeasterly, crossing diagonally through the city. The tracks entered Grand Avenue at Eucalyptus Drive (where the depot was situated) and continued on Grand to Concord Street.

MILEAGES:

South Los Angeles	9.88
Delta (Vermont Avenue)	10.76
Cypave	12.88
Hawthorne	14.42
El Segundo	18.87

FREQUENCY OF SERVICE — 1916: 7 round trips daily.

RUNNING TIME — not available.

Other Southern District Lines

The following lines did not use the "main" Southern District artery from Los Angeles or otherwise reach Los Angeles. Instead, these lines connected other cities with the Southern District.

LONG BEACH-SAN PEDRO LINE

Passenger service on this line began June 25, 1910, and ended January 2, 1949. *Route:* the line went from the Pacific Electric station on Ocean Boulevard and Pacific Avenue in Long Beach on Pacific to Broadway, on Broadway to Pine Avenue, on Pine to Third Street, and on Third to the Los Angeles River, where a private right-of-way on the east side of the river carried tracks to a private bridge adjacent to the Seventh Street bridge. After 1940, the route was west on Ocean Boulevard from Pacific Avenue and over the river. The private right-of-way went up the west bank of the river to approximately Eighth Street and turned northwesterly, crossing Anaheim Street just west of Hayes Avenue. The private right-of-way divided "I" Street from Nicholson Avenue to Mahar Avenue in Wilmington and then continued for five blocks, where it joined the line from Los Angeles (see *San Pedro via Dominguez Line*) and contined to San Pedro.

MILEAGES:

Long Beach	0.00
East Wilmington	4.05
Wilmington (Canal Street)	5.23
San Pedro	7.85

FREQUENCY OF SERVICE — 1911: every 60 minutes (18 round trips daily);

1922: every 40 minutes; 1928: every 30 minutes; 1940: 35 round trips daily; 1941: every 30 minutes; 1944: every 20 minutes; 1948: every 40 minutes.

RUNNING TIME — 1911: 19 minutes to Wilmington and 27 minutes to San Pedro; 1926: 28 minutes to San Pedro; 1932: 23 minutes to San Pedro; 1942: 31 minutes to San Pedro; 1943: 33 minutes to San Pedro; 1948: 30 minutes westbound (to San Pedro) and 31 minutes eastbound (to Long Beach).

SANTA ANA-HUNTINGTON BEACH-BALBOA LINE

Passenger service began in 1907 from Santa Ana to Balboa via Huntington Beach and ended in mid-1912 to points beyond Huntington Beach and to all points in 1922. *Route:* tracks went south from the Pacific Electric station at 421 East Fourth Street in Santa Ana over a private right-of-way to First Street, south in Maple Street to Myrtle Street, and then in a private right-of-way adjacent to Maple Street to Central Avenue. The private right-of-way then curved southeasterly and paralleled Talbert Avenue from Bristol Street to Talbert (later renamed Fountain Valley), continuing south and then easterly. The Pacific Electric station was situated on Lake Avenue at Chicago Street in Huntington Beach. The private right-of-way continued from there to the Los Angeles-Balboa tracks of the Pacific Electric. The line used these tracks to reach Balboa.

MILEAGES:
Santa Ana	0.00
New Delhi	2.69
Acelga	5.60
Talbert (Fountain Valley)	8.16
Bushard	10.53
Huntington Beach	13.31
Newport Beach	18.67
Balboa	20.85

FREQUENCY OF SERVICE — 1911: eight round trips daily plus one round trip between Santa Ana and Huntington Beach only; 1914: 10 round trips daily; 1916: six round trips daily; 1918: one round trip daily; 1921: two round trips daily.

RUNNING TIME 1911: 38 minutes from Santa Ana to Huntington Beach and 51 minutes from Santa Ana to Balboa.

HUNTINGTON BEACH-LA BOLSA LINE

Using a portion of Southern Pacific trackage that was electrified, passenger service started in February, 1911, and ended November 9, 1928. *Route:* from the Pacific Electric station at Chicago Street in Huntington Beach, a private right-of-way paralleled Lake Avenue to Seventeenth Street and then continued northward to the line's terminus at sugar beet processing plants.

MILEAGES:
Huntington Beach	0.00
La Bolsa	1.7
Wiebling	2.84

FREQUENCY OF SERVICE — 1911: 7 outbound and 6 inbound trips daily.

RUNNING TIME — not available for this line.

SANTA ANA-ORANGE LINE

Passenger service on this line began in 1886 and 1887 when it was constructed by the Santa Ana, Orange, and Tustin Street Railway as a horse car line. Henry E. Huntington's Los Angeles Inter-Urban Railroad acquired the line and electrified it in 1906. Passenger service ended on September 14, 1930. *Route:* from the Southern Pacific depot on Fourth Street in Santa Ana, the tracks were on Fourth to Main Street, on Main to a private right-of-way starting approximately across the street from Bullocks' Department Store in Fashion Square, and on the right-of-way to Lemon Street at La Veta Avenue in Orange. The tracks went in a private right-of-way paralleling Lemon to Chapman Avenue, where the line ended.

MILEAGES:
Santa Ana	0.00
Hargraves	2.92
Orange	4.04

FREQUENCY OF SERVICE — 1911: 14 round trips daily; 1916: every 15 minutes from 5:15 a.m. to 6:06 p.m. and every 40 minutes until 11 p.m.; 1921: every 20 minutes during daylight hours and every approximately 45 minutes in the evening.

RUNNING TIME — not available.

LONG BEACH-SEAL BEACH LINE

Passenger service from downtown Long Beach to the Alamitos Bay area started in 1904 and was extended to Seal Beach in 1913. Passenger service ended February 24, 1940. *Route:* from Pacific Avenue near Ocean Boulevard the tracks went in Pacific to Broadway, on Broadway to Pine Avenue, north on Pine to Third Street, east on Third to Alamitos Avenue, turning on Alamitos to Broadway, on Broadway to approximately Orizaba Avenue, and then southeasterly over a private right-of-way going diagonally to Grand Avenue and Ocean Boulevard, and then on a private right-of-way, dividing Ocean to the San Gabriel River, and over the river on a private bridge to Ocean Avenue in Seal Beach. The tracks went on Ocean to the line's terminus at Ocean and Main Street in Seal Beach.

FREQUENCY OF SERVICE — 1911: every 20 minutes from 6:05 a.m. to 7:25 a.m., and then every 30 minutes until midnight; 1932: every half hour.

RUNNING TIME: 1930: 22 minutes.

NORTHERN DISTRICT

The Pacific Electric's Northern District covered the lines operating in the Pasadena area and stretching eastward as far as Ontario. From downtown Los Angeles, cars travelled a common route to Echandia Junction. Interurbans then rolled directly to their destinations or went through one or as many as five more junctions to reach the ends of the lines. Besides Echandia, the junctions were Valley (originally called Covina Junction), Sierra Vista, Oneonta Park, El Molino, and San Marino.

ECHANDIA JUNCTION: BASIC LOS ANGELES "EXIT" ROUTE

The common route from the Pacific Electric Building at Sixth and Main Streets in downtown Los Angeles was via tracks in Main Street to First Street, in First to Los Angeles Street, in Los Angeles to Aliso Street, and in Aliso (including a bridge over the Los Angeles River) to a private right-of-way paralleling Ramona Boulevard. This right-of-way went north to Echandia Junction (at approximately Mission Road and Marengo Street). After opening of the elevated tracks from the P. E. Building to San Pedro Street, tracks went up San Pedro to Aliso Street. Some routes then went on San Pedro exclusively, while others utilized only Main Street and some used a combination of the two streets for entry and exit.

MILEAGES:
Pacific Electric Station	
6th and Main, L.A.	0.00
1st and Main	.63
Aliso and San Pedro Sts.	1.04
Echandia Junction	2.38

SOUTH PASADENA LINE

Passenger service began May 1, 1895 (as the area's first electric interurban route, built by the Pasadena and Los Angeles Railway Company) and ended January 2, 1935. *Route:* from Echandia Junction, the tracks went on Daly Street to Pasadena Avenue, on Pasadena to a private right-of-way, on this private right-of-way to Roble Avenue, on Roble to a private right-of-way to Mission Street, on Mission to Fair Oaks Avenue, and up Fair Oaks to Colorado Street.

MILEAGES:
Echandia Junction	2.38
Roble Avenue and Avenue 64	7.32
Mission and Fair Oaks	9.24

FREQUENCY OF SERVICE — 1911: every 10 to 20 minutes (approximately 130 round trips daily).

RUNNING TIME — not available.

Valley (formerly "Covina") Junction

From Echandia Junction, a private right-of-way paralleled Ramona Boulevard to Valley Junction (at approximately Ramona Boulevard and Marengo Street). Cars bound for Covina, Pomona, or the San Bernardino and Riverside areas continued eastward through Valley Junction. Trolleys headed for Pasadena or other San Gabriel Valley points went northeasterly through Sierra Vista Junction.

MILEAGES:
Echandia Junction	2.38
Valley (Covina) Junction	3.13

Sierra Vista Junction

From Echandia Junction, a private right-of-way paralleled Ramona Boulevard through Valley Junction (at approximately Ramona and Marengo Street) and then paralleled Soto Street to Huntington Drive. The tracks followed a private right-of-way dividing Huntington Drive to Sierra Vista Junction (at Huntington Drive and Main Street).

MILEAGES:
Echandia Junction	2.38
Valley (Covina) Junction	3.13
Bairdstown	6.16
Sierra Vista	7.42

ALHAMBRA-SAN GABRIEL-TEMPLE CITY LINE

Passenger service to Alhambra and San Gabriel began June 21, 1902, and service on the extension to Temple City started July 29, 1924. Passenger service ended November 29, 1941. *Route:* from Sierra Vista Junction, the tracks were in a private right-of-way dividing Main Street to the Southern Pacific right-of-way (at Raymond Avenue). The tracks then continued eastward in Main, which became Las Tunas Drive in San Gabriel, to the Masonic Home (later the San Gabriel Country Club) between Country Club Drive and California Street. Tracks of the San Gabriel branch went south from Main Street in Mission Drive, passed San Gabriel Mission, were in Junipero Street from the mission to Broadway, and were in a private right-of-way dividing Junipero to San Marino Avenue. The tracks connected to those on Las Tunas via San Marino Avenue. The tracks went eastward on Las Tunas to San Gabriel Boulevard and then followed a private right-of-way dividing Las Tunas to Rosemead Boulevard. From here, the tracks went on Las Tunas to the Pacific Electric station at the northeast corner of Las Tunas and Kauffman Avenue.

MILEAGES:
Sierra Vista Junction	7.42
Palm Avenue	8.21
S. P. Pasadena Branch	8.38
S. P. Monrovia Branch	8.63
Mission Street Junction	10.42
Masonic Home (San Gabriel Valley Country Club)	12.12
Temple City	14.67

FREQUENCY OF SERVICE — 1911: every 15 to 60 minutes (approximately 35 round trips daily); 1924: 51 outbound and 53 inbound trips daily; 1940: approximately 50 round trips daily.
RUNNING TIME — 1911: 17 minutes to Valley (Covina) Junction, 24 minutes to Sierra Vista Junction, 28 minutes to West Alhambra, 37 minutes to Union Street in Alhambra, 45 minutes to San Gabriel Mission, and 50 minutes to the Masonic Home (San Gabriel Valley Country Club); 1940: 52 minutes outbound and 48 minutes inbound (to and from Union Street).

Oneonta Park Junction

The route was to Sierra Vista Junction and then northward on a private right-of-way dividing Huntington Drive to Oneonta Park Junction (at Fair Oaks Avenue).

MILEAGES:
Sierra Vista Junction	7.42
Oneonta Park Junction	8.31

EL MOLINO JUNCTION

The route was to Oneonta Park Junction and then eastward in a private right-of-way dividing Huntington Drive to El Molino Junction (at Oak Knoll Avenue).

MILEAGES:
Oneonta Park Junction	8.31
El Molino Junction	10.04

PASADENA SHORT LINE

Passenger service began in 1902 and ended September 30, 1951. *Route:* from Oneonta Park Junction, the route was north in a private right-of-way dividing Fair Oaks Avenue to Monterey Road and then north on Fair Oaks to California Street, on California to Raymond, on Raymond to the Pacific Electric car barns at Fair Oaks and Mary Avenue. Cars leaving Pasadena went down Fair Oaks from Mary Avenue and followed the inbound line after passing California Avenue.

MILEAGES:
Oneonta Park Junction	8.31
Mission and Fair Oaks	9.26
Raymond Hotel	9.87
Colorado and Fair Oaks	11.20

FREQUENCY OF SERVICE — 1911: every 10 to 30 minutes (approximately 70 round trips daily); 1949: every 15 to 60 minutes (approximately 40 round trips daily).
RUNNING TIME — 1911: Los Angeles to Mission and Fair Oaks Avenue, 30 minutes, and Los Angeles to Colorado and Fair Oaks, 38 minutes; 1951: 47 minutes.

PASADENA OAK KNOLL LINE

Passenger service began in 1906 and ended September 30, 1951. *Route:* the line from Los Angeles went to El Molino Junction and then continued northward on a private right-of-way paralleling Oak Knoll Avenue. The tracks entered Oak Knoll Avenue at approximately Wentworth Avenue, and went on Oak Knoll to Arden Road. The tracks went on Arden to Lake Avenue, north on Lake to Colorado Street, and west on Colorado to Fair Oaks Avenue.

MILEAGES:
El Molino Junction	10.04
Colorado and Lake	11.96
Colorado and Fair Oaks	13.90

FREQUENCY OF SERVICE — 1911: every 15 to 60 minutes (40 round trips daily); 1946: every 15 to 60 minutes (49 round trips daily).
RUNNING TIME — 1911: 17 minutes to Valley (Covina) Junction, 24 minutes to Sierra Vista Junction, 26 minutes to Oneonta Park Junction, 29 minutes to El Molino Junction, and Colorado and Fair Oaks, 45 minutes; 1949: 59 minutes to Colorado and Fair Oaks.

MOUNT LOWE LINE

The line opened July 4, 1893, became a Pasadena and Los Angeles Railway property in 1896, and was acquired by the Pacific Electric in 1902. Service ended after the mountain section of the railway was destroyed by rains in March, 1938. *Route:* the line followed the Pasadena Oak Knoll route to Fair Oaks Avenue and Colorado Street, and then went north on Fair Oaks to Mariposa Street, Altadena. The tracks went east on Mariposa to Lake Avenue, and north on Lake to a private right-of-way beginning approximately 2,600 feet north of Mariposa. This right-of-way led to Rubio Canyon, at Rubio Canyon Road and Loma Alta Drive. Passengers transferred here to the incline railway, which carried them to Echo Mountain. There they boarded narrow gauge trolleys that wound on a right-of-way on the mountains to the Alpine Tavern on Mount Lowe.

MILEAGES:
El Molino Junction	10.04
Pasadena	13.00
Altadena	17.11
Rubio Canyon	18.88
Echo Mountain	19.38
Cape of Good Hope	20.25
Dawn	20.61
Circular Bridge	21.15
Granite Gate	22.00
Alpine Tavern	22.95

FREQUENCY OF SERVICE — 1911: 5 round trips from Los Angeles and 2 round trips from Pasadena.
RUNNING TIME — 1911: 17 minutes to Valley (Covina) Junction, 24 minutes to Sierra Vista Junction, 26 minutes to Oneonta Park Junction, 30 minutes to El Molino Junction, 50 minutes to Pasadena, 65 minutes to Altadena, 75 minutes to Rubio Canyon, 90 minutes to Cape of Good Hope, 95 minutes to Dawn, 100 minutes to Circular Bridge, 106 minutes to Granite Gate, and 120 minutes to Alpine Tavern.

San Marino Junction

From El Molino Junction, the route was on a private right-of-way dividing Huntington Drive to Sierra Madre Boulevard.

MILEAGES:
El Molino Junction	10.04
San Marino Junction	11.35

SIERRA MADRE LINE

Passenger service began March 19, 1904, and ended October 6, 1950. *Route:* the line followed the one from Los Angeles to San Marino Junction and then turned north on a private right-of-way to Sierra Madre Boulevard to Michillinda Avenue. From there, the track continued in Sierra Madre to Kersting Court. The track went on

Kersting to Baldwin Avenue (where the station was situated) and then continued over a private right-of-way to its terminus at Mountain Trail Avenue.

MILEAGES:

San Marino Junction	11.35
El Camino	13.15
El Rincon	14.27
Sierra Madre	16.70
Wilson Trail	17.03

FREQUENCY OF SERVICE — 1911: every 20 to 60 minutes (18 round trips daily); 1946: 19 round trips daily; 1948: 11 trains outbound and 9 trains inbound daily.

RUNNING TIME — 1911: 17 minutes to Valley (Covina) Junction, 26 minutes to Sierra Vista Junction, 32 minutes to El Molino Junction, 34 minutes to San Marino, and 52 minutes to Sierra Madre; 1948: 63 minutes to Sierra Madre.

MONROVIA-GLENDORA LINE

Passenger service began March 1, 1903, to Monrovia and in April, 1907, to Glendora. Passenger service ended September 30, 1951. *Route:* the line followed the one from Los Angeles to San Marino Junction. The tracks then continued eastward in a private right-of-way dividing Huntington Drive through San Marino and Arcadia, where at approximately San Rafael Road the tracks curved northward on a private right-of-way and at Santa Anita Avenue went eastward on Santa Clara Avenue to to Second Avenue. The tracks continued eastward on a private right-of-way that would have been an extension of Santa Clara. The tracks entered Chestnut Avenue at Esplanade Avenue, continuing east on Chestnut past the Pacific Electric station (at the northeast corner of Chestnut and Myrtle Avenue) to Canyon Boulevard. The tracks continued eastward on a private right-of-way following what would have been an extension of Chestnut to approximately Mountain Avenue, where the tracks curved northward to a private right-of-way paralleling Royal Oaks Drive. At Fish Canyon Road (Las Lomas Avenue), the private right-of-way turned southeasterly, and after entering Azusa paralleled Crescent Drive from Vernon Avenue to Orange Avenue, where the tracks entered Ninth Street. The Pacific Electric station was south of Ninth between Angeleno and Azusa Avenues. The route was on Ninth to approximately Pasadena Avenue, where a private right-of-way continued eastward, paralleling the Santa Fe right-of-way to approximately Trayer Avenue in Glendora. The tracks entered Glendora on Mountain View Avenue and ended at Pennsylvania Avenue.

MILEAGES:

San Marino Junction	11.35
Sunnyslope	14.46
Arcadia	16.24
Monrovia	18.26
Duarte	19.82
Puente Largo	21.56
Azusa	23.32
Glendora	25.99

FREQUENCY OF SERVICE — 1911: 29 outbound trains daily to Monrovia (11

of which continued to Glendora) and 31 inbound trains daily to Monrovia (12 of which started in Glendora; 1943: 47 round trips daily (25 of which continued to Glendora).

RUNNING TIME — 1911: 31 minutes to San Marino, 42 minutes to Arcadia, 47 minutes to Monrovia, 51 minutes to Duarte, 60 minutes to Azusa, and 68 minutes to Glendora; 1943: 37 minutes to San Marino, 51 minutes to Arcadia, 57 minutes to Monrovia, 78 minutes to Azusa, and 80 minutes to Glendora.

Valley (formerly "Covina") Junction

The route from Echandia Junction was over a private right-of-way paralleling Ramona Boulevard to Valley Junction (at approximately Cornwell Street). Much of the right-of-way was covered by the San Bernardino Freeway.

MILEAGES:

Valley (Covina) Junction	3.13

COVINA-POMONA LINE

Passenger service to Covina began in 1907 and to Pomona on August 31, 1912. *Route:* the line was over a private right-of-way paralleling Ramona Boulevard from Valley Junction to approximately Rockwell Avenue in El Monte. Portions of the San Bernardino Freeway have covered many parts of the right-of-way. From Rockwell, a private right-of-way went eastward, paralleling San Bernardino Road (which became Ramona Boulevard in Baldwin Park) from Valley Boulevard to approximately Harlan Avenue. From Harlan, a private right-of-way divided Ramona Boulevard to Downing Avenue. The private right-of-way then cut northeasterly, paralleling Los Angeles Avenue from approximately Elton Avenue to Azusa Canyon Road. The tracks then continued eastward on a private right-of-way to Grand Avenue in Covina. The right-of-way then cut northeasterly and at Valley Center Avenue headed eastward. In La Verne, the right-of-way turned southwesterly, paralleling Orange Street to the P. E. station between "D" and "E" streets. From here, the tracks curved southward on a private right-of-way between White Avenue and Huntington Boulevard, passing the Los Angeles County Fairgrounds and Ganesha Park. The tracks went down White Avenue to Holt Avenue, on Holt to Garey Avenue, south on Garey to Franklin Avenue, and east on Franklin to the route's terminus at Palomares Avenue.

MILEAGES:

Valley (Covina) Junction	3.13
Granada Park	6.40
Ramona	8.15
Wilmar	9.51
El Monte	13.14
Baldwin Park	18.00
Covina	21.79
San Dimas (P. E. Station)	26.29
San Dimas (S. P. Station)	26.35
Lordsburg (La Verne)	28.53
Pomona Junction	30.89
Pomona	31.89

21 round trips daily, of which 1 went only to and from El Monte and seven went to and from San Dimas; 1912: 12 round trips daily to Pomona; 1920: 19 round trips daily to Pomona and 31 round trips daily to Covina; 1940: 18 round trips daily to Pomona; 1946: 5 round trips daily to Covina and 43 round trips daily to Baldwin Park.

RUNNING TIME — 1911: 23 minutes to Granada Park, 31 minutes to Wilmar, 39 minutes to El Monte, 49 minutes to Baldwin Park, 60 minutes to Covina, and 72 minutes to San Dimas; 1916: 22 minutes to Granada Park, 30 minutes to Wilmar, 39 minutes to El Monte, 60 minutes to Covina, 65 minutes to San Dimas, and 83 minutes to Pomona; 1920: 84 minutes to Pomona; 1946: 36 minutes to Wilmar, 46 minutes to El Monte, and 61 minutes to Baldwin Park.

Other Northern District Interurban Routes

The following routes also were operated in the Pacific Electric's Northern District, linking cities within the area. They did not, however, connect directly to Los Angeles.

ONTARIO-SAN ANTONIO HEIGHTS LINE

The Ontario and San Antonio Heights Railway Company was established in 1887 and used mules to haul passener cars. (The mules pulled the cars up the line and got a free ride down on a platform.) Acquired by the Ontario Electric Company, the line was electrified in 1895 and became part of the Pacific Light and Power Company when it absorbed Ontario Electric in 1908. Pacific Electric purchased the railway in 1912 and merged it into the P. E. system. Passenger service was discontinued to 24th Street on July 4, 1924, to Upland on November 1, 1924, and on the balance of the line on October 6, 1928. *Route:* the line was from Emporia Street and Euclid Avenue in Ontario up a private right-of-way dividing Euclid to La Cima (24th Street), where the right-of-way turned west and continued to San Antonio Heights.

MILEAGES:

Ontario	0.00
Upland	2.59
San Antonio Heights	7.54

FREQUENCY OF SERVICE — 1916: 20 round trips daily.

RUNNING TIME — 1916: 9 minutes from Ontario to Upland, and 25 minutes from Upland to San Antonio Heights.

POMONA-UPLAND LINE

The line was built in 1910 by the Ontario and San Antonio Heights Railway Company, which was acquired in 1912 by the Pacific Electric. Passenger service began January 1, 1911, and ended January 1, 1933. *Route:* the line was from the Pacific Electric station at Third Street and Garey Avenue in Pomona north on Garey to Walnut Street, where tracks went in a private right-of-way to the P. E. main line between Los Angeles and San Bernardino.

The route followed this line to Euclid Avenue in Upland.

MILEAGES:

Pomona (Salt Lake R.R. Station)	0.00
Claremont	.50
West Upland	6.87
West Ontario	8.07
Upland	11.69
Ontario	10.50
San Antonio Heights	13.07

FREQUENCY OF SERVICE — 1916: 33 round trips daily (of which 10 ended at North Pomona).

RUNNING TIME — 1916: 12 minutes to North Pomona, 17 minutes to Claremont, 27 minutes to Upland, and 39 minutes to Ontario.

EASTERN DISTRICT

The lines the farthest from Los Angeles operated in the Pacific Electric's Eastern District, which covered trolley lines in San Bernardino County east of Ontario and those in Riverside County. The electric cars followed the line to Pomona as far as Lordsburg (LaVerne).

SAN BERNARDINO LINE

Passenger service to San Bernardino began June 11, 1914, and ended November 1, 1941. *Route:* the line from Los Angeles followed the one to Pomona to the P. E. station on Orange Street between "D" and "B" streets in LaVerne. From here, a private right-of-way curved northeasterly and then headed east, paralleling the Santa Fe Railroad right-of-way through Claremont to approximately Berkeley Avenue, where the tracks paralleled First Street to approximately Mills Avenue. There the tracks entered a private right-of-way dividing Huntington Drive to Benson Avenue, where the private right-of-way continued midway between Arrow Highway and Ninth Street. The tracks entered San Bernardino on Third Street and the P. E. station was on the south side of Third between "E" and "F" streets.

MILEAGES:

Lordsburg	28.75
North Pomona	30.32
Claremont	31.82
Upland	35.91
Alta Loma	39.39
Etiwanda	43.71
Fontana	49.17
Rialto	52.92
San Bernardino	57.41

FREQUENCY OF SERVICE — 1916: 7 round trips daily; 1934: 8 round trips daily; 1937: 9 round trips daily; 1940: 4 round trips daily.

RUNNING TIME — 1916: 125 minutes; 1931: 110 minutes; 1935: 119 minutes; 1940: 105 minutes.

SAN BERNARDINO-RIVERSIDE LINE

Passenger service began October 14, 1913, and ended May 8, 1939. *Route:* the line from the Pacific Electric station on the south side of Third Street between "E" and "F" Streets went south on a private right-of-way midway between "E" and "F" to Mill Street, and continued south in a private right-of-way dividing Mount Vernon

Avenue to "I" Street in Colton. From here, the tracks went down Ninth Street to "O" Street and then south over a private right-of-way to approximately West Highgrove Street in Riverside, where the right-of-way paralleled La Cadena Drive (formerly Colton Avenue) to First Street; the line went west on First to Main Street, and south on Main to 14th Street.

MILEAGES:

Riverside (14th and Main)	0.00
Vine	1.42
Market Junction	1.62
Palmyrita	3.11
Grand Terrace	5.44
Revino	5.87
Congress	6.99
Colton (S. P. Crossing)	7.63
Mount Vernon	8.43
Shop Siding	10.63
San Bernardino	10.94

FREQUENCY OF SERVICE — 1935: every 37 to 60 minutes (13 round trips daily).

RUNNING TIME — 1935: 9 minutes to Colton and 34 minutes to Riverside (14th and Main Streets).

REDLANDS LINE

Passenger service between Redlands and San Bernardino began March 3, 1903, and between Redlands and Los Angeles on June 11, 1914. Passenger service ended July 20, 1936. *Route:* from the Pacific Electric station on the south side of Third Street between "E" and "F" Streets in San Bernardino, the line was east on Third Street to "A" Street, curving onto a private right-of-way paralleling Mill Street to Mountain View Street, south on a private right-of-way adjacent to Mountain View to San Bernardino Avenue, on a right-of-way adjacent to Mountain View to Orange Avenue, and south on Orange to the terminus at Citrus Avenue.

MILEAGES:

San Bernardino	0.00
Allen Street	.91
Race Track	2.14
Amen	2.84
Gravel Pit	3.31
Marigold	4.62
Crown Jewel	6.08
Sunkist	7.09
Lugonia	8.16
Casa Loma	8.56
Redlands (P. E. Station)	9.16

FREQUENCY OF SERVICE — 1903: every 40 to 50 minutes (20 round trips daily); 1908: every 30 to 45 minutes (25 round trips daily); 1912: every 40 minutes (29 round trips daily); 1916: every 60 minutes; 1935: 6 outbound and 5 inbound trips daily.

RUNNING TIME — 1903: 40 minutes outbound and 35 minutes inbound; 1908: 32 minutes outbound and 28 minutes inbound; 1935: 26 minutes.

RIVERSIDE-REDLANDS LINE

Passenger service began in 1916 and ended May 8, 1939. *Route:* the line was composed of through-routing of the line from Riverside to San Bernardino and San Bernardino to Redlands.

MILEAGES:

Riverside (14th and Main)	0.00
Vine	1.42
Market Junction	1.62
Palmyrita	3.11
Grand Terrace	5.44
Revino	5.87
Congress	6.99
Colton (S. P. Crossing)	7.63
Mount Vernon	8.43
Shop Siding	10.63
San Bernardino	10.94
Allen Street	11.85
Race Track	13.08
Amen	13.78
Gravel Pit	14.25
Marigold	15.56
Crown Jewel	17.02
Sunkist	18.03
Lugonia	19.10
Casa Loma	19.50
Redlands (P. E. Station)	20.10

FREQUENCY OF SERVICE — 1927: every 40 to 60 minutes; 1935: 7 round trips daily.

RUNNING TIME — 1935: 50 minutes.

SAN BERNARDINO-COLTON LINE

The line was built by the San Bernardino Valley Traction Company and opened for service February 22, 1902. Passenger service ended February 22, 1942. *Route:* the line from San Bernardino was from "D" Street west on Third Street to Mount Vernon Avenue, south on Mount Vernon to Hubbard Street, and then over a private right-of-way to Eighth Street in Colton. The tracks went south in Eighth Street to "J" Street and east on "J" to Ninth Street.

MILEAGES:

San Bernardino ("D" and Third)	0.00
P. E. Station	.14
Santa Fe Station	.86
La Cadena	2.87
Colton ("J" and Ninth)	4.24

FREQUENCY OF SERVICE — 1903: every 30 to 60 minutes (approximately 30 round trips daily); 1912: every 20 to 40 minutes (approximately 30 round trips daily); 1924: every 15 to 30 minutes (approximately 75 round trips daily).

RUNNING TIME — 1903: 20 minutes.

ARROWHEAD SPRINGS LINE

Built by the San Bernardino Valley Traction Company, the line opened March 15, 1907. Passenger service ended January 2, 1925. *Route:* the line went from the Pacific Electric station on the south side of Third Street between "E" and "F" Streets east on Third Street to "D" Street, north on "D" to Highland Avenue, east on Highland to Mountain View Avenue, and then north in a private right-of-way dividing Mountain View. From Mountain View, the track followed a private right-of-way to Arrowhead Springs.

MILEAGES:

San Bernardino (P. E. Station)	0.00
Highland Avenue	2.55
Severance	5.00
Arrowhead Springs	7.25

FREQUENCY OF SERVICE — 1907: 7 round trips daily; 1912: 8 round trips daily; 1914: 6 round trips daily; 1920: 5 round trips daily; 1922: 6 round. trips daily.

RUNNING TIME — 1921: 35 minutes outbound and 28 minutes inbound.

HIGHLAND-PATTON LINE

The line was constructed in 1903 by the San Bernardino Traction Company, and passenger service began August 13, 1903. Passenger service to Patton ended June 1, 1924, and to Highland on July 20, 1936. *Route:* the line went from the Pacific Electric station on the south side of Third Street between "E" and "F" Streets east on Third Street to "D" Street, north on "D" to Seventh Street, east on Seventh to "A" Street and then southeasterly over a private right-of-way to Waterman Avenue and Sixth Street. The right-of-way then went easterly over a private right-of-way representing an extension of Sixth to Pepper Avenue; the line went north on Pepper to Second Street (Harlem Springs), east on Second to Central Avenue, north on Central to Pacific Avenue, and east on Pacific to Palm Avenue in Highland. The Patton Line went north from Patton Junction (Central and Pacific Avenues) on Central to Patton.

MILEAGES: (To Highland)

San Bernardino (P. E. Station)	0.00
"C" Street	.20
Cemetery	.90
Antill	2.02
Sterling	3.33
Harlem	5.25
Patton Junction	6.05
Highland	6.56

MILEAGES: (To Patton)

Patton Junction	6.05
Patton	6.57

FREQUENCY OF SERVICE — 1912: every 60 minutes (18 round trips daily, of which half made the side trips to Patton when inbound); 1921: 11 round trips daily (4 of the trips when to Patton); 1924: 6 round trips daily; 1932: 3 round trips daily.

RUNNING TIME — 1924: 22 minutes outbound and 25 minutes inbound.

LOS ANGELES-RIVERSIDE LINE

Passenger service between Riverside and the Riverside Portland Cement Company at Crestmore began in 1908, to Bloomington on May 20, 1911, and to Rialto on March 24, 1914. Passenger service between Los Angeles and Riverside started March 15, 1915, and service was discontinued June 9, 1940. *Route:* the line from Los Angeles followed the one from Los Angeles to San Bernardino to Rialto Junction, and then turned south on a private right-of-way dividing Riverside Avenue in Rialto. The private right-of-way then turned southwesterly to Bloomington, and then headed southeasterly through Crestmore. Cars left the right-of-way and entered Riverside on Market Street, going south on Market past the Pacific Electric station on the east side of Market between Seventh and Eighth Streets to 14th Street.

MILEAGES:

Rialto	52.92
Poole	53.92
Bloomington	56.42
Cement Plant	58.82
Alvarado	60.91
Alamo	61.37
Hancock	61.81
Riverside (P. E. Station)	62.50
Riverside (14th and Market)	63.08

FREQUENCY OF SERVICE — 1916: five outbound and six inbound trips between Los Angeles and Riverside daily; 1938: one round trip daily.

RUNNING TIME: 1916: 137 minutes.

RIVERSIDE-RIALTO LINE

Passenger service began May 20, 1911, to Bloomington and March 24, 1914, to Rialto. Passenger service ended June 9, 1940. *Route:* the line followed the Los Angeles-Riverside route between Rialto and Riverside.

MILEAGES: (*See Los Angeles-Riverside Line*)

FREQUENCY OF SERVICE — 1914: approximately 10 round trips daily; 1931: 9 round trips daily; 1939: 4 round trips daily; 1940: 1 round trip daily.

RUNNING TIME — 1914: 28 minutes to Bloomington and 38 minutes to Rialto.

RIVERSIDE-CORONA LINE

Passenger service began on February 17, 1915. Passenger service between Arlinton and Corona ended August 31, 1931, and from Riverside to Arlington on January 10, 1943. *Route:* from Sixth and Main Streets in Riverside, the line was south on Main to 14th Street, and then south on Magnolia Avenue to Arlington; the tracks then followed a private right-of-way dividing Magnolia Avenue to Corona, where the line went in Third Street to Merrill Avenue.

MILEAGES:

Riverside (6th and Main)	0.00
Central Avenue	2.25
Arlington	6.62
May Tower	12.60
Corona (3rd and Merrill)	14.53

FREQUENCY OF SERVICE — 1913: every 20 minutes to Arlington; 1927: every two hours to Corona; 1943: every 30 minutes to Arlington.

RUNNING TIME — 38 minutes outbound and 43 minutes inbound between Riverside and Arlington; 1924: 20 minutes outbound and 23 minutes inbound; 1927: 37 minutes between Riverside and Corona.

WESTERN DISTRICT

The Pacific Electric's Western District was formed through the consolidation of the Los Angeles Pacific Railroad routes, which served Hollywood, Beverly Hills, Santa Monica, Venice, and adjacent areas, and the Los Angeles and Redondo Railway. The Glendale Line, part of Henry Huntington's original Pacific Electric, also was included in the district since the route was westerly from downtown Los Angeles. The lines to the San Fernando Valley and Burbank, constructed after the formation in 1911 of the consolidated Pacific Electric, also operated within the Western District.

Many Western District lines operated from the Hollywood Subway after its opening in 1925. The subway began beneath the Subway Terminal Building at 417 South Hill Street in downtown Los Angeles and extended 4,325 feet, emerging southeast of Beverly Boulevard and Glendale Boulevard. Cars entered Glendale Boulevard, going on Glendale to Sunset Boulevard where they resumed their previous routes.

SANTA MONICA VIA SAWTELLE LINE

Passenger service from Los Angeles to Santa Monica began in 1897 and to Venice in 1901. Service ended July 7, 1940. *Route:* the line followed the Venice Short Line to Vineyard Junction. From here, the tracks were in a private right-of-way in the center of San Vicente Boulevard to Burton Way and in a private right-of-way adjacent to Burton Way from there to Santa Monica Boulevard; the line continued in a private right-of-way dividing Santa Monica Boulevard to Sepulveda Boulevard. The tracks then went in Santa Monica Boulevard to Ocean Avenue, and in Ocean Avenue and Trolleyway to Windward Avenue.

MILEAGES:

Vineyard Junction	5.56
Carthay Center	7.73
Beverly Hills	10.18
Sawtelle	13.36
Santa Monica	17.12
Ocean Park (Pier Avenue)	18.49
Venice (Windward Avenue)	19.33

FREQUENCY OF SERVICE — 1911: every 30 minutes (38 round trips daily); 1934: every 40 minutes.

RUNNING TIME — 1911: 23 minutes to Vineyard, 32 minutes to Beverly Hills, 38 minutes to Sawtelle, 52 minutes to Santa Monica, 60 minutes to Ocean Park, and 64 minutes to Venice; 1934: 60 minutes to Santa Monica.

HOLLYWOOD-VENICE LINE

Passenger service began in the late 1890's and ended on August 23, 1941. *Route:* from Fourth and Hill Streets in downtown Los Angeles, the tracks went north on Hill to Sunset Boulevard, west on Sunset to Hollywood Boulevard, west on Hollywood to La Brea Avenue and south through Crescent Junction (originally Gardner Junction) over a private right-of-way emerging through Crescent Heights Boulevard onto Santa Monica Boulevard, and then over a private right-of-way dividing Santa Monica Boulevard on the line used by the Beverly Hills via Sawtelle Line to Venice.

MILEAGES:

Los Angeles (4th and Hill)	0.00
Bonnie Brae Street	2.65

Gardner (Crescent) Junction	
(La Brea Avenue)	8.70
Beverly Hills	12.19
Sawtelle	15.37
Santa Monica	19.13
Ocean Park	
(Pier Avenue)	20.50
Venice (Windward Avenue)	21.34

FREQUENCY OF SERVICE — 1911: every 30 minutes (approximately 40 round trips daily); 1920: approximately 20 trips daily

RUNNING TIME — 1911: Los Angeles to: Hollywood, 31 minutes, Beverly Hills, 48 minutes, Sawtelle, 54 minutes, Santa Monica, 68 minutes, and Venice, 80 minutes; 1927: Los Angeles to Venice, 93 minutes.

VENICE SHORT LINE

Passenger service began in 1903 and was discontinued September 17, 1950. *Route:* from the Hill Street station at Fourth and Hill Streets in downtown Los Angeles, the line originally went south on Hill Street to Venice Boulevard, on Venice to Pacific Avenue, over a private right-of-way to Normandie Avenue, on Venice Boulevard to Arlington Avenue, over a private right-of-way and Blaine Street to Concord Street, and then along a private right-of-way to Vineyard Junction (between Pico and Venice Boulevards and Highland Avenue and West Boulevard). The line then went on a private right-of-way paralleling Venice Boulevard to Pacific Avenue in Venice, on Pacific to Windward Avenue, on a private right-of-way paralleling Pacific Avenue to Ocean Avenue and on Ocean to Pico Boulevard. From there, the tracks went over a private right-of-way to the Pacific Electric station at Third Street and Santa Monica Boulevard.

MILEAGES:
Los Angeles	0.00
Vineyard	5.56
Culver City.	9.25
Palms	10.05
Ocean Park Heights	11.95
Venice (Windward Avenue)	14.81
Ocean Park (Pier Avenue)	15.65
Santa Monica (Santa Monica Blvd. and Broadway)	17.02

FREQUENCY OF SERVICE — 1911: every 15 to 30 minutes (53 round trips daily); 1948: every 7 to 20 minutes (55 round trips daily).

RUNNING TIME — 1911: 22 minutes to Vineyard, 30 minutes to Palms, 38 minutes to Venice, 42 minutes to Ocean Park, and 50 minutes to Santa Monica; 1941: 64 minutes to Venice.

WESTGATE LINE

Passenger service began in 1906 and ended June 30, 1940. *Route:* the line followed the Santa Monica via Beverly Hills line to Sawtelle, where it turned north at Purdue Avenue onto a private right-of-way. From Wilshire Boulevard, this track was on a right-of-way dividing San Vicente Boulevard to Ocean Avenue in Santa Monica. The line then went on

Ocean Avenue to its terminus at Santa Monica ʼBoulevard.

MILEAGES:
Sawtelle	13.36
Santa Monica	19.42

FREQUENCY OF SERVICE — 1911: every 60 minutes between 7:25 a.m. and 6:25 p.m.; 1913: 2 round trips daily; 1927: every 30 minutes during rush hours (approximately 40 round trips daily.)

RUNNING TIME — 1927: Los Angeles to: Beverly Hills, 40 minutes, Sawtelle, 48 minutes, and Santa Monica, 75 minutes.

INGLEWOOD LINE

Passenger service began in 1902 over trackage built in 1887 by the Santa Fe Railroad and leased for electrification to the Los Angeles and Pacific. Passenger service ended in 1928. *Route:* from Ocean Park, the line went on a private right-of-way paralleling Neilson Way to Loma Avenue in Venice, and then paralleling Washington Boulevard to Washington Way; from here, the right-of-way went east, paralleling Jefferson Boulevard from a point just west of Grosvenor Boulevard to Centinela Avenue, curving on a parallel with Florence Avenue to Centinela Avenue and following Centinela to approximately the 5900 block. The right-of-way paralleled Thornburn Street from Alvern Street to Venice Way, Hyde Park Boulevard from Venice Way to Glenway Drive, and Ballona Boulevard to the Pacific Electric station on Eucalyptus Avenue.

MILEAGES:
Ocean Park	0.00
Milwood Junction	.64
Machado	2.04
Alla	2.66
Inglewood	7.23

FREQUENCY OF SERVICE — 1911: one round trip daily.

RUNNING TIME — not available.

SANTA MONICA AIR LINE

Passenger service began in 1908 on this line, developed on the right-of-way of the Los Angeles and Independence Railroad opened in 1875 between Santa Monica and Los Angeles and acquired in 1877 by the Southern Pacific. The S. P. leased the line to the Los Angeles and Pacific, which electrified it. Passenger service was discontinued on October 26, 1953. *Route:* from the Pacific Electric Building at Sixth and Main Streets in downtown Los Angeles, cars followed the Long Beach line to Amoco Junction (at 25th Street) and then went southwesterly over a private right-of-way; at Figueroa Street, this right-of-way divided Exposition Boulevard to 34th Street in Santa Monica. The right-of-way continued, paralleling Colorado Avenue from 20th Street to Lincoln Boulevard; the tracks went on Lincoln to Ocean Avenue, and on Ocean to Ocean Park.

MILEAGES:
Los Angeles	0.00
Amoco Junction	2.62

San Pedro Street	3.76
Grand Avenue	4.54
U.S.C.	5.40
Culver Junction	11.16
Palms	12.19
Santa Monica	16.85
Ocean Park	19.20

FREQUENCY OF SERVICE — 1911: 1 round trip daily; 1913: every 60 minutes; 1920: every 30 to 90 minutes to Culver Junction and 1 round trip daily to Santa Monica;

RUNNING TIME — 1911: 40 minutes.

REDONDO BEACH-DEL REY LINE

Passenger service to Playa del Rey began in 1902 and to Redondo Beach in 1903. Passenger service ended May 12, 1940. *Route:* from Los Angeles, the line followed the Venice Short Line to Culver City. The tracks then were in a private right-of-way dividing Culver Boulevard to Lincoln Boulevard, and from there followed a private right-of-way to Vista del Mar Boulevard in Playa del Rey. The tracks went in Vista del Mar to the ocean front and then went in a private right-of-way paralleling the coast to Homer Avenue in Hermosa Beach. The private right-of-way continued, paralleling Shakespeare Avenue to Hawthorne Avenue; from here, the right-of-way divided Hermosa Avenue to Redondo Beach. The tracks went in Hermosa Avenue to a junction with the Santa Fe Railroad line at Pacific Avenue, and then went on Pacific to Catalina Avenue, and on Catalina to Clifton.

MILEAGES:
Culver Junction	9.25
Playa del Rey	15.10
Manhattan Beach	20.59
Hermosa Beach	22.29
Redondo Beach	24.06
Clifton	25.07

FREQUENCY OF SERVICE — 1911: 30 round trips daily; 1931: 24 outbound and 22 inbound trips.

RUNNING TIME — 1911: Los Angeles to Vineyard Junction, 23 minutes; Los Angeles to Playa del Rey, 43 minutes, Los Angeles to Manhattan Beach, 53 minutes, and Los Angeles to Redondo Beach, 63 minutes; 1940: 87 minutes.

SAN FERNANDO VALLEY LINE

Passenger service started to Van Nuys on December 16, 1911, to Owensmouth (Canoga Park) on December 7, 1912, and to San Fernando on March 22, 1913. Service to Owensmouth and San Fernando was discontinued June 1, 1938 and service to Van Nuys ended December 28, 1952. *Route:* the line originally went from Fourth and Hill Streets in downtown Los Angeles north to Sunset Boulevard. When the Subway Terminal opened in 1925, the route was from there via the subway to Glendale Boulevard, on Glendale to Park Avenue, on Park to Sunset Boulevard, on Sunset to Santa Monica Boulevard, on Santa Monica to Highland Avenue, and on Highland to Cahuenga Pass. A private right-of-way paralleled the highway through the pass and along Cahuenga

Boulevard to Vineland Avenue. The route was up Vineland to Weddington Street, where the tracks turned onto a private right-of-way dividing Chandler Boulevard. The line followed Chandler to Van Nuys Boulevard. The route was then on a private right-of-way in Van Nuys to the Southern Pacific tracks near Aetna Street, where the tracks continued in Van Nuys Boulevard. The private right-of-way in Van Nuys Boulevard resumed at Van Owen Street and continued to Sherman Circle, where the tracks curved into a private right-of-way in Sherman Way. They continued in Sherman Way to Etiwanda Avenue, where they were laid in Sherman Way to Vanalden Avenue. There they resumed the private right-of-way dividing Sherman Way, continuing to Variel Avenue. The tracks were laid in Sherman Way to Topanga Canyon Boulevard, terminus of the line.

MILEAGES: (To North Sherman Way Junction)
Los Angeles	0.00
Highland and Santa Monica	7.09
Highland and Hollywood Boulevard	7.84
Cahuenga Pass	8.56
Hollywood Way	9.99
Universal City	11.10
Rio Vista	11.59
North Hollywood	14.17
Kester Junction	16.17
Circle Drive	17.72
Van Nuys	19.11
North Sherman Way	19.89

MILEAGES: (To San Fernando)
North Sherman Way Junction	19.89
Mission Acres	22.81
Plummer	23.81
San Fernando	27.47

MILEAGES: (To Owensmouth)
North Sherman Way Junction	19.89
Reseda	24.91
Owensmouth (Canoga Park)	29.10

FREQUENCY OF SERVICE — 1912: 10 round trips daily to Van Nuys; 1913: 7 round trips daily to Owensmouth (Canoga Park); 1913: 6 round trips daily to San Fernando (City); 1918: 10 round trips daily to San Fernando (City); 1929: 27 cars daily left Los Angeles for the San Fernando Valley and after alternate switching or division of two-car trains, 17 cars went to Owensmouth (Canoga Park) and 16 went to San Fernando (City); 1944: every 20 minutes.

RUNNING TIME — 1912: to Van Nuys, 70 minutes outbound and 65 minutes inbound; 1913: to Owensmouth (Canoga Park), 95 minutes; 1913: to San Fernando (City), 80 minutes outbound and 78 minutes inbound; 1931: to San Fernando (City), 78 minutes; 1952: to Van Nuys, 89 minutes outbound and 87 minutes inbound.

GLENDALE-BURBANK LINE

Passenger service to Glendale began April 6, 1904, and to Burbank on September 6, 1911. Passenger service ended June 19, 1955. *Route:* the line originally went from the Southern Pacific's Arcade Station at Fifth, Central, and Ceres Streets in downtown Los Angeles on Ceres to Sixth Street, on Sixth to Olive Avenue, on Olive to Seventh Street, on Seventh to Figueroa Street, on Figueroa to Second Street, and on Second to Glendale Boulevard. After opening of the Subway Terminal in 1925, cars left through the Subway to Glendale Boulevard, and at Sunset Boulevard entered a private right-of-way dividing Glendale Boulevard. This right-of-way continued to Effie Street, where tracks returned to Glendale Boulevard. At Alessandro Street, the tracks entered a private right-of-way through the Ivanhoe Hills and spanning the Los Angeles River by a bridge. The tracks then resumed a private right-of-way dividing Glendale Boulevard; at San Fernando Road (city limits of Glendale), Glendale Boulevard became Brand Boulevard, with the tracks continuing in Brand to Mountain Street. Burbank Branch: at Arden Junction, the line turned from Brand and went west in a private right-of-way dividing Glenoaks to Eton Drive.

MILEAGES: (Glendale)
Los Angeles	0.00
Ivanhoe	5.71
San Fernando Road	6.85
Tropico Avenue	7.22
Ninth Street	7.75
Lomita Avenue	8.00
Glendale (Fourth Street)	8.39
Arden Avenue	9.50
Casa Verdugo	9.64
Bliss	9.88

MILEAGES: (Glendale to Burbank)
Arden Avenue	9.50
Cypress Avenue	13.41
Eton Drive	15.11

FREQUENCY OF SERVICE — 1911: every 20 to 30 minutes (54 round trips daily) to Glendale; 1941: every 2 to 20 minutes (approximately 150 round trips daily, with about 50 continuing to Burbank).

RUNNING TIME — 1911: 24 minutes to San Fernando Road, 28 minutes to Lomita Avenue, 30 minutes to Broadway, 33 minutes to Arden Avenue, and 34 minutes to Casa Verdugo; 1941: 25 minutes to Glendale (Broadway) and 44 minutes to Burbank.

Pacific Electric interurbans wait at Naples, the community of canals by Alamitos Bay in Long Beach. This picture was made in about 1906 when Naples was a feature of the Triangle Trolley Trip sightseeing tour.

Hotel Napoli, Naples, Cal.

B. 1901 P. E. Articles of Incorporation

Here are the articles of incorporation of the Pacific Electric Railway filed November 10, 1901, with the California Secretary of State. The corporation consolidated the electric railroad holdings of Henry E. Huntington and his associates. It was the instrument for expanding interurban lines. The 1901 Pacific Electric Railway corporation was consolidated into a new Pacific Electric Railway incorporated in 1911.

ARTICLES OF INCORPORATION
OF THE
PACIFIC ELECTRIC RAILWAY COMPANY

KNOW ALL MEN BY THESE PRESENTS: That we, the undersigned, a majority of whom are citizens and residents of the State of California, have this day voluntarily associated ourselves together for the purpose of forming a corporation under the laws of the State of California,

AND WE HEREBY CERTIFY:

FIRST. That the name of said corporation shall be PACIFIC ELECTRIC RAILWAY COMPANY.

SECOND. The purpose for which said corporation is formed are:

To construct, or acquire by purchase or lease or otherwise, and to operate and maintain, railroads, and to acquire all rights of way and lands necessary for and to construct and maintain all tracks, switches, turnouts, adjuncts, depots, car-houses, power-houses, terminal accommodations, machinery, appurtenances, appliances and equipment, necessary to properly construct, improve, maintain and operate, such railroads; and to sell, convey, lease, convey in trust, or mortgage the same. The places from and to which said railroads are intended to be run are as follows:

Commencing in the City of Los Angeles, In Los Angeles County, State of California, and running thence in a northerly and easterly direction by the way of and through the City of Monrovia, and the Town of Duarte in said County of Los Angeles, and the Cities of San Bernardino and Redlands in San Bernardino County and the City of Riverside in Riverside County, to and in the City of Santa Ana in Orange County, all in the State of California; with an intermediate branch extending from the line above described in or near the City of Azusa in Los Angeles County, by the way of and through the Town of Covina, to and in the City of Pomona in said Los Angeles County; and with an intermediate branch extending from the line above described in the City of San Bernardino to Highlands in said San Bernardino County, the estimated length of said line and intermediate branches being one hundred and forty-five (145) miles.

Also commencing at or near Colorado street in the City of Pasadena in said Los Angeles County and running in a northerly and easterly direction to and in the town of Sierra Madre in said County, the estimated length of the last described line being seven (7) miles.

Also commencing in the City of South Pasadena, in Los Angeles County, and running easterly to East San Gabriel in said County, the estimated length of the last described line being five (5) miles.

Also commencing in the City of Los Angeles in said Los Angeles County, and running south-easterly by the way of and through the City of Whittier in said County, to and in the City of Santa Ana in Orange County, in said State of California, with an intermediate branch extending from the last described line in a north-easterly direction to and in the City of Pomona, the estimated length of said line and intermediate branch being sixty (60) miles.

Also commencing in said City of Los Angeles, and running southerly and easterly by the way of and through the City of Long Beach in said Los Angeles County, to and in the said City of Santa Ana in Orange County, State of California, with an intermediate branch extending from the last described line to and in the City of San Pedro in said Los Angeles County; and also an intermediate branch extending from said main line north-easterly to the Town of Covina, situate upon the Covina branch of the Southern Pacific Railroad, the estimated length of said main line and the intermediate branches being eight-five (85) miles.

Also commencing in said City of Los Angeles, and running southerly to and in the City of San Pedro, with an intermediate branch extending from the last described line, to and in the Town of Redondo in said Los Angeles County, the estimated length of said line and intermediate branch being thirty-five (35) miles.

Also commencing in the City of Los Angeles and extending northerly to the City of Santa Barbara in Santa Barbara County, State of California, the estimated length of said main line being one hundred and fifteen (115) miles.

The aggregate length of the lines proposed to be constructed hereunder being four hundred and fifty-two (452) miles.

Also to acquire by purchase, or lease or otherwise, and to hold, own and use, all lands necessary or proper for the erection and operation of power-houses and electric poles and wires, and also all franchises, rights and privileges necessary or proper for the erection, construction and operation of all machinery and appliances necessary or proper for the production, manufacture, use distribution and sale of electric motive power, heat and illuminating lights of every description, and to produce, manufacture, use, distribute and sell the same; and to sell, convey, lease, convey in trust, or mortgage all such property.

Also to acquire by purchase or lease or otherwise, any patents or patent rights relative to the business hereinbefore mentioned.

Also to purchase or otherwise acquire, and hold, sell or otherwise dispose of, shares of the capital stock of other corporations.

THIRD. That the place where the principal business of said corporation is to be transacted is the City of Los Angeles, Los Angeles County, State of California.

FOURTH. That the term for which said corporation is to exist is fifty (50) years from and after the date of its incorporation.

FIFTH. That the number of Directors of said Corporation shall be seven (7), and that the names and residences of the Directors who are appointed for the first year, and to serve until the election and qualification of such officers are as follows, to-wit:

NAMES	WHOSE RESIDENCE IS AT
H. E. Huntington	City and County of San Francisco, State of California
I. W. Hellman	City and County of San Francisco, State of California
A. Borel	City and County of San Francisco, State of California
C. De Guigne	City and County of San Francisco, State of California
Epes Randolph	City of Los Angeles, State of California
John D. Bicknell	City of Los Angeles, State of California
J. S. Slauson	City of Los Angeles, State of California

SIXTH. That the amount of the capital stock of said corporation is ten million dollars ($10,000,000.00), and the number of shares into which it is divided is one hundred thousand (100,000), of the par value of one hundred dollars ($100.00) each.

SEVENTH. That the amount of said capital stock which has been actually subscribed is Four Hundred and Fifty-two Thousand Dollars and the following are the names of the persons by whom the same has been subscribed, to-wit:

NAMES OF SUBSCRIBERS	NUMBER OF SHARES	AMOUNT
H. E. Huntington	986	$98,000
I. W. Hellman	678	$67,800
A. Borel	678	$67,800
C. De Guigne	678	$67,800
Epes Randolph	500	$50,000
John D. Bicknell	500	$50,000
J. S. Slauson	500	$50,000

EIGHTH—That the subscribers for the capital stock herein-before mentioned have elected E. B. Holladay Treasurer of the proposed corporation and that at least ten per cent (10%) of the capital stock subscribed has been paid to said Treasurer of this Corporation, aggregating the sum of Forty-five Thousand Two-Hundred dollars, which is now held by him for the benefit of this intended Corporation.

IN WITNESS WHEREOF we have hereunto set our hands and

seals, this 29th day of October, 1901.

H. E. Huntington
Isaias W. Hellman
Chr. De Guigne
Epes Randolph
John D. Bicknell
J. S. Slauson
A. Borel

C. 1911 P. E. Articles of Incorporation

Below are the articles of incorporation of the Pacific Electric Railway filed September 1, 1911, as the corporate instrument of The Great Merger by which the Southern Pacific consolidated eight Southern California electric railroads, including the Pacific Electric formed by Henry E. Huntington in 1901. The articles themselves covered fifty-seven printed pages in a six by nine inch book. An additional eighty-nine pages in the book provided space for signatures of the officers and notary forms as well as statements concerning the ownership of the new and old companies' stock.

ARTICLES OF INCORPORATION AND CONSOLIDATION

made and executed on this 24th day of August 1911, by and between Pacific Electric Railway Company, a corporation incorporated, organized and existing under the laws of the State of California, the party of the first part, Los Angeles Inter-Urban Railway Company, a corporation incorporated, organized and existing under the laws of the State of California, the party of the second part, Los Angeles and Redondo Railway Company, a corporation incorporated, organized and existing under the laws of the State of California, the party of the third part, The Riverside & Arlington Railway Company, a corporation incorporated, organized and existing under the laws of the State of California, the party of the fourth part, The San Bernardino Valley Traction Company, a corporation incorporated, organized and existing under the laws of the State of California, the party of the fifth part, Redlands Central Railway Company, a corporation incorporated, organized and existing under the laws of the State of California, the party of the sixth part, San Bernardino Inter-Urban Railway Company, a corporation incorporated, organized and existing under the laws of the State of California, the party of the seventh part, and Los Angeles Pacific Company, a corporation incorporated, organized and existing under the laws of the State of California, the party of the eighth part,

WITNESSETH:

WHEREAS, the said party of the first part, the Pacific Electric Railway Company, is the owner of certain railroads constructed within the State of California, hereinafter in Subdivision First, of Article VIII, particularly described;

AND, WHEREAS, the said party of the second part, the Los Angeles Inter-Urban Railway Company; is the owner of certain railroads constructed within the State of California, hereinafter in Subdivision Second, of Article VIII, particularly described;

AND, WHEREAS, the said party of the third part, the Los Angeles and Redondo Railway Company, is the owner of certain railroads constructed within the State of California, hereinafter in Subdivision Third, of Article VIII, particularly described;

AND, WHEREAS, the said party of the fourth part, The Riverside & Arlington Railway Company, is the owner of certain railroads constructed within the State of California, hereinafter in Subdivision Fourth, of Article VIII, particularly described;

AND, WHEREAS, the said party of the fifth part, the San Bernardino Valley Traction Company, is the owner of certain railroads

constructed within the State of California, hereinafter in Subdivision Fifth, of Article VIII, particularly described;

AND, WHEREAS, the said party of the sixth part, the Redlands Central Railway Company, is the owner of certain railroads constructed within the State of California, hereinafter in Subdivision Sixth, of Article VIII, particularly described;

AND, WHEREAS, the said party of the seventh part, the San Bernardino Inter-Urban Railway Company, is the owner of certain railroads constructed within the State of California, hereinafter in Subdivision Seventh, of Article VIII, particularly described;

AND, WHEREAS, the said party of the eighth part, the Los Angeles Pacific Company, is the owner and lessee of certain railroads constructed within the State of California, hereinafter in Subdivision Eighth, of Article VIII, particularly described;

AND, WHEREAS, said several parties are also the owners of franchises, rights, privileges and other property, real and personal, appurtenant to and exercised and used in connection with their several lines of railroad hereinbefore described;

AND, WHEREAS, pursuant to the laws of the State of California in such cases made and provided, the respective Boards of Directors of said corporations, parties hereto, have agreed upon the consolidation of said corporations, their capital stocks, properties, roads, equipments, adjuncts, franchises, claims, demands, contracts, agreements, obligations, debts, liabilities and assets of every kind and description, upon the terms and in the manner hereinafter set forth in full;

AND, WHEREAS, stockholders of said respective corporations, parties hereto, representing more than three-fourths of the subscribed capital stock of their respective corporations, have, in writing, consented to and ratified and confirmed said consolidation upon the terms and in the manner hereinafter set forth in full, which said consent, ratification and confirmation by said stockholders of the parties hereto is evidenced by the written memoranda annexed hereto, which said memoranda are respectively signed by stockholders representing all of issued capital stock and all of the subscribed capital stock of their respective corporations, parties hereto, as aforesaid.

NOW THEREFORE, know all men by these presents: That the parties hereto, pursuant to the laws of the State of California in such cases made and provided, do hereby consolidate their capital stocks, properties, roads, equipments, adjuncts, franchises, claims, demands, contracts, agreements, obligations, debts, liabilities and assets of every kind and description, and, in pursuance of said consolidation, and in order more fully to carry the same into force and effect, do hereby adopt the following

ARTICLES OF INCORPORATION AND CONSOLIDATION.
ARTICLE I

The name of said new and consolidated corporation shall be "PACIFIC ELECTRIC RAILWAY COMPANY."

ARTICLE II

The purpose for which said consolidated corporation is formed is as follows, to-wit:

To construct, or acquire by purchase, or lease, or otherwise, railroads, and to operate and maintain the same; and to acquire all franchises, rights of way and lands necessary for, and to construct, maintain, purchase and lease all tracks, turnouts, switches, adjuncts, depots, car-houses, power-houses, terminal accommodations, appurtenances, appliances, and equipment necessary to properly construct, improve, maintain, and operate such railroads; and to sell, convey, lease, convey in trust, or mortgage the same.

Also, to acquire by purchase, or lease, or otherwise, and to hold, own and use, all lands necessary or proper for the erection and operation of power houses and electrical poles and wires, and also, all franchises, rights, and privileges necessary or proper for the erection, construction, and operation of all machinery and appliances necessary or proper for the production, manufacture, use, distribution, and sale of electric motive power, heat and illuminating lights of every description, and to produce, manufacture, use, distribute, and sell the same; to construct, build, charter, or otherwise acquire, steamers, tugs, vessels and barges, to run in connection with said railways for coasting and foreign business, and to operate the same; and to build, construct, buy, lease, or otherwise acquire, docks, wharves, warehouses and stations; and to sell, convey, lease, convey in trust, and mortgage all such property.

Also, to acquire by purchase, or lease, or otherwise, patents or patent rights relative to the business hereinbefore mentioned.

Also, to purchase, or otherwise acquire, and hold, sell, or otherwise dispose of, bonds and shares of the capital stock of other corporations; and to acquire all property, real and personal, that may be now or hereafter permitted by law.

The kinds of railroads to be constructed, acquired, purchased, leased, operated, maintained, sold, conveyed, conveyed in trust, and mortgaged as aforesaid, are commercial, street and inter-urban railroads having either a standard gauge or a narrow gauge and one or more tracks, with all necessary switches, side-tracks, turnouts, turntables, terminal accommodations, station houses, machine-shops, power-houses, and all other adjuncts and appliances necessary or convenient to the operation of the same; said railroads to be operated by electricity or other lawful motive power.

And generally to all and everything necessary, suitable, convenient or proper for the accomplishment of the purpose or the attainment of any one or more of the objects herein enumerated, or incidental to the powers herein named, or which shall at any time appear conducive to, or expedient for the protection or benefit of the corporation, either as holder of or as interested in any property or otherwise, with all the powers now or hereafter conferred by the laws of the State of California.

The foregoing clauses shall be construed both as objects and powers; and it is hereby expressly provided that the foregoing enumeration of specific powers shall not be held to limit or restrict in any manner the powers of the corporation.

ARTICLE III

The place where the principal business of said corporation is to be transacted is the City of Los Angeles, in the County of Los Angeles, State of California.

ARTICLE IV

The term for which said corporation is to exist is fifty (50) years from and after the date of the filing of a certified copy of the articles of incorporation and consolidation in the office of the Secretary of State.

ARTICLE V

The number of Directors of said corporation shall be five, and the names and residences of the persons appointed to act as such until their successors are elected and qualified are as follows:

NAMES	RESIDENCES.
WM. F. HERRIN	San Francisco, California
R. C. GILLIS	Los Angeles, California
W. C. MARTIN	San Francisco, California
EPES RANDOLPH	Tucson, Arizona
PAUL SHOUP	Los Angeles, California

ARTICLE VI

The amount of the capital stock of said corporation shall be One Hundred Million Dollars ($100,000,000.00), divided into ten hundred thousand shares of the par value of one hundred dollars ($100.00) each, which said amount of capital stock does not exceed the amount actually required for the purposes of said corporation, and is the amount actually required and ascertained to be necessary for acquiring, constructing, completing, equipping operating and maintaining its roads and branches, and is so estimated by competent engineers, as will appear by the written estimate of such engineers, duly signed and acknowledged by them, and attached hereto.

ARTICLE VII

The amount of said capital stock which has been actually subscribed is One Hundred Million Dollars, consisting of one million

shares, which have been subscribed by and allotted in accordance with the terms of said consolidation hereinafter set forth in full. in the following proportions and amounts, to-wit:

To the stockholders of the Pacific Electric Railway Company, 399,950 shares.

To the stockholders of the Los Angeles Inter-Urban Railway Company, 250,000 shares.

To the stockholders of the Los Angeles and Redondo Railway Company, 50,000 shares.

To the stockholders of The Riverside & Arlington Railway Company, 10,000 shares.

To the stockholders of The San Bernardino Valley Traction Company, 20,000 shares.

To the stockholders of the Redlands Central Railway Company, 5,000 shares.

To the stockholders of the San Bernardino Inter-Urban Railway Company, 15,000 shares.

To the stockholders of the Los Angeles Pacific Company, 250,000 shares.

Together with such other and further appendages, adjuncts and terminal facilities to the hereinbefore described lines and projected lines of railroad, including sidings, turnouts, industrial spurs and spur-tracks, as the Board of Directors of said Consolidated Company may from time to time direct.

ARTICLE VIII

The termini of the road or roads and branches of said consolidated company are as follows:

First. (Pacific Electric Railway Company) A double track electric railway commencing at a point in Main Street in the City of Los Angeles, County of Los Angeles, State of California, 190 feet southerly from the center line of Sixth Street; then southerly along Main Street to Ninth Street; thence easterly along Ninth Street to beginning of curve to right at a point about 130 feet westerly from the center line of Tennessee Street; thence southerly along said curve and along course south 20° 54' west to beginning of four track line on private right of way between Long Beach Avenue and Tennessee Street, at a point 310 feet south of center line of Ninth Street; thence on private right of way south 2° 54' west; thence along 3° curve to right; thence south 17° 58' west approximately parallel to Long Beach Avenue and about 80 feet westerly therefrom, to a point about 70 feet southerly from south line of Sixteenth Street in said city; thence, continuing along private right of way on 5° curve to left; thence south 3° 08' west, approximately parallel to Long Beach Avenue; thence along 2° curve to left intersecting north line of Washington Street, at a point 57 feet westerly from west line of Long Beach Avenue; thence on private right of way along the following courses and curves: South 1° 09' west; 1° curve to right; south 0° 31' west; south 0° 49' west; south 0° 18' west to south boundary line of City of Los Angeles at a point about 154 feet east of east line of Encino Street; thence south 0° 11' east; south 0° 15' east to City of Watts in said County, end of four track line; thence on 3° curve to left; south 23° 36' east; 3° curve to right; south 3° 16' east to City of Compton on private right of way to Wilmington Street; 3° curve to left; south 19° 08' east; 1° 30' curve to left; south 29° 08' east; 1° 30' curve to right; south 20° 47' east; curve to right; thence south on private right of way on American Avenue to Anaheim Street in the City of Long Beach in said County; thence continuing south on American Avenue in said city to Ocean Park Avenue; thence westerly on Ocean Park Avenue to Golden Street in said city.

Also, commencing at a point in Ninth Street in said City of Los Angeles, about 130 feet westerly from the center line of Tennessee Street; thence easterly along Ninth Street to Santa Fe Avenue.

Also, commencing at a point in the center line of the Los Angeles Inter-Urban Railway Company's Newport Beach Line, about 190 feet southeasterly from the south line of Anaheim Road in the County of Los Angeles; thence southeasterly along a 7° 30' curve to the right; then southerly along a private right of way 30 feet in width on Redondo Avenue to Anser Street; thence continuing southerly across Anser Street and on private right of way generally forty feet in width; thence on curve to left to a point on private right of way eighty feet in width between Park Avenue and Second Street in the City of Long Beach, about 50 feet east of the east line of Redondo Avenue.

Also, beginning at Redondo Avenue and Anser Street; thence westerly along Anser Street; thence westerly along Anser Street and Railway street to Railway Street and Paloma Avenue in said City of Long Beach.

Also, commencing at American and Ocean Park Avenues, in said

City of Long Beach; thence east along double track line on Ocean Park Avenue and Ocean Avenue in said city to end of double track line at Esperanza Avenue to double track line on private right of way on Railway Street; thence east along double track line on private right of way on Railway Street to a point just west of Paloma Avenue; thence along curve to right; thence on private right of way eighty feet in width along the following courses and curves: south 51° 18′ east; 5° curve to left; north 72° 19′ east; 6° curve to left; north 12° 43′ west; curve to left to a point in the center line of the main tracks of the Los Angeles Inter-Urban Railway Company's Newport Beach Line just east of Nieto Avenue.

Also, commencing at Esperanza and Ocean Avenues in said City of Long Beach; thence easterly along double track line on Ocean Avenue and on private right of way just south of Ocean Boulevard to the end of double track line and beginning of single track line on private right of way sixty feet wide, along the following courses and curves: south 53° 20′ 45″ east; 4° curve to left; south 64° 22′ 45″ east; 0° 30′ curve to right; south 57° 57′ 45″ east to end of single track line just west of entrance to Alamitos Bay.

Also, commencing at Alamitos Avenue and Railway Street in said City of Long Beach; thence east on private right of way on Railway Street to Esperanza Avenue.

Also, commencing at a point in the Pacific Electric Railway Company's Long Beach Line at Ocean Park Avenue and Daisy Avenue, in said City of Long Beach; thence southwesterly on curve to left; thence south 74° west on private right of way seventy-four feet in width to east line of Golden Avenue, about 157 feet south of south line of said Ocean Park Avenue; thence, continuing south 74° west; thence on curve to right to point in private right of way forty feet in width on Santa Cruz Avenue; thence westerly along said right of way to Mitchell Avenue; thence on curve to right and continuing on said right of way; thence north 66° 42′ west; thence on curve to left; thence south 83° 18′ west parallel to and twenty feet southerly from the south line of Pacific Boulevard to a point just west of Mendocino Avenue.

Also, commencing at a point in the center line of the Pacific Electric Railway Company's Long Beach Line on private right of way on American Avenue in said City of Long Beach, about 300 feet north of the north line of Fourteenth Street; thence on curve to right; thence westerly on private right of way, sixty feet wide, on Fourteenth Street to Chestnut Avenue; thence on curve to left; thence southerly to point about 170 feet north of the north line of Tenth Street; thence on curve to right; thence southwesterly; thence on curve to left to Magnolia Avenue; thence southerly on Magnolia Avenue to Ocean Park Avenue.

Also, commencing at or near the intersection of Pine Avenue and Ocean Park Avenue in said City of Long Beach; running north on Pine Avenue to Fourteenth Street.

Also, beginning at or near the intersection of Railway Street and Esperanza Avenue, in said City of Long Beach; thence north on Esperanza Avenue to Bishop Street; west on Bishop Street to Alamitos Avenue, across Alamitos Avenue to Third Street; west on Third Street to the west end thereof at Cerritos Slough.

Also, beginning at Ocean Park and Pacific Avenue, in said City of Long Beach; thence north on Pacific Avenue to First Street; thence east on First Street to and across Alamitos Avenue to the west end of Second Street; thence along Second Street to Esperanza Avenue.

Also, commencing at Seventh Street and Redondo Avenue in said City of Long Beach; thence west along single track line on Seventh Street to beginning of double track line just east of Alamitos Avenue; thence continuing west on Seventh Street to the west end thereof at Cerritos Slough.

Also, commencing at Fair Oaks Avenue and Colorado Street in the City of Pasadena, in said county; thence westerly along Colorado Street to Orange Grove Avenue; thence northerly and northeasterly along Orange Grove Avenue to Fair Oaks Avenue.

Also, commencing at Bellevue Drive and Raymond Avenue in said City of Pasadena; thence northerly along Raymond Avenue to Chestnut Street; thence easterly on Chestnut Street to a point about 50 feet east of the east line of said Raymond Avenue.

Also, commencing at Colorado Street and Los Robles Avenue in said City of Pasadena; thence southerly along Los Robles Avenue to California Street; thence easterly on California Street to Lake Avenue; thence northerly on Lake Avenue to Colorado Street.

Also, commencing at Lake Avenue and California Street in said City of Pasadena; thence easterly along California Street to a point about 1720 feet east of the center line of said Lake Avenue.

Also, commencing at Colorado Street and Los Robles Avenue in said City of Pasadena; thence northerly along Los Robles Avenue to Villa Street; thence easterly on Villa Street to Lake Avenue; thence southerly on Lake Avenue to Colorado Street.

Also, commencing at Villa Street and Lake Avenue in said City of Pasadena; thence northerly along Lake Avenue to West Lake Street.

Also, commencing at Fair Oaks Avenue and Colorado Street in said City of Pasadena; thence northerly along double track line on Fair Oaks Avenue to north city boundary of said City of Pasadena; thence along private right of way thirty-two feet wide, north 0° 09′ east; curve to right; north 21° 36′ 30″ east; curve to right; thence east; curve to left; north 59° 36′ 30″ east to end of private right of way at Mariposa Street; thence east on Mariposa Street to Lake Avenue; north on Lake Avenue and along curve to right, to beginning of private right of way about 2600 feet north of Mariposa Street; thence continuing curve to right; thence along 51′ E.; curve to right; north 78° 06′ E.; curve to left; north 42° 51′ E.; curve to right; north 82° 24′ E.; curve to left; north 49° 04′ E.; curve to left; north 1° 26′ W.; curve to right; S. 59° 13′ E.; curve to left; south 77° 48′ E.; curve to left; north 49° 04′ E.; curve to left; north 1° 26′ W.; curve to right; S. 59° 13′ E.; curve to left; south 77° 48′ E.; curve to left; north 79° 32′ E.; curve to right; thence south 28° 00′ east to beginning of incline railway at Rubio Canyon; thence in a generally northwesterly, northerly and easterly direction, following various curves and courses along and over private right of way 200 feet in width, through Sections 2 and 3, Township 1 north, Range 12 west, S. B. B. & M., and Sections 34, 27, and 26, Township 2 north, Range 12 west, S. B. B. & M., to the end of single track line in the southwest Quarter of said Section 26, from which point the corner of Sections 3, 4, 33 and 34, Townships 1 and 2 north, Range 12 west, S. B. B. & M., bears south 47° 37′ 17″ W., 10,358.76 feet distant.

Also, commencing at a point in the Pacific Electric Railway Company's Monrovia Line, about 280 feet easterly from the West line of Section 33, Township 1 north, Range 11 west, S. B. B. & M.; thence easterly on private right of way generally sixty feet and eighty-five feet in width, along curve to right; thence south 78° 33′ east; on curve to left; thence north 89° 24′ east; thence around loop just west of Santa Anita Ave.

Also, commencing at a point in the center line of the main tracks of the Pacific Electric Railway Company's Monrovia Line, distant north 66° 28′ east along said center line about 650 feet from the San Bernardino Base Line; thence on private right of way thirty-two feet wide along the following curves and courses: Northerly on curve to left; north 11° 51′ 30″ west; 7° curve to right; north 49° 07′ 15″ east; 4° curve to right; north 3° 12′ 15″ east; 1° curve to left; north 00° 08′ 15″ west; thence on curve to left to end of private right of way on East Colorado Street about 900 feet west of Santa Anita Road; thence west on East Colorado Street to Fair Oaks Avenue in said City of Pasadena.

Also, commencing at Mission Road and Daly Street in the City of Los Angeles; thence northerly along Daly Street to Pasadena Avenue; thence northerly along Pasadena Avenue to end of double track line and beginning of single track line near Avenue 35 in said City; thence continuing northerly on Pasadena Avenue crossing the Arroyo Seco to end of Single Track line and the beginning on Pasadena Avenue and private right of way and northeasterly on Pasadena Avenue and private right of way to end of double track, about 400 feet easterly of Avenue 66 in said City of Los Angeles; thence easterly, crossing the Arroyo Seco, to end of single track and beginning of double track at a point in Arroyo Drive about 400 feet westerly from Sycamore Avenue; thence in a generally easterly direction along Arroyo Drive and private right of way to Pasadena Avenue; thence northeasterly on Pasadena Avenue to Mission Street; thence easterly along Mission Street to aFir Oaks Avenue (formerly Palermo Avenue) in the City of South Pasadena.

Also, commencing near the intersection of Mission Street and Meridian Avenue in the City of South Pasadena, California; thence northeasterly on private right of way generally twenty-five feet wide, and on Oak Hill Avenue to an end of Double Track and beginning of single track near the north line of Magnolia Drive; thence northerly on Oak Hill Avenue and on private right of way to end of single track and beginning of double track line at a point 250 feet southerly from Buena Vista Street; thence northerly over private right of way along Fair View Avenue to Columbia Street in said City of Pasadena; thence easterly along Columbia

Street, about 1200 feet; thence northeasterly to a point in Fair Oaks Avenue about 450 feet north of the south boundary line of said City of Pasadena.

Also, that double track electric railway commencing at a point in Main Street in said City of Los Angeles, said point of beginning being southerly 190 feet from the center line of Sixth Street; thence northerly along Main Street to First Street; easterly along First Street to Los Angeles Street; northerly along Los Angeles Street to Aliso Street; easterly along Aliso Street to a point just west of the intersection of Aliso Street and Anderson Street.

Also, commencing at a point in said City of Los Angeles which is west about 600 feet from a point in the east boundary line of said City of Los Angeles, the said last mentioned point being about 2400 feet south along said boundary line from the southeasterly line of Mission Road in said city; thence along four-track line on private right of way, generally from 60 to 100 feet in width, along the following courses and curves: north 9° 53' east; 8° curve to right; north 37° 32' east; 5° curve to right; 2° curve to right; south 76° 22' east; 8° curve to left; north 63° 34' east, continuing on private right of way; 3° curve to right; north 81° 25' east; 4° curve to left; north 51° east; 5° 30' curve to left; north 1° 31' east; crossing Alhambra Road at a point about 900 feet west of Fremont Avenue in the City of Alhambra, California; 5° curve to right to Oneonta Park in the City of South Pasadena; thence north 89° 57' east; 5° curve to left; north 54° 32' east, crossing the easterly boundary line of the City of South Pasadena at a point about 300 feet northwesterly from Wilson Avenue; 1° curve to left; north 51° 48' east to end of four-track line and beginning of double track line near Oak Knoll Avenue; thence continuing north 51° 48' east to end of four track line and beginning of double track line near Oak Knoll Avenue; thence continuing north 51° 48' east; 3° curve to right; N. 66° 08' north 81° 19' east; 1° curve to right; north 85° 31' east, approximately parallel to and about 650 feet northerly from the main track of the Southern Pacific Railroad Company's Monrovia Branch, to the west boundary line of the City of Arcadia; thence through the City of Arcadia continuing said course of N. 85° 31' east; 2° curve to right; south 86° 41' east; 3° curve to left; north 37° 59' east, paralled to and 50 feet northwesterly from said Main Track of the Monrovia Branch of the Southern Pacific Railroad Company; 5° curve to right; N. 89° 25' east; 3° curve to left; north 83° 05' east; 1° curve to right, crossing the east boundary line of the City of Arcadia and the west boundary line of the City of Monrovia at a point about 500 feet north of the said Main Track of the Southern Pacific Railroad Company's Monrovia Branch; thence through the City of Monrovia, north 89° 27' east, continuing on private right of way; thence on 8° curve to left; north 60° 27' east; 8° curve to right; north 89° 27' east to intersection of Mayflower and Olive Avenues; then easterly along Olive Avenue in said City of Monrovia to California Avenue.

Also, commencing in the center line of the Pacific Electric Railway Company's Pasadena Short Line on private right of way about 650 feet northeasterly from the north and south center line of Section 8, T. 1 S., R. 12 W., S. B. B. & M.; thence on private right of way, generally sixty feet in width, along double track line on the curves and courses as follows: 5° curve to right; north 89° 45' east; 5° curve to right; south 44° 22' east; 7° 30' curve to left to Railroad Avenue and Main Street in the City of Alhambra, California; then easterly and northeasterly along said Main Street, to end of double track and beginning of single track at a point about 540 feet easterly from the east boundary line of the City of Alhambra; thence along single track line on curve to the right; thence on County Road to a point in County Road about 30 feet east of the east line of San Gabriel Mission.

Also, commencing at a point in private right of way on Huntington Drive, in the City of South Pasadena, about 350 feet east of the east line of Fremont Avenue; thence along curve to the left; thence northerly on private right of way on Fair Oaks Avenue to Monterey Road; thence northerly on Fair Oaks Avenue to Colorado Street in the City of Pasadena.

Also, commencing at Daly Street and Mission Road in said City of Los Angeles; thence southerly over private right of way along the southerly produced center line of Daly Street; thence along a 10° curve to right; thence southerly, parallel to and 35 feet westerly from the westerly line of Echandia Street; thence on a 10° curve to the right; thence southwesterly to a point in the center line of that certain railway of the Los Angeles Inter-Urban Railway Company known as the "San Gabriel Valley Rapid Transit Railway," about 335 feet southwesterly from the intersection of said

last mentioned center line with the westerly end of Echandia Street.

Also, commencing at a point in Main Street in said City of Los Angeles, said point of beginning being north about 70 feet from the center line of Seventh Street; thence southeasterly along a curve to the left; thence easterly along Seventh Street to a point about 132 feet west of Alameda Street.

Second. (Los Angeles Inter-Urban Railway Company) Commencing at a point in the center line of the main tracks of the Pacific Electric Railway Company's Long Beach Line, distant southerly about 40 feet from the center line of Slauson Avenue in said City of Los Angeles; thence southeasterly over private right of way to a point in Santa Fe Avenue in the City of Huntington Park; thence continuing through the City of Huntington Park, over private right of way approximately parallel to and about 1300 feet distant northerly from the Laguna and Florence Road; thence southeasterly over private right of way to a point in the west line of Downey and Rivera Road, distant southerly along said west line about 768 feet from the south line of Main Street, Rivera; thence continuing easterly and southeasterly over private right of way to a point in the west line of the Norwalk and Puente Mills Road, distant northerly about 560 feet from the northeasterly line of the right of way of the Santa Fe Railway Company's San Diego Branch; thence northeasterly over private right of way to the end of said private right of way at the Los Angeles and Whittier Road; thence southerly along said road to Philadelphia Street in the City of Whittier, California; thence east on Philadelphia Street in the City of Whittier, California; thence east on Philadelphia Street in said City to Greenland Avenue; thence south on Greenleaf Avenue and east over private property to the end of track between Greenleaf and Bright Avenues just north of Penn Street in said City of Whittier.

Also, commencing at a point in the center line of the main tracks of the Pacific Electric Railway Company's Long Beach Line, about 450 feet northerly from the center line of Merrill Avenue; thence southwesterly along a curve to the right; thence south 89° 32' west to Central Avenue.

Also, commencing at a point in the center line of the main tracks to the Pacific Electric Railway Company's Long Beach Line in the City of Watts, in said Los Angeles County; thence southeasterly on private right of way, generally 100 feet and 120 feet in width, to a point on the boundary line between Los Angeles and Orange Counties, about 10 feet south of the southeast corner of the southwest Quarter of the southwest Quarter of Section 5, Township 4 south, Range 11 west, S. B. B. & M.; thence continuing southeasterly over private right of way to a point in the west line of the City of Santa Ana, County of Orange, California, about 1000 feet northeasterly from the north line of Fifth Street in said City of Santa Ana; thence continuing along private right of way to Fourth Street in said City of Santa Ana; thence easterly along said Fourth Street to the end of track just east of Evergreen Street in said City of Santa Ana.

Also, commencing at Fourth and Main Streets in said City of Santa Ana; thence northerly along Main Street in said City to a point about 100 feet north of the Santiago Creek.

Also, commencing at a point in Main Street in said City of Santa Ana, about 100 feet north of the northerly line of Santiago Creek; thence along single track line northerly and then easterly to La Veta Avenue in the City of Orange, County of Orange, California; thence continuing easterly along said La Veta Avenue to Glassell Street; thence northerly along Glassell Street to the Plaza in said City of Orange.

Also, commencing at a point in the center line of the main tracks of the Pacific Electric Railway Company's Long Beach Line, about 600 feet distant northerly from the intersection of said center line with the Main Track of the Southern Pacific Railroad Company's San Pedro Branch; thence in a southwesterly direction over private right of way to the intersection of Seventh and McFarland Streets, Wilmington; thence in a southwesterly direction across Wilmington, and continuing southwesterly and southerly over private right of way to the end of track at a point just east of the southerly end of San Pedro Street in what was formerly the Town of San Pedro, California.

Also, commencing at Fourth and Palos Verdes Streets, San Pedro, thence east on Fourth Street to Front Street; south on Front Street to Sixth Street; west on Sixth Street to Pacific Avenue; and north on Pacific Avenue to First Street.

Also, commencing at Fifth and Beacon Streets, in San Pedro; thence south on Beacon Street to Thirteenth Street; west on Thirteenth Street to Palos Verdes Street; and south on Palos Verdes

Street to Crescent Avenue.

Also, commencing at Beacon Street and Crescent Avenue; thence southwesterly on Crescent Avenue to Twenty-second Street.

Also, commencing at Sixth Street and Pacific Avenue, San Pedro; thence south on Pacific Avenue to private right of way north of Thirty-sixth Street; along private right of way sixty feet in width on 4° curve to left; thence south 25° 18′ east; on curve to right to end of private right of way; thence continuing on curve to right on Pacific Avenue to a point in the west line of the City of San Pedro as same existed prior to annexation to the City of Los Angeles.

Also, commencing at a point in the center line of the main track of the Pacific Electric Railway Company's Long Beach Line about 800 feet northerly from the center line of Willow Street, in said County of Los Angeles; thence in a general southeasterly direction along the double track line on private right of way of various widths from 80 feet to 200 feet, to a point in the west line of the City of Huntington Beach, California, about 2400 feet south from the north Quarter section corner of Section 4, Township 6 south, Range 11 west, S. B. B. & M.; thence continuing in a southeasterly direction over a private right of way varying in width from 100 feet to 250 feet, to the end of double track line and beginning of single track line, at a point on private right of way between Ocean Avenue in said City of Huntington Beach and the shore line of the Pacific Ocean; thence along single track line in a general southeasterly direction over private right of way, generally sixty feet in width, and along private right of way on Bay Avenue in the City of Newport Beach, and along private right of way sixty feet in width on Central Avenue in said City of Newport Beach, to the end of single track line about 120 feet west of "B" Street in said City of Newport Beach, in the County of Orange, in said state.

Also, commencing at a point in the private right of way sixty feet in width immediately west of Vermont Avenue in said County of Los Angeles, and thirty feet northerly from the south line of Section 1, Township 3 south, Range 14 west, S. B. B. & M.; and running thence southerly along said private right of way to a point about 850 feet north of the east and west center line of Section 12, Township 3 south, Range 14 west, S. B. B. & M.; and running thence southerly along said private right of way to a point about 850 feet north of the east and west center line of Section 12, Township 3 south, Range 14 west, S. B. B. & M.; then on 4° curve to the left; thence southerly; thence on 4° curve to the right; thence southerly along Vermont Avenue to a point about 400 feet north of the north line of Rancho San Pedro; thence on 4° curve to right; thence southerly; thence on 4° curve to left to private right of way immediately west of Orange Avenue, Gardena, California; thence southerly on said private right of way to Palm Street, Gardena; thence westerly on Palm Street to Vermont Avenue; thence southerly on Vermont Avenue to private right of way sixty feet in width immediately west of said Vermont Avenue; thence in a general southeasterly direction to Ancon Street in San Pedro, California; thence southerly on Ancon Street to First Street; thence easterly on First Street to Front Street; thence southerly on Front Street to Second Street; thence westerly on Second Street to Beacon Street; thence southerly on Beacon Street to Fifth Street; thence easterly on Fifth Street to Front Street; thence northerly on Front Street to a point south south of Fourth Street.

Also, commencing at Broadway and Colorado Streets, in said City of Pasadena; thence south on Broadway to Bellevue Drive; west on Bellevue Drive to Raymond Avenue; south on Raymond Avenue to California Street; west on California Street to end of track on Arroyo Drive.

Also, commencing at Fair Oaks Avenue and East Orange Grove Avenue, in said City of Pasadena; running thence along East Orange Grove Avenue to Los Robles Avenue.

Also, single track line on East Orange Grove Avenue, between Lake Avenue and Allen Avenue, Pasadena.

Also, commencing at Villa Street and Los Robles Avenue, Pasadena; thence north on Los Robles Avenue to Washington Street; thence east on Washington Street to Lake Avenue.

Also, commencing at West Lake Street and Lake Avenue, Pasadena; thence north on Lake Avenue to Mariposa Street.

Also, commencing at a point in East Colorado Street, Pasadena, about 70 feet west of the west line of Huntington Drive, Los Angeles County; thence easterly on East Colorado Street to the west line of Daisy Street.

Also, commencing at a point in Sixth Street in said City of Los Angeles, about sixty-five feet westerly from the center line of Main Street; thence easterly along Sixth Street to Ceres Avenue;

thence northerly on Ceres Avenue to Central Avenue; thence northerly along Central Avenue to a point about 25 feet northerly from the center line of Fifth Street; thence, curving to the right, leaving Central Avenue; thence easterly over the private right of way about 100 feet to the Arcade Depot of the Southern Pacific Railroad Company.

Also, commencing at a point in Central Avenue in said City of Los Angeles about 25 feet northerly from the center line of Fifth Street; thence northerly along Central Avenue to Towne Avenue.

Also, commencing at a point in the Pacific Electric Railway Company's Pasadena Main Line, at Avenue 64, in said City of Los Angeles; thence northerly along said Avenue 64 to the northern boundary line of said City of Los Angeles; thence continuing northerly along Mountain Avenue to a point about 2630 feet northerly from the northern boundary line of said City of Los Angeles.

Also, commencing at Huntington Drive and East Colorado Street, in the County of Los Angeles; thence northwesterly across said East Colorado Street to beginning of private right of way, generally forty feet, fifty feet and sixty feet in width; thence along said private right of way in a northeasterly direction to the end of private right of way in a northeasterly direction to the end of private right of way at west end of Central Avenue, Sierra Madre, California; thence east on said Central Avenue to a point just west of Baldwin Avenue; thence on a 20° curve to left; thence north on Baldwin Avenue; thence on a 19° curve to right of private right of way; thence northeasterly on private right of way to end of track at Mountain Trail Avenue in said City of Sierra Madre.

Also, commencing at Olive and California Avenues, in the City of Monrovia, California; thence along a double track line on private right of way in a general easterly direction to Ninth Street in Azusa, California; thence easterly on said Ninth Street to Pasadena Avenue in Azusa; thence easterly on 1° curve to right on said Ninth Street to east end of said Ninth Street and a private right of way eighty feet in width to end of double track and beginning of single track line at a point near the east line of said City of Azusa; thence along private right of way, generally eighty feet in width, in an easterly direction to Minnesota Avenue, Glendora, California, about 230 feet south of the south line of Meda Avenue.

Also, commencing at a point in private right of way in Lot 10, of Florence Terrace Tract, in said City of Los Angeles, about 350 feet south of Marengo Street and 130 feet west of Breed Street; thence in an easterly direction along private right of way to a point in the east line of said City of Los Angeles about sixty feet south of the southerly line of Lancaster Avenue; thence along private right of way in a general easterly direction to El Monte, California; thence along private right of way in a general easterly and northeasterly direction to and through Vineland in said County of Los Angeles to Azusa Street and Badilla Avenue; thence easterly along Badillo Avenue on private right of way sixty feet in width to Hollenbeck Street; thence easterly on Badillo Avenue, in the City of Covina, California, to Barranca Street.

Also, commencing at California Street and Lake Avenue in said City of Pasadena; thence southerly on said Lake Avenue to Oak Knoll Avenue; thence on curve to right; thence south 70° 59′ on private right of way 35 feet in width; thence on curve to left to Oak Knoll Avenue; thence southerly along private right of way 35 feet in width on said Oak Knoll Avenue, to a point in the east line of said Oak Knoll Avenue about 270 feet north of Old Mill Road; thence southeasterly on curve to left; thence south 87° 16′ east; thence on curve to right; thence south 16° 29′ west; thence on curve to right to point in the center line of the Pacific Electric Railway Company's Monrovia Line on private right of way opposite south end of Oak Knoll Avenue.

Also, commencing at a point in the center line of the Los Angeles Inter-Urban Railway Company's Newport Beach Line about 260 feet southeasterly from the southeasterly line of Ravenna Way, Naples, in Los Angeles County; thence southwesterly on private right of way along curve to left; thence southwesterly along private right of way parallel to Ravenna Way; thence on curve to left; thence southerly to the southerly line of the Esplanade in said Naples.

Also, commencing at a point in private right of way 32 feet in width in Main Street, San Gabriel, California, about 400 feet east of the center of Shorb Road; thence southwesterly along a 10° curve to left; thence on private right of way generally forty feet in width in a southwesterly direction to a point in County Road about 30 feet easterly from the east line of the San Gabriel Mission.

Also, commencing at a point in the Pacific Electric Railway Company's Alhambra Line on Main Street, about 550 feet east of the east line of the City of Alhambra, California; thence easterly along private right of way thirty-two feet in width, adjoining Main Street, to San Gabriel Boulevard in East San Gabriel.

Also, commencing at Railroad Avenue and Main Street in said City of Alhambra; thence southwesterly and southerly over private right of way thirty-four feet in width, adjoining Palm Avenue to a point about 200 feet southerly of Chestnut Street; thence southwesterly along a 16° curve to right to the south line of San Gabriel Road about 250 feet west of said Palm Avenue.

Also, commencing at a point in Main Street about 60 feet southerly from Sixth Street in said City of Los Angeles; thence along curve to left to a point in said Sixth Street; thence westerly along Sixth Street to Figueroa Street; thence northerly along Figueroa Street to Second Street; thence northerly and westerly along Second Street and Lake Shore Avenue to Sunset Boulevard; thence along and over private right of way, crossing north patent boundary line of said City of Los Angeles at a point about 420 feet west of the intersection of said boundary line with the center line of Alvarado Street in said City; thence in a general northerly direction to and through the City of Glendale in said County of Los Angeles to Mountain Avenue in the Glendale Boulevard Tract.

Also, commencing at a point in Aliso Street, immediately west of the intersection of Aliso and Anderson Streets in said City of Los Angeles; thence northwesterly along curve to left, leaving Aliso Street; thence over private right of way, generally 60 feet to 120 feet in width, in a general easterly direction, crossing Marengo Street at a point about 250 feet easterly from Cornwell Street in said City of Los Angeles to a point in said city which is west about 600 feet from a point in the east boundary line of said city, said last mentioned point being about 2400 feet south along said boundary line from the southeasterly line of Mission Road in said city.

Also, commencing at a point in Mountain Avenue about 2630 feet northerly from the northern boundary line of said City of Los Angeles and running thence northerly along said Mountain Avenue about 2700 feet to end of line.

Also, commencing at Fifth Street and Pacific Avenue, San Pedro, California; thence west on Fifth Street to Bay View Avenue; thence westerly over private right of way thirty-four feet wide to end of line at Third Street.

Also, commencing at a point in the Pacific Electric Railway Company's Long Beach Line, about 110 feet northerly from the northerly line of Adams Street in said City of Los Angeles; thence northeasterly along a curve to the right over private right of way; thence north 63° 44' east, approximately parallel to the Southern Pacific Railroad Company's Santa Monica Branch, and about 50 feet southerly therefrom; thence along a 15° curve to the right; thence north 89° 12' east, approximately parallel to about 220 feet northerly from the south charter boundary of said City of Los Angeles; thence along a 10° curve to the left; thence north 55° 31' east; thence along a 15° curve to the right; thence north 89° 44' east to a point in the west line of Santa Fe Avenue, opposite Butte Street in said City of Los Angeles.

Also, commencing at a point in the main track of the Whittier Branch of the Los Angeles Inter-Urban Railway in said County of Los Angeles, about 200 feet easterly from the Norwalk and Puente Mills Road; thence in a southeasterly direction over private right of way to a point in the main track of the Southern Pacific Railroad Company's Whittier Branch, distant northeasterly along said track about 1815 feet from the crossing of said track with the main track of the Santa Fe Railway Company's Branch to San Diego; thence in a southeasterly direction over private right of way to a point in the boundary line between Los Angeles and Orange Counties, California, distant northerly along said line about 1320 feet from the east and west center line of Section 7, Township 3 south, Range 10 west, S. B. B. & M.; thence continuing along private right of way in a general easterly direction to the end of track at a point in the west line of Section 11, Township 3 south, Range 10 west, S. B. B. & M., at or near Station of Pillsbury in the County of Orange, California.

Also, two electric railway tracks, adjacent to and lying one each side of the Pacific Electric Railway Company's Long Beach Main Line, beginning just south of Ninth Street in said City of Los Angeles, and running thence along and parallel to said Main Line of the Pacific Electric Railway Company's Long Beach Line to the City of Watts.

Also, the two electric railway tracks commencing just south of Mission Road in said City of Los Angeles, and running thence easterly on both sides of the double track line of the Pacific Electric

Railway and parallel and adjacent thereto, to El Molino Station, in said County of Los Angeles.

Third. (Los Angeles and Redondo Railway Company) Commencing at a point in the center line of the Inglewood division of the Inglewood Division of the Los Angeles and Redondo Railway Company, opposite the station at the Plaza in the Town of Hawthorne, Los Angeles County, California; thence southerly over private right of way of varying widths from 50 feet to 100 feet to a point, said point being the point of beginning of a 50° 45' curve to the right; thence along said curve to the right to an intersection with the north line of the Rancho San Pedro, said north line of the Rancho San Pedro being the center line of Moneta Road; thence from said point along said curve to the right, over a sixty foot right of way and intersecting streets to the end of said curve; thence southerly on a tangent to said curve, over a 60 foot right of way to an intersection with the Gardena Division of the Los Angeles and Redondo Railway Company at Belvidere.

Also, commencing at a point in the Gardena Division of the Los Angeles and Redondo Railway Company, said point being in Vermont Avenue at Vermont Heights, Los Angeles County, California; thence southerly from said point along Vermont Avenue to a point in the center line of Rosecrans Avenue; thence southerly from said point, over private right of way to a point of a reverse curve; thence along said reverse curve to a point in the northerly line of the Rancho San Pedro; thence continuing along said reverse curve over private right of way to the end of said curve; thence southerly over said right of way and across intersecting streets to the point of beginning of a 10° curve to the right, said point of beginning being distant northerly 75 feet, a little more or less, from the northerly line of Palm Avenue, in what was formerly the Town of Gardena, now part of the City of Los Angeles; thence along said curve to the right, over private right of way, to the end of said curve; thence westerly along private right of way to easterly line of Centinella Avenue; thence from said point westerly over and along San Pedro Street on the route of a franchise granted by the County of Los Angeles, to a poir , said point being the point of beginning of a 10° curve to the left; thence along said curve to the left to a point in the southerly line of San Pedro Street, distant easterly 75 feet, a little more or less, from the easterly line of Flint Avenue; thence continuing along said curve over private right of way and intersecting streets to Perry Station; thence along Electric Street westerly to the beginning of a 10° curve to the left; thence along said curve to the left to a point in the southerly line of Electric Street, distant easterly 350 feet, a little more or less, from the northeast corner of Block 8, of the McDonald Tract; thence from said point along said curve to the end of said curve; thence southerly to a point in the easterly line of Block 8 of the McDonald Tract, distant 410 feet, a little more or less, from the northeasterly corner of said Block 8; thence in a general westerly direction to a point in the easterly boundary of the Townsite of Redondo Beach; thence from said point westerly over private right of way to a point, said point being the point of beginning of a 5° 10' tapered curve to the right; thence along said curve, over private right of way and across intersecting streets, to the end of said curve; thence northwesterly tangent to said curve, over private right of way and across intersecting streets, to a point, said point being the point of beginning of a 3° 15' curve to the left; thence along said curve to the end of said curve; thence westerly on a tangent to said curve, over private right of way and across intersecting streets, to a point, said point being the point of beginning of a curve to the left; thence along said curve to the end of said curve; thence westerly to a point in the westerly line of Gertruda Avenue in the Townsite of Redondo Beach; thence westerly on Diamond Street in the City of Redondo Beach to Pacific Avenue; thence southerly along Pacific Avenue to a point opposite the general office building of the Los Angeles and Redondo Railway Company in the City of Redondo Beach.

Also, commencing at a point in the intersection of the center line of Moneta Division of the Los Angeles and Redondo Railway Company with the center line of Paloma Avenue, as shown on map of Bowen's Main, Moneta and Figueroa Tract, in said County of Los Angeles; thence from said point of beginning on a curve to the right over an 80-foot private right of way to the end of said curve over said right of way and across intersecting streets to a point, said point being the point of beginning of a 2° 30' curve to the left; said point being also northerly 160.7 feet, a little more or less from the intersection of Olympia, Laconia, and Compania Boulevards in Athens, in said County of Los Angeles; thence southerly along a tangent to said curve over private right of way to a point, said point being the point of beginning of a 12° curve to the right; thence westerly along said curve to the end of said curve; thence along a tangent to said curve, said tangent being parallel and distant northerly forty feet from the northerly line of the Rancho San Pedro, over an 80-foot private right of way to a junction with the Gardena Division of the Los Angeles and Redondo Railway Company and Vermont Avenue.

Also, commencing at a point, said point being the point of intersection of the center line of Catalina Avenue and Opal Street in the City of Redondo Beach; thence easterly along said Opal Street and over a right on streets reserved in the Townsite of Redondo Beach to an intersection with Jasper Street; thence northeasterly along Jasper Street to Maria Avenue; thence northerly along Maria Avenue to an intersection with the Main Line of the Los Angeles and Redondo Railway Company.

Also, commencing at a point in the center line of Diamond Street in the City of Redondo Beach, 31.93 feet, a little more or less, from the intersection of the center line of Diamond Street with the Tangent of Broadway produced southerly to said intersection; thence southwesterly across lots owned by the Los Angeles and Redondo Railway Company in Block 178 of the Townsite of Redondo Beach to an intersection with the center line of Catalina Avenue over a right reserved on streets in the Townsite of Redondo Beach to an intersection with the southerly line of Marguerita Avenue; thence southerly along Catalina Avenue, over a perpetual right, to "I" Street in Clifton-by-the-Sea.

Also, those certain spur-tracks located in Blocks 146, 147, and 171, of the Townsite of Redondo Beach, on Broadway from Diamond Street to Pacific Avenue, and on Blocks 142, 143, 144, 77, 78, 79, 113 and 114, and on Pacific Avenue adjacent to said blocks in said Townsite.

Also, spur beginning at the easterly line of Hermosa Avenue in said Townsite of Redondo Beach and thence across Lots 155, 154, 153, 229 and 228, and easterly along Eighth Street in the Ocean Beach Subdivision of said Townsite, and across intersecting streets to a point just west of Lake View Avenue. Also spur-track on Railway Avenue, between Sixth and Eighth Streets of Ocean Beach Subdivision of said Townsite; also those spur tracks along the water front from Diamond Street in said Townsite to a point south of Wharf No. 3, and on wharves Nos. 1, 2, and 3, at Redondo Beach; also spur to gravel pit; also commencing at a point opposite Diamond Street in the Townsite of Redondo Beach, and thence across Lots 136, 135 and 134 and 133, of the Ocean Beach Subdivision of said Townsite, and across Hermosa Avenue, and over property of the Los Angeles and Redondo Railway Company and over property of the New Liverpool Salt Company, and over that certain property leased to the Montgomery and Mullen Lumber Company.

Also, commencing at the Pacific Sandstone & Brick Company's plant on Lot 12, of Block 74, of the Second Addition to Hermosa Beach, in said County of Los Angeles; thence southerly across Blocks 74, 91 and 76, of said Second Addition, and across intersecting streets, to the intersection with the north boundary line of the City of Redondo Beach; thence over a 20-foot right of way parallel and adjacent to Lake View Avenue and across intersecting streets, to a point in the westerly line of Lake View Avenue; thence southerly along said Lake View Avenue to property of the Los Angeles and Redondo Railway Company; and thence across said property to an intersection with lumber yard spur near Beryl Street.

Fourth. (The Riverside and Arlington Railway Company) Commencing at Van Buren Street and Magnolia Avenue, in the City of Riverside, County of Riverside, State of California; thence northeasterly along Magnolia Avenue to Arlington Avenue; thence east on Arlington Avenue to Brockton Avenue; north on Brockton Avenue to Fourteenth Street; east on Fourteenth Street to Main Street; northerly along Main Street to the end of double track just northerly of First Street, on private property; thence on curve to left through private property, along single track line to east end of Houghton Avenue; thence westerly on Houghton Avenue to end of track on Cedar Street.

Also, commencing at Seventh Street and Rubidoux Boulevard in said City of Riverside; thence along Seventh Street to beginning of double track line at Market Street; thence continuing east on Seventh Street to end of double track line just east of Evergreen Street in said City.

Also, commencing at Fourteenth Street and Main Street, in said City of Riverside; thence east on Fourteenth Street to Lime Street; thence south on Lime Street to Olivewood Avenue; thence south on Olivewood Avenue to Cridge Street; east on Cridge Street to Myrtle Avenue; south on Myrtle Avenue to Temperance Street; and thence southerly to the end of single track line.

FIFTH. (The San Bernardino Valley Traction Company) Commencing at the intersection of the center line of Third Street and the center line of "D" Street in the City of San Bernardino, San Bernardino County, California; thence easterly along Third Street to a point near the intersection of "A" Street with said Third Street, said point being at the beginning of a curve to the left having a radius of 400 feet; thence along said curve to the end of said curve; thence easterly on a tangent to said curve 75.91 feet to a point, said point being the beginning of a curve to the right having a radius of 400 feet; thence along said curve to the end of said curve; thence easterly along Third Street to the beginning of a 10° curve to the right, the beginning of said curve being distant westerly 25 feet, a little more or less, from the westerly line of Allen Street; thence along said curve to a point in the southerly line of Allen Street, thence along said curve to a point in the southerly line of Third Street distant 622 feet westerly from the northeast corner of Block "E" of Daly Tract; thence continuing along said curve, over 60-foot right of way and across intersecting streets, to a point, said point being the point of beginning of a 1° curve to the right; thence along said curve, over 60-foot right of way, to the end of said curve; thence southeasterly on a tangent to said curve, over 60-foot right of way, to a point, said point being the point of beginning of a compound curve to the left; thence along said curve to a point in the north line of Mill Street, 75 feet, a little more or less, westerly from the southeast corner of Lot 6; thence continuing along said curve to the end of said curve; thence easterly on a tangent to said curve, said tangent being parallel and adjacent to Mill Street, over private right of way, to a point, said point being the beginning of a 7° curve to the right, and said point being distant westerly 2090 feet, a little more or less, from the westerly line of Sterling Street; thence from said point along said curve to the end of said curve; thence southeasterly on a tangent to said curve 808.85 feet, a little more or less, to a point; thence southeasterly over 60 foot right of way to a point, said point being point of beginning of a 6° curve to the right; thence along said curve to the end of said curve in Sterling Street, said point being near the northerly end of the San Bernardino Valley Traction Company's bridge over the Santa Ana River; thence southerly along Sterling Street to a point, said point being the point of beginning of a 11° curve to the left; thence along said curve to the intersection of same with the easterly line of Sterling Street; thence continuing along said curve over a 60-foot right of way to an intersection with the northerly line of San Bernardino Avenue; thence continuing along said curve to the end of said curve and over San Bernardino Avenue; thence easterly along San Bernardino Avenue to an intersection with the westerly boundary of the City of Redlands; thence continuing easterly along said San Bernardino Avenue in the City of Redlands to an intersection with Orange Street; thence southerly along Orange Street to Cajon Street; thence southerly along Cajon Street to Olive Street.

Also, commencing at the center line of "D" Street with the center line of Third Street in said City of San Bernardino, and running thence northerly along Third Street to Highland Avenue; thence easterly along Highland Avenue to a point, said point being distant easterly 700 feet, a little more or less, from the center line of "C" Street; thence from said point northerly over 60-foot private right of way and across intersecting streets to the point of beginning of a 1° 30' curve to the left; distant southerly 80 feet, a little more or less, from the southerly line of the Muscupiobo Land and Water Company's property; thence along said curve to the left to the end of said curve; thence northwesterly on a tangent to said curve to a point, said point being the beginning of a 1° 30' curve to the right; thence along said curve to the end of said curve, over 60-foot right of way to the point of beginning of a 7° curve to the right; thence along said curve over a 60-foot right of way to a point in the westerly line of the property of John L. Hall and distant Southerly 260 feet, a little more or less, from an iron post at the intersection of the Muscupiobo Rancho line and the westerly line of the property of John L. Hall; thence along said curve over a 100-foot right of way to the end of said curve; thence easterly on a tangent to said curve, over private right of way, to the point of beginning of a 2° curve to the right; thence along said curve to the right, over private right of way to the end of said curve; thence southeasterly along a tangent to said curve, over private right of way, to point in the westerly line of the property of George Emerich, said point being distant southerly 380 feet, a little more or less, from the corner between Sections 10, 11, 14 and 15, of Township

1 north, Range 4 west, S. B. B. & M.; thence over private right of way from said point southeasterly to a point, said point being the point of beginning of a 2° curve to the left; thence along said curve over said right of way to a point in the easterly line of the property of George Emerich; thence along said curve over private right of way to the end of said curve; thence easterly on a tangent to said curve, over private right of way to the point of beginning of a 14° curve to the left; thence along said curve to the end of said curve; thence northwesterly on a tangent to said curve over 60-foot right of way, to the point of beginning of a 12° curve to the right; thence along said curve over private right of way to the end of said curve; thence northeasterly, on a tangent to said curve, over private right of way, to the point of beginning of a 9° curve to the right; thence along said curve over private right of way to the end of said curve; thence southeasterly on a tangent to said curve, over private right of way, 74.35 feet to the point of beginning of a curve to the left; thence along said curve to the end of said curve; thence easterly on a tangent to said curve over a private right of way 309.57 feet.

Also, commencing at the intersection of the center line of "D" Street and the center line of Third Street in said City of San Bernardino; thence westerly along Third Street to Mount Vernon Avenue; southerly on Mount Vernon Avenue to a point south of Mill Street; thence southwesterly over private right of way to Eighth Street, in the City of Colton, California; thence southerly along Eighth Street in said City to "I" Street; thence easterly along "I" Street to Ninth Street.

Also, commencing at the intersection of Pacific and Central Avenues in the County of San Bernardino, and running thence northerly along Central Avenue to Highland Avenue.

Also, commencing at the intersection of Olive Avenue and Cajon Street, in said City of Redlands, and running thence southwesterly along Olive Avenue to Railroad Avenue; thence southeasterly along Railroad Avenue to Laurel Avenue.

Also, commencing at the intersection of Olive Avenue and Cajon Street in said City of Redlands, and running thence southeasterly along Cajon Street to Garden Street; thence easterly and southeasterly over private right of way, parallel to and adjacent to Garden Street, to a point east of Lot 2, in Denman's Subdivision.

Also, commencing at the intersection of Cajon Street and Cypress Avenue, in said City of Redlands, and running thence southwesterly along Cypress Avenue to Center Street; southeasterly along Center Street to Cedar Avenue; southwesterly along Cedar Avenue to a point in Cedar Avenue easterly of the southwest corner of Lot 2, of Block "V," of West Redlands; thence northwesterly over private right of way to the point of beginning of a curve to the left; thence along said curve to the end of said curve; thence westerly on a tangent to said curve to the point of beginning of a curve to the right; thence along said curve to the end of said curve; thence northerly on a tangent to said curve to a point, said point being the point of beginning of a curve to the left; thence along said curve to the end of said curve; crossing Palm Avenue; thence northwesterly on a tangent to said curve to an intersection with Clifton Avenue; thence southwesterly along Clifton Avenue to Sunnyside Avenue; thence northwesterly along Sunnyside Avenue to Fern Avenue; southwesterly along Fern Avenue to Railroad Avenue; northwesterly along Railroad Avenue to Laurel Avenue, and southwesterly along Laurel Avenue to Crescent Boulevard.

Also, commencing at the intersection of the center line of Orange Street and Citrus Avenue, in said City of Redlands; running thence easterly along Citrus Avenue to the car house of The San Bernardino Valley Traction Company located at the southwest corner of Citrus Avenue and Sixth Street.

Also, commencing in the center line of Third Street distant easterly 133 feet, a little more or less, from the easterly line of "B" Street, in said City of San Bernardino; thence northeasterly over private right of way to an intersection with "A" Street; thence northerly along "A" Street to a point about midway between Sixth and Seventh Streets, said point being the beginning of a curve to the right; thence along said curve over private right of way to the end of said curve; thence along a tangent to said curve to the intersection of Waterman Avenue with Sixth Street; thence easterly along Sixth Street three miles, a little more or less, to a County Road; thence northerly along said County Road to a point in Base Line Street, said point being also the point of beginning of a curve to the right; thence along said curve to the right over private right of way to the end of said curve; thence easterly on a tangent to said curve over private right of way to the point of beginning of a curve to the left; thence along said curve over private right of way

to a point in the westerly line of Central Avenue; thence northerly along Central Avenue to Pacific Avenue; thence easterly along Pacific Avenue for one-half mile, a little more or less.

Also, commencing at the intersection of third and "E" Streets in said City of San Bernardino; thence southerly along "E" Street to Colton Avenue; and southwesterly along Colton Avenue to Urbita Springs Park.

Also, commencing at the intersection of Mill and "E" Streets in said City of San Bernardino; thence easterly along Mill Street to an intersection with the Redlands Division of The San Bernardino Valley Traction Company at a point distant easterly 1750 feet, a little more or less, from the easterly line of Waterman Avenue.

Also, commencing at the intersection of the center line of "D" Street with the center line of Seventh Street, in said City of San Bernardino; thence easterly along Seventh Street to an intersection with the Highlands Division of The San Bernardino Valley Traction Company just east of "A" Street.

SIXTH. (Redlands Central Railway Company) Commencing at the intersection of Dearborn Street and Citrus Avenue in said City of Redlands, California, and running thence westerly along Citrus Avenue to Brookside Avenue; and southwesterly along Brookside Avenue to Myrtle Avenue.

SEVENTH. (San Bernardino Inter-Urban Railway Company) Commencing at the intersection of the center line of Main and First Streets, in the City of Riverside, California; thence easterly along First Street in said City to the easterly line of Colton Avenue; thence northerly over 50-foot right of way, parallel to Colton Avenue, to the boundary line between Riverside and San Bernardino Counties, in said state.

EIGHTH. (Los Angeles Pacific Company) Beginning at the intersection of the center lines of Fourth and Hill Streets in the City of Los Angeles, Los Angeles County, California; thence southerly along Hill Street to 16th Street; thence westerly along 16th Street to west line of Pacific Avenue; thence along private right of way as follows:—along tangent bearing westerly to a point about 340.0 feet westerly from center line of Grover Street; along a 1° curve to the left; along tangent bearing westerly to the east line of Normandie Avenue; thence westerly along 16th Street to Arlington Avenue; thence westerly along private right of way and Blaine Street to beginning of a 3° 25' curve to the right; around said curve to Blaine Street and Crossing Concord Street; thence along private right of way as follows:—westerly along tangent to the west City Limits of Los Angeles at Vineyard Power Station; westerly by a tangent crossing Pico Street to the beginning of a 5° curve at Gayland; around said curve to the right; northwesterly along a tangent to the beginning of a 5° 10' curve at Wilshire Boulevard; around said curve to the right; thence on private right of way as follows:—northwesterly along a tangent to the beginning of a 7° curve at Sherman Junction; around said curve to the left; westerly along a tangent to the beginning of a 5° curve at Beverly; around said curve to the left; southwesterly along a tangent parallel to Santa Monica Boulevard to Aliso Avenue; southwesterly along same tangent parallel to Railroad Avenue to the beginning of a 4° 06' curve to the right; around said curve to Lima; southwesterly along tangent parallel to Railroad Avenue to the easterly City Limits of Sawtelle, being the end of the private right of way; thence along Oregon Avenue in the City of Sawtelle, crossing Southern Pacific Railroad Soldiers Home Branch to the West City Limits of Sawtelle, being also the easterly City Limits of Santa Monica; thence in the City of Santa Monica continuing southwesterly along Oregon Avenue to Ocean Avenue connecting by curve to the left with the Lagoon Division.

Also, beginning at an intersection with the Hollywood Division near north portal of Tunnel No. 2, in the City of Los Angeles; thence southeasterly along Sunset Boulevard to and into the Buena Vista Freight Yards at corner of North Broadway and Sunset Boulevard.

Also, beginning at the intersection of Echo Park Road with Sunset Boulevard, in the City of Los Angeles; thence in a general northeasterly direction by curve and tangents in Echo Park Road to the end of said line in Cerro Gordo Street, about 6600 feet.

Also, beginning at the intersection of the center lines of Fourth and Hill Streets in the City of Los Angeles; thence northeasterly along Hill Street, passing through Tunnel No. 1 to the northerly line of Temple Street; thence northerly and passing through Tunnel No. 2 to Sunset Boulevard; thence in a general northwesterly direction along Sunset Boulevard crossing Figueroa Street, Beaudry Avenue, and other streets to Lake Shore Avenue, crossing overhead the Pacific Electric Glendale Line; thence westerly to curve to right at

Mohawk Street; thence northwesterly continuing on Sunset Boulevard to beginning of private right of way on westerly line of Childs Avenue; thence northwesterly on 25-foot private right of way in center of Sunset Boulevard to Sanborn Junction; thence northwesterly on 25-foot private right of way in center of Sunset Boulevard to end of private right of way in south line of Hollywood Boulevard; thence along Hollywood Boulevard westerly, crossing Western Avenue, Vine Street, Highland Avenue and other streets to beginning of 35-foot private right of way in westerly line of La Brea Avenue; thence southwesterly along a tangent on said private right of way to beginning of a 10° 30' tapered curve to the right; thence along said curve to northerly line of Michigan Avenue, being the end of said 35-foot private right of way; thence along Michigan Avenue to end of said curve; westerly along a tangent in Michigan Avenue to end of said curve; westerly along a tangent in Michigan Avenue to the beginning of a 5° 04' tapered curve to the left; along said curve to southerly line of Michigan Avenue; thence along same curve over 35-foot private right of way; thence southwesterly on tangent over 35-foot private right of way passing through Gardner Junction to South City Limits of Hollywood, now City of Los Angeles; thence along same tangent over 35-foot private right of way to Crescent Junction, this being the end of the private right of way; thence westerly along Santa Monica Boulevard to beginning of 7° curve to the left; thence along said curve to the southerly line of Santa Monica Boulevard; thence over 40-foot private right of way parallel to Sherman Avenue as follows: continuing along said 7° curve to end thereof; southwesterly along tangent to the beginning of a 2° curve to the left; along said curve to Sherman Yards; thence along said curve and southwesterly along tangent across the northwesterly side of Sherman Yards; thence on same tangent over 35-foot private right of way parallel to Sherman Avenue to Clearwater Canyon Road; thence across said Road to beginning of 60-foot private right of way; thence along same tangent over said 60-foot private right of way to intersection with Main Line in Beverly Drive to Beverly.

Also, beginning at the intersection of the Melrose Cutoff with the Colegrove Division in Santa Monica Boulevard, a point which is about 100 feet easterly from the easterly line of Avery Street, in the City of Los Angeles; thence along a curve to the right having a radius of 442 feet to a point in the northerly line of Santa Monica Boulevard; thence along 35-foot private right of way to the end of said curve; thence along a tangent northwesterly in 35-foot private right of way to a point which is about 40 feet northerly from the northerly line of Sunset Boulevard; thence along a 12° 30' curve to the right to the end of the private right of way in the easterly line of Vermont Avenue; thence along Vermont Avenue by a continuation of said curve to the right, a northerly tangent and a curve to the left, to a point in the westerly line of Vermont Avenue about 220 feet southerly from the center line of Hollywood Boulevard; thence along same curve to its intersection with the Hollywood Division.

Also, beginning at intersection with the Hollywood Division at Gardner Street, known as Gardner Junction; thence westerly along Sunset Boulevard to the west limits of Hollywood, now City of Los Angeles; thence westerly along Sunset Boulevard to the intersection of the Laurel Canyon Division with the Quint Cutoff; thence westerly about 250 feet to the end of the northerly half of Sunset Boulevard; thence northwesterly to the easterly line of the Los Angeles Pacific Land Company's property; thence within said property to the gravel pit.

Also, beginning at a point which is approximately the intersection of the center lines of Sixth Street and Oregon Avenue in the City of Sawtelle, Los Angeles County, California; thence along a curve to the right to a point in the northerly line of Oregon Avenue; thence over private right of way by curve and tangent a distance of about 225 feet to the beginning of double track line; thence northwesterly on a tangent, to the Northerly City Limits of Sawtelle; thence along curves and tangents through the southwest corner of the Sawtelle Soldiers' Home Grounds to Federal Avenue; thence along 50-foot private right of way in the center of San Vicente Road to the northeasterly City Limits of Santa Monica; thence continuing along said private right of way in the center of San Vicente Road to Ocean Avenue; thence along 28-foot private right of way which adjoins Ocean Avenue on the westerly side thereof to the northerly line of Montana Avenue; thence in Ocean Avenue along the westerly side thereof to Oregon Avenue.

Also, beginning at a point about 30 feet westerly from the intersection of the center lines of Santa Monica Boulevard and Western Avenue, in the City of Los Angeles; thence southerly along private

right of way as follows:—tangent to the southerly line of Temple Street; along curve to the left having a radius of 318 feet to a point which is about 30 feet easterly from the westerly line of Temple Street; along curve to the left having a radius of 318 feet to a point which is about 30 feet easterly along a tangent to a point which is about 137 feet westerly from the center line of Oxford Boulevard; easterly along a tangent to a point which is about 137 feet westerly from the center line of Alexander Avenue; along a curve to the left having a radius of 280 feet; northeasterly along a tangent; along a curve to the right having a radius of 275 feet to a point about 77 feet westerly from the center line produced southerly of Windermere Avenue; thence easterly along a tangent a distance of about 342 feet; all the above private right of way being of an average width of 30 feet; thence along same tangent parallel to Temple Street, to the center line of Vermont Avenue; thence easterly along Temple Street to the easterly line of Juanita Avenue; thence along same tangent parallel to Temple Street to the beginning of a curve to the right; thence along tangents and curves following contour of ravine to end of track, a distance of about 2870 feet.

Also, beginning at a point on the Lagoon Division in the City of Santa Monica, Los Angeles County, California, known as North Beach; thence easterly along Utah Avenue to Third Street; thence northerly along Third Street to Montana Avenue; thence easterly along Montana Avenue to a point which is about 170 feet westerly from the center line of 7th Street.

Also, extending from the center line of Santa Monica Boulevard, in the County of Los Angeles, northerly along Sunset Boulevard to intersection with Laurel Canyon Div., all being in 25-foot private right of way.

Also, beginning at the intersection of the center line of the Rodeo Division with the center line of the Main Line (Sawtelle Division) at Beverly, Los Angeles County, California; thence northwesterly by curves and tangents on private 30-foot right of way along the center of Rodeo Drive to its intersection with Sunset Boulevard; thence northeasterly on private 32-foot right of way in center of said Sunset Boulevard to a point in Sunset Boulevard about 407 feet northeasterly from the intersection of the center lines of Sunset Boulevard and Beverly Drive; thence northeasterly in Sunset Boulevard to end of said line, a distance of about 1400 feet.

Also, beginning at Vineyard at a point in the westerly line of Sherman Drive produced southerly, which point is about 90 feet easterly from the westerly boundary line of the City limits of the City of Los Angeles; thence along private right of way of an average width of 70 feet by tangents and curves as follows:— tangent westerly; 2° 45' tapered curve to left; tangent westerly; 1° 30' 30" tapered curve to left; tangent southwesterly; 0° 30' curve to right; tangent southwesterly to City Limits Ocean Park; tangent southwesterly; 1° 30' curve to left; curve to right connecting with Lagoon Division.

Also, beginning at Sanborn Junction at a point about 50 feet southeasterly from the center line of Defrees Street, in the City of Los Angeles; thence along curve to left in Belvedere Street to beginning of private right of way; thence southwesterly along same tangent; thence along curve to right to easterly line of Hoover Street, being end of private right of way; thence along same curve to westerly line of Hoover Street; thence westerly along Santa Monica Boulevard to West City Limits of Los Angeles; thence along Santa Monica Boulevard to intersection with Hollywood Division at Crescent Junction.

Also, beginning at the intersection of Western Avenue with Santa Monica Boulevard, in the City of Los Angeles; thence northerly along Western Avenue to Franklin Avenue; thence westerly along Franklin Avenue to Argyle Avenue; thence southerly along Argyle Avenue to Larquier Avenue; thence westerly along Larquier Avenue to Vine Street; thence southerly along Vine Street to intersection in Hollywood Boulevard with Hollywood Division.

Also, beginning at the intersection of Highland Avenue with Santa Monica Boulevard; thence northerly along Highland Avenue to the northerly line of Fountain Avenue, it being the southerly line of the City of Hollywood, now a part of the City of Los Angeles; thence northerly along Highland Avenue by tangents and curves to the north boundary of the City of Hollywood, now a part of the City of Los Angeles.

Also, beginning at Sherman Junction, in Los Angeles County, California, at a point on the Main Line; thence northwesterly along private right of way to Fourth Street; across Fourth Street on a reverse, having a reverse tangent of about 45 feet; thence again northwesterly along private right of way to Sherman Yards; thence through Sherman Yards to the intersection with the Hollywood Division.

Also, beginning at Ivy Junction, in Los Angeles County, California, thence over 60-foot private right of way in a general southwesterly direction as follows:—along tangent to beginning of 0° 40′ curve to the right; along said curve; along tangent crossing Washington Street, County Road, Elenda Street, Berryman Avenue, Santa Monica Road, Columbus Avenue, right of way Inglewood Division at Alla, to beginning of a 5° curve to the right; along said curve, along tangent to beginning of 3° 11′ 36″ curve to the left; along said curve; southerly along tangent at Del Rey to beginning of an 8° 36′ curve to the left; along said curve; southerly along tangent to beginning of a 2° 52′ 52″ curve to the right; along said curve; southerly along tangent to beginning of a 5° curve to the left; along said curve; southerly along tangent in Vista Del Mar Boulevard to end of 60-foot private right of way in northerly line of Moscow Avenue, Del Rey Townsite; thence along Vista Del Mar Boulevard to north line of Section 3, T. 3 S., R 15 W., thence on 60-foot private right of way southerly on tangent to beginning of a 0° 30′ curve to the right; along said curve; southerly along tangent to southerly line of above mentioned Section 3; thence over 50-foot private right of way as follows:— along same tangent to beginning of 0° 18′ curve to the left; along said curve; southerly along tangent in Sections 10 and 11, T. 3 S., R 15 W. to northerly line of Section 14, T. 3 S., R. 15 W.; southerly along tangent in said Section 14 to beginning of 0° 20′ curve to the right; along said curve; southerly along tangent to beginning of 0° 20′ curve to right; along said curve to southerly line of said Section 14; along curves and tangents parallel to The Strand through Manhattan Beach to the northerly limits of Hermosa Beach City; thence southerly along same 50-foot private right of way to Homer Avenue in Hermosa Beach City; thence southerly on 40-foot private right of way parallel to Shakespeare Avenue to Hawthorne Avenue; thence southerly on 50-foot private right of way in Hermosa Avenue to the southerly City Limits of Hermosa Beach City, being also the northerly City Limits of Redondo Beach, said common boundary line of the two cities being the center line of Eleventh Street in the City of Redondo Beach and marking the end of private right of way; thence along Hermosa Avenue in the City of Redondo Beach to a point about 200 feet northerly from the Santa Fe Railroad crossing; thence continuing as a single track line across the Santa Fe Railroad and along Pacific Avenue to the end of Redondo Division, a distance of about 2000 feet.

Also, beginning at a point near the intersection of the Inglewood and Southern Pacific Divisions near 5th Street in the City of Santa Monica, Los Angeles County, California; thence in a southerly direction over private right of way by curves and tangents to the northerly line of Fremont Avenue; thence southeasterly across Fremont Avenue and along Main Street in the City of Santa Monica to the southerly line of Hollister Avenue; thence southeasterly over private right of way of varying width, parallel to the Lagoon Division and about 150 feet northeasterly therefrom to the South City Limits of Santa Monica, being also the North City Limits of Ocean Park; thence southeasterly by curves and tangents over private right of way of varying width to the westerly line of Lake Avenue; thence easterly across Lake Avenue and along 50-foot private right of way parallel to Electric Avenue to Venice Avenue; thence around 3° 30′ curve over private right of way to the right; thence southeasterly along 50-foot private right of way crossing the Short Line to beginning of 3° curve to the left; thence on 50-foot private right of way around said curve to Venice Junction; thence to end of said curve over 60-foot private right of way; thence over 60 foot private right of way as follows; southeasterly along tangent to beginning of 1° curve to the left; around said curve; southeasterly along tangent to City Limits of Ocean Park at the Southeast corner of said City; along same tangent to Panama Street in Los Angeles County; thence along private right of way of an average width of 90 feet crossing the Redondo Division to beginning of 3° 0′ curve to the left; thence around said curve over same 90-foot private right of way and crossing Playa Street; into 50-foot private right of way as follows:—easterly along tangent crossing County Road near Playa Street to beginning of 3° curve to the right; around said curve; southeasterly along tangent to easterly line of Rancho Sausal Redondo; thence over 30-foot private right of way along same tangent about 900 feet; thence over 50-foot private right of way as follows:—along same tangent to beginning of 4° curve to the left; around said curve; southeasterly along tangent to beginning of 4° curve to the right; around said curve; southeasterly along tangent to beginning of 4°, 6°, 4° compound curve; around said curve

crossing West City Limits of City of Inglewood; easterly along tangent parallel to Ballona Street to beginning of 4°, 6°, 4° compound curve; around said curve; southeasterly along tangent to end of Inglewood Division on line of Santa Fe Railroad property. This division includes numerous spurs and sidings.

Also, beginning at the intersection of Oregon and Ocean Avenues in the City of Santa Monica, Los Angeles County, California; thence southerly past North Beach Depot, crossing overhead the Southern Pacific Tunnel at Colorado Avenue; along Ocean Avenue to the south line of Fremont Avenue; thence southerly along private right of way of varying width by curves and tangents to the south boundary of the City of Santa Monica, being also the north boundary of the City of Ocean Park; thence continuing southerly over private right of way of varying width by curves and tangents through the City of Ocean Park to the southerly City Limits thereof; thence southerly over private right of way by curves and tangents to connection with Redondo Division between "A" and "B" Street in Del Rey Townsite.

Also, beginning at a point on Lagoon Division near Windward Avenue, City of Ocean Park, Los Angeles County, California; thence easterly by curves and tangents over private right of way of varying width to beginning of 50-foot private right of way at Rivera Street; thence easterly along tangent parallel to Mildred Avenue to beginning of curve to left connecting with Short Line; thence on tangent last above mentioned over 50-foot private right of way crossing Short Line to intersection with Inglewood Division at Venice Junction. Also other tracks in Venice Freight Yards, including among others, one track to wharf along Lorelei Avenue, and another connecting Freight Branch to Lagoon Division.

Also, beginning on Franklin Avenue at a point about 73 feet west of the center line of Hartford Avenue, in the City of Hollywood, now a part of the City of Los Angeles; thence around curve to the right into private right of way of varying width; thence northerly over said private right of way by tangents and curves crossing Frostless Belt Road to a point in the westerly line of Hartford Avenue; thence along Hartford Avenue to Canyon Drive; thence northerly along Canyon Drive; thence in a general northerly direction by tangents and curves over private right of way of varying width to North City Limits of Hollywood now City of Los Angeles; thence by curves and tangents a distance of about 2200 feet with various sidings and spurs for the commercial purposes of the Los Angeles Stone Company.

Also, leased line commencing at or near Clement Junction in the City of Los Angeles, California, being the intersection of the

Southern Pacific San Pedro Line and the Southern Pacific Santa Monica Line; thence over private right of way a width of fifty (50) feet to one hundred (100) feet, or over, as follows:—southwesterly by curve and tangent to east of Compton Avenue in the City of Los Angeles, connecting with Pacific Electric at or near Amco Station on Pacific Electric Line; thence westerly and curve to the right; thence northwesterly across San Pedro Street in the City of Los Angeles; thence curve left and westerly across Main Street, Figueroa Street, Vermont Avenue, Normandie Avenue, in the City of Los Angeles, to a point west of Western Avenue; thence on curve right and tangent to Sentous; thence westerly along tangent crossing Washington Street and Short Line at Ivy Junction to Palms; around curve to the right; northwesterly along tangent; around curve to the left; northwesterly along tangent; around curve to the left; northwesterly along tangent; around curve to the right; northerly along tangent; around 4° curve to left crossing 1st Street, Palms; westerly along tangent to 0° 24′ curve to the left at Home Junction; along said curve; westerly along tangent crossing South City Limits of Sawtelle to West City Limits of Sawtelle; thence into 700 feet wide material yard of Southern Pacific Company to beginning of 0° 29′ 30″ curve to left; along said curve to East City Limits of Santa Monica; thence along same curve over 100-foot private right of way to end of curve; thence southwesterly along tangent over said 100-foot private right of way to Santa Monica Freight Yards; thence by tangents and curves, including sidings and spurs, through said yards to East Line of Ocean Avenue; thence around curve to the right through Tunnel under Ocean and Colorado Avenues to 50-foot private right of way; thence over said 50-foot private right of way; thence over 50-foot private right of way by curves and tangents along the Ocean Front to a point about 100 feet northwesterly from the North City Limits of Santa Monica; thence over private right of way of varying width to beginning of curve to left approaching Long Wharf; thence along Long Wharf to the end of same.

Also, leased line, beginning with the east and west legs of the "Y" at Home Junction; thence northwesterly over 40-foot private right of way in the City of Sawtelle parallel to the East City Limits of Sawtelle, crossing the Main Line of Sawtelle Division on Oregon Avenue to the North City Limits of Sawtelle, being the south boundary of the Soldiers' Home Grounds; thence by curves and tangents including loop, sidings and spurs at north end, within the Soldiers' Home Grounds.

Also, commencing at a point in the City of Santa Monica, Los Angeles County, California, on Oregon Avenue northeasterly to its intersection with Chelsea Street; thence running in a general southeasterly direction to a connection with the Southern Pacific Santa Monica Branch at or near 23rd Street, length of this line being about 2550 feet.

Also, beginning at the intersection of Highland Avenue with the North City Limits of Hollywood, now City of Los Angeles, Los Angeles County, California; thence over 50-foot private right of way along the following courses and curves:—N. 7° 06′ E.; 2° 30′ curve to the left; N. 14° 54′ W.; 3° curve to the left; N. 27° 02′ W.; 1° 30′ curve to the left; N. 48° 42′ W.; 6° curve to the right; N. 28° 23½′ W.; 2° curve to the left; N. 39° 58′ W.; 5° curve to the left; N. 75° 04′ W.; 1° curve to the right; N. 68° 06′ W.; 3° curve to the right; N. 48° 32′ W.; 2° curve to the left, crossing San Fernando Avenue, to a point on said curve; thence over 70-foot private right of way along the following courses and curves: continuing along 2° curve to the left; N. 64° 10′ W.; 10° curve to the right crossing Vineland Avenue; N. 0° 26½′ E. to and across Los Angeles River; changing from 70 ft. to 60 ft. private right of way at a point in the river; thence along said course over said 60-foot private right of way parallel to Vineland Avenue and adjoining it on the west to a point in Second Street, N. 0° 22½′ E. crossing San Fernando Avenue and Fourth Street to Weddington Avenue; thence over private right of way of varying width around 10° curve to the left crossing Weddington and Wilcox Avenues into Southern Pacific Railroad Right of Way Chatsworth Park Branch; thence westerly through Town of Lankershim along said Chatsworth Park Branch right of way to beginning of 3° tapered curve to the right; southeasterly from Kester siding; thence in a northerly and westerly direction to the Townsite of Van Nuys. Also branch line from above described line to and through the Townsite of Van Nuys. Also two branch lines from above described main line easterly and westerly through the Townsite of Van Nuys.

NINTH. (Proposed Lines of Consolidating Systems) All those other certain projected lines of railway described as follows:

Commencing at the Town of Glendora, in said County of Los Angeles, and running thence in a general easterly direction to the City of San Bernardino, in the County of San Bernardino, in said state.

Also, commencing at the Town of Covina, in said County of Los Angeles, and running thence in a general easterly direction to and through the City of Pomona, and and in the City of Riverside, in the County of Riverside, in said State of California.

Also, commencing at a point on the main line of the Los Angeles Inter-Urban Railway Company's railway from Los Angeles to Covina, in said County of Los Angeles, and running thence in a general southwesterly direction to the City of Long Beach in said County of Los Angeles.

Also, commencing at a point in the La Habra Line of said Los Angeles Inter-Urban Railway Company, in the County of Orange, in said state, and running thence in a general easterly direction through the Santa Ana Canyon to and in the City of Riverside, in said County of Riverside, California; with a branch from said last mentioned line in the County of Orange, running to and in the City of Santa Ana, in said County of Orange.

Also, commencing at the City of Los Angeles, and running thence in a general northwesterly direction by the most practicable route through the San Fernando Valley, to and into the City of Santa Barbara, in Santa Barbara County, in said state; with an intermediate branch commencing on the main line last above described in said County of Los Angeles, and extending in a northerly direction to or near the Town of San Fernando in Los Angeles County.

Also, commencing at or near the present terminus of the Glendale Line of said Los Angeles Inter-Urban Railway Company, and running thence in a northwesterly direction to and through the Town of Burbank, in said County of Los Angeles.

Also, commencing at a point on the main line of the Pacific Electric Railway Company running from the City of Los Angeles to the City of Long Beach; thence running in a general southwesterly

direction to and in the City of Redondo Beach, Los Angeles County, California.

Also, commencing in the City of Santa Monica, Los Angeles County, California; and running thence in a general northwesterly direction by the most practicable route, to and in the City of San Buenaventura, Ventura County, California.

Also, commencing at a point in that portion of the City of Los Angeles, Los Angeles County, California, that formerly was the City of San Pedro, and running thence by the most practicable route, to and in the City of Redondo Beach, Los Angeles County, California.

Also, commencing at a point in the City of Santa Ana, Orange County, California; running thence in a general southeasterly direction by the most practicable route, to and in the City of San Diego, San Diego County, California.

Also, commencing in that portion of the City of Los Angeles, Los Angeles County, California, formerly City of San Pedro; running thence by the most practicable route to the most southeasterly extension of the San Pedro Outer Harbor.

Also, commencing at a point in the four-track line of the Pacific Electric Railway Company known as the Pasadena Short Line, said point being just east of the easterly city boundary of the City of Los Angeles, Los Angeles County, California; and running thence by the most practicable route in a general northerly direction, to and in the City of South Pasadena, Los Angeles County, California.

Together with such other and further appendages, adjuncts and terminal facilities to the hereinbefore described lines and projected lines of railroad, including sidings, turnouts, industrial spurs and spur-tracks, as the Board of Directors of said Consolidated Company may from time to time direct.

ARTICLE IX

The total length of constructed railway lines and branches of said Consolidated Corporation is eight hundred and seventy-five miles, and the estimated length of the projected railways and branches of said Consolidated Corporation is one thousand miles.

ARTICLE X

The names of the constituent corporations are Pacific Electric Railway Company; Los Angeles Inter-Urban Railway Company; Los Angeles and Redondo Railway Company; The Riverside & Arlington Railway Company; The San Bernardino Valley Traction Company; Redlands Central Railway Company; San Bernardino Inter-Urban Railway Company; and Los Angeles Pacific Company; each and all of said corporations having been incorporated, organized and existing under the laws of the State of California.

ARTICLE XII

The terms and conditions of said consolidation in full, and as the same are set forth in the agreement of consolidation between the Boards of Directors of the several constituent corporations, are as follows, to-wit:

First. That the said consolidation shall be made at once, and that the name and style of said consolidated corporation shall be "PACIFIC ELECTRIC RAILWAY COMPANY"; that it shall continue in existence for a period of fifty years from and after the date of filing of a certified copy of these Articles of Incorporation and Consolidation in the office of the Secretary of State of the State of California.

Second. Upon the filing of the Articles of Incorporation and Consolidation in the offices prescribed by law, the constituent companies named herein shall be deemed and held to have become extinct in all courts and places, and said Consolidated Corporation shall succeed to all the several stocks, properties, roads, equipments, adjuncts, franchises, claims, demands, contracts, agreements, assets, choses and rights in action of every kind and description, both at law and in equity, held, owned, or possessed by each of said constituent corporations, and shall be entitled, to possess, enjoy, and enforce the same and every thereof, as fully and completely as either and every of said constituent corporations might have done had no consolidation taken place. Said consolidated or new corporation shall also become subrogated to its several constituents and each thereof in respect to all their contracts and agreements with other parties, and all their debts, obligations and liabilities, of every kind and nature, to any persons, corporations, or bodies politic, whomsoever, or whatsoever, and shall sue, and be sued, in its own name in any and every case in which any or either of its constituents might have sued or might have been sued at law or in equity had no such consolidation been made. Said several capital stocks, properties, roads, equipments, adjuncts, franchises, claims, demands, contracts, agreements, obligations, debts, liabilites, and assets of every kind and description held, owned or possessed by each of said constituent corporations shall be vested in said consolidated corporation, PACIFIC ELECTRIC RAILWAY COMPANY, as fully as the same are now severally held and enjoyed by them respectively, subject, however, to all conditions, stipulations, contracts, liens, claims, and charges thereon, and to all debts and obligations of said respective corporations.

Third. Of the said shares of stock of said consolidated corporation, Wm. F. Herrin, W. C. Martin, R. C. Gillis, Paul Shoup and Epes Randolph shall each subscribe for, and there shall be issued to them, ten shares each, and the several stockholders of each of said constituent corporations shall have issued to them, out of the shares hereinbefore in Article VII set forth, subscribed for and allotted to said stockholders, such proportion of said shares as the number of shares owned by such stockholders in their respective constituent corporations, bears to the whole issued and outstanding capital stock of such constituent corporation, in exchange for their stock in the constituent companies which shall thereupon be surrendered and cancelled.

Fourth. The objects, the purposes, the capital stock, the Board of Directors, and the principal place of business of said new consolidated corporation, and all other matters and things hereinbefore set forth, shall be as expressed in these Articles of Incorporation and Consolidation, which said Articles of Incorporation and Consolidation were by the terms of said agreement of consolidation made a part of said agreement and were authorized to be signed and countersigned by the presidents and secretaries of the several constituent corporations, and sealed with the respective corporate seals of said constituent corporations.

IN WITNESS WHEREOF, the said parties have caused these presents to be signed and countersigned by their respective presidents and secretaries, and their respective corporate seals to be hereunto affixed, pursuant to resolutions of their respective Boards of Directors heretofore made and adopted, the day and year first above written.

> Pacific Electric Railway Company
>   William F. Herrin, President
>   H. A. Culladen, Secretary
> Los Angeles Inter-Urban Railway Company
>   William F. Herrin, President
>   H. A. Culladen, Secretary
> Los Angeles and Redondo Railway Company
>   Paul Shoup, President
>   H. A. Culladen, Secretary
> The Riverside and Arlington Railway Co.
>   George Frost, President
>   L. F. Martin, Secretary
> The San Bernardino Valley Traction Company
>   William F. Herrin, President
>   H. A. Culladen, Secretary
> Redlands Central Railway Company
>   William F. Herrin, President
>   H. A. Culladen, Secretary
> San Bernardino Inter-Urban Railway Co.
>   William F. Herrin, President
>   H. A. Culladen, Secretary
> Los Angeles Pacific Co.
>   Paul Shoup, Vice President
>   George L. Bugbee, Secretary

This scene at Travel Town, in Los Angeles' Griffith Park, shows a P. E. locomotive and Big Red Car preserved as reminders of the era when Southern California had an efficient commuter system. (Photo by the Author)

D. Population of Area Served by the Red Cars

This table details the population from 1850 to 1950 of Southern California cities served by Pacific Electric Railway. Statistics for the four counties served by the system as well as for the State of California are included for comparative purposes. Source of this information is the United States Department of Commerce Bureau of the Census.

THE COUNTIES. Los Angeles County was one of California's original twenty-seven counties. San Bernardino County was formed in 1853 from portions of Los Angeles and San Diego Counties, Orange County was organized in 1889 from territory which had been part of Los Angeles County. Riverside County was formed in 1893 from portions of San Diego and San Bernardino Counties.

THE CITIES. Statistics are shown for the towns only after their incorporation as cities inasmuch as the absence of fixed boundaries for unincorporated communities prevents accurate comparisons from year to year. Consequently, numerous cities with substantial populations after 1950 are missing because they were not legally incorporated until after that time. Prior to incorporation many of these cities were widely known by their historical community names (given by the original real estate developers or early day settlers), but had no legal status. The date following the name of each city on the table indicates the year of incorporation.

Many areas existing briefly as cities but later annexed to larger municipalities were excluded because of the lack of means to compare growth. Belmont Heights was incorporated in 1908 and became part of Long Beach in 1909. Casa Verdugo, organized as a municipality in 1925, was annexed to Glendale a year later. The City of Los Angeles, famed for its immense physical area, absorbed many one-time cities. Among these communities were Hollywood, Eagle Rock, San Pedro, Wilmington, and Venice.

In analyzing the table, it should be noted that population gains of all cities ordinarily cannot be credited only to the influx of new residents. Most cities annexed surrounding territory from time to time, thus adding to their total populations.

COUNTY	1850	1
Los Angeles	3,530	11
Orange		(Fo
Riverside		(Fo
San Bernardino	(Formed 1853)	3
Total (of Four Counties)	3,530	15
California State Total	92,597	379

THE CITIES	1850	18
Alhambra (1903)		
Arcadia (1903)		
Azusa (1903)		
Bell (1927)		
Beverly Hills (1914)		
Brea (1917)		
Burbank (1911)		
Claremont (1907)		
Colton (1887)		
Compton (1888)		(F
Corona (1896)		
Covina (1901)		
Culver City (1917)		
El Monte (1912)		
El Segundo (1917)		
Fullerton (1904)		
Gardena (1930)		(
Glendale (1906)		
Glendora (1911)		
Hawthorne (1922)		
Hermosa Beach (1907)		
Huntington Beach (1909)		
Huntington Park (1906)		
Inglewood (1908)		
La Habra (1925)		
La Verne (1906)		
Long Beach (1897)		
Los Angeles (1850)	1,610	
Lynwood (1921)		
Manhattan Beach (1912)		
Maywood (1924)		
Monrovia (1887)		
Montebello (1920)		
Monterey Park (1916)		
Newport Beach (1906)		
Ontario (1891)		
Orange (1888)		
Pasadena (1886)		
Pomona (1888)		
Redlands (1888)		
Redondo Beach (1892)		
Rialto (1911)		
Riverside (1883)		
San Bernardino (1869)		
San Fernando (1911)		
San Gabriel (1913)		
San Marino (1913)		
Santa Ana (1886)		
Santa Monica (1886)		
Seal Beach (1915)		
Sierra Madre (1907)		
Signal Hill (1924)		
South Gate (1923)		
South Pasadena (1888)		
Torrance (1921)		
Upland (1906)		
West Covina (1923)		
Whittier (1898)		

* Less Than 1,500

		THE AREA						
1870	1880	1890	1900	1910	1920	1930	1940	1950
15,309	33,381	101,454	170,298	504,131	936,455	2,208,492	2,785,643	4,151,687
		13,589	19,696	34,436	61,375	118,674	130,760	216,224
		17,897	34,696	50,297	81,024	105,524	170,046	
5,551	7,786	25,497	27,929	56,706	73,401	133,900	161,108	281,642
20,860	41,167	140,540	235,820	629,969	1,121,528	2,542,090	3,183,035	4,819,599
560,247	864,694	1,208,130	1,485,053	2,377,549	3,426,861	5,677,251	6,907,387	10,586,223

1870	1880	1890	1900	1910	1920	1930	1940	1950
				5,021	9,096	29,472	38,935	51,284
				696	2,239	5,216	9,122	23,041
				1,477	*	4,808	5,209	11,042
						7,884	11,264	15,206
					674	17,429	26,823	28,915
					2,435	2,567	2,562	3,208
				600	2,913	16,622	34,337	78,318
				1,114	*	2,719	3,057	6,327
		1,315	1,285	3,980	4,282	8,014	9,686	14,465
in 1910)				922	1,478	12,516	16,198	47,893
			1,434	3,540	4,129	7,018	8,764	10,223
				1,652	*	*	3,049	3,956
					503	5,669	8,976	19,646
				550	*	3,479	4,746	8,103
					*	3,479	3,738	8,011
				1,725	4,415	10,860	10,442	13,958
in 1940)							5,909	14,418
				2,746	13,536	62,736	82,582	95,398
					*	2,761	2,822	3,988
						6,596	8,263	16,278
				679	2,327	4,796	7,197	11,766
				865	1,687	3,690	3,738	5,237
				1,299	4,513	25,591	28,648	29,376
				1,536	3,286	19,480	30,114	46,046
						2,273	2,499	4,961
				*	*	2,860	3,092	4,198
			2,252	17,809	55,593	143,032	164,271	244,072
5,728	11,183	50,395	102,479	319,198	576,673	1,238,048	1,504,277	1,970,358
						7,323	10,982	25,534
					859	1,891	6,398	17,534
						6,794	10,731	13,193
		907	1,205	3,576	5,480	10,890	12,807	20,247
						5,498	8,016	21,754
					4,108	6,406	8,531	20,113
				445	894	2,203	4,438	12,120
			722	4,274	7,280	13,583	14,197	22,872
		866	1,216	2,920	4,884	8,066	7,901	10,027
		4,882	9,117	30,291	45,354	76,086	81,864	104,087
		3,634	5,526	10,207	13,505	20,804	23,539	35,157
		1,904	4,797	10,449	9,571	14,177	14,324	18,429
			855	2,935	4,913	9,347	13,092	25,208
					961	1,642	1,770	3,156
		4,683	7,973	15,212	19,341	21,696	34,696	47,764
	1,673	4,012	6,150	12,779	18,721	37,481	43,646	12,992
					3,204	7,567	9,094	12,858
					2,640	7,224	11,867	20,204
					584	3,730	8,175	11,199
		3,628	4,933	8,429	15,485	30,322	31,921	71,299
		1,580	3,057	7,847	15,252	37,146	53,500	71,595
					669	1,156	1,553	3,553
				1,303	*	3,550	4,581	7,273
						2,932	3,184	4,040
						19,632	26,945	51,116
		623	1,001	4,629	7,652	13,730	14,350	16,950
						7,271	9,950	22,206
				2,384	4,713	6,316	9,050	22,241
						769	1,072	4,499
			1,590	4,550	7,997	14,822	16,115	23,866

Steam engines helped haul freight over the well-constructed P. E. system during World War II. This 2-6-0 (Southern Pacific Engine No. 1721) pulls approximatly 40 cars of rock for Los Angeles Harbor. (Carl Blaubach Collection)

E. Digest of P. E. Financial Reports

The adjoining table digests the basic financial information for the Pacific Electric (formed in late 1911 by the merger of major Southern California electric railroads) from 1912 through 1962. The information was supplied by the California Public Utilities Commission (successor to the California Railroad Commission) and the Interstate Commerce Commission. The major expenses deducted as "fixed charges" were the interest payments on the company's bonds; smaller amounts included in this category covered miscellaneous items such as other interest, loss of property, and rental for the use of trucks owned by other railroads.

Year	Gross Revenue	Passenger Revenue	Earnings or (Loss) Before Fixed Charges	Profit or (Loss) After Fixed Charges	Total Passengers Carried	Rail Passengers Carried
1912	$ 8,864,873	$ 6,677,289	$3,114,585	$ 71,204	69,751,537	69,751,537
1913	9,605,878	7,328,047	3,240,360	477,816	78,803,806	78,803,806
1914	9,467,483	7,366,661	2,446,500	(610,101)	82,084,429	82,084,429
1915	8,922,638	6,893,205	2,399,359	(683,521)	72,092,530	72,092,530
1916	8,856,797	6,705,709	2,383,930	(821,734)	71,240,033	71,240,033
1917	9,267,130	6,730,706	2,556,043	(885,116)	72,305,287	72,305,287
1918	10,331,016	7,469,559	1,843,163	(1,748,191)	74,584,736	74,584,736
1919	11,278,016	8,119,267	1,032,596	(2,767,726)	73,810,416	73,810,416
1920	15,346,345	10,828,804	2,805,843	(1,158,045)	91,048,268	91,048,268
1921	17,096,117	11,956,812	3,296,807	(799,632)	96,142,694	96,142,694
1922	18,307,733	12,885,131	3,640,421	(575,989)	94,113,239	94,113,239
1923	21,641,553	14,515,318	4,680,044	330,915	106,963,592	106,963,592
1924	20,729,483	$13,677,320	4,006,514	(592,185)	109,185,650	109,185,650
1925	19,514,325	12,592,345	2,895,937	(42,438)	102,921,794	102,921,794
1926	19,111,164	12,324,394	1,944,949	(1,096,033)	101,526,203	101,526,203
1927	19,614,542	12,166,609	2,393,843	(1,233,053)	100,607,634	86,227,855
1928	18,310,988	11,543,662	1,680,727	(596,079)	103,417,260	86,861,181
1929	18,417,335	11,632,978	2,182,062	(1,233,053)	107,180,838	88,232,749
1930	15,692,360	10,689,197	941,997	(1,968,822)	100,797,255	81,669,330
1931	13,281,619	9,210,400	513,055	(2,254,487)	89,703,821	71,929,929
1932	10,533,656	7,368,927	75,971	(2,597,546)	75,742,135	60,080,409
1933	9,062,840	6,313,867	36,501	(2,614,402)	67,695,352	52,922,330
1934	9,004,701	6,259,966	(164,665)	(2,779,322)	69,079,875	53,575,072
1935	9,780,615	6,658,591	22,499	(2,562,423)	73,484,169	56,302,311
1936	10,957,158	7,247,134	298,331	(2,284,505)	80,572,757	59,756,955
1937	11,648,939	7,573,662	(426,846)	(2,982,382)	84,886,506	60,304,692
1938	11,061,479	7,195,050	(699,628)	(3,248,384)	78,258,538	53,592,261
1939	11,295,462	7,260,467	(470,608)	(2,918,734)	75,515,301	49,773,804
1940	12,063,285	7,496,716	(44,666)	(2,543,120)	79,839,650	48,071,234
1941	13,423,114	7,801,818	648,538	(1,663,835)	77,766,224	49,464,879
1942	19,751,111	11,232,457	3,606,818	1,546,807	99,125,745	60,324,100
1943	31,796,925	17,432,579	7,599,845	5,602,315	137,404,976	84,071,038
1944	36,886,919	21,134,222	3,605,439	1,922,194	168,427,103	104,124,721
1945	36,411,955	21,805,708	1,751,325	356,264	177,996,137	109,101,535
1946	32,351,171	20,822,398	1,153,723	(218,879)	174,082,830	103,081,713
1947	33,798,485	19,860,892	(467,800)	(1,760,073)	163,408,138	90,369,385
1948	34,313,463	20,355,012	1,313,506	33,180	143,920,644	75,280,914
1949	31,027,937	18,275,458	385,506	(894,092)	125,697,986	66,350,103
1950	29,629,648	16,077,659	999,784	(279,681)	109,320,571	54,151,982
1951	30,501,731	15,574,695	1,217,103	(61,295)	101,582,333	36,762,072
1952	31,104,326	16,330,209	527,670	(435,897)	92,719,375	28,704,881

Information supplied by the governmental agencies noted that not until 1927, when the Pacific Electric began to turn to the use of busses, were records maintained indicating that passengers were carried by means other than rail.

Statistics covering operations in 1953 were not available because of the sale that year of the passenger service to Metropolitan Coach Lines. In 1954, Metropolitan Coach Lines carried a total of 66,099,549 passengers — of which 13,692,556 traveled by rail. The company carried 7,731,-911 rail passengers (out of a total of 56,425,714) in 1955, while in 1956 it serviced 5,604,820 rail travelers (and carried a total of 60,721,361 commuters).

F. Los Angeles "Local" Trolley Service

Below are the routings of the Los Angeles local streetcar lines as they existed in 1912, as the trolley era neared its peak. Additional tracks were laid in subsequent years, only to be removed as the electric car age was doomed. This information is based on "Investigation of Los Angeles Electric Railway Traffic Conditions," a thesis presented in May, 1914, to the University of Southern California by Roscoe E. Shonerd as a requirement for a degree of bachelor of science in electrical engineering. These lines were operated by Henry Huntington's Los Angeles Railway.

The local lines of the Pacific Electric were described in that corporation's 1911 by-laws.

AVENUE 20 LINE.
From S. P. Shops via Lamar, N. Main, Ave. 20, N. Broadway, San Fernando and Ann St. to Main.

EAGLE ROCK VALLEY & HAWTHORNE LINE
From Hawthorne via private right-of-way, Santa Barbara, private right-of-way, Grand, Jefferson, Main, Spring, Main, Marchessault, Pasadena Ave., Avenue 20, Dayton Ave., Avenue 28, Cypress Ave., private right-of-way, Central Ave., Colorado St., to Townsend Ave.

GEORGIA ST LINE
Arlington and Santa Barbara via Santa Barbara, Vermont, 24th & Hoover, Burlington, 16th, Georgia, 11th, Figueroa, 8th, Hill and 3rd St. to Los Angeles St.

VERMONT AVE. BRANCH OF GEORGIA LINE
From Santa Barbara, Vermont via Santa Barbara Ave. to Florence Ave.

GRAND AVE. & N. BROADWAY LINE
From 54th & Mesa via 54th private right-of-way 48th, Hoover, Santa Barbara, private right-of-way, Grand, Seventh, Broadway, 1st, Spring, Main, San Fernando, Belview Ave., N. Broadway & Pritchard St. to East Lake Park.

GRIFFITH & GRIFFITH LINE
From Vernon and McKinley via McKinley; Jefferson, Griffith Ave., 14th, Stanford Ave., 12th, Main, San Fernando, Bellview Ave., N. Broadway, Pasadena Ave., Avenue 26, and Griffith Ave. to Avenue 45.

ARCADIA & WEST 6TH LINE
From Arcade Depot via 5th, Spring, 7th, Hoover, Wilshire Blvd., Commonwealth Ave., 6th, private right-of-way 4th, and private right-of-way to Melrose Ave.

UNIVERSITY AND CENTRAL
From 45th and Dalton via Dalton, Santa Barbara, Vermont, McClintock, 32nd, Hoover, Union, 23rd, Estrella, Washington, Flower, 10th, Main, Spring, 2nd, Central Ave. to Slauson, 39th branch from 39th & Vermont via 39th to Western Ave., Washington, etc.

WASHINGTON AND MAPLE
Washington St. to Figueroa, 6th, Olive, 5th, Maple, Woodlawn, Santa Barbara, Wall, 53rd to San Pedro St.

WEST ADAMS AND HOOPER
Adams St., Normandie Ave., 24th, Hoover, Burlington, 16th, Hill, 3rd, Main, 12th, Tennessee, Hooper, private right-of-way and Ascot Ave. to 51st.

11TH ST. LINE
10th and Grammercy Place via 10th, Hoover, 11th, Main, Broadway, 2nd, Stephenson, 3rd, and Santa Fe Ave. to S. F. Station.

JEFFERSON AND N. MAIN
From Jefferson & Arlington via Jefferson, Main, Spring, N. Main to East Lake Park.

WEST 9TH AND BROOKLYN
From Harvard Boulevard via 8th, Vermont, 9th, Spring, N. Main, Macy, Brooklyn Ave. to Evergreen.

HOMEWARD & VERMONT
From Homeward and Moneta Ave. via Moneta, Main, Spring, 4th, Broadway, Main, Jefferson, Grand, private right-of-way, Santa Barbara, Hoover and Vermont Ave. to Monte Vista Ave. Vermont Heights.

BOYLE HEIGHTS AND SEVENTH ST. LINE
Route: First, Broadway, 7th, Alvarado, 6th, Rampart and private right-of-way to Bimini Hot Springs. Thence via 3rd, Vermont Ave., 4th, Western Ave. to Melrose Avenue.

Euclid Ave. Extension: Via Evergreen, 4th, Euclid Ave. to Stephenson Ave.

Heliotrope Extension: From Bimini — West 1st, private right-of-way, West Temple, Austin, Heliotrope Drive, Melrose Ave. to Normandie Ave.

Rowan Street Extension: Via 1st, Rowan, Hammel and Gage Streets.

WEST 8TH AND EAST 4TH LINE
Route: From 7th and Lake via Lake, 8th, Hill, 3rd, Stephenson Ave., Merrick, Fourth, Fresno to 1st St.

SAN PEDRO STREET LINE
Route: South Park Ave., San Pedro, 5th, Main to Temple Block.

E. SEVENTH AND SANTA FE STATION LINE
Route: From 7th and Broadway via 7th, Mateo and Santa Fe Ave. to Santa Fe Station.

TEMPLE STREET LINE
Route: From Edgemont and Benefit Sts. via Benefit, Avery, Virgil, Clinton, Hoover, Temple, Broadway and 1st to San Pedro Street.

WEST 1ST AND 6TH ST. LOOP
Route: From 6th and Alvarado via 6th, Olive, 5th, Spring, 2nd, Olive, 1st, Bonnie Brae, Ocean View and Alvarado.

EAST 14TH ST. LINE
Route: From Tennessee St. via 14th and 11th Sts. to Santa Fe Ave.

PICO HEIGHTS LINE
Route: Pico, Main, Broadway, 2nd to Spring, thence south on Spring, 4th, Broadway and south.

NORTH DEPOT LINE
Route: 5th, San Pedro, 4th, Spring, 1st, Cumming to Boyle and Stephenson Aves.

SANTA FE AVE. LINE
Route: From 7th and Broadway via 7th, Mateo, 9th, Santa Fe Ave., Pacific Boulevard to Saturn Ave., Huntington Park.

SEVENTH & STEPHENSON LINE
Route: From 1st and Virgil via 1st, Commonwealth, 6th, Alvarado, 7th, and Lake via 7th, Boyle Ave., Stephenson Ave., Downey Road to Cemeteries, Indiana Street Division from Stephenson and Indiana via Indiana St. to 1st Street.

ANGELENO & CROWN HILL LINE
Route: From Douglas St. and Kensington Road via E. Edgeware, Bellevue Ave., Beaudry, Alpine, Figueroa, Boston, Bunker Hill, California, N. Broadway, First, Hill, Fifth, Olive, Sixth, Flower, Third, Crown Hill, Columbia, W. Second, Loma Drive, Belmont, Temple, Echo Park Ave., Bellevue Ave., to E. Edgeware.

MAIN STREET LINE
Route: From Ascot Park, via 61st, Moneta Ave., Main, San Fernando, Bellevue Ave., North Broadway, Pasadena Ave., Ave 20, Dayton Ave., Marmion Way, private right-of-way, Monte Vista, Ave. 61, Piedmont Ave., and Eagle Rock Ave., to Eagle Rock Park.

54th Street Extension: From 54th and Moneta, via 54th St., to Denker Ave.

York Boulevard Extension: From Pasadena and Piedmont via York Boulevard to Avenue 50.

THE INDEX

Accidents, (148), 149-55, (153), (154, (155)
Advertising, 61, (178), 179 ff., (180), (181)
"Air Line," Santa Monica, 206, 233
"Alabama" (Huntington's private car), 190, (194)
Alamitos Bay, 25, 63, 80, 94
Alhambra, 50, 53, 58, 60, 63, 75, 94, 100, 110, 113, 158, 176, 201, 206, (206), 229, 239, 240-41; population, 248-49
Alhambra Advocate, (quoted), 149
All-Year Club of Southern California, 132
Alpine Tavern, 128
Altadena, 75, 128
Alta Loma, 231
American Car Company, 190
Amoco Junction, 233
Anaheim, 97, 63
Angel's Flight Railway, (27), 29, 219
Annandale Line, 162
Anza, Juan Bautista de, 17
Arcadia, 100, 175, 176, 230, 239; population, 248-49
Arlington, 65, 104, 176, 232
Army Corps of Engineers, 25
Arrowhead Springs, 65, (87), 90, 104, 173, 175, 204, 231
Artesia, 77, 226
Atchison, Topeka, and Santa Fe Railroad, see "Santa Fe Railroad"
Automatic block signals, 154
Automobiles, 132, 103, 157 ff., 203, 212
Azusa, 90, 230, 235; population, 248-49
Azusa Ranch, 53

Baker, Donald N., 204
Balboa, 78, 173, 226
Baldwin Park, 230
Ballonna Bay, 25
Balloon Route Excursion, 128, 132
Baltimore, 30
Barney and Smith Car Co., 190
Barthlomew, Emil, 151 ff.
Base Line, 129
Bay City, see "Seal Beach"
Belding, Don, 180-82
Bell, 226; population, 248-49
Bellflower, (199), 209, 226
Belmont Heights (city), 100, 248
Beach Land Co., 109
Belmont Shore, 115
Belvidere, 163
Beverly Hills, 37, 114, 115, (125), 161, 174, 176, 232 ff.; population, 248-49
Beverly Hills-Santa Monica Line, 114, (206)
Bicknell, John, (49), 72
Bicycle Freeway, 29 ff., (30)
Biddle, Lem, 135
Big Creek, 63, 183-84
"Big Four," 21
Birney trolley cars, 187, 192-94, (193)
Bloomington, 176, 232
"Blue Boy," (painting by Gainsborough), 185

Board of Public Utilities, Los Angeles, 100 ff., 159
Borel, Antoine, 53, 54, 71, 72
Boston, 30
Bradbury Block, 54
Brand Boulevard, 114
Brand, L. C., 75 ff., 116
Brea, 103, 226 ff.; population, 248-49
Brill, J. G. Co., 190
Brotherhood of Railroad Trainmen, 139 ff.
Brown, John, 68
Bugbee, George L., 247
Bunker Hill, (27), 29, 160
Bunker Hill Tunnel, (161)
Burbank, 75, 115, 161, 173, 176, 192, 232, 234, 246; population, 248-49
Business districts' development, 114
Busses, 177, 196, 197, 204, (205), 209; map of routes, (208)

Cable streetcars, 27 ff., 30
Cahuenga Pass, (114), (118), 117, (119), 206, (207), 233
Cahuenga Valley Railroad, 122
"California Car," 188
California Club, 44
California Pacific Railway, 49, 64
California Public Utilities Commission, see "California Railroad Commission"
California Railroad Commission, 196, 200-04, 208-09, 250
Cajon Pass, 23
Canoga Park, 233--34
Carr, Harry, 52
Cars, see "Rolling Stock"
Carson Investment Co., 113
Casa Verdugo, (restaurant), 132; (city), 248
Catalina Island, 29, 128, 132, 162, 167, 173, (203)
Catick, Mayor J. W., 104
Central Business District Association, 204
Central Pacific, 21 ff., 140
Chaffey, George, 14
Chandler, Harry, 14, 117, 161
Charts, (176), 201, (206)
Chavez, Cesar, 144
Chesapeake and Ohio Railroad, 42, 145
Chicanos, 140 ff.
Chittenden, Henrietta, 152 ff.
Church, E. Dwight, 184
Cincinnati Car Co., 190
Clara Barton Hospital, 152
Claremont, 231; population, 248-49
Clark, Eli, 14, 33, (34), 45, 76 ff., 82 ff., 95, 97, 109, 122, 211, 215
Clark, Senator William A., 24, (64), 64, 71
Clearwater, see "Paramount"
Clifton, 163, 227
Collisions, see "Accidents"
Colorado River, 219
Colton, 68, 75, 104, 129, 176, 231; population, 248-49

"Commodore," (private car) (137)
Commuter fares, 201-02
Commuters School of Southern California, 204
Competition between railroads, 61
Compton, 58, 151, 201, 225; population, 248-49
Conductors, see "Trolleymen"
Consolidation of trolley lines, see "Great Merger"
Construction (of P. E. system), 58, (105), 105 ff., (114), (143); costs, 76, 104
Corona, 65, 94, 104, 175, 176, (202), (203), 232; population, 248-49
Covina, 53, 65, (73), 75-77, 94, 100, 103, 131, (159), 235 ff., 246; population, 248-49
Covina Junction, see "Valley Junction"
Crescent City Railroad, 65 ff.
Crescent Junction, 232 ff.
Crestmore, 65 ff., 232
Crocker, Charles, 21
Crowther, Bosley, (quoted), 125
Crump, Mrs. Jessie Person, (126), John Spencer, (215); Spencer, (126), (215); Victoria Elizabeth Margaret, (215)
Culladen, H. A., 247
Culver City, 125, 174, 222, 233; population, 248-49
Curtiss, Glenn, 131
Cycleway, 29 ff., (32)
Cypress, 77, 226

Daft, Leo, 30, 32
"Day for a Dollar," 129
Depression (of the 1930's), 202 ff.
DeGuigne, Christian, (48), 53, 54, 71, 72
Del Rey, see "Playa del Rey"
DeLongpres, Paul, 129
Development (of Southern California), see "Growth"
Dobkins, Horace, 29 ff., 219
Dominguez Air meet, 131
Dominguez Junction, 90, 131, 174, 225 ff.
Downey, 97
Drake, Colonel Charles R., 48 ff., 58
Duarte, 230, 235
Due, John F. (quoted), 197
Dunn, William E., 68 ff., (69), 88, 115, 184, 186

Eagle Rock, 248, 252
East Side Railway Co., 34
Eastern District (of P. E. operations), 176, 231 ff.
Echandia Junction, (212), 228 ff.
Echo Mountain, 28 ff., 128
Eddy, J. W., 29
Edendale Line, 162
Edison, Thomas, 30
"Electric Interurban Railways in America" (quoted), 197
Electric streetcars (development), 30 ff.
Electric power stations, (map), (200)
Electric Railway Historical Association, 133, 224
Electric Railway Homestead Tract, 32

"Electric Tract," 110
Elevated system (proposed for Los Angeles), 161 ff.; drawing, (171); map, (167)
El Molino Junction, 75, 162, 228 ff.
El Monte, 230; population, 248-49
El Segundo, 104, 176, 227; population, 248-49
Escondido, 65
Etiwanda, (31), 231
Excursionists, see "Sightseers"

Fairmount Park, 65
Fares, 61 ff., 160, (181), (198), 198, 201-02, (201)
Farmers and Merchants Bank, 54
Federal Railway Labor Act, 139
Finances, 198, (201), 201-02, 206, 208 ff., 250-51
Fontana, 140, 176, 231
Foote, Cone, and Belding (advertising agency), 180
Foster, Joseph, 153
Fountain Valley, 112, 228
Fox, Fontaine, 102
Franchise for $100,000, 68 ff
Franklin's autobiography, 185
Freeways, 206 ff., (211)
Freight, 202; cars, (60), (71), 188, 192
Fremont, John C., 33
Fresno, 63-64, 91, 184
Fresno Traction Co., 91
Friedman, Eugene, 153
Frost, George, 247
Fullerton, 104, 115, 176, 206, 227; population, 248-49

Gaffney, John, 81
Gardena, 163, 174, 227, 241-43; population, 248-49
Garden Grove, 77, 106, 226
Gardner Junction, see "Crescent Junction"
Garland, William, 13 ff., (15), 97, 113 ff., 219
Gauges, discussion of railroad, 45
"The General," (motion picture), 125
Gilmore, Edward W., 87 ff.
Glendale, 24, 75 ff., 100, (105), 110, 114, 116 ff., 132, (134), 557-58, 161, (165), 170, 173, 176, 192, 201, 204, 209, 232, 234, 241, 246; population, 248-49
Glendale-Burbank Line, (10), (190), (190)
Glendora, 75, 107, (154), 175-76, (206), 209, 230, 240, 246; population, 248-49
Glendora Gleaner, (quoted), 107
Glenwood Mission Inn, see "Mission Inn"
Gould, George, 87 ff.
Grade Crossings, 158 ff.
Graves, J. A., (quoted), 54, 72
"Grease" car, (107)
"Great Merger," 91 ff., 104, 109 ff., 130, 136, 179, 188, 190, 204, 236 ff.
Growth, 30 ff., 47, 59 ff., 75 ff. ff., 157-58, 167, 173 ff., 211 ff., 248-49; factors for, 144 ff.
Guinn, J. M., (quoted), 100
Gutenberg Bible, 184

Hamilton, H. H., 50
Hammond Lumber Co., 145
Harbor development, 24 ff., 45 ff., 59 ff., 78, 81 ff., 94
Harlem Springs, 65
"Harold Lloyd's World of Comedy," (motion picture), (122)
Harriman, Edward Henry, 42, (44), 45 ff., 61, 63 ff., 70 ff., 77, 82 ff., 85 ff., 109, 159-60, 215
Harriman, W. Averell, 45
Hatzfeldt-Wildenberg, Princess, see "Huntington, Clara"
Hawthorne, 163, 241, 252; population, 248-49
Hearst, William Randolph, 88, 149, 166
Hellman, Isaias W., 38, (53), 53-54, 60, 64 ff., 71 ff., 219
Henry, Charles L.; 34
Hermosa Beach, (38), 100, 163, 176, 201-02, 206, 233, 242; population, 248-49
Herrin, William, 72 ff., 92, (94), 247
Hertrich, William, 44, 146, 185, 188
Highland, 53, 65, 75, 104, 129, 173, 204, 232, 235
Hilton, George W. (quoted), 197
Hoffman, Charles, 153
Holabird, W. H., 50, 105
Holladay, W. H., 76
Hallidie, Andrew, 27 ff.
Hollywood, 37, (45), (46), 68, (92), 94, 97, 100, 117, (118), 122 ff., 125, 161, (165), 73-74, 176, 194, 209, 232, 246, 248
Hollywood Freeway, 206
"Hollywood Rajah," (quoted), 125
Hollywood Subway, 124, 160 ff., (161), (165), 173, 176, (195), 204, 209, 220, (223), 232-34, (234); construction, (195)
Hollywood-Venice Line, 233
Home Junction, 246
Hook, William Spencer, 34, 48 ff., 50, 64, 68 ff., 215, 211; T. J., 68 ff.
Horse streetcars, 30
Howland, Charles H., 32, 219
Huntington, Arabella Worsham, 42, 85 ff., 145 ff., 185-86, (185)
Huntington, Archer, 185 ff., 215-16
Huntington Beach, 25, 39, 45, 63, 75 ff., 78, 90, (110), 110-12, 128, 131, 176, (205), 209, 225, 228, 240; population, 248-49
Huntington Building, see "Pacific Electric Building"
Huntington, Clara, 85 ff.
Huntington, Collis P., 21, 25 ff., (26), 38 38 ff., 85, 88, 105, 186
Huntington, Henry Edwards, 13 ff., 26, 38 ff., (39), 54, 58 ff., ff., 85 ff., 97 ff., 145 ff., (185); 211; art and book collection, 147, 183 ff., automobile ownership, 159; directorships, 145; divorce, 85 ff.; labor relations, 135 ff., 143; private railroad cars, 146-47, 190, (194); railroad construction background, 105; role in developing San Fernando Valley, 117; San Marino estate, (146), (183); second marriage, 145 ff.
Huntington, Howard, 74, 135, 184, 186

Huntington Land Co., 110, 184
Huntington Library and Art Gallery, 39, 147 ff., 183 ff.
Huntington, Marian, (86
Huntington, Mrs. Mary, 42, 85 ff., (86)
Huntington Memorial Hospital, 186
Huntington Park, 39, (54), 100, 158, 174, 204, 226-27, 239; population, 248-49
Huntington, Solon, 42

Imperial Valley, 219
Ince, Thomas, 104
Ingersoll, I. M., (quoted), 101
Inglewood, 100, 163, 176, 233; population, 248-49
Inland Shopping Center, 131
Interurban, origin of term, 34

Jackson, Helen Hunt, 79
James, George Wharton, (quoted), 101
Jewett Car Co., 190-91
"Jobs for Long Beach," 102
Johnson, Arthur T., (quoted), 101
Johnson, G. G., 68 ff.
Jonathan Club, 44, 146
Jones, Senator John P., 36 ff.

Keaton, Buster, 124 ff.
Kelly, George B., 179
Kinney, Abbot, 38, 79 ff., (80), 109, 129, 215
Kruttschmitt, Julius, 103

Laborers (for P. E.), 105 ff., 135 ff.
La Grande Station, (33)
La Habra, 75, 77, 103, 107, 226-27, 246; population, 248-49
Land prices, 58, 109 ff.
Lankershim, 246
La Verne, 100, 230-31; population, 248-49
Lawndale, 163
Laurel Canyon, 125
Lindberg, Charles A., 186
Lloyd, Harold, (122), 123
"Local" trolley service, 75, 91 ff., 193 ff., 252
Locomotives, electric, (70), (220)
London underground railway, 30
Long Beach, 24-25, 45, (47), 47 ff., (55-56), 56 ff., (56-57), (59), 61, 68, 75, (76), 77, 94, 97, 102, 103, 105 ff., 110, 112, 114, (115), 128-29, 131, 133, (137), 151, 155, 158 ff., 173-74, 176, 179, 187, 190-92, 194, 196, (197), 201, 204, (206), 209, (211), 224, 225 ff., 237-38, (234), 240, 246; American Avenue (later Long Beach Boulevard), (49); Freeway, (211); Harbor, 94, 161; "Local" trolley lines, 94; Marine Band, 100; population, 248-49
Long Beach Press, (quoted), 61, 106, 109, 112
Lord and Thomas (advertising agency), 179-80
Lordsburg, see "La Verne"
Los Angeles, 13 ff., 18, 25, (25), (28), 32, (33), 37, (52), 64, (100,), 102, 109 ff., 111-12, 116, 117 ff., 124, 125, 128 ff., 140, 149

ff., (153), 157 ff., 159-60, 163, 173 ff., 180, 184, 187, 192, 204 ff., (224), 225 ff., 246; growth, 30 ff., 248-49; Harbor, 132; "Local" trolley lines, 95, 252; population, 248-49
Los Angeles and Independence Railway, 37, 233
Los Angeles and Pasadena Railway, 35 ff., 38, 188
Los Angeles and Redondo Railway, 60-61, 77-78, 80 ff., 92 ff., 102, 190, 236 ff., 241-42; map, (83)
Los Angeles and San Fernando Valley Railway, 118 ff.
Los Angeles aqueduct, 117 ff.
Los Angeles Board of Public Utilities, 100 ff., 159
Los Angeles Chamber of Commerce, 109
Los Angeles Consolidated Railway, 34 ff., 38
Los Angeles City Council, 159-60, 166
Los Angeles County, 97 ff., 157-58, 173; population, 248-49
Los Angeles County Fair, 132-33, 176, 180, 209
Los Angeles Daily News, 166
Los Angeles Examiner, (112), (148), (152), (157); (84), 88, 166; cartoon, 157; (quoted), 85 ff., 88, 166
Los Angeles Evening Express, 166
Los Angeles Herald, 166; (quoted) 62, 135
Los Angeles Illustrated Daily News, 166
Los Angeles Inter-Urban Railway, 74 ff., 77-78, 82, 91 ff., 109, 236 ff., 246
Los Angeles Metropolitan Transit Authority, 96, 132, 140, 155, 196-97, 212, 224
Los Angeles Metropolitan Water District, 177
Los Angeles and Pacific Railroad, 52, 61, 78 ff., 85 ff., 92 ff., 97, 109, 111, 115, 122, 128-29, 150, 159-60, 179, 196, 232, 236, 246; map, (81)
Los Angeles Railway Co., 35, 38, 68, 91 ff., 145, 184, 252
Los Angeles Record, 52, (152), 166; headlines, (82), (84); (quoted), 44 ff., 46, 80, 113, 143; 5
Los Angeles River, 94, 164, 246; franchise, 86 ff., 146
Los Angeles Suburban Homes Co., 117
Los Angeles Terminal Railroad, 48-49, 63
Los Angeles Times, 14, 52, (111), 117, 132, 161, 166, (170), 170; (quoted), 43., 46, 61, 64 ff., 72, 104, 109, 111, 135, 166
Los Angeles Traction Co., 34
Los Angeles Transit Lines, 96
Los Nietos, 226-27
Lowe, Mount, see "Mount Lowe"
Lowe, Thaddeus S. C., 28 ff., 128, 219
Lowe, W. W., 50
Lynwood, 226; population, 248-49

Maclay School of Theology, 116

Macy Street Yard, 192
Maintenance, (137)
Manhattan Beach, 163, 176, 202, 206, 233; population, 248-49
Maps, (81), (83), (93), (167), (168-69), (200), (208)
Marcosson, Isaac F., 39 ff.
Market Street Railway, 53-54
Marler, Harry O., 111, 124, 127 ff., 130 ff.
Martin, James R., (quoted), 115
Martin, L. F., 247
Maywood, population, 248-49
McAleer, Mayor Owen, 88 ff.
McGroarty, John Steven, 104, 132
McKinley, President William, 26
McMillan, James, 91
Methodists, 47
Metro-Goldwyn-Mayer, 125
Metropolitan Coach Lines, 140, 197, 202, 209, (222), 250-51
Metropolitan Transit Authority, see "Los Angeles Metropolitan Transit Authority"
Mexican-Americans, 140-44, (141), (143), 144
Miller, Frank A., 65
Minneapolis and Saint Louis Railway, 145
Mission Inn, 65, 131
Mission Play, 104, 132, 176, 180
Missions, Spanish, 17
Model trolleys, 102
Moneta, 163
Monrovia, 52, 60, 63, 75, (97), 100, 102, 130, 150-51, 158, 175, 209, 239, 230, 235; population, 248-49
Montebello; population, 248-49
Monterey Park, population, 248-49
Morgan, J. P., 113
Mosher, Leroy E., 26
Motion pictures, 122 ff., (122), 124, 125
Motormen, see "Trolleymen"
Motor Transit Co., 137, 177
Mount Lowe, 28 ff., 65, 75, 95, (126), 128, (128), (129), 131, 132 ff., (132), (133), 173, 176, 179, (192), (209), 219-20, 229
Muir, John, 68
Mulholland, William, 14, 117 ff.
Museums, 102 ff.; also see "Orange Empire Trolley Museum"
"My Sixty Years in California," (quoted), 112
Nadeau, Remi, (quoted) 102
Naples (Long Beach), 80, 128-29, 226, (234)
Narrow-gauge trolley lines, 94, 105, 128
National City Lines, 95 ff.
National Orange Show, 104, 132, 175, 180
Nestor Film Co., 122
Nevada Bank, 54
Newmark, Harris, 20
Newport, 25, 45, 60, 77 ff., 109, (116), 137, (150), 174, 176, (206), 226, 240; population, 248-49
Newport News Shipbuilding and Drydock Co., 145, 184
New York City, 30, 186, 212, 215
New York Times, (quoted), 146
Nixon, Frank, 137, (137); Hannah Milhous, 137; President Richard, 137

Nordhoff, Charles, 18, 22
Northern District (of P. E. operations), 176, 230 ff.
North Hollywood, 234
Northwestern Pacific, 194
Nylander, Martha, 152 ff.

Oak Knoll Line, 162
O'Brien, George, 124
Ocean Park, 38, 79, 95, 115, 163, 233
Ogle, Joel, 139
Old Mission Trolley Trip, 128, 131-32
Olinda, 63, 110
Omnibus, 27
Oneonta, N. Y., 39, 186
Oneonta Park Junction, (63), 162, 228 ff.
Ontario, (19), 75, 158, 175-76, 230-31; population, 248-49
Ontario and San Antonio Heights Railway Co., 230
Orange, (city), 75, 77, 158, 235, 239; population, 248-49
Orange County, 77 ff., 157-58, 173, 228, 246; population, 248-49
Orange Empire, 65 ff.; also see "Riverside County" and "San Bernardino County"
Orange Empire Trolley Museum, 102 ff., (215), (220), 220
Oregon City, Ore., 34
Ostrich Farm, 128
Otis, Harrison Gray, (15), 117
Owensmouth, see "Canoga Park"
Owens Valley, 117 ff.

Pacific City, see "Huntington Beach"
Pacific Electric, articles of incorporation, 92 ff., 235 ff., construction, 58, (105), 105 ff., (114), (143); financing, 54, 72, 198 ff., 206, 250-51; formation, 48, 52 ff., 92 ff., 176; labor relations, 135 ff., 143; map, (93), (208), (216-17); operations, 173 ff.; proposed construction, 92 ff.
Pacific Electric Building, (75), 78, (79), 133, 146, 164, (165), 173, 177, (213), 220, (222)
Pacific Electric Club, 136-37
Pacific Electric Land Co., 74 ff., 77
Pacific Electric Magazine, 102, (128), (135), 137, (139), (141), (quoted), 144, (150), (160), (172), (quoted), 175, 176 ff.; (178), (186), (208)
"Pacific Electric Tract," 110
Pacific Light and Power Co., 63, 91, 145, 183-84
Palos Verdes Hills, 81, 94
Paramount, 226
Paramount Pictures, 124
Paris, France, 146
Pasadena, (16), 24, 29 ff., (32), 35 ff., 48, 50, 58, 60-61, (66-67), 75, 97, 114, 128, 131, (147), 157, 162, 173, 175, (175), 176, 187, 190, 194, 202, 204, (206), 209, 235, 238-39, 240; "Local" trolley service, 94 ff.; population, 248-49
Pasadena and Mount Lowe Railroad, 52
Pasadena and Pacific Railway, 36

Pasadena Evening Star, (quoted), 187
Pasadena Oak Knoll Line, 209, 229
Pasadena Short Line, 35, 60, 209, 229, 239, 246
Pasadena Villa Tract, 113
Passenger volume, (167), 173 ff., 177, 203 ff., 206, (206), 206, 250-51
Patton (city), 173, 232
Patton, George, 45, (69), 74, 219
"PCC" cars, (190), 192, 194, (210)
Peninsular Railroad (of Santa Clara County), 64, 91
Perris, 102, 220
Philadelphia, 212
Phoenix Railway, 34
Pickering Park, 131
Pico Boulevard Heights Tract, 114
Pico-Rivera, see "Rivera"
Pierce, C. M., 127 ff., 218
Pillsbury, George, 74, 84, 107
Pillsbury (station), 84, 241
"Pinkie" (painting by Lawrence), (166), 185
Playa del Rey, 109, 129, 163, (172), 176, 233
Plaza, Los Angeles, 164, 166 ff.
"Poinsettia Route," 129 ff., (131)
Point Fermin, 81, 128, 131
Pomona, 53, 90, 94, 103, 114, 131-32, 158, 173, 175-76, 209, 220, 230 ff., 246; "Local" trolley service, 95; population, 248-49
Pomona Progress, (quoted), 103
Pontius, David W., 139, 158-59, 161, 164-66, 175, (177), 204
"Poppy" car, 130
Population (of areas served by P. E.), 78, 97 ff., 157-58, 173 ff.; tabulated by city, 248-49
Portland, Ore., 34
Port Los Angeles, 25 ff.
Powers, Dr. J., 143
President's Conference Committee Cars, see "PCC Cars"
Prentice, Mrs. Clara, 85
Prescott and Arizona Railroad, 34
Private cars, (137), 146-47, 186-87, 190, (194)
Proposed P. E. lines, 246
Pullman-Standard Car Co., 190
Punch designs, (138)

Randolph, Epes, 43, (48), 50, 53, 58, 60, 62 ff., 72, 74, 76, 82 ff., 219
Randolph (station), 84; also see "Brea"
Rannert, Oscar, 153
Rapid transit proposals, 204
Raymond Hotel, (16)
Real estate and trolleys, 109 ff., 113, 116; advertising, (111), (112), (117)
"Red Cars," discussion of how color selected, 188; painting, (189)
Redlands, (39), (40-41), 52, 61, 65, 75, (78), (89), 90, 104, 129, 150, 173, 175, 176, 194, 204, 231, 235-36, "Local trolley service, 95; population, 248-49
Redlands Central Railway, 65, 92 ff., 236 ff., 242-43, 236 ff., 246

Redondo Beach, 25, 45, 53, 76 ff., 79 ff., 94, 100, 131, 163, (172), 174, 176; 201-02, 206, 227, 233, 235, 241-42, 246 ;population, 248-49
Redondo Beach-Del Rey Line, 233
Redondo Land Co., 80 ff.
Rialto, 90, 176, 231-32; population, 248-49
Richmond, Va., 30
"Ride the Big Red Cars" slogan, 173, 179 ff.
Right-of-ways, 158 ff., (207), 220, 225 ff.
Rivera, 226, 239
Riverside (city), 53, 61, 65 ff., 68, 75, 77, 90, 94, 104, 131, 175-76, 192, 194, 206, 220, 231 ff., 235, 243 ff., 246; "Local" trolley service, 95; population, 248-49
Riverside and Arlington Railway, 65 ff., 92 ff., 242, 246
Riverside County, 65 ff., 157, 173, 235, 246; population, 248-49
Riverside Portland Cement Co., 65 ff., 232
Rogers, Will, (quoted), 203
Rolling stock, (187), 187 ff., 193 ff.; costs, 196; maintenance, 192, 194, 197
Roosevelt, President Theodore, 24, 61
Rose, Mayor H. H., 104
Rose Parade, see "Tournament of Roses"
Routes of Pacific Electric, 173 ff., 225 ff.
Rowan, V. J., 118
Rubio Canyon, 28, 128, (209), 220

Sacramento Northern Railway, 190
Safety, see "Accidents"
Saint Albans, W. Va., 42
Saint Louis Car Co., 188, 190-91
Saint Louis Railway Co., 145
Salt Lake Railroad, 24, 45, 61, 64, 71 ff., 87, 151, 201
San Antonio Heights, 173, 230-31
San Bernardino, (city), 52, 63, 65 ff., 68, 75, 77, 90, 103-04, 114, 125, 128 ff., 131-32, 158, 173, 175-76, 180, 184, 187, 191-92, 194, 204, 231 ff., 243, 235, 246; Local "trolley" service, 95; population, 248-49
San Bernardino County, 157-58, 173, 235, 246; population, 248-49
San Bernardino Freeway, 209
San Bernardino Inter-Urban Railway, 68, 92 ff., 236 ff., 246
San Bernardino Mountains, 65, 90, 137
San Bernardino Sun, (quoted), 103 ff.
San Bernardino Valley Traction Co., 63, 65 ff., 90, 92 ff., 104, 231-32, 236 ff., 242, 246
San Buenaventura, see "Ventura"
San Diego, (city), 65, 94, 246
San Diego County, 246
San Dimas, 103, 151, 175-76
Sandusky, Milan, and Norwalk Railway, 34
San Fernando, (city), 54, 116, 204; population, 248-49
San Fernando Mission Land Co., 116 ff.

San Fernando Valley, 64, 75, 94, 110, (114), 116 ff., (117), (123), 161, 173-74, 176, 194, 204, (207), 232-34, 246
San Francisco, 17, 27 ff., 35, 43, 53-54, 64, 85 ff., 157
San Francisco Call, (quoted), 85
San Francisco Examiner, (quoted), 85 ff.
San Gabriel, 114, 132, 176, 209, 235; population, 248-49
Sau Gabriel Mission, 128, 239-40
San Gabriel Mountains, 29, 65
San Gabriel Valley, 60-61, 63 ff., 110, 116, 161, 175, 191, 209
San Gabriel Valley Railroad, (21), 239
San Joaquin Valley, 144
San Marino, 44, 60, 85, 110, 145 ff., 184 ff., 188, 190, 225 ff.; population, 248-49
San Marino Junction, 228 ff.
San Pedro, 24 ff., 45, 48, 53, 64, 68, (71), 75, 81, 90, 103, 105, 131, 173-74, 176, 194, 201, 209, 225 ff., 235, 239-40, 246, 248; "Local" trolley service, 95
San Pedro Times, (quoted), 105
Santa Ana, 52-53, 60, 75, (77), 77 ff., 90, 94, 100, 110, 114, 128, 131, 137, 158, 174, 176, (196), (206), 209, 226 ff., 235, 239, 246; "Local" rtolley service, 95; population, 248-49
Santa Ana Blade, (quoted), 77, 107
Santa Ana Canyon, 65, 94, 246
Santa Ana River, (150), (218)
Santa Barbara, 53, 64, 75, 80, 94, 235, 246
Santa Clara County, 64, 91
Santa Fe Railroad, 24, 36, 53, 76, 65, 87, 161

Santa Monica, 25 ff., (29), (35), 36 ff., 45, 54, 58, 60, 79 ff., 87, 94, 97, (113), 114, 151, 157, 159, 161, 163, 163, 174, 176, 187, 194, 204, 206, 222, 233, 246; "Local" trolley service, 95; population, 248-49
Santa Monica "Air Line," 206, 233
Santa Monica Bay, 78 ff., 232 ff.
Santa Monica-Beverly Hills Line, 114, (206)
"Saturday Night Kid," (motion picture), 124
Sawtelle, 100, 232-33, 243, 246
Schad, Robert O., (cited), 185
Scedules, 225 ff.
Schindler, A. H., 82
Seal Beach, 78, 110-11, 220, 226, 228; population, 248-49
Security Pacific National Bank, 54
Semi-Tropical Park, (150)
Shaw, F. E., 110
Sherman, Moses, 14, 32 ff., (34), 45, 76 ff., 82 ff., 95, 97, 109, 117, 122, 211, 215
Sherman (interurban shops), (89)
Shippey, Lee, (quoted), 176
Shonerd, Roscoe E., (study quoted), 252
Shoup, Carl, 102
Shoup, Paul, 92, (95), 102-04, 136, 153 ff., 219, 247
Sierra Madre, 75, (98-99), 100, 115, 175, 229-30, 235, 240; population, 248-49

The Venice canals were a thing of beauty and a major attraction on the P. E.'s famous Balloon Trolley Trip. Oil-drill- *ing helped destroy the area's beauty in the 1930's. (Security Pacific National Bank)*

"Sierra Madre Mountains," (misnomer), 29
Sierra Nevada, 184
Sierra Vista Junction, 162, 228 ff.
Sightseers, 100, 127 ff., 130, (126-27), (130), 179, (209)
Signal Hill, population, 248-49
Silver Spike ceremony, 104
Slauson, John, (49), 53
Slauson Junction, (51-52), (54), 174, 225 ff.
Smith, Oscar A., 13, 60, 137, 140, (182), 188, 204, 206
South Gate, population, 248-49
South Pasadena, 35, 60, (63), 75, 97, 114, 128, 176, 228 ff., 235, 238-9, 246; population, 248-49
Southern California Edison Co., 184
Southern California Railway, 76
Southern District (of P. E. operations), 176, 225 ff.
Southern Pacific, 22 ff., 30 ff., 35, 36 ff., 39 ff., 47 ff., 53-54, 61 ff., 63 ff., 68, 78, 82 ff., 85 ff., 91 ff., 103, 107, 109, 116, 143, 145, 161, 186, 196, 198, 202, 209, 233
Sprague, Frank J., 26 ff., 30, (30), 32, 34, 219
Stanford, Leland, 21
Standard Steel Car Co., 191
Stanton, 77, 226
Stations, (98-99), (113), (125), (134), 175, (182), (205), (222)
Stephenson, Terry, (quoted), 106
Strikes, 136 ff.
Subways, 159 ff.; see "Hollywood Subway"
Subway Terminal, construction, (195); Building, 161, (161), (165), 232
Sunday "Pass," 132, 176 ff., (177)

Sunset Bay, 63
Sunset Beach, 111
Sunset Boulevard, 122-23, 160
Sunset Magazine, 92, 136
Suydam, E. and Co., 102

Talbert (community), see "Fountain Valley"
Talbert, Thomas B., 112
Telford, Edward T., (quoted), 159
Temple, D. W., 114
Temple City, 114, 229
Terminals, 161 ff., 170, 225 ff.; see "Stations"
Terminal Island, (216-17)
Thalberg, Irving, 125
Tichenor Tract, 109
Time Magazine, (quoted), 159
Timetables, 162-63, (179)
Tingler, Dewey, (142)
Titcomb, H. B., 136, 200
Toonerville Trolley (cartoon), (101), 102
Torrance, 103, 174, 176, 206, 229; population, 248-49
Tourists, 127 ff., 179
Tournament of Roses, 131, 133, 175
"Tower" car, (104)
Traffic problems, 158 ff.
Traffic volume (on interurbans), 68
Tract 1,000, see "San Fernando Valley"
Transportation, development of urban, 27 ff.
Travel Town, 102
Triangle Trolley Trip, 128
Trolleymen, (73), (134), 135 ff., (135), (138), (142); wages, 202

"Trolleys," origin of name, 30
"Trolley Song," 102
Trolleyway, 37
Tustin, 77

Union Pacific Railroad, 24, 42, 161
Union Passenger Railway, 30
Union Passenger Terminal (Los Angeles), 170
Unions, 136 ff.
United States Bureau of Labor Statistics, 135 ff.
United States Naval Academy, 130
Universal City, 234
University of Southern California, 34, 54, 115-16, 144, 233; studies cited, 142 ff.
Upland, 173, 176, 230; population, 248-49
Urbita Hot Springs, 129, 131

Valley Junction, 228 ff.
Van Dyne, S. S., see "Wright, Willard"
Van Nuys, 201, 204, 233-34, 246
Venice, 37, 79 ff., 100, 109, 129, 151, 159, 161, 163, (172), 174, 176, 194, 202, 209, 222, 232 ff., 248
Venice Short Line, 114, 151 ff., 233
Ventura, (city), 80, 94, 246
Ventura County, 246
Vernon, 100
Veysey, Laurence R., (study cited), 177
Victoria Hill, 65
Vineyard Junction, (144), 151 ff., 163, 232 ff.

Walthers, William K., Inc., 102
Wages, of trolleymen, 135 ff.; 142 ff.
Watts, 75, 77, (91), 100, 112, 162, 174, 176, (199), 225 ff.; riot, 96
Wells Fargo Nevada Bank, 54
West Coast Land and Water Co., 63
West Covina, population, 248-49
West Los Angeles, 115, (144), (160), 176
Western District (of P. E. operations), 176, 232 ff.
Western Pacific Railroad, 87
Westgate Line, 233
White, J. Gustin, 204
White, Miss Hortense, 26
White, Senator Stephen, 26, 45, 219
Whitsett, W. P., 118
Whittier, 53, 61, 64, 75-76, 90, 97, 106 ff., 137, 174, 176, 204, 226, 235 ff., 239; population, 248-49
Whittier Register, (quoted), 188
Widney, Robert M., 19 ff., (20), 34, 47 ff., 54, 113, 116, 211, 215
Wiggins, Frank, 14, 109
Wiley, John L., (quoted), 102, 130
Willmore City, see "Long Beach"
Willmore, William Erwin, 47
Wilmington, 100, 227-28, 240, 248
World War II, 132, 173, 194-96, 206
Wright, Willard, 137 ff.
Wrigley, William, 167

Yorba Linda, 90, 103, 137, 174, 176, 204, 226-27, 234
Young Men's Christian Association, 204